UNLOCKING THE PUZZLE

UNLOCKING THE PUZZLE

The Keys to the Christology and Structure
of the Original Gospel of Mark

David Oliver Smith

RESOURCE *Publications* · Eugene, Oregon

Resource Publications
An Imprint of Wipf and Stock Publishers
199 W. 8th Ave., Suite 3
Eugene, OR 97401

www.wipfandstock.com

PAPERBACK ISBN: 978-1-5326-0556-7
HARDCOVER ISBN: 978-1-5326-0558-1
EBOOK ISBN: 978-1-5326-0557-4

Manufactured in the U.S.A.   NOVEMBER 9, 2016

To the woman with the alabaster flask.

Contents

Contents

Preface

PAPIAS OF HIEROPOLIS IN the early second century wrote that the presbyter, John, said that Mark did not report the events in the life of Jesus in the correct order in his Gospel. Some eighteen hundred years later C.H. Weisse and H.J. Holtzmann proposed that there had been a simpler UrMarcus Gospel before the Canonical Gospel of Mark was published. In 1990 Helmut Koester wrote that possibly the entire Bethsaida Section of Mark's Gospel (6:45—8:27) was a later interpolation into the original Gospel.

Using literary tools, this book demonstrates that these commentators on Mark's Gospel were on the right track. The Gospel of Mark is replete with parallel and chiastic structures, and triplets with a unique Markan structure. These literary structures intentionally created by Mark can be analyzed and used to excise interpolated pericopae and verses from Mark's Original Gospel and to replace relocated pericopae into their original Markan context.

Once these exorcisms and relocations are accomplished, a different Christology emerges from Mark's Original Gospel and a coherent structure of the Gospel reveals itself. This emergent Christology in Original Mark provides a basis on which to make informed speculation on the nature of the theological differences between Paul and the Jerusalem apostles that Paul referenced in his epistles. In the Gospel Mark uses Jesus's disciples as the literary embodiment of the Jerusalem apostles. With the exposition of Mark's intended Christology, the reasons why Matthew and Luke modified Mark's Christology in composing their versions of Jesus's ministry begin to become clear.

It appears that a single redactor made a number of modifications to the Gospel originally written by the person we call "Mark." By comparing the text interpolated into Mark by this redactor with Luke's redactions to Mark's text found in The Gospel of Luke, the author of Luke beomes the prime suspect of being the redactor of Mark's Original Gospel. It may be that the redactions to Original Mark were Luke's first attempt to obfuscate Mark's Christology as originally presented in the first written Gospel.

During the journey to discover Mark's Original Gospel, the reader will see Mark's exposition of Paul's Christology, disparagement of the disciples/Jerusalem apostles, adaptations of Old Testament stories, and the presentation of Markan structural puzzles the author planted to engender in the reader a deeper understanding of the first written Gospel.

David Oliver Smith
La Quinta, California
2016

Acknowledgments

Thanks to Robert M. Price, Bill Cummings and C.J. Ransom for their encouragement and advice.

Abbreviations

ABD	Anchor Bible Dictionary
BCE	Before the Common Era
BTB	Biblical Theology Bulletin
CE	Common Era
EKKNT	Evangelisch-katholischer Kommentay zum Neuen Testament
FRLANT	Forschungen zur Religion und Literatur des Alten und Neuen Testaments
HCGM	Historical Commentary on the Gospel of Mark
JSNT	Journal for the Study of the New Testament
LXX	Septuagint
MLM	Midrash and Lection in Matthew
MMLP	Matthew, Mark, Luke and Paul
NAB	New American Bible
NASB	New American Standard Bible
NICNT	New International Commentary on the New Testament
NIGTC	New International Greek Testament Commentary
NRSV	New Revised Standard Version
NT	New Testament
PRSt	Perspectives in Religious Studies
OT	Old Testament
SBL	Society of Biblical Literature
WBC	Word Biblical Commentary

Part I

Literary Structures

1

Introduction

THE GOSPEL OF MARK is a puzzle. Reading it, especially for the first time, one gets the impression that it is disjointed. The narrative proceeds from baptism to controversies with the authorities, to the killing of John the Baptizer, to teaching the multitude, to trekking to Jerusalem, to a plot against Jesus, to arrest, to trials, to crucifixion, to an empty tomb, in an orderly fashion. But around that narrative there are teachings, miracles, boat trips, and journeys happening "immediately" one upon another. It can be quite confusing.

Until scholars generally recognized that Mark was the first written Gospel, the usual opinion among New Testament (NT) scholars was that Mark was a pedestrian work merely setting out the basic story of Jesus's ministry and crucifixion. Mark was criticized because the Greek was poor, the ideas simple, and there were a number of mistakes. During the twentieth century Mark has become more and more appreciated by scholars as they plumb the depths of the first written Gospel.

Literary Structures

Herein three techniques are used to detect interpolations into the Original Gospel. The first consists of identifying large chiastic and parallel literary structures created by the author that extend over several pericopae and containing up to twenty stiches. These terms are defined in chapter 2. A break or gap in a chiastic structure alerts the investigator to a possible interpolation or repositioning of pericopae. The second consists of utilizing Mark's penchant for creating triplets. Over eighty triplets (words or phrases used only three times in the Gospel) and sextets (words or phrases used only six times in the Gospel) are identified in Appendix 2 and there are probably more. In a Markan triplet there are, of course, three elements, but the middle element differs slightly from the first and third elements. For example, Mark uses the Roman monetary unit "denarius" three times, at Mark 6:37, 12:15, and 14:5. The first and third times he uses the plural "denarii" but in the middle element at 12:15 he uses the singular, "denarius." Knowing this pattern allows the investigator to identify interpolated text that may have inadvertently destroyed the Markan triplet pattern. It can also suggest in a gross fashion when a pericope may have been moved. The third technique consists of qualitatively analyzing the style of writing in a suspected interpolation to determine if it comports with Mark's sparse style. In other words, if a suspected interpolation gives colorful details or repeats facts, it bears scrutiny.

The question naturally arises as to why Mark would create long chiastic structures that readers would have trouble discerning because of the literary distance between the matching elements. Further, few people could read nineteen hundred years ago, and most people would have only heard the Gospel read aloud. It would have been virtually impossible for listeners of Mark's Gospel to have picked up on the long structures, especially those structures where words or concepts in the beginning of the Gospel matches words or concepts at the end of the Gospel.

There are two possible answers to this. The first is that some of Mark's literary constructions may have had the purpose of foiling attempts to redact or interpolate into the Original Gospel. Unfortunately, either Mark was too subtle for the redactor, or the redactor did not care, or the redactor thought no one would notice. It is clear that ancient authors feared that their works would be redacted or interpolated. The author of Revelation testifies to this at Rev 22:18–19:

> 18 I warn everyone who hears the words of the prophecy of this book: if anyone adds to them, God will add to that person the plagues described in this book; 19 if anyone takes away from the words of the book of this prophecy, God will take away that person's share in the tree of life and in the holy city, which are described in this book.

In his Gospel Mark did not put a curse on anyone who changed his words, but it appears he may have laid chiastic traps so that chiasms would be destroyed if his text were added to or deleted. If this was his plan, it did not work.

Bart D. Ehrman forcefully makes the point in his book, *Forged*,[1] that forgery, or passing off one's work as being that of a more famous and respected author, was universally condemned in the ancient world. Interpolation is not exactly writing an entire work and passing it off as having been written by one of Jesus's disciples or another famous person, and the real name of the author of Mark is unknown. But the point is forgery, interpolation, and redaction were well known in the ancient world and frowned upon.

Mark was the first written Gospel, and Matthew and Luke made extensive use of it in creating their Gospels. The authors of the Gospel of Matthew and the Gospel of Luke added to and rearranged Mark's Gospel for their own purposes. So if Mark was concerned about possible redaction, the other two Synoptic Gospels demonstrate that he was justified in his fear. It appears that Matthew and Luke did not like what Mark was saying in his Gospel and set out to lessen its influence. Why they disapproved of Mark's Gospel will be made clear.

---

1. Ehrman, *Forged*, 36–40.

In late first-century Koine Greek there was no punctuation and no spaces between words; therefore, a written work would not show literary units an author might want to indicate. There were, however, chiastic and parallel structures used in ancient literature, especially the Bible, a book Mark was very familiar with.[2] Perhaps ancient readers were trained to be more adept than modern readers to spot repeated words, phrases, and concepts. The author of Mark may well have used these literary structures to delineate separate units in his work. These literary structures reveal how the author originally organized the Gospel and further reveal his Christology. Analysis of these structures will demonstrate that there has been a sizable interpolation into the Gospel and that several pericopae have been moved from their original positions to their present locations in Canonical Mark.

The second reason why the author of Mark might have created these hard-to-discern literary structures is that he enjoyed it. He did it because he could. Whether or not a reader understood these structures may have been unimportant to him. He was an artist, and he was creating art the best way he knew how. To give a trivial example of this, a modern mystery writer did something similar in a recent book.

In the book *The Promise* by Robert Crais[3] one character is trying to convince another character, Rollins, that the police are not going to discover them. The text has, "'They gonna roll over us and keep on rollin'.' Rollins gathered his thoughts."[4]

Two sequential words are homographs–rollin' and Rollins. The writer did that for fun. Some will notice it. Others readers will not. In a later passage the writer described the working of the Major Crimes Division (MCD) of the Los Angeles Police Department. The protagonist had been talking to a female detective, Furth, who was in the Metro Division and was upset because MCD took the case away from her. The author wrote, "MCD detectives caught way more nightly news time than a divisional dick like Furth would ever see."[5]

The narrator calls the police woman a "dick," slang for "detective" used earlier in the sentence but also slang for "penis," which the female detective does not have in addition to no camera time on the nightly news. This is a joke between the author and his reader. If the reader missed it, no problem. If the reader got it, it is an enhanced experience for the reader. The author did it because he could. Perhaps Mark created his structures because he enjoyed doing it.

This work will use the terms "Original Gospel," "The Original Gospel of Mark," and "Mark's Original Gospel" to refer to the Gospel as originally written by the author. The term "Canonical Gospel" and "The Canonical Gospel of Mark" will be used to refer to the Gospel as found in the Bible today. Also in this work when the reader finds

---

2. McCoy, "Chiasmus."

3. Crais, *The Promise*.

4. Ibid., 10.

5. Ibid., 37.

an unattributed chapter and verse, e.g., 8:27, that should be understood to be Mark 8:27. For all other scriptural references the book name will be used, e.g., Matt 23:15.

Christology of the Original Gospel

Canonical Mark is clearly Pauline in outlook.[6] By using literary structures to discover the Original Gospel of Mark, the Pauline tone becomes more pronounced. Mark also accuses Jesus's disciples of misunderstanding Jesus's message. The Gospel as originally written by Mark subtly suggests the Christology that Mark accuses Jesus's disciples of not understanding. Mark takes Paul's side in Paul's dispute with the Jerusalem apostles, Peter, James, and John.[7] Mark's Original Gospel makes the point that Peter, James, and John did not understand Jesus's message. This implies that the misunderstanding of Jesus's message by his disciples as described by Mark is the identical misunderstanding of which Paul accuses the Jerusalem apostles. The further ramification is that at the time Mark wrote his Gospel the Paul/Jerusalem apostle dispute was still an active controversy between Christian groups. It had not been resolved. There is a report of a rapprochement between Peter and Paul described in Acts 15:6–11, which, if historically accurate, would be an indication that this assessment is not correct. If Acts is historically accurate, this rapprochement occurred long before Mark wrote his Gospel. This rapprochement is probably fiction.

There is persuasive evidence that Acts 15 does not accurately represent history. The entire book of Acts appears to be designed to bring the Pauline and Petrine factions of Christianity together. In other words it is propaganda. Acts 15 appears to relate the same events as Gal 2, but the two are incompatible. Lastly, the fact that Mark wrote a Gospel long after this putative rapprochement that disparages the twelve disciples and promotes Pauline Christianity, indicates that the conflict was not over at the time Mark wrote his Gospel.

It is important to realize that Paul never reveals in his epistles the fundamental difference between his Christology and that of the Jerusalem apostles. We know little more than the Jerusalem apostles insisted that Christians be circumcised and adhere to Jewish law and Paul thought that was unnecessary. Paul did say that those from Jerusalem were "false apostles"[8] and they were preaching "another Jesus."[9]

Paul and the Jerusalem apostles agreed that they were waiting for the Danielic Son of Man to descend from heaven with the clouds to save the elect and establish the kingdom of God. Paul never used the term "Son of Man" in his epistles, but it is clear from his description of his Christ Jesus coming to Earth that he was describing

---

6. Koester, *Ancient Gospels*, 26; See also, Dykstra *Canonizer*; Smith, *MMLP.*

7. Gal 2:4–15, 3:1.24; 2 Cor 11:1–24.

8. 2 Cor 11:13.

9. 2 Cor 11:4.

the Danielic Son of Man.[10] Paul said that he and the Jerusalem apostles had points of agreement.[11]

The epistles of Paul show that he and the Jerusalem apostles disagreed with re-gard for whom God was going to send this salvation. This work will present the theory that the Jerusalem apostles believed that God was going to send the Danielic Son of Man to rescue the Jews, the elect according to the Jerusalem apostles, and create the kingdom of God, a Jewish-dominated world. Otherwise it makes no sense to pros-elytize on the basis one must become Jewish in order to be a Christian. On the other hand, Paul's Christology was that this savior, Christ Jesus, earned the honor of being the Danielic Son of Man by first being the Isaiac Suffering Servant and being crucified for all mankind as an atonement sacrifice, for Jews and gentiles alike. Paul cites Isaiah more than any other OT book in his seven authentic epistles, ninety-one times. And he cites Isaiah's Suffering Servant seven times. Both Paul and the Jerusalem apostles were anticipating the coming of Christ Jesus, the Messiah, the Son of Man, to set up the kingdom of God and save the elect. For Paul the elect were the baptized; for the Jerusalem apostles the elect were the circumcised.

There is a virtually unanimous opinion in Markan scholarship that Mark com-piled his Gospel by collecting oral stories of Jesus and editing them together into a coherent narrative.[12] If that were true, it could be one of the reasons for the disjointed feel of the Gospel. However, evidence will be presented herein that that is not what happened. There were no oral stories of Jesus circulating in early Christianity because there had been no earthly Jesus who gathered twelve apostles, preached a gospel of loving one's neighbor as oneself, and was crucified by the authorities. Chapter 15 documents that the events in Jesus's life as created by Mark were based upon Old Testament (OT) stories. Mark used OT stories as the source for his events in the life of Jesus. Since Matthew and Luke copied Mark's narrative of the story of Jesus's life, this means that there were no earlier stories of Jesus as a historical person. John, no doubt, used those three Gospels as a template for his version of Jesus's life.

In Paul's Christology the crucifixion of Jesus occurred in one of the lower levels of heaven,[13] not on Earth, and it was revealed to Paul by God's word in the OT.[14] That is the reason Mark used the OT as his source to create the events in the life of his Jesus. Another point of agreement between Paul and the Jerusalem apostles was that when the Son of Man came to Earth it would be the first time he was on Earth. They were not waiting for a second coming; they were waiting for the first coming.

The Original Gospel of Mark is Adoptionist, not because Mark thought Jesus had been a real person, but because he needed a literary device to place Jesus in the

---

10. 1 Thess 4:15–17.

11. Gal 2:7–10.

12. Larsen, "Structure of Mark's Gospel," 144; Dewey, *Public Debate*, 25.

13. Doherty, *Jesus, Neither*, 101.

14. Rom 1:2, 16:25; 1 Cor 2:7–8; Gal 3:1.

historical context of Pontius Pilate, Herod Antipas, and John the Baptizer. In Mark's Christology Jesus is adopted by God at his baptism but only fully accepts his role as God's adopted son in Gethsemane when he repeats Paul's phrase that adopted sons of God use, "Abba, Father."[15]

Structure

Scholars have puzzled for many years over the question of whether there is an over all structure to Mark's Gospel apart from the straight-line narrative. In a 2004 article[16] Kevin W. Larsen reviewed the varied theories. Some say there is no structure.[17] Others have a geographical structure.[18] Many commentators emphasize theological themes.[19] At least two exegetes have considered the situation of the recipients for whom it was written.[20]

The literary/rhetorical aspects of Mark's Gospel have been proposed by a number of commentators.[21] Among those advocating the literary aspect, several scholars have proposed a chiastic structure for Mark.[22] These chiastic structures typically try to match the general intent of sections in the first half of the Gospel with sections in the second half, the second half sections repeating the first half sections in reverse order, e.g., a miracle healing matching another one, a controversy matching another one. These chiastic structures are usually centered on "Peter's Confession at Caesarea Philippi" (8:27–33). The matches are necessarily subjective and some seem far-fetched.

Since at least 1838 there has been a suspicion in NT scholarship that Canonical Mark may be the result of redaction and/or interpolation into an earlier, simpler Gospel. C.H. Weisse proposed the "UrMarkus Hypothesis,"[23] in that year. His hypothesis was that Canonical Mark is the result of some editing of an original first draft. H.J. Holtzmann[24] took up the theory in 1863, but later abandoned it. These scholars were proposing the UrMarkus theory in their attempts to solve the Synoptic problem. The

15. Rom 8:15; Gal 4:6.

16. Larsen, Structure of Mark's Gospel.

17. Nineham, *St. Mark,* 29.

18. Taylor, *According to St. Mark,*; Hedrick, "What is a Gospel," 257; Lane, *The Gospel*; and France, *Gospel of Mark.*

19. Achtemeier, *Mark*; Myers, *Binding the Strong Man*; Peace, *Paul and the Twelve*; Robbins, *Jesus the Teacher*; Gnilka, *Markus*; Heil, *Model for Action*; Manicardi, *Il cammino*; Farrer, *A Study*; Hobbs, *Mark and Exodus*; Swartley, "*Hodos*;" Derrett, *Making of Mark*; Watts, *Exodus in Mark.*

20. Bowman, *Christian Jewish Passover*; Carrington, *Primitive Christian Calendar.*

21. Guelich, *Mark 1–8.26*; Shepherd, *Markan Sandwich Stories*; Teleford, *The Barren Temple*; Witherington, *The Gospel of Mark,*; Schmidt, *Der Rahmen der Geschichte Jesu*; Perrin, "Towards an Interpretation," 7–13.

22. Standaert, *Ĺevangile selon Marc*; Brett, "Suggestions for an Analysis," 174–90; Humphrey, *He is Risen?*; Scott, "Chiastic Structure," 17–26; Krantz, *Mark's Chiastic Gospel.*

23. Weisse, *The Gospel History.*

24. Holtzmann, *The Synoptic Gospels.*

Synoptic problem is the puzzle in NT scholarship regarding which of the Synoptic Gospels, Matthew, Mark, and Luke, was written first and what sources the Synoptic evangelists used in writing their Gospels. The purpose of this work is not concerned with the Synoptic problem, although the conclusions may provide a piece of the puzzle.

For the record, the Two-Source Theory solution to the Synoptic problem does not seem viable. That theory states that Mark was written first and Matthew and Luke independently used Mark and an as-yet undiscovered hypothetical Gospel called "Q." Rather, the Farrar-Goulder Theory makes more sense. The Farrar-Goulder Theory is that the Q document never existed; Mark was indeed written first, but Matthew used only Mark as a source, creating his own additions; and Luke used both Matthew and Mark, creating some of his own additions.[25] As shown the book *Matthew, Mark, Luke, and Paul*, all three Synoptic evangelists also used Paul's epistles as a source.[26]

Helmut Koester, professor emeritus of New Testament and Ecclesiastical History at Harvard Divinity School, revised the Urmarkus Hypothesis. He wrote:

> The cumulative evidence of these peculiarities may allow the conclusion that an earlier version of Mark, which was used by Luke, did not contain the 'Bethsaida Section' (Mark 6:45—8:26) . . .[27]

While Koester identified a number of "peculiarities" in the text of the Bethsaida Section as indicators that it might be a later interpolation into Mark's original first draft, he did not perform any analysis of the literary structures found in Mark. This work takes a critical look at the literary structures of Mark and, based on that analysis, determines what may or may not be original to the Gospel of Mark. The conclusion based on that analysis is that Koester's position is fairly close to being correct, with modifications. There is evidence that that Luke's copy of Mark did include Mark 6:44–8:26. Chapter 11 provides the evidence that the author of Luke's Gospel is the redactor of Mark's Gospel. A section is included in chapter 11 on why Luke failed to copy most of the Bethsaida Section as well as "Killing John the Baptizer" (Mark 6:12–29) and "Leaven of the Pharisees" (Mark 8:13–21). Luke did apparently use a small part of the Bethsaida Section. Modifications to Koester's assessment are derived from the analysis of the literary structures in Mark.

Analysis of Mark's literary structures and devices can reveal the Original Gospel of Mark. It is important to determine the Original Gospel so that it can be judged for itself as a literary composition. The plot may become smoother, the structure more easily discernible, and the Christology and theology clearer. Also the difference between Canonical Mark and Original Mark presents an interesting historical mystery, the answer to which it appears that Mark purposely left clues. As indicated, the overwhelming majority of NT scholars believe that Mark's Gospel was the first one

25. Goodacre, *Case Against Q*.

26. Smith, *MMLP*. See also, Goulder, *MLM*.

27. Koester, *Ancient Christian Gospels,* 285.

written and was used by Matthew and Luke as the basis for their Gospels. Therefore, discovering Mark's first draft may give clues to how and why Matthew and Luke wrote their Gospels and what sources they used.

If Koester is fundamentally correct that all or part of the Bethsaida Section of Mark was interpolated, that should have a major effect on the opinions of the scholars mentioned above who have tried to discern the basic structure of Mark's Gospel. Part II sets forth the theory regarding the structure and Christology of the Original Gospel of Mark.

In addition to a confusing structure, the text of Canonical Mark raises other questions. Odd or apparently inartful constructions are found in Canonical Mark. John Meagher tried to explain what he calls Mark's "clumsy constructions."[28] Fowler used a different theory to explain odd aspects of Markan style.[29] Additionally, Canonical Mark raises a number of questions that contribute to the disjointed feel:

1. Why would Mark write an overly long episode at 6:12–29 about the killing of John the Baptizer? It is an unusually long intercalation between Jesus sending out the apostles and their return. Additionally, the killing of John does not seem to be related to the apostles' journey as the other intercalations are related.

2. Why at Mark 6:45–53 does Jesus order his disciples to Bethsaida, but they go to Gennesaret? As Larsen puts it:

> For example, in Mk 6.45 Jesus instructs his disciples to go to Bethsaida while he remains behind. After Jesus rejoins his disciples, the reader finds them landing at Gennesaret. Interpreters have offered suggestions to explain the discrepancy. Malbon (1984) suggests that the discrepancy is theologically motivated—Bethsaida represents Gentile territory and the fear of the disciples is their reluctance to go to the gentiles. Achtemeier (1970), followed by Kelber (1974), suggests that the geographical confusion is due to the rearrangement of traditional material. However, these are only suggestions or, as Achtemeier calls them, 'non-Markan guesses' (1986: 13).[30]

3. Why at Mark 7:1–23 would scribes and Pharisees go all the way from Jerusalem to Gennesaret to debate Jesus?

4. Why did Mark include a strange healing of a blind man that took two tries with the blind man seeing men "as walking trees" at 8:23–26?

5. What happened 6 days before the Transfiguration at 9:2?[31]

---

28. Meagher, *Clumsy Constructions*.

29. Fowler, *Let the Reader*.

30. Larsen, "Structure of Mark," 147.

31. 9:1 And he said to them, "Truthfully I say to you, there are some standing here who will in no way taste of death, until they see the kingdom of God coming with power." 9:2 And after six days Jesus

6. Why does it appear that the disciples are hearing "rise from the dead" for the first time at 9:10 when they heard it at 8:31?

7. What happened at Jericho at 10:46?

8. Why does Mark report that Jesus goes into Jerusalem at 11:11 and immediately turns around and leaves?

It hardly can be doubted that the author of Mark's Gospel was a literary genius, as modern NT scholarship demonstrates. This work will show that the Gospel was very carefully constructed with an amazing attention to the detail of the words utilized. There are some factual errors in Mark with regard to OT Scriptures, but it appears that these errors were deliberate. Mark was more concerned with form than with accuracy. There are discernible literary divisions pointing to the overall structure and objective of this master work.

When a Greek word used by the author of the Gospel is significant the transliteration into the English alphabet will be given. The translation of the Gospel of Mark is my own, based on the American Standard Version. If a quotation of NT scripture is not attributed to a recognized biblical translation, the translation is my own. Even though in reconstructing the Original Gospel some text of Canonical Mark is eliminated and some pericopae are repositioned, the traditional chapter and verse identifications of Mark's Gospel are retained for ease of reference by the reader. For purposes of this book each separate pericope-level chiastic structure is regarded as a separate pericope, even though two adjoining pericope-level chiastic structures may be parts of the same event. Appendix 3 sets out the seventy-eight pericopae that make up The Original Gospel of Mark. For comparison purposes Appendix 4 contains the eighty-three pericopae found in The Canonical Gospel of Mark. Each pericope has been given a name and will be referred to as such enclosed in quotation marks and usually followed by the encompassing chapter and verses in parentheses, such as: "The Transfiguration" (9:2–8).

The structure of the drama of the Original Gospel of Mark is much like a play. As a result, the major units in the Original Gospel are called "Acts" herein. Unsurprisingly, there are three acts in Mark's Original Gospel, with the first and third acts being relatively short and the second act quite long. In Mark's Original Gospel "Peter's Confession At Caesarea" (8:27—9:1) is not the turning point. As originally designed the turning point comes in the middle of the second act as Jesus ends his Galilean ministry and starts the trek to his fate in Jerusalem. There is also a discernible prologue beginning at 1:2. The prologue ends with Jesus beginning his ministry in Galilee. A matching epilogue begins at Jesus's death. The epilogue ends at 16:8, the original ending of the Gospel.

---

takes with him Peter, and James, and John, and brings them up into a high mountain by themselves.

2

Markan Literary Techniques

Every Pericope Has a Chiastic Structure

THE SMALLEST LITERARY STRUCTURAL unit in a Gospel as written at the end of the first century is the pericope, a scene or event with a discernible beginning and end. So how did Mark, writing the first Gospel in Koine Greek, show his literary units? He used literary structures. Every pericope in the Gospel has a chiastic structure, although some of the interpolated and redacted pericopae employ unsatisfactory chiastic structures. To complicate matters, in the Original Gospel parallel structures are sometimes found embedded within the chiastic structures. These have special significance. One long parallel structure in the Gospel has been identified, which delineates the prologue and epilogue. There are also five long chiastic structures that overlap each other and provide clues as to where interpolations and movements of pericopae have occurred.

The term "pericope-level chiastic structure" will be used to indentify those chiasitic structures by which the pericope are defined. Appendix 1 sets out my translation of The Original Gospel Of Mark showing the chiastic structure of every pericope (the pericope-level chiastic structures). A new pericope begins with an A hemistich which is the A' hemistich of the prior pericope. Mark's Original Gospel has seventy-eight pericopae. Canonical Mark has eighty-three. This analysis eliminates five pericopae from Canonical Mark, repositions three multi-pericopae passages, and redacts three others to eliminate probable interpolations.

A chiastic structure, also called a "chiasm" or "chiasmus," is a literary construction where words or concepts in the first half are repeated in reverse order in the second half. These are also called "ring structures" and "concentric structures." For example, "The first shall be last, and the last first." First, last; last, first—a short, simple chiastic structure. A famous chiasm from John F. Kennedy's Inaugural Address is "Ask not what your country can do for you, rather ask what you can do for your country."

A chiasm is typically diagramed as follows:

A Ask not what your country

  B can do

    C for you

C' ask what you

B' can do

A' for your country.

Each matching pair (A, A') (B, B') (C, C') is called a "stich" and each half is a "hemistich."

In Mark's chiastic structures it is not necessarily words or phrases that are repeated in reverse order; sometimes concepts denote chiastic structure:

A 10:13 And they were bringing to him little children so that he would touch them.

B And the disciples admonished them.

C 10:14 But Jesus seeing it became indignant, and said to them, "Allow the little children to come to me; do not forbid them. For the kingdom of God belongs to such as these.

C' 10:15 Truthfully, I say to you, Whoever will not receive the kingdom of God as a little child, there is no way he will enter into it."

B' 10:16 And he took them in his arms, and blessed them, laying his hands upon them.

A' 10:17 And going on the journey one ran up to him and kneeled to him, and asked him, "Good Teacher, what should I do that I may inherit eternal life?"

In the (B, B') stich there are no repeated significant words. The relationship between the two hemistiches is a concept—how to treat people. Not only that, they are opposites. The disciples admonish the people; Jesus took the children in his arms and blessed them. Mark used this type of ironic opposition often in his chiastic matches. Some matches of Mark make theological points.

As to the entire chiasm, the (A, A') stich is united by movement into and out of the pericope, or more accurately into the next pericope. This structure interlocks the pericopae and keeps the action moving. The A' hemistich of this pericope is the A hemistich of the next pericope. The (B, B') stich is united by how to treat people. The (C, C') stich is united by the lesson that one should be childlike to deserve the kingdom of God, with "kingdom of God" being a phrase found in both hemistiches.

In the pericopae-level chiastic structures Mark's stiches often would match words of Jesus. That is, Jesus may have said something in the C hemistich and then said something that relates to it in the C' hemistich. Or a question might be asked in the first half of the stich and answered in the second half of the stich. The same person may be mentioned in both halves of the stich. There are a number of ways that Mark found to match the two halves of a stich. It cannot be emphasized too strongly that Mark not only used parallel concepts as matches, but he also used opposing concepts as matches. Reading scholarly articles on chiastic structure one could get the impression that a chiasm only exists if the concepts are parallel or if there are exact word matches. Those are relatively easy to discern. But Mark is not easy. He matches opposites, persons speaking, persons spoken about, questions asked and answered, and theological concepts in addition to similar subjects and words throughout his chiasms.

By studying the pericope-level chiastic structures carefully, one can get a feel for the workings of the mind of the author of Mark's Gospel with respect to relationships that he thought created a satisfactory chiasm, such as in the (B, B') stich above where the author has "the disciples admonished them" (mathētai epetimēsan autois) matching "and he took them in his arms" (enankalisamenos auta). In detecting Markan chiasms one must be alert for any type of relationship, even a theological relationship such as baptism and dying:

> Rom 6:3 Or are you ignorant that all we who were baptized into Christ Jesus were baptized into his death? 6:4 We were buried therefore with him through baptism unto death. That as Christ was raised from the dead through the glory of the Father, so we also might walk in newness of life.

The two halves of a stich may have very dissimilar lengths. Sometimes in a long sermon of Jesus, consisting of several sentences, the second hemistich will be matching a much shorter first hemistich. For example Mark 2:18–22:

> B And they come and say to him, "Why do John's disciples and the disciples of the Pharisees fast, but your disciples do not fast?"
> B' 2:19 And Jesus said to them, "Can the sons of the bride chamber fast while the bridegroom is with them? As long as they have the bridegroom with them, they cannot fast. 2:20 But the days will come, when the bridegroom will be taken away from them. And then will they fast at that time. 2:21 No one sews a piece of unshrunken cloth on old clothing, because the new patch would tear away from the old and makes a worse tear. 2:22 And no one puts new wine into old wineskins because the wine will burst the wineskins. And the wine and the wineskins are destroyed. Put new wine into new wineskins."

The sermon of B' answers the question asked in B. The lengths are not comparable. The B' hemistich follows rule 6 below that speeches, regardless of length are usually one hemistich.

Markan Rules for Pericope Chiasitic Structures

In his online book, *Historical Commentary on the Gospel of Mark*,[1] Michael A. Turton showed a chiastic structure for essentially every pericope in Canonical Mark. He developed a set of rules for determining the beginning and ending of Markan hemistiches. This work expands those rules and alters some of Turton's chiasms. There

---

1. Turton, *HCGM*, ch 1, "Excursus: Chiastic Structures in Mark."

are thirteen rules that the author of the Gospel of Mark follows in constructing his chiasms:

1. The A' hemistich of a pericope is always the A hemistich of the following pericope, except for the end of the Gospel.

2. The pericope-level chiastic structures in the Gospel of Mark have twinned centers. Some of the centers are more complex with parallel structures at the centers, such as (A, B, CA, CB, CA', CB', B', A').

3. Parallel centered structures signal the beginning or ending of a major division or theological section of the Gospel.

4. A new pericope begins when the location or the cast of characters changes. This change signals the A' hemistich of the ending pericope and the A hemistich of the following pericope.

5. Separate actions usually constitute separate hemistiches.[2]

6. Speeches, regardless of length, are usually single hemistiches, so long as they are one speech directed at one audience. There are a number of long hemistiches, usually in the B' hemistich, ending a pericope, which are sermons by Jesus.

7. There are exceptions to rule 6. A command such as "watch out," "be careful," "look," etc., in the middle of a speech signals a new hemistich. This is especially noticeable in "The Olivet Discourse" (Mark 13:3–37) that is all one speech, but has four separate stiches, eight hemistiches.

8. Speeches may also be broken into more than one hemistich if there appears to be a natural demarcation between two parts, usually when the audience has shifted. This typically takes place when there is a shift from an address to persons present in the narrative, to an aphorism, often signaled by a formula like "Truly I say" or "But I tell you," as above at 10:15 in the (C, C') stich. While it is one speech by Jesus, it is two hemistiches, one directed at his disciples and one the aphorism.

9. "And immediately" (kai euthys) usually, but not always, signals a new hemistich. There are six exceptions, three of which are in the middle of speeches.

10. Actions plus speeches may comprise one hemistich.[3]

---

2. For example:
E And they laid hands on him, and took him,
  F But one of them standing by drawing his sword struck the servant of the high priest."
  F' And cut off his ear.

3. For example:
B 14:44 Now the one delivering him up had given them a signal saying, "Whoever I kiss, he is the one; take him, and lead him away safely."

11. Actions plus speech followed by actions and/or descriptions are usually separate hemistiches.[4]

12. Where the text turns back on itself—usually by way of explanation—a new hemistich is indicated.[5]

13. Where a verse involves a movement from one place to another, positing an interval of time between, a new hemistich is signaled.[6]

Parallel Centers

The author of Mark's Gospel not only used chiastic structures; he also used parallel structures. As mentioned earlier, some of the twinned centered pericope-level chiastic structures are parallel. For example:

A 1:14 And after John was delivered up Jesus came into Galilee, proclaiming the gospel of God, 1:15 and saying, "The time is complete, and the kingdom of God is at hand: repent, and believe in the gospel."
>BA 1:16 And passing by the sea of Galilee, he saw Simon and Andrew the brother of Simon throwing a net in the sea; for they were fishers.
>BB 1:17 And Jesus said to them, "Follow me, and I will make you fishers of men."
>BC 1:18 And immediately they left the nets and followed him.
>BA' 1:19 And going on a little farther, he saw James the son of Zebedee and John his brother and they were in the boat mending the nets.
>BB' 1:20 And immediately he called them:
>BC' and they left their father Zebedee in the boat with the hired servants and went after him.
>A 1:21 And they go into Capernaum.

Without a parallel center the above pericope is a simple (A, B, B', A') chiastic structure. Looking closely at Jesus calling Peter and Andrew and then James and John, Mark has written that

4. For example:
C 14:45 And immediately on arriving, he came to him and says, "Rabbi"
>D and kissed him.
Whenever "and" (kai) signals a new action, appended to the end of the verse, a new hemistich begins.
5. For example:
E 5:25 And a woman, who had an issue of blood twelve years, 5:26 and had endured many things from many physicians, and had spent all she had, and was no bettered, but rather was worse, 5:27 having heard things about Jesus, she came in the crowd behind and touched his robe.
>F 5:28 For she said, "If I just touch his robe, I will be cured."
The "for" (gar) signals the beginning of a new stich.
6. For example:
B 11:13a And seeing in the distance a fig tree in leaf, he went to see if he could find anything on it.
>C When he came to it, he found nothing but leaves, for it was not the season for figs.

1. Jesus saw two brothers who are fishermen with nets,

2. he calls them, and

3. they follow him.

This pericope is significant structurally because it signals the end of the prologue and the beginning of Jesus's ministry. Those scholars who disparage Mark's style of writing, complaining that there is no purpose for reporting that James and John were in the boat mending nets have failed to see the parallelism Mark was making for this pericope, and how it fits in to the Gospel structure. The prologue encompasses 1:2–15 with the 1:14–15 hemistich being the A' hemistich ending the prologue. The pericopae with parallel center constructions are:

1. 1:2–3 "Messenger to Prepare the Way"

2. 1:14–20 "Calling the First Four Disciples" (Three parallel elements)

3. 2:1–12 "Healing the Paralytic"

4. 2:23–28 "Plucking Grain on the Sabbath"

5. 4:36–41 "Calming the Sea"

6. 5:1–20 "Healing the Gerasense Demoniac"

7. 6:34–37; 8:5–9 "Feeding the Multitude"

8. 8:22–26 "Healing the Blind Man of Bethsaida"

9. 10:17–31 "The Rich Man"

10. 10:35–41 "James and John Ask a Favor"

11. 7:1–15 "Controversy on Tradition" (Three parallel elements)

12. 12:12b–17 "Rendering unto Caesar"

13. 14:53–72 "Sanhedrin Trial, Peter's Denials"

14. 15:20b–39 "The Crucifixion" (Two parallel structures)

The last pericope with a parallel center uniquely contains two parallel structures signaling the beginning of the epilogue and the end of Jesus's ministry. The significance of these pericopae is explained in chapter 12. There are fifteen parallel stiches in the pericope-level chiastic structures. We will see throughout this book that Mark creates many structures based on three and multiples of three: six, nine, twelve, and fifteen.

Triplets

It is fairly obvious that Mark's Gospel contains a number of triplets. There are three Passion Predictions, three Parousia Predictions, and three favorite disciples. Jesus enters Jerusalem and the temple three times, Jesus finds his disciples sleeping at

Gethsemane three times, Peter denies knowing Jesus three times, and three women go to Jesus's tomb. These triplets are easily discerned. There are many more triplets that are less obvious. Appendix 2 documents over eighty triplets and sextets, and there may be more. Some sextets are actually two triplets, while some are straight sextets.

Later in this chapter the argument is presented that Mark did not repeat himself when narrating plot information, and yet here it is stated that there are phrases repeated three or six times, and there are special cases where there are more. But this is not inconsistent. Mark does repeat phrases or concepts three or six times, but he is not being repetitious. That is, he is not giving the same information about what is happening in the plot or in the pericope multiple times. It is not Mark's style to write three times that Jesus and his disciples were going to the desert, or three times that the disciples forgot bread. He did is use phrases such as "kingdom of God" more than once to create an image. That is different from giving the reader duplicate narrative information.

In creating his triplets Mark writes the first and third elements with identical or nearly identical wording or structure while the middle element is slightly different in some aspect, but recognizably so. For example, Mark uses the phrase "in those days" (ekeinais tais humērais) at 1:9, 13:17, and 13:24. With the first and third elements (1:9 and 13:24) Mark tells the reader what happened with the phrase "in those days" preceding the event. In the middle element (13:17), Mark has Jesus tell his disciples about an event with the event preceding the phrase "in those days." So that the triplet is "in those days (x)," "(y) in those days," "in those days (z)."

Another example of a phrase used three times is "all things are possible with God." This is a paraphrase of Gen 18:14 where God tells Abraham and Sarah that Sarah will have a son, even at her advanced age. This is a story mentioned by Paul in Rom 4:19. Mark paraphrases Gen 18:14 at 9:23, 10:27, and 14:36. At 9:23 and 14:36 Mark has Jesus use a pronoun: "all things are possible for *him* who believes" at 9:23 and "all things are possible for *you*" (praying to God) at 14:36, but in the middle iteration at 10:27, Jesus says "all things are possible with God," not using a pronoun.

Mark's triplets can also be a tool used to detect redaction. If a phrase or concept is used four times, one of them may be an interpolation, and the middle-element-is-different structure can sometimes be used to choose which is the interpolation. Ideally there will also be other indicators of interpolation. Appendix 2 enumerates the triplets discovered at the time of publication. Sentences which have three part actions such as: 10:50 "And he, throwing away his tunic, leaped up, and came to Jesus" are not consided triplets. Mark is replete with this kind of sentence structure where the reader is told that three actions occur. Mark loved threes.

Long Chiastic Structures

There are a least five long chiastic structures in Original Mark, the shortest of which encompasses eleven pericopae. The longest one encompasses the entire second half of the Gospel, and another one of similar length overlaps that one and runs from the Parable Discourse to Jesus praying in Gethsemane.

These long structures are not like the chiastic structures Markan scholars posit as being the basic structure of the Canonical Gospel. Markan scholars generally observe that one healing matches another healing and one controversy matches another controversy. In the long chiastic structures specific word matches, specific concept matches, and specific concept opposites are found similar to those found in the pericope-level chiastic structures. For example, the heavens tearing open and the spirit descending like a dove to enter Jesus at 1:10 matches the temple curtain tearing open and the spirit departing Jesus at 15:37–38. Another stich in this same structure has Jesus telling an unclean spirit to be silent at 1:25 matching Jesus standing silent before Pilate at 15:5. These are very specific matches, not the generalized type found in scholarly literature on Markan structure.

With respect to the chiastic structures posited by Markan scholars, of special note is *Markan Public Debate*[7] by Joanna Dewey. She proposes a chiastic structure for Mark 2:1—3:6. She is of the opinion that "Healing the Paralytic" (2:1–12) matches "Healing the Man with the Withered Hand" (3:1–6) because both are healing controversies, that is, they are healing miracles with a controversy in the middle.[8] She notes similar words: "hearts" (kardias) and "arise." Dewey also notes that both pericopae have chiastic structures, although she simplifies them to (A, B, A') (presentation of afflicted – controversy – healing afflicted).

She then matches "Call of Levi"/"Eating with Sinners" (2:13–17) with "Plucking Grain On The Sabbath" (2:23–27) because they are both about eating. Then "Lesson On Fasting" (2:18–22) is the center. So she finds an (A, B, C, B', A') chiastic structure, having five elements and spanning six pericopae-level chiastic structures since "Call of Levi" has a separate chiastic structure from "Eating with Sinners."[9] What Dewey has identified is a Pauline section in Mark's Gospel. This will be expained in chapter 17 on the structures in the Gospel.

Dewey also believes that the Parable Discourse (4:1–34) has a chiastic structure. She outlines the Parable Discourse as (A, B, C, B', A') with the elements being: Introduction – Parable – Sayings – Parable – Conclusion. She also notes repeated words such a "birds" and "bring forth fruit."[10] In contrast the chiastic structure of

---

7. Dewey, *Public Debate*.
8. Ibid., 111.
9. Ibid., 110.
10 41 Ibid., 147 et seq.

"The Parable Discourse" analyzed in chapter 8 has six stiches with the typical Markan twinned center (F, F'). The chiastic matches are mainly word matches.

Dewey is not wrong. "The Parable Discourse" is structured as she has set it out. The analysis in chapter 8 is more specific, and perhaps gets to a deeper understanding of the pericope. Dewey concludes that chiastic or concentric structure is a deliberate literary technique used by the author of the Gospel of Mark.[11] Her assessment is correct. To a limited extent Dewey anticipates the methodology used in this work. She sees chiastic structures of relatively short length but extending over several pericopae.

The matches in the long chiastic structures documented herein are very specific. Consequently, when there is a long stretch of text with no matching elements and then a resumption of matching elements, it can safely be surmised that there has been an interpolation or a repositioning of pericopae. However, the conclusions reached herein do not rely soley on chiastic matches.

Long Parallel Structure

There is one significant, long parallel structure in the Gospel of Mark. It demonstrates beyond any reasonable doubt that 16:8 is the ending of The Original Gospel of Mark. This structure is detailed in the next chapter.

The Artistry Of Mark

The writing style of the author of the Gospel of Mark is similar in several ways to that of modern screenwriters. Mark is very sparse. He does not tell the reader much; he leaves the details up to the reader's imagination, just as modern screenwriters leave it up to the actor to infuse the emotional component into a script.

A scene is the screenwriter's analog to a Markan pericope. When writing a scene, screenwriters are taught to enter the scene late and leave early. That means in a well-written scene the writer should not have the characters expound on details and background at the beginning of the scene and not linger in the scene with a long explanatory denouement after one of the main characters has achieved his or her objective for the scene. Mark wrote his pericopae like that. He encourages the reader to fill in the blanks.

This is not to say Mark never repeats himself. There is repetition in Mark, but for the most part it is Jesus repeating the elements of a sermon. Often he makes his point three times is slightly different words. There is virtually no repetition in the narrative of the Original Gospel. There are repeated words making chiastic matches, but new information is given. The reader is rarely, if ever, told the same fact twice.

---

11. Ibid., 132.

Below is an example of Mark's repetition while making a chiastic match. The pericope are set out as chiastic structures are normally shown in scholarly works. The separate hemistiches are lettered (A, B, C, D, D', C', B', A') with the (A, A') stich at the far left, the (B, B') stich indented from that, the (C, C') stich indented from that, etc. until the twined center used by Mark. The A' hemistich of a pericope is the A hemistich of the next pericope.

At 1:21–28 – "Unclean Spirit In The Synagogue":

A 1:21 And they go into Capernaum.

  B And immediately on the Sabbath he entered into the synagogue and taught.

    C 1:22 And they were astonished at his teaching. For he taught them as having authority, and not as the scribes.

      D 1:23 And immediately in their synagogue there was a man with an unclean spirit.

        E And he shouted, 1:24 saying, "What are we to you, Jesus, the Nazarene? Have you come to destroy us? I know who you are, the Holy One of God."

        E' 1:25 And Jesus admonished him, saying, "Be silent and come out of him."

      D' 1:26 And having thrown the man into convulsions the unclean spirit shouted with a loud voice and came out of him.

    C' 1:27 And they were all amazed, such that they asked each other, saying, "What is this? New teaching? He commands with authority, and the unclean spirits obey him."

  B' 1:28 And immediately the news about him went out everywhere into all the surrounding region of Galilee.

A' 1:29 And immediately, when they had come out of the synagogue, they came into the house of Simon and Andrew, with James and John.

The reader is told that Jesus had authority (exousian) first in his teaching then in commanding the unclean spirit. Mark made a chiastic match for the (C, C') stich. "Astonished/amazed" (exeplēssonto/ethambēthēsan) and "authority" are in both hemistiches. This is repetition, but from a slightly different perspective in that it adds new information. If one finds the same exact fact repeated in the narrative, it is a tell-tale sign of interpolation by a redactor who was not as sparse as Mark. For example:

> 6:30 And the apostles gather together with Jesus; and they told him about every thing, what they had done, and what they had taught. 6:31 And he says to them, "Come down into the *desert* and rest a while." For many were coming and going, and they had no opportunity to even eat. 6:32 And they went away in a boat to their private *desert* place. 6:33 And many saw them going, and recognized them, and they all ran there on foot from all the cities, and got there before them. 6:34 And he got out and saw a large crowd, and he had pity on them because they were as sheep without a shepherd: and he began to teach

them many things. 6:35 And when the hour became late his disciples came to him and said, "This place is *desolate*, and the hour is late.

Within six verses the reader has been told they are going to the desert, on their way to the desert, and are in the desert. This does not seem to be the same author who does not tell the reader how Jesus was tempted in the wilderness at Mark 1:12 or why Jesus wants demons and people who are healed to keep silent about him. With the narrative fact of going to the desert being used three times, we may begin to suspect that a redactor has had a hand in this sequence.

As a further example of Mark's economy of words at 4:37–38 he wrote:

4:37 And there arises a large windstorm, and the waves washed into the boat, so that the boat was already filling. 4:38 And he was in the stern sleeping on the cushion: and they awaken him, and say to him, "Teacher, do you not care that we are going to die?"

The disciples do not tell Jesus that a storm is filling the boat with water. The reader has already been told that, so Mark has them ask Jesus if he cares they are going to die. Those ten words communicate so much about the fear and desperation the disciples are experiencing. Mark does not engage in unnecessary dialogue.

Jesus never tells his disciples or the crowd that he is going to cure an afflicted person. He just does it. The author of Mark is succinct. If we find text where there is reiteration of facts or motives, we should suspect that a redactor who was wordier than the taciturn Mark has introduced an interpolation.

Mark is also subtle in his chiastic matches. The chiastic matches are obvious when the exact same words are used in a stich, but matching concepts can be obscure. For example:

A 1:29 And immediately, when they had come out of the synagogue, they came into the house of Simon and Andrew, with James and John.

B 1:30 But Simon's mother-in-law was sick with a fever; and immediately they tell him about her.

C 1:31 And he came and took her by the hand and raised her up. And the fever left her, and she served them.

D 1:32 And at evening, when the sunset, they brought all the sick to him, and those that were possessed with demons.

D' 1:33 And the entire city was gathered together at the door.

C' 1:34 And he healed many that were sick with various diseases, and cast out many demons.

B' And he did not allow the demons to speak, because they knew him.

A' 1:35 And very early, a long time before daylight, he woke up and went out, and departed into a deserted place, and was praying there.

The (B, B') stich matches are 1. they tell Jesus that Simon's mother-in-law is sick and matching that, he did not allow the demons to speak—telling and not speaking, a match of opposites, and 2. Simon's mother-in-law is sick, which conceptually matches demon possession.

In the (C, C') stich Jesus heals Simon's mother-in-law and he heals those that come to the house.

In the (D, D') stich they brought the sick to Jesus and the entire city was at the door. In a Markan center stich typically one of the hemistiches is much longer than the other with the shorter being a summary of the longer one.

Word matching is easy to spot, especially if the word is unusual. Concepts are not as easy to recognize, and opposing concepts can be easily overlooked. Occasionally the concepts are Christian theological concepts and take some thinking before the recognition hits. Then there are questions asked and answered, stiches wherein the character who is speaking matches the character spoken about. All of this enhances the reader's experience in building to the center and waning from the center to the end of the pericope. There are some rather linear pericopae that build to the end with Jesus giving a sermon and an aphorism at the end.

3

The Prologue and Epilogue Parallel Structure

MARK SIGNALED MAJOR DIVISIONS in his Gospel with parallel constructions in the center stich of the pericope-level chiastic structure of some significant pericopae. The parallel center of the pericope "Calling the First Four Disciples" (1:14–20) was pointed out above. Here is the pericope to begin the Gospel and the prologue:

1:1 The beginning of the gospel of Jesus Christ, Son of God

A 1:2 As it is written in Isaiah the prophet,

BA "Look, I send my messenger ahead of you,

BB who will prepare your way."

BA' 1:3 A voice proclaiming in the wilderness,

BB' "Prepare the way for the Lord. Make his way straight."

A' 1:4 Appeared John the Baptizer in the wilderness proclaiming the baptism of repentance for remission of sins.

Identifying the chiastic structure of this initial pericope resolves a question scholars have had as to whether verse 1:1 is the title/incipit or whether it is the first line of the text. The beginning of the initial pericope-level chiastic structure is at 1:2 with the mention of Isaiah. This makes clear that 1:1 is not part of the text. It must be the incipit, the title of the Gospel. Analysis of Markan triplets and sextets also demonstrates that 1:1 is not part of the text. All of the words found in 1:1 except "Jesus" are found in triplets or sextets within the text if the occurrence of the word in 1:1 is ignored. "Beginning" (archē) is found three times in the text, ignoring the occurrence at 1:1. "Gospel" (euangelou) is found in the text, ignoring the occurrence 1:1, three times before the turning point at 10:32 and three times after the turning point, a Markan sextet. The word "Christ" (christos) is found in two triplets ignoring the occurrence at 1:1. All elements of the "Christ" triplet are combined with the verb "to say" (legō). "Son of God" (huiou Theou) is also used three times in the text ignoring the occurrence at 1:1. Since these two triplets and two sextets are located between 1:2 and 16:8 and there are over eighty other triplets and sextets in this text, as documented in Appendix 2, it is evident that 1:1 is an incipit and not part of the text. As further evidence the four incipit phrases are in the order: triplet (beginning), sextet (gospel), sextet (Christ), triplet (Son of God)—a chiastic structure.

With over eighty triplets and sextets in the Original Gospel, using words and phrases such as "Satan," "prophet," and "all things are possible," it is inconceivable that important words and phrases like "gospel," "Christ" and "Son of God" would not be parts of triplets or sextets. Therefore, 1:1 must be an incipit and not part of the text of the Original Gospel.

The first pericope of the Gospel begins at 1:2. In this special case there is no movement into the scene or change of cast in the A hemistich since there is no prior scene. The A' hemistich has John appearing in the wilderness, a definite location and the introduction of a cast member. The (BA, BA') stich matches "sending a messenger" with "a voice in the wilderness." The (BB, BB') stich matches "preparing the way."

Mark signaled the limits of the prologue in another way. The first words spoken by Jesus as he enters Galilee are, "The time has been completed and the kingdom of God is at hand. Repent and believe in the gospel." This is a clear demarcation of the prologue: from "the gospel" (tou evangeliou) in the incipit at 1:1 to "believe in the gospel" (tou evangeliou) at 1:15. Immediately thereafter Jesus begins his ministry by recruiting Simon, Andrew, James, and John.

There is an identifiable epilogue in Mark's Gospel for those who recognize the signals. Francis J. Moloney identifies 16:1–8 as the epilogue.[1] There is not much discussion in the literature about an epilogue in Mark, other than by the minority of scholars who claim either the long or the short ending (16:9–20) is the epilogue.

In Greek tragedy an epilogue is a short concluding scene, generally involving a substantial shift of tone and/or a *deus ex machina.* The young man in the open tomb is a *deus ex machina.* He may have been the one who rolled the stone away and let Jesus out of the tomb. He tells the women that the tomb is empty; that Jesus has risen from the dead (this is the third time "risen" in the sense of "to rise from the dead" is used outside of the Passion Predictions) and that Jesus is on his way to Galilee. There is also a definite shift in tone at the end, but where does that shift begin?

Between 1:13 and 15:38, the narrative is about Jesus: what he says, what he does, what others say to him, what others do to him. There are minor digressions, such as the killing of John the Baptizer by Herod, Pharisees consulting with the Herodians, two unnamed disciples fetching a colt, two unnamed disciples hiring a room for the Passover meal, and Judas consulting with the high priests. Before 1:13 the narrative is mainly about John the Baptizer and after 15:39 the narrative is about Joseph of Arimathea and the women. The tone changes at 15:39 as Jesus dies.

A And they lead him out to crucify him.

1. Moloney, *Gospel of Mark,* 352.

B 15:21 And they compel a passer by, Simon of Cyrene, coming from the country, the father of Alexander and Rufus, to carry his cross. 15:22 And they take him to Golgotha which is being translated, "The place of a skull."

CA 15:23 And they gave him wine mingled with myrrh: but he did not take it.

CB 15:24 And as they were crucifying him

CC they divided his garments among them, throwing dice for them, what each should take.

    D 15:25 And it was the third hour, and they crucified him.

      E 15:26 And the inscription of the charge against him was written over, "The King of the Jews."

        F 15:27 And with him they crucify two robbers, one on his right hand, and one on his left. 15:28.

          GA 15:29 And those that passed by called him names, shaking their heads, and saying, "Ha! You that destroys the temple, and builds it in three days,

          GB 15:30 save yourself, and come down from the cross."

          GA' 15:31 Likewise also the chief priests ridiculing him among themselves with the scribes said, "He saved others; he cannot save himself.

          GB' 15:32 Let the Christ, the King of Israel, now come down from the cross, that we may see and believe."

        F' And those being crucified with him insulted him.

      E' 15:33 And at the sixth hour darkness came over the entire land until the ninth hour.

    D' 15:34 And at the ninth hour Jesus shouted with a loud voice, "Eloi, Eloi, lama sabachthani?" which is, being interpreted, "My God, my God, why have you abandoned me?"

CA' 15:35 And some of those that standing there, hearing it, said, "Look, he calls Elijah." 15:36 And one ran and filled a sponge full of vinegar, put it on a rod, and gave it to him to drink, saying, "Let him have it. See if Elijah comes to take him down."

CB' 15:37 And Jesus uttered a loud sound, and the spirit departed from him.

CC' 15:38 And the curtain of the temple was torn in two from the top to the bottom.

B' 15:39 And the centurion standing across from him, seeing that the spirit departed from him said, "Truly this man was a Son of God."

A' 15:40 And there were also women looking on from a distance: among whom Mary Magdalene, and Mary the mother of James the less and of Joseph, and Salome;

The last words of the incipit before the initial pericope of the prologue are "Son of God" (huiou Theou). The last words of "The Crucifixion" pericope before the next pericope starts at 15:40 are "Son of God" stated by the centurion. This comes immediately after Jesus dies with the centurion recognizing who Jesus is. This is exactly where one might expect an epilogue of a Gospel about Jesus to begin—immediately after the tragic death of the main character.

In addition to being alerted by the parallel stiches that a major division is occurring, the prologue is defined by the inclusio "the gospel." The beginning of the prologue and epilogue can be identified by the words "Son of God."

The last words of both 1:1 and at 15:39 are "Son of God," this repetition signals the beginning of a large parallel structure. To test this hypothesis let us examine the ends of the proposed prologue and epilogue to see if there are matching words or concepts. What is found is that at the end of the prologue Jesus proclaims the gospel of God. At the end of the proposed epilogue the women keep silent because they are afraid. This makes a good opposing ironic match—proclaiming and keeping silent. We will see later how the women keeping silent affects the Messianic Secret. There are also significant repeated words near the ends of both the prologue and the epilogue. At 1:14 Jesus came "into the Galilee" to translate the Greek literally, and at 16:7 the women are told by the young man that they should tell the disciples and Peter that he (Jesus) goes before them "into the Galilee," using the exact same three words. These identical words are near the end of the prologue at 1:14 and near the end of the Gospel at 16:7. In fact, there are twenty-three Greek words from "Galilee" to the end of the prologue and twenty-two Greek words from "Galilee" to the end of the Gospel.

The prologue and the epilogue form a parallel structure, with either repeated words, repeated concepts, opposite or ironic concepts, and interestingly, using both halves of a stich to make references to an included Markan passage and a Pauline passage. Chiasmus dominates the literary structures of Mark's Gospel, but parallel structures signal important divisions. Comparing the prologue and epilogue line by line reveals a number of matching hemistiches.

Since this structure is long (fifteen stiches), it will be set out in a table of parallel columns. Each stich will comprise a row of the table. The left hand column will have the first half of the structure, the prologue, (A, B, C, etc.) hemistiches and the right hand column with have the second half of the structure, the epilogue, (A', B', C', etc.) hemistiches.

The table has my translation of Mark of the subject passages with the matching elements in *italics*. Below the table will be a stich-by-stich notation of the matching elements between the hemistiches and commentary. After the commentary there will be an analysis section clarifying what the subject structure has established and other evidence that may support any changes to Canonical Mark.

The Prologue and Epilogue Parallel Structure

A 1:1 The beginning of the gospel of Jesus Christ, *Son of God.*

A' 15:39 And the centurion standing across from him, seeing that the spirit departed from him said, "Truly this man was a *Son of God.*"

B 1:2a As it is written in Isaiah the prophet, Look, *I send my messenger ahead of you,*

B' 15:40 And there were also women looking on from a distance: among whom Mary Magdalene, and Mary the mother of James the less and of Joseph, and Salome; 15:41 who when he was in Galilee *followed him,* and served him. And many other women *came up with him to Jerusalem.*

C 1:2b who will *prepare* your way. 1:3 A voice proclaiming in the wilderness, *Prepare* the way for the Lord, Make his way straight;

C' 15:42 And evening having arrived, since it was the *Preparation,* that is, the day before the Sabbath,

D 1:4a *Appeared John the Baptizer* in the wilderness

D' 15:43a *Arrived Joseph from Arimathea, a Sanhedrin member of honorable estate,*

E 1:4b and proclaiming the *baptism of repentance* for forgiveness of sins.

E' 15:43b who also himself was expecting the *kingdom of God;* arrived

F 1:5a And all the country of Judea *went out to him,* and all of Jerusalem;

F' 15:43c and he boldly *went in to Pilate,* and petitioned for the body of Jesus.

G 1:5b And they were *baptized* by him in the Jordan River, confessing their *sins.*

G' 15:44 And *Pilate* wondered if he were already *dead:* and calling to him the *centurion,* he questioned him whether he was already *dead.* 15:45 And learning of it from the *centurion,* he granted the corpse to Joseph.

H 1:6 And John was *dressed in camel's hair, and a leather belt around his hips,* and he ate locusts and wild honey.

H' 15:46a And buying a linen cloth, and taking him down, he *wrapped him in the linen cloth,* and laid him in a tomb which had been hewn out of a rock.

I 1:7 And he preached, saying, "After me there comes someone who is mightier than I. I am not fit to *bend down and loosen the buckle of his sandals.*

I' 15:46b And he *rolled a stone against the door of the tomb.* 15:47 And Mary Magdalene and Mary the mother of Joseph saw where he was laid.

J 1:8 I *baptized you* in *water;* he will *baptize you* in the *Holy Spirit.*"

J' 16:1 And with the Sabbath passing Mary Magdalene, and Mary the mother of James, and Salome, bought *spices,* that they might come and *anoint him.*

K 1:9 And it happened in those days, that *Jesus the Nazarene* came from Galilee, and was baptized by John in the Jordan.

K' 16:6a And he says to them, "Do not be astonished. You are looking for *Jesus the Nazarene* who was crucified.

L 1:10 And immediately *coming up out of the water,* he saw the heavens tearing open, and the Spirit like a dove descending into him: 1:11 And a voice came out of the heavens, "You are my beloved Son, in whom I am well pleased."

L' 16:6b He is *risen.*

M 1:12 And immediately the Spirit drives *him out into the wilderness.* 1:13 And he was in the wilderness forty days tempted by Satan; And he was with the wild animals. And the angels served him.

M' 16:6c *He is not here.* Look at the place where they laid him!

N 1:14a And after John was delivered up Jesus came *into Galilee,*

N' 16:7 But go, tell his disciples and Peter, he goes ahead of you *into Galilee.* You will see him there just as he told you."

O 1:14b *proclaiming* the gospel of God, 1:15 and *saying,* "The time has been completed, and the kingdom of God is at hand: repent, and believe in the gospel."

O' 16:8 And going out they fled from the tomb for trembling and astonishment had come over them: and they *told no one anything* for they were afraid.

Commentary

A (1:1), A' (15:39)

"Son of God" is found in both hemistiches. Technically, this "Son of God" match is not part of the prologue or epilogue. As previously discussed, the words "Son of God" are only used four times in Mark's Gospel, including in the incipit. These two uses signal the beginning of the parallel structure. Both hemistiches are the words immediately before the beginning of the first pericope of the prologue and the first pericope of the epilogue. In other words, the prologue and the epilogue begin with the next sentence (1:2 and 15:40).

B (1:2A), B' (15:40–41)

"I send my messenger ahead of you" in the first hemistich matches "followed him" in the second. This match is one of opposites, depending on how it is viewed. In 1:2 the reader is told that God sent a messenger before Jesus to prepare the way by quoting Mal 3:1 and Exod 23:20. In 15:41 the reader is told that the women followed Jesus to Jerusalem. In 1:2 Jesus presumably will follow John the Baptizer and in 15:41 the women followed Jesus into Galilee and came with him to Jerusalem. There is the action of following in both hemistiches. While the words are not exactly alike, the concept is, and there is a relationship between sending a messenger ahead and following. This concept match occurs within a few words after the repetition of an exact phrase, "Son of God." The young man in the tomb tells the women that Jesus "goes ahead of you into Galilee." This is no doubt a reprise of "I send my messenger ahead of you."

C (1:2b), C' (15:42)

"Prepare" is found twice in the first hemistich and once in the second. In 1:2b Mark continues his quote of Mal 3:1 and mixes in Exod 23:20 and Isa 40:3. In making a match with "prepare" at 1:2b Mark uses "kataskeuasei," a future tense verb, while at 15:42 is "paraskeue," a singular noun with the same root (skeuazo). These are the only two times "skeuazo" is used in Mark. Within the first two verses of the prologue and the epilogue there are words almost never used by Mark outside of this provisional structure. It seems as if Mark is intentionally matching words.

In 15:42 Mark tells the reader that it was "the Preparation," the day before the Sabbath. This is a proper noun used in Greek to denote the day before the Sabbath or any feast. This word "paraskeue" is used in all four canonical Gospels and in Josephus.[2] Therefore, Mark was linguistically required to use that term. As mentioned above Mark quoted a conflation of Mal 3:1, Exod 23:20, and Isa 40:3. The Septuagint (LXX) uses "hetoimazate" as the word for "prepare" or "make ready" in both Exod 23:20 and Isa 40:3. "Epibilepsetai" is used in Malachi for "prepare" which means closer to "survey" and makes sense when speaking about a road or path. Neither of those would match "paraskeue;" therefore, Mark deliberately misquoted Mal 3:1 to match 15:42. Then he properly quoted Isa 40:3. It appears that Mark was deliberately matching words to create a parallelism.

D (1:4a), D' (15:43a)

"Appeared John the Baptizer" in the first hemistich matches "Arrived Joseph from Arimathea, a Sanhedrin member of honorable estate." In the very next verses of the prologue and epilogue the reader is introduced to new characters forming the (D, D') stich. At 1:4 Mark used "he appeared" (egeneto). At 15:43 he used "he arrived" (elthon) to describe the action of Joseph from Arimathea. At 15:43 Joseph appears out of nowhere much like John the Baptizer. While exact words are not used in both hemistiches, there are two characters introduced out of nowhere and inserted into the story. There is also an unusual Greek construction in Mark: "Egeneto Ioannes ho baptizon" usually translates "appeared John, baptizing" or "appeared John who baptized." These translations miss the nominative masculine singular article "ho." It looks like Mark perhaps meant an appositive, "John, the one baptizing." The NRSV has "John the baptizer appeared." If Mark intended an appositive, the constructions of 1:4a and 15:43a are also parallel with "the baptizing" or "the baptizer" parallel to "a Sanhedrin member of honorable estate." There are other affinities between John and Joseph. John puts Jesus under water; Joseph puts Jesus in the tomb. John is not fit to unbuckle Jesus's sandal; Joseph wraps Jesus in a linen cloth (both actions of dressing). John prepares Jesus for his ministry; Joseph prepares Jesus for burial.

2. J.A. 16:6:2.

E (1:4B), E' (15:43B)

"Baptism of Repentance" in the first hemistich matches "Kingdom of God" in the second. One might well question how these passages are related. Significantly, 1:4b mentions "repentance" (metanoias) immediately after John the Baptizer is introduced and 15:43b mentions "kingdom of God" immediately after Joseph of Arimathea is introduced. This may be a Markan internal reference to 1:15, the end of the prologue and beginning of Jesus's ministry. Jesus uses both "repent" and "kingdom of God" in the first words spoken by him in Mark's Gospel. There are only three occurrences of "repent/repentance" in Mark and 1:4 and 1:15 are two of them (6:12 is the other). According to Mark's Jesus, those who want to attain the kingdom of God must repent. "Repentance" and "the Kingdom of God" are inextricably linked. Mark linked them at 1:15 and also linked them in the matching hemistiches of the prologue and the epilogue. Further, 15:43 is near the end of the Gospel and the words of Jesus at 1:15 "believe in the gospel" take on a greater meaning after Jesus's crucifixion.

F (1:5A), F' (15:43C)

In the first hemistich the people of Judea and Jerusalem "went out to John" and in the second Joseph "went in to Pilate." Movement in opposite directions is the match.

G(1:5B), G' (15:44–45)

"Baptism" and "sin" in the first hemistich are a match for "dead" found twice in the second. Significantly, "Pilate" and "centurion" are Romans. It is not immediately obvious that there is a relationship between 1:5b and 15:44–45. Why do "baptism" and "sin" match "dead"? In *Matthew, Mark, Luke, and Paul* abundant evidence is presented that Mark knew Paul's epistles.[3] This stich is a reference by Mark to Rom 6:3–8:

> 6:3 Or are you ignorant that all we who were *baptized* into Christ Jesus were *baptized* into his *death*? 4 We were *buried* therefore with him through *baptism* unto *death*. That like as Christ was raised from the *dead* through the glory of the Father, so we also might walk in newness of life. 5 For if we have become united with him in the likeness of his *death*, we shall be also in the likeness of his resurrection 6 Knowing this, that our old man was *crucified* with him, that the body of *sin* might be done away, that so we should no longer be in bondage to *sin*; 7 for he that has *died* is justified from *sin*. 8 But if we *died* with Christ, we believe that we shall also live with him.

Paul tells the Romans that at baptism Christians die with respect to sin. Mark has the people of Judea and Jerusalem being baptized and confessing their sins at 1:5b, while

---

3. Smith, *MMLP.*

at 15:44–45 Pilate learns that Jesus has died unexpectedly early. When Christians are baptized they "die" unexpectedly early in Paul's theology. The Roman governor, Pilate, learns this from a Roman Centurion. With his use of Roman characters, Mark has consciously referred to Paul's Epistle to the Romans! The combination of 1:5b and 15:44–45 specifically mentions all three elements: "baptism," "sins," and "death," and Romans discusses these elements. It is difficult to believe that this just coincidentally reflects Rom 6:3–8. Chapter 15 demonstrates that one of Mark's purposes in writing his Gospel was to promote Pauline Christianity. If that is true, it is not surprising that Mark would make a parallel match based upon Paul's epistle to the Romans.

H (1:6), H' (15:46A)

"Dressed in camel's hair, and a leather belt around his hips" in the first hemistich matches "wrapped him in a linen cloth" in the second hemistich.

At 1:6 Mark tells how John was dressed by making a reference to 2 Kings 1:8 and the description of Elijah, using a direct quote of that verse from the LXX. Matching the way John is dressed at 15:46a, Mark tells the reader how Joseph dresses Jesus for burial. Mark includes a description of John the Baptizer's clothing as a way of indicating that John is a reappearance of Elijah and forerunner to the coming of the kingdom of God as prophesied at Mal 4:5. The description of dressing Jesus's body for burial seems unnecessary, but it conveniently provides a match for John's clothing at 1:6. Of course, winding Jesus's body with a linen cloth provides colorful detail in the story of Jesus's burial, but it is not necessary. And it parallels "a leather belt around his hips." Not only does it provide the match, but also it shows a contrast of John wearing rough animal skins and Joseph providing expensive linen for Jesus.

Mark's Gospel tells his readers how someone is dressed seven times:

1. John's costume is described,

2. Jesus tells his disciples what to wear when he sends them out,

3. Jesus's clothes are described at the transfiguration,

4. A young man becomes naked at Jesus's arrest,

5. The Roman soldiers dress Jesus in a purple robe,

6. Joseph of Arimathea wraps Jesus's body in linen, and

7. The clothing of the young man in the tomb, who may be the same person as the naked young man, is described.

Three of these seven "dressings" are in the prologue and epilogue.

I (1:7), I' (15:46B)

"Bend down and loosen the buckle of his sandals" in the first hemistich matches "rolled a stone against the door of the tomb." This stich contains the opposing concepts of opening and closing. At 1:7 John preaches about a coming mighty one and that John is not worthy of loosening his shoe latchets. At 15:46b Joseph is mighty enough to roll a stone against the door of the tomb to keep it closed so that it will not come loose. We learn later at 16:4 that the stone was "exceedingly great," indicating how mighty Joseph was to have rolled it by himself. In both hemistiches we have something closed, sandals with a latchet and a tomb door with a large stone rolled in front. John is not worthy of loosening the shoe latchets, but the reader discovers later that Jesus or the young man has loosened the tomb door.

J (1:8), J' (16:1)

"Baptized you" found twice in the first hemistich matches "anoint him" in the second. "Water" and "Holy Spirit" in the first hemistich match "spices" in the second. This stich matches the similar concepts of baptism and anointing. In 1:8 John says he baptizes the people while at 16:1 the women intend to anoint Jesus with oil and spices. There is a physical relationship between baptizing and anointing. The baptism of John consists of putting the baptized person's entire body in water, while the anointing for burial with oil and spices (aleipho) consists of bathing the entire body in the oil and spice mixture. "Christos" means "anointed one" in Greek, but comes from a different verb "chriō"—to anoint in a religious sense—which would have been inappropriate for the women to do to Jesus's body.

K (1:9), K' (16:6A)

"Jesus the Nazarene" in the first hemistich matches "Jesus the Nazarene" in the second. In this stich there is "Iesous," (Jesus) and either "Nazarēnou" or "Nazaret" (Nazareth). Was Jesus a Nazarene or from Nazareth? It is possible that Mark's Original Gospel at 1:9 had "Nazarene," and "Nazaret" is a later redaction. There are a several reasons that the use of "Nazaret" in this verse is suspicious:

1. Mark identified Jesus as "Nazarēnou" four times (there are different endings for the different cases) and 1:9 is the only time "Nazaret," is used. While absolute consistency is not required, it is curious that 1:9 is different from the other four times.

2. Matthew eliminated Mark's "Nazarene" in all of Matthew's passages that are parallel to Mark's use of "Nazarene." At Matt 3:13 when Jesus is coming to be baptized he describes Jesus as "the Jesus from the Galilee" eliminating the "Nazarene" or "of Nazareth," whichever was there originally in Mark. At Matt 2:23 Matthew says that Jesus and family move

from Egypt to Nazareth, and he adds that this fulfills the prophesy that he would be called a "Nazōraios" (Nazorean) but this is slightly different from Mark's "Nazarēnos" (Nazarene) for the same case (nominative masculine singular). For some reason the writer of Matthew, who some scholars think was a Jewish-Christian scribe,[4] did not like Mark's "Nazarene" and Matt 2:23 is his only use of the term. There is no obvious prophesy in the OT that the messiah would be called a Nazarene.

3. Mark usually used an article before "Jesus" as he did at 1:14 "came *the* Jesus into the Galilee," as did Matthew at Matt 3:13, just quoted. However, an article is not found before "Jesus" at 1:9 in Canonical Mark. This may be evidence of a later redaction.

4. If "of Nazareth" found at 1:9 was originally "Nazarene," there would be an exact match of three words in the (K, K') stich. This, of course, is a self-fulfilling prophesy, but given the previous ten matches, it could well be that Mark intended an exact word match with this stich. Perhaps in the original Gospel both 1:9 and 16:6 identified Jesus as a "Nazarene."

Chapter 12 demonstrates that the five uses of "Nazarene" are combined with a subtle textual reference to form a sextet, in true Markan fashion. This Markan structural puzzle is powerful evidence that Mark's Original Gospel had "Nazarene" at 1:9.

L (1:10), L' (16:6B)

"Coming up out of the water" in the first hemistich matches "he is risen." After John baptizes Jesus he comes up out of the water at 1:10, while at 16:6b the young man tells the women that Jesus is risen. The physical act of moving upward makes this an obvious match.

M (1:12), M' (16:6C)

"Him out into the wilderness" in the first hemistich matches "he is not here" in the second. At 1:12 Jesus immediately left the scene of his baptism, and apparently at 16:6 he immediately left the scene of his entombment without waiting around for his disciples or the women to find him. In both cases Jesus left. Location is described in both hemistiches.

N (1:14A), N' (16:7)

"Into Galilee" is found in both hemistiches. This is a match of an exact three Greek word phrase "into the Galilee" (eis tēn Galilaian) near the end of the prologue and near the end of the epilogue. In addition to that at 16:7 the young man tells the women that Jesus had prophesied that he would go before them into Galilee after he was raised

---

4. Goulder, *MLM*, 5.

up. At 14:28 Jesus uses the exact words "into the Galilee." The young man at the tomb quotes Jesus word for word. These are two elements in a triplet of the phrase "into Galilee."

O (1:14B), O' (16:8)

"Proclaiming" and "saying" in the first hemistich is an ironic opposite to "told no one anything" in the second. This is the final match and an ironic opposite to end the literary unit and the Gospel. Jesus comes into Galilee preaching and telling people to repent and believe in the gospel. The young man implores the women to tell the disciples and Peter that Jesus will see them in Galilee. They say nothing because they are afraid. This is an ironic juxtaposition found frequently in Mark. The failure of the women to comply with the young man's directive has bothered Christians for almost nineteen hundred years, so much so that alternative endings were added to Mark in the fourth century to make the ending more palatable.

Matching Language

There are too many consecutive parallel relationships between the prologue 1:1–15 and the epilogue 15:39—16:8 to be coincidental. Recognizing the parallel structure found uniting the prologue and the epilogue exposes a coherent literary unit and provides additional layers of meaning. There are two hundred forty-five Greek words in the prologue and three hundred six Greek words in the epilogue. They produce fifteen consecutive directly parallel matches. A match every twenty words.

These matches could not possibly have resulted by chance. The following is a table of the matching language, leaving out the non-matching words.

A *Son of God*	A' *Son of God*
B *I send my messenger ahead of you.*	B' *followed him, came up with him to Jerusalem*
C *prepare, prepare*	C' *preparation*
D *Appeared John the Baptizer,*	D' *Arrived Joseph of Arimathea, a Sanhedrin member of honorable estate*
E *repentance*	E' *the kingdom of God*
F *went out*	F' *went in*
G *baptized, sins*	G' *Pilate, dead. Centurion, dead, Centurion*
H *dressed in camel's hair and a leather belt around his hips*	H' *linen cloth, wrapped him in the linen cloth*
I *bend down and loosen the buckle of his sandals*	I' *rolled a stone against the door of the tomb*
J *baptized you, water, baptize you, Holy Spirit*	J' *spices, anoint him*
K *Jesus the Nazarene*	K' *Jesus the Nazarene*

L *coming up out of the water*	L' *he is risen*
M *out into the wilderness*	M' *he is not here*
N *into Galilee*	N' *into Galilee*
O *proclaiming, saying*	O' *They told no one anything*

Looked at this way, without the non-matching words impeding observation, it looks as if Mark has deliberately made a parallel construction using matching words, matching concepts, and opposite concepts. Admittedly, the self-referential match to Mark 1:15 and the reference to Rom 6:3–8 in the parallel construction are somewhat obscure, but like all great authors, Mark wrote on multiple levels that can be appreciated by readers with differing sophistications.

Ending The Gospel with "Gar"

Mark 16:8 ends with "ephobounto gar" (for they were afraid). "Gar" is a conjunction in Greek, and it seems odd to end a book with a conjunction. However, this is essentially the same phrase found ending a sentence at Genesis 18:15 (LXX) describing why Sarah lied to God. (Mark uses the third-person plural while Genesis uses the third-person singular.) Curiously, the vast majority of books and articles about the ending of Mark have focused on "gar" and have largely ignored "ephobounto." One scholar noted that the most impressive parallel ending a sentence with "gar" is Gen 18:15. In fact he calls it "strikingly similar."[5] No scholar has expressed the idea that Mark was deliberately referencing Gen 18:15. Mark's abrupt ending at 16:8 is intended for literary effect and he is deliberately referencing Gen 18:15 (LXX). Chapter 16 below documents numerous quotes from and references to the OT in Mark.

Clearly Mark was familiar with the LXX, having referenced it numerous times throughout his Gospel. What does Gen 18:15 have to do with the women at Jesus's tomb on Easter morning? In Gen 18:15 God told Abraham that even at his and Sarah's advanced ages, Sarah would give birth to a son. Sarah laughed to herself, and God asks Abraham why Sarah laughed. For Sarah's benefit, God asks Abraham the rhetorical question of whether he thinks that it would be difficult for God to do. Sarah denied she laughed, and then the text says, "for she was afraid" (ephobēthē gar) and the sentence ends. God then says to her, "Yes you did laugh." Apparently Sarah was afraid because she realized that God could read her thoughts.

Mark used "ephobounto gar" to make a theological point. God's rhetorical question to Abraham, but meant for Sarah, at Gen 18:14 is: Is anything too difficult for God? This expresses the same idea as the triplet found at Mark 9:23, 10:27, and 14:36: "all things are possible with God." At Mark 16:8 the writer was reminding his readers that with God all things are possible. The women at the tomb and the reader should

5. Iverson, "A Further Word," 87.

not be surprised that Jesus had been raised from the dead. Not only is Gen 18:15 a precedent for ending a sentence with a conjunction, it was the source for Mark's decision to end his Gospel with a conjunction. Mark was in the habit of locating "gar" after the verb in his sentences. He may well have thought that such an odd end to a sentence would be familiar to readers of the LXX and his use of the same phrase would be an instant reference to Gen 18:9–15. Mark was directing the reader to the surrounding text and especially Gen 18:14 and God's rhetorical question to Abraham for Sarah's benefit, essentially saying that all things are possible with God. Mark is assuring his reader that the women might not believe it, they might be afraid, but rest assured God can raise dead people from the grave.

This ending also provides a solution to one of Mark's structural puzzles that is discussed in chapter 12. Amazingly, this ending is also a reference to Rom 4:18–21.

With the concluding verse 16:8, there is also an ironic opposing parallel with the entire prologue. In the prologue there is a voice crying in the wilderness, John the Baptizer preaching, a voice out of the heavens, and Jesus preaching and proclaiming the gospel of God's son, while at the culmination of the Gospel and the epilogue there are frightened women who say nothing to anyone.

The above analysis shows that there are fifteen matches between Mark 1:1–14 and Mark 15:39—16:8. The only significant gap is that there are no matches for this structure from 16:2–5. However, these four verses provide two matches for a separate chiastic structure that is analyzed in the next chapter. Even if one is of the opinion that the proposed matches of the (E, E') stich and the (G, G') stich are not credible, there are still thirteen matches in parallel order within 14 verses of Mark 1 and within 17 verses of Mark 15 and 16. The odds against such an occurrence being accidental must be very great.

The logical conclusion is that Mark constructed the prologue and epilogue to be parallel. He wanted the epilogue to be an echo of the prologue. Parallel structures in the center stich of a pericope-level chiastic structure are significant, and 16:8 is definitely the original end of the Gospel.

The parallel structure under discussion clearly delineates the prologue and epilogue. Now we can begin to outline the Original Gospel. Appendix 3 sets out and numbers all seventy-eight pericopae in Original Mark. The Prologue – Epilogue Parallel Structure described in this chapter establishes that pericopae numbers 1–5, 77 and 78 were part of Original Mark. The next chapter confirms those pericopae and adds several more.

4

The Beginning and Passion Chiastic Structure

CHAPTER 3 DEMONSTRATES THAT the prologue and epilogue of Mark's Gospel are defined by a parallel structure containing fifteen matching stiches. This chapter will analyze an even larger chiastic structure uniting the beginning and ending of Mark's Gospel. The first half of the structure runs from Mark 1:2 to 1:38. The second half of the structure runs from Jesus's praying at Gethsemane at 14:32 to the women fleeing from the tomb at 16:8.

The previous chapter demonstrated unequivocally that 16:8 is the end of the Original Gospel since it matches the end of the prologue. This chapter adds further proof that 16:8 is, in fact, the original end of the Gospel because this chiasmus begins at 1:2 with a chiastic match to 16:8. The beginning of the Gospel matches chiastically with the end of the Gospel, proving again that 16:8 is the end of the Gospel.

Except for pericope-level chiastic structures, the traditional format for showing a chiastic structure by indenting from one stich to the next will not be used from this point on. The structures are so large, taking up multiple pages, that readers may have difficulty appreciating the matching language. Therefore, the format used in the previous chapter containing only the matching language will be continued so that the chiasm can be more easily discerned. In this case the left hand column runs from 1:2 through 1:38 including Jesus's baptism, the beginning of his ministry, calling his first disciples, healing a man possessed by an unclean spirit, healing Simon's mother-in-law and going out into the desert to pray. The right hand column will be recording the blocks of verses in reverse order from 16:8 to 14:32. This sequence includes (in reverse Gospel order) the women discovering an empty tomb, Jesus's burial, his crucifixion, his trial before Pilate, Peter's denial of Jesus, Jesus's trial before the Council, and his arrest. Only the matching language will be shown in *italics*. Readers desiring to consult the full text of any particular block of text may refer to Appendix 1, which contains my translation of Mark's Original Gospel. Below the table is a commentary on the matching elements.

The Beginning and Passion Chiastic Structure

A 1:2a *As it is written*

A' 16:8 . . . *told no one anything*

B 1:2b *I send my messenger ahead of you*

B' 16:7 *But go, tell his disciples and Peter he goes ahead of you.*

C 1:3 *A voice proclaiming . . . "Prepare the way for the Lord . . ."*

C' 16:6 *he says, . . . "Jesus, the Nazarene, who was crucified. He is risen."*

D 1:4 *Appeared John the Baptizer in the wilderness . . . 1:6 . . . dressed in camel's hair, and a leather belt around his hips.*

D' 16:5 . . . *a young man sitting on the right, dressed in a white robe.*

E 1:7 And *he preached, saying, ". . . who is mightier than I . . . bend down and loosen the buckle of his sandals."*

E' 16:3 *they were saying, ". . . Who will roll the stone away from the door of the tomb . . ."*

F 1:8 *"I baptized . . . water . . . baptize . . ."*

F' 16:1 . . . *spices . . . anoint*

G 1:9 . . . *Jesus the Nazarene came from Galilee*

G' 15:41 . . . *he was in Galilee . . . came up with him*

H 1:10 . . . *coming up out of the water . . . heavens tearing open . . . spirit as a dove descending into him*

H' 15:37 . . . *spirit departed from him* 15:38 . . . *curtain of the temple was torn in two . . . top to the bottom.* 15:39 . . . *the spirit departed from him*

I 1:11 . . . *voice came out of the heavens, "You are my beloved son, in whom I am well pleased."*

I' 15:34 . . . *voice, "Eloi, Eloi, lama sabachthani? Which is, being interpreted, My God, my God, why have you abandoned me?"*

J 1:13 . . . *forty days tempted by Satan . . . angels served him*

J' 15:29 And *those that passed by called him names, shaking their heads, and saying, "Ha! You that destroys the temple, and builds it in three days,* 15:30 *save yourself, and come down from the cross."*

K 1:16a . . . *saw Simon and Andrew, the brother of Simon*

K' 15:27 . . . *two robbers*

L 1:16b *throwing a net in the sea; for they were fishers . . . 1:18 . . . they left the nets, and followed him*

L' 15:24 *And crucifying him they divided his garments . . . throwing dice for them*

M 1:19 . . . *James the son of Zebedee, and John his brother*

M' 15:21 . . . *Simon of Cyrene, coming from the country, the father of Alexander and Rufus*

N 1:21 . . . *he entered into the synagogue . . . 1:22 And they were astonished at his teaching . . . having authority . . .*

N' 15:16 . . . *took him inside the court, that is, the Praetorian . . . 15:17 And they dressed him in a purple tunic, and braiding a crown of thorns, they put it on him. 15:18 and they began to salute him, "Hail, King of the Jews!" 15:19 And they struck his head with a rod, and spat upon him, and on bended knees worshipped him.*

O 1:24 *saying, "What are we to you, Jesus, the Nazarene? Have you come to destroy us? . . . the Holy One of God."*

O' 15:12 . . . *answered and said to them, "What then shall I do to him whom you call the King of the Jews?" 15:13 . . . "Crucify him." 15:14 . . . "Crucify him."*

P 1:25 . . . *"Be silent . . ."*

P' 15:4 . . . *"Do you have nothing to say? . . ."* 15:5 *But Jesus answered nothing . . .*

Q 1:26 . . . *spirit shouted with a loud voice*

Q' 15:2b . . . *answering says . . .*

R 1:27 . . . *asked each other, ". . . He commands with authority . . ."*

R' 15:2a *And Pilate interrogated him. " . . . King of the Jews?"*

S 1:32 . . . *the sun went down . . . entire city was gathered together . . .* 1:34 . . . *and he did not allow the demons to speak, because they knew him.*

S' 14:66 . . . *"You also were with the Nazarene, Jesus."* 14:68 *But he denied, saying, "I neither know, nor understand what you are saying." . . .* 14:69 . . . *those standing there, "This is one of them."* 14:70 *But he again denied it . . . those standing there . . . "Truly you are one of them; for you are a Galilean."* 14:71 *But he began to curse and swear, "I do not know this man you are talking about."* 14:72 . . . *the cock crowed.*

T 1:35 . . . *into a deserted place, and was praying there.* 1:36 *And Simon and those that were with him searched . . .* 1:37 *And they found him . . . "Everyone is looking for you."* 1:38 . . . *"into the neighboring towns, so that I may preach there also; for this is why I came."*

T' 14:32 . . . *come to a place that was named Gethsemane . . . "Sit here while I pray." . . .* 14:35 . . . *and prayed that . . .* 14:37 *And he comes and finds them sleeping, . . .* 14:39 . . . *he prayed, saying the same words.* 14:40 . . . *he found them sleeping . . .* 14:42 . . . *"Look, he that delivers me is coming."* 14:43 . . . *Judas, one of the twelve, comes and with him a bunch from the chief priests and the scribes and the elders with swords and clubs . . .* 14:49 *"I was with you in the temple teaching every day, . . . But let the scriptures be fulfilled."*

Commentary

A (1:2A), A' (16:8)

"As it is written" in the first hemistich matches its opposite, "told no one anything." This match is one of ironic opposites. While Isaiah (or in this case partially Malachi) published his pronouncements to the world, the women told no one anything, or as the literal Greek reads, "to none nothing they said."

B (1:2B), B' (16:7)

"I send my messenger ahead of you" in the first hemistich matches "but go, tell his disciples and Peter he goes ahead of you." In 1:2b God sent a messenger and in 16:7 the young man instructed the women to be a messenger to the disciples and Peter. The OT quote at 1:2 is a conflation of Mal 3:1 and Exod 23:20. No doubt Malachi was quoting Exod 23:20 and was adapting it for his own purposes. Mark seems to be using both. Chapter 3 shows why Mark used a Greek word for "prepare" different from the one found in Malachi (LXX) and different from the word that is found in Exodus

(LXX). The young man in Jesus's tomb tries to recruit the women as messengers to tell the disciples that Jesus has gone ahead of them to Galilee. The women refuse the task.

C (1:3), C' (16:6)

There are three matching elements in this stich:

1. "Voice proclaiming" in the first hemistich matches "he says" in the second.
2. "Prepare the way" in the first hemistich matches "who was crucified. He is risen" in the second.
3. "The Lord" in the first hemistich matches "Jesus, the Nazarene" in the second.

This part of the Gospel's opening quotation is from Isa 40:3. With the accomplishment of the crucifixion and Jesus's rising, the way is prepared as prophesized in Isaiah. While Isaiah means Yahweh when he says "the Lord," it is also a title for Christ as used by Paul, and Jesus says the Son of Man is "Lord of the Sabbath" at 2:28.

In Mark's Original Gospel, no one addresses Jesus as "Lord." The one time it occurs in Canonical Mark is in the pericope "Healing the Syro-Phoenician Woman's Daughter" (7:24–30), which the evidence will show is interpolated. Jesus refers to himself as "the Lord" when he instructs two disciples to get a colt for him to ride in "Getting a Colt for Jesus" (11:1–6). In Mark's Christology Jesus becomes Lord and the Danielic Son of Man at his resurrection. Therefore linking crucifixion and rising with "prepare the way for the Lord" is part of Mark's Christology. It is also Paul's Christology. Paul preaches Christ crucified and risen from the dead.[1]

D (1:4–6), D' (16:5)

There are three matching elements in this stich:

1. "Appeared John, the Baptizer" in the first hemistich matches the women "saw a young man" in the second.
2. "In the wilderness" in the first hemistich matches "sitting on the right" in the second.
3. "Dressed in camel's hair and a leather belt around his hips" in the first hemistich matches "dressed in a white robe."

The matching elements are in the same order (who, where, how dressed) in both hemistiches. The texts describe how both John and the young man are dressed in detail, using different Greek words for "dressed." The description of how John is dressed is a word-for-word quote from 2 Kings 1:8 (LXX), a description of Elijah. Here Mark

---

1. 1 Cor 15:3–4.

hints to the sophisticated reader who knows the LXX that John is Elijah, the forerunner of the coming of the kingdom of God, as prophesied at Malachi 4:5.

E (1:7), E' (16:3)

There are three matching elements in this stich:

1. "He preached, saying" in the first hemistich matches "they were saying" in the second.

2. "Who is mightier than I" in the first hemistich matches "who will . . . for us" in the second.

3. "Bend down and loosen the buckle on his sandals" in the first hemistich matches "roll the stone away from the door of the tomb" in the second.

John says someone mightier than he is coming, and the women wonder who mightier than they will help them. In the actions described in both hemistiches there are three sub-elements given:

a. "bend down" matches "away from the door,"

b. "loosen the buckle" matches "roll the stone," and

c. "of his sandals" matches "of the tomb."

In both cases there is an opening of something closed. "Bend down" is an unnecessary thing for John to say, but Mark typically describes actions in three stages and it conveniently matches the women's question about the tomb door.

F (1:8), F' (16:1)

"Water" in the first hemistich matches "spices" in the second, and "baptized" and "baptize" in the first hemistich match "anointing" in the second. John baptizes Jesus by immersing his entire body in the water. The women plan to anoint Jesus's entire body with oil and spices.

G (1:9), G' (15:41)

There are three matching elements in this stich:

1. "Jesus" in the first hemistich matches "he" in the second.

2. "Jesus came" in the first hemistich matches "women came" in the second.

3. "Galilee" is in both hemistiches.

Jesus came to his baptism from Galilee, and the women came up to Jerusalem from Galilee with Jesus. Jesus went from Galilee to Jerusalem to meet his destiny. This turn of events had been set in motion by his baptism.

H (1:10), H' (15:37–39)

There are three matching elements in this stich:

1. "Coming up out of the water" in the first hemistich matches its opposite, "from the top to the bottom" in the second.

2. "The heavens tearing open" in the first hemistich matches "the curtain of the temple was torn in two" in the second.

3. "The spirit as a dove descended into him" in the first hemistich matches "the spirit departed him" found twice in the second.

Since the matching elements of this stich are in reverse order, one could say that each element is in a separate stich. All three are in one stich because they were all in only one verse in the baptism pericope.

The verb meaning "split" or "tear" or "divide," (schizō) is used in both hemistiches for the tearing of the heavens and the temple curtain. The tearing of the curtain is symbolic of mankind no longer being separated from God. The curtain in second temple Judaism separated the worshipers from the "holy of holies" that could only be entered by the high priest on the Day of Atonement.[2]

At Jesus's baptism the spirit descends into him, and at death the spirit departs from him. The Greek root is "pneuma" which can mean "spirit" or "breath" or "wind." Mark repeated the phrase that the spirit departed Jesus twice: at 15:37 and 15:39 bracketing the tearing of the temple curtain. In many English translations of 15:37 and 15:39 at Jesus's death, the translation says that Jesus "breathed his last." This is an acceptable translation, but it misses the chiastic and theological point Mark was making that the spirit went into him at his baptism and out of him at his crucifixion. Translating the word "exepneusen" (out spirit or out breath) as "breathed his last" makes it appear that the spirit that left Jesus at the crucifixion was his soul and something completely different from the spirit that infused him at his baptism and drove him into the wilderness. This chiastic match makes it clear that the spirit leaving him is the same one that went into him at baptism.

The spirit entering Jesus at baptism is an Adoptionist element. Adoptionism was a heresy in the early church. There were two branches of Adoptionism. Adoptionists believed that Jesus was born human and was adopted by God either at his baptism or upon resurrection.

---

2. Heb 9:7.

Many translations of Mark 1:10 say "as a dove descending *onto* him." The Greek word used by Mark is "eis," which means "in" or "into," emphasizing the chiastic match, and agreeing with Baptismal Adoptionism. "Epi" is the Greek preposition that usually denotes the English "onto." Isaiah 42:1 (LXX) has "ep" meaning onto. The versions which translate "eis" as "onto" appear to be assuming that Mark made a mistake in copying Isa 42:1 (LXX) that says, "I have put *my* spirit *upon* him." For example, Randel Helms says that Mark's usage of "the spirit" instead of "my spirit" shows his ineptness.[3] Helms fails to note that Mark used "eis" instead of "ep," apparently assuming Mark made a mistake. Obviously, Helms did not appreciate the chiastic and theological point Mark was making. Mark deliberately changed Isa 42:1 to make his theological point. Both Matthew and Luke in copying this passage from Mark changed the Greek "eis" to "ep" to match Isa 42:1 (LXX). Helms suggests that Matthew and Luke were embarrassed by Mark's mistake. It may be that they were consciously changing Mark's Adoptionism. This may also be the reason they added nativity stories to Mark. Mark made the deliberate choice to write "into" (eis) in order to make a chiastic and a theological match with the spirit entering Jesus at baptism and leaving Jesus at his crucifixion. Once the chiastic structure is appreciated, Mark's motive for writing "eis" becomes clear.

I (1:11), I' (15:34)

"Voice" is in both hemistiches. "You are my beloved son, in whom I am well pleased" in the first hemistich matches "Eloi, Eloi, lama sabachthani?" which is, being interpreted, "My God, my God, why have you abandoned me?" in the second.

A voice comes out of the heavens calling Jesus, and Jesus in a loud voice calls God. God's voice says, " . . . in whom I am well pleased," while Jesus voices ironic disappointment with God. The voice from heaven partially quotes Isa 42:1; Jesus quotes Ps 22:1. The father calls his son at baptism/adoption; the son calls his father at crucifixion. Mark expected his readers to know he was quoting from the OT and would be familiar with the quotes and surrounding passages. Much of the crucifixion pericope is based upon Ps 22.

J (1:13), J' (15:29–30)

There are three matching elements in this stich:

1. "Forty days" in the first hemistich matches "three days" in the second.

2. "Angels served him" in the first hemistich matches its ironic opposite "those that passed by called him names shaking their heads" in the second.

---

3. Helms, *Who Wrote*, 15

3. "Tempted by Satan" in the first hemistich matches "Those that passed by . . . saying Ha! You that destroys the temple, and builds it in three days, 15:30 save yourself, and come down from the cross."

God's messengers, angels, serving Jesus in the wilderness matches its ironic opposite—the human witnesses of his crucifixion verbally abusing him. Both hemistiches contain time periods measured in days, forty days in the wilderness matching the false accusation of claiming to rebuild the temple in three days. The false accusation is a reiteration from Jesus's trial before the Council. Tempting by Satan is a match to the taunting by the crowd tempting Jesus to come down from the cross. Presumably both are tempting Jesus to ignore God's will.

K (1:16A), K' (15:27)

"Simon and Andrew" in the first hemistich matches "two robbers" in the second.

As Jesus begins his ministry his first two companions are Simon and Andrew, his first disciples. As Jesus dies, his last two companions are unnamed robbers—two and two. Mark knew from Paul's epistles that Peter, James and John were the pillars of the Jerusalem church.[4] Therefore, they become the first disciples called. At Gal 2:7 Paul said that Peter was the apostle to the circumcised (Jews), so it was reasonable that Mark have him be the first one called. On the other hand, he needed two disciples to be called first to match the two robbers being crucified with Jesus. Therefore, Mark added Andrew as the brother of Simon Peter. Andrew is never mentioned as an individual again until the Olivet Discourse.

The second two disciples called are brothers James and John, not coincidentally the names of the other two Jerusalem apostles Paul identifies in Galatians. One of Mark's objectives in writing his Gospel was to discredit the Jerusalem apostles. Therefore, to make their misunderstanding of Jesus's message more egregious, Mark made Peter, James, and John Jesus's special confidants. It also stands to reason that he would make them the first disciples to be called.

Robert Eisenman writes that James, the leader of the Jerusalem apostles, and James son of Zebedee were the same person.[5] This makes good sense. Eisenman opines that James the Just was the biological brother of Jesus and leader of the Jerusalem apostles. If Jesus was not a historical person, he did not have a biological brother. The identification of the leader of the Jerusalem apostles as Jesus's brother is based upon Gal 1:19 wherein Paul writes that he went to Jerusalem and saw "James, the brother of the Lord." Earl Doherty makes a convincing case that "brother of the Lord" is not a sibling designation, but a title.[6] Paul does not call James "brother of Jesus." In

---

4. Gal 2:9.

5. Eisenman, *James,* 96–98.

6. Doherty, *Jesus Neither,* 60–63.

addition, "Lord" is ambiguous in Paul's epistles. It can either mean Christ or God. It is clear from Gal 2:12 that James is the leader of the Jerusalem apostles. Acts also makes it clear that the leader of the Jerusalem church was James.[7] Mark knew that the Jerusalem pillars mentioned by Paul in Galatians were Peter, James and John. Mark writes at 6:3 that Jesus has a brother named James. This does not appear to be an interpolation, but it may be. Jesus's brother James is not one of the twelve apostles as are James, son of Zebedee and James, son of Alphaeus as listed at 3:17–18. Mark also makes it clear that Peter, James and John are special because Jesus gives them epithets.

Acts 12:2 states that "King Herod" killed James son of Zebedee, and that Herod is traditionally identified as Herod Agrippa, because Herod Antipas had been banshished to Spain by Roman Emperor Cagligula (Caius in Josephus) in 39 CE. Herod the Great had died in 4 BCE. So the "Herod" identified in Acts could not be either of those Herods. By default historians assume Acts means Herod Agrippa. There is no historical evidence that Agrippa killed James son of Zebedee, only that dubious statement in Acts. Josephus reports that Agrippa was a most honorable man, one to be emulated.[8] Josephus seemed to enjoy reporting on foul deeds done by people in high places, and he has no report of Agrippa doing anything like that. The author of Acts, presumably Luke, apparently thought he needed to kill off James son of Zebedee so that James, brother of Jesus, could be identified as the head of the Jerusalem apostles. Mark, on the other hand, writing long after James, son of Zebedee is supposedly killed, gives no hint that James, son of Zebedee, is a different James from the leader of the Jerusalem apostles. Mark realized that "brother of the Lord" found at Gal 1:19 was a title and not a designation of siblinghood to Jesus, since his Jesus was a fictional character. Mark, wanting to make the Jerusalem apostles appear more incompetent, made them the special confidants of Jesus.

L (1:16b–18), L' (15:24)

There are four matching elements in this stich:

1. Throwing or casting is in both hemistiches,

2. "They were fishers" in the first hemistich matches "they" (soldiers) in the second.

3. "Left their nets" in the first hemistich matches "divided his garments" in the second.

4. "Followed him" in the first hemistich matches its ironic opposite "crucifying him" in the second.

Simon and Andrew throw (ballō) a net into the sea, leave their nets and follow Jesus, and in the reverse order the soldiers crucify Jesus, divide his garments and throw

7. Acts 15:13–20. Although it is not clear from Acts which James the leader is. It cannot be James, son of Zebedee, according to Acts, since he was killed at Acts 12:2.

8. J.A., 18:5:3.

(ballō) lots or dice to gamble for Jesus's clothes. Opposites of following and crucifying, opposites of leaving nets and taking clothes, and a parallel of throwing nets and dice comprise the matches here.

John Meagher sees 1:16 as one of the "clumsy constructions" in Mark, opining that it was unnecessary to write that Simon and Andrew were throwing their net into the sea and that they were fishers.[9] He failed to appreciate that Mark was making a chiastic match between fishers who throw nets, leave them, and follow Jesus, as opposed to soldiers who crucify Jesus, throw dice, and divide his clothes. In addition, Meagher fails to appreciate that Mark typically describes actions as occuring it sets of threes. Therefore, it is not unusual for Mark to write at 1:16–18 that as Jesus is (1) passing by the sea of Galilee, he (2) sees Peter and Andrew casting their net (3) for they were fishers. These three descriptive elements match Jesus (1) going on a little farther, (2) he saw James the son of Zebedee and John his brother, and (3) they were in the boat mending the nets at 1:19–20. These two sets of threes are the (BA, BA') stitch of the parallel center of the pericope-level chiastic structure.

M (1:19), M' (15:21)

"The son of Zebedee and John his brother" in the first hemistich matches "the father of Alexander and Rufus" in the second. It is curious that Mark identifies Simon of Cyrene by the names of his children. Mark has given the reader no hint who Alexander and Rufus might be. It is usual to identify children by the name of their father as James and John are at 1:19 unless the children have been introduced earlier in the narrative. The reason for mentioning Simon's sons is to provide a chiastic match between Simon's two sons and the two sons of Zebedee. Matthew and Luke either did not appreciate the chiastic match or decided to ignore it when writing their Gospels.

Also "father of Alexander and Rufus" makes a chiastic match with "Son of God" at 15:39 (father and son), which is the (B, B') stich of the pericope-level chiastic structure.

N (1:21–22), N' (15:16–19)

There are three matching elements in this stich:

1. "He entered into the synagogue" in the first hemistich matches "took him inside the court, that is the Praetorian" in the second.

2. "They were astonished at his teaching" in the first hemistich matches its ironic opposite, "And they dressed him in a purple tunic, and braiding a crown of thorns, they put it on

---

9. Meagher, *Clumsy Constructions*, 44.

him. And they began to salute him, "Hail, King of the Jews!" And they struck his head with a rod, and spat upon him, and on bended knees worshipped him."

3. "Having authority" in the first hemistich matches "King of the Jews" in the second, although ironic.

All three of these matches have an opposing elemcent. Jesus enters the the synagogue voluntarily, but he is taken into the Praetorian forcibly. Jesus impresses the congregation with his first miracle, and the soldiers mock him. "Having authority" is parallel to "King of the Jews" on its face, but the salute is sarcastic and degrading.

O (1:24), O' (15:12-14)

In this stich there are four matching elements:

1. "Saying" in the first hemistich matches "answering" in the second.

2. "Have you come . . .?" in the first hemistich matches "What then shall I do with him?" in the second.

3. "The Holy one of God" in the first hemistich matches "whom you call King of the Jews" in the second.

4. "Destroy us" in the first hemistich matches "crucify him" found twice in the second.

The unclean spirit correctly identifies Jesus as the "Holy One of God" while Pilate incorrectly identifies him as "King of the Jews." Notice that the unclean spirit did not say "Son of God" which would have been the fourth instance of this title and destroyed Mark's "Son of God" triplet. Therefore, he intentionally avoided using "Son of God" in this first miracle, basing this quote on 1 Kgs 17:18 and what the widow of Zaraphath says to Elijah. Both hemistiches deal with killing.

P (1:25), P' (15:4-5)

"Jesus admonished him" in the first hemistich matches "Pilate again questioned him" in the second, and "be silent" in the first hemistich matches "do you have nothing to say" and "Jesus answered nothing" in the second. Jesus admonishes the unclean spirit to be silent in his first miracle, and at his trial before Pilate Jesus remains silent although Pilate wants him to speak.

Q (1:26), Q' (15:2B)

"Spirit shouted with a loud voice" in the first hemistich matches "answering says" in the second. As Jesus casts out the unclean spirit in the synagogue, it shouts with a loud voice, matching Jesus responding to Pilate's first question. Both of these contradict the silence of the preceding stich.

R (1:27), R' (15:2A)

"Asked each other" in the first hemistich matches "Pilate interrogated him" in the second, and "commands with authority" in the first hemistich matches "King of the Jews" in the second. The members of the synagogue's congregation question among themselves, and Pilate questions Jesus at the trial. Again "authority" matches "King of the Jews" in an ironic manner.

S (1:32), S' (14:66–72)

There are four matches in this stich:

1. "Sun went down" in the first hemistich matches "the cock crowed" in the second.
2. "Entire city gathered together" in the first hemistich matches "those standing there" found twice in the second.
3. "Did not allow the demons to speak" in the first hemistich matches "You also were with the Nazarene, Jesus," "This is one of them" and "truly, you are one of them; for you are a Galilean."
4. "They knew him" in the first hemistich ironically matches "but he denied, saying 'I neither know nor understand what you are saying;'" "he again denied it" and "I do not know this man you are talking about."

In the first hemistich the sun sets matching its opposite, the cock crowing for the second time signaling sunrise. In both hemistiches there are witnesses, the city population and the bystanders.

Meagher cites 1:32–34 as another of Mark's clumsy constructions. He assumes Mark mentions the sun setting so that Jesus would not be curing sick people on the Sabbath, although Meagher notes that Jesus has cured Simon's mother-in-law and cast out an unclean spirit earlier in the day. He also thinks Mark is being clumsy in writing that Jesus forbade the demons to speak. These criticisms fail to take into account that Mark is making chiastic matches. They are both opposites: sunset opposite of the cock crowing for the second time, and the servant girl and the bystanders trying to get Peter to talk being the opposite of Jesus not allowing the demons to speak. The statement that the demons knew who Jesus was matches Peter's denial of knowing Jesus. This chiastic match may be Mark hinting that Peter is possessed by a demon. In the first half of the Gospel there is a twelve-element structure using the word "demon," no doubt referring to the twelve disciples. Jesus calls Peter "Satan" at 8:33.

T (1:35), T' (14:32–49)

There are seven matching elements in this final stich of the structure:

1. "Into a desert place" in the first hemistich matches "come to a place named Gethsemane" in the second.

2. "Was praying there" in the first hemistich matches "sit here while I pray," "was praying that" and "he prayed saying the same words" found in the second.

3. "Simon and those that were with him searched for him" in the first hemistich matches "Judas, one of the twelve, comes and with him a bunch from the chief priests and the scribes and the elders with swords and clubs" in the second.

4. "They found him" in the first hemistich matches "he comes and finds them sleeping" and "he found them sleeping" in the second.

5. "Everyone is looking for you" in the first hemistich matches "Look, he that delivers me is coming" in the second.

6. "Into the neighboring towns so that I may preach there" in the first hemistich matches "I was with you in the temple teaching every day" in the second.

7. "For this is why I came" in the first hemistich matches "let the scriptures be fulfilled" in the second.

Jesus going to a deserted place matches his going to Gethsemane. While in English the word "place" seems to be a match, in the first hemistich the Greek word for place (topos) means "region" or "area" and in the second hemistich (chōrion) means "field" or something more particular, perhaps "garden."

In both hemistiches people are looking for Jesus. Simon, who is with others, says prophetically, "Everyone is looking for you," matching Judas and others arriving with swords and clubs looking for Jesus. In both cases there are disciples looking for Jesus. Mark makes it clear that Judas is one of the twelve.

Simon and his companions find Jesus, ironically matching Jesus finding Simon James and John sleeping after he told them in "The Olivet Discourse" that the master may come unexpectedly and find them sleeping and to be vigilant.[10] In the first hemistich Jesus tells Simon he (Jesus) should go preaching in neighboring towns, matching Jesus telling the arresting group that he was teaching in the temple everyday. The final match of "this is why I came" and "let the scriptures be fulfilled" makes the theological point that Jesus came to Earth fulfilling scriptural prophecy. There is a hidden irony here in that at the beginning of the Original Gospel Jesus is not yet aware of his true mission. Until "The Transfiguration" (9:2–8) he believes that he is the Danielic Son of Man who has been sent to establish the kingdom of God. Talking to Moses and Elijah on the mountain of the transfiguration, Jesus discovers that his mission is to be an

---

10. Mark 13:36–37.

atoning sacrifice for all mankind, and the kingdom of God would come after he had risen from the dead. This final match of the structure matches Jesus's original idea of his mission with the actual mission in the process of being accomplished.

Conclusion

This long twenty-stich structure with its first half at the beginning of the Gospel runs through four pericopae past the end of the prologue, covering Jesus's baptism, calling his disciples and his first two miracles. The second half at the end of the Gospel runs from the last three pericopae of Act II and all of Act III including the epilogue, covering Jesus's arrest, both trials, crucifixion, burial and the frightened women fleeing the tomb. The first half of the structure begins at 1:2, the beginning of the Gospel text. It ends at 16:8, the end of the Gospel text. This structure provides additional evidence that 1:1 is the incipit and the Gospel text begins at 1:2.

 With this many matches in exact chiastic order, it is impossible that this structure is a coincidence or that matching concepts are being manufactured where they do not exist. Many of the chiastic matches are opposites:

1. The tone for this structure is set with the first stich of "as it is written" matching with "they told no one anything."

2. God sends his messenger, but the women refuse to be the messengers to the disciples.

3. John is dressed in a rough desert costume while the young man is dressed in a luxurious white robe. The young man wears a "stolēn," a flowing robe worn by the elite.

4. John baptizes with water symbolizing a new life, and the women come to anoint the dead body with spices.

5. Jesus comes up out of the water, and the temple curtain is torn down.

6. The spirit descends into Jesus, and the spirit departs from Jesus.

7. The voice from heaven says it is pleased with Jesus, and Jesus asks why God has abandoned him.

8. The angels in the wilderness serve Jesus, and the witnesses to his crucifixion abuse him.

9. Simon and Andrew leave their nets and follow Jesus, and the soldiers take his clothes and crucify him.

10. James and John are identified by the name of their father, and Simon of Cyrene is identified by the names of his sons.

11. The congregation at the Capernaum synagogue admires Jesus's teaching, and the soldiers ridicule him.

12. The unclean spirit knows that Jesus is the "Holy One of God," and Pilate misidentifies him as "King of the Jews." Both phrases contain three words in Greek.

13. Jesus tells the unclean spirit to be silent, and Pilate asks Jesus to speak.

14. Jesus does not allow the demons to speak the truth, and Peter falsely denies that he knows Jesus.

In twenty matching stiches, fourteen of them have an element of opposition. These opposing concepts compare the optimism of Jesus's baptism and the beginning of his ministry with the degradation and hopelessness of his crucifixion. The question was posed earlier as to why Mark would separate the chiastic structure over such a long literary distance. Here we see that Mark wanted to emphasize a contrasing mood. He added to the contrasting mood by making the text match in reverse. He trusted that the reader would feel the emotion of the contrast enhanced by the chiastic structure, if not intellectually realize it.

It is amazing that not only has Mark made elements match in opposite directions; two-thirds of his matching elements have an opposite direct statement or tone. In addition, consider that for a considerable portion of this structure, he also made them match in parallel. The critics of Mark's Gospel who have said it is simple and basic are wrong.

With the demonstration of the discussed chiastic structure, pericopae numbers 6–8 and 63–77 as listed in Appendix 3 can be confirmed to be part of The Original Gospel of Mark.

5

The Beginning and Transfiguration
Chiastic Structure

THE NEXT LITERARY STRUCTURE is a chiastic structure that encompasses Act I and part of Act II. This structure has nineteen stiches. We have seen that the beginning of Mark's Gospel is part of two literary structures uniting it with the end of the Gospel, one parallel and one chiastic. The beginning is also a part of a third structure with "The Transfiguration" and "Leaving the Mountain" (9:2–13) pericopae and several others that precede them.

In the table describing this structure, the left column of the table runs from 1:2 to 2:26 encompassing the beginning of Jesus's ministry, healing a leper, healing a paralytic and Jesus being involved in two controversies. The right column of the table runs backwards from 9:13 to 3:14 encompassing (in reverse Gospel order) Jesus and three disciples coming down the mountain, the transfiguration of Jesus on the mountan, the twelve returning from their journey, Herod killing John the Baptizer, Jesus sending out the twelve to preach, Jesus preaching in his home town, healing Jairus's daughter and a woman who had been bleeding for twelve years, the calming of a storm at sea, a disagreement between Jesus and his family, a controversy about Beelzebul, and Jesus choosing the twelve apostles. This structure demonstrates that major revisions have been made to Mark's Gospel since it was originally written. This structure suggests that "The Parable Discourse" (4:1–34) and "The Transfiguration" through "Answering the Disciples" (9:2–29) have been relocated from their original positions in the Gospel.

As with the previous chiastic structure table, only the matching language in italics will be included so that the reader will be able to get a sense of what passages are matching each other. The (Q, Q') stich below is a special case based on a matching form. As previously mentioned, the complete text of Mark's Original Gospel can be found in Appendix 1 for reference.

The Beginning and Transfiguration Chiastic Structure

A. 1:2a *As it is written . . .*

A' 9:13b *. . . as it is written* of him.

B 1:2b *Look, I send my messenger ahead of you . . . 1:3 A voice proclaiming . . . for the Lord . . .*

B' 9:12 *. . . "Elijah indeed having come first . . . is it written of the Son of Man . . . 9:13a . . . Elijah has come*

C 1:4a *John the Baptizer appeared . . .*

C' 9:11 *. . . Elijah must come first*

D 1:4b *proclaiming . . . 1:5 . . . they were baptized . . . 1:8 I baptized you . . . 1:9 . . . was baptized by John . . .*

D' 9:9b *. . . tell no one . . . rise from the dead. 9:10 . . . discussing among themselves what "rising from the dead" is.*

E 1:10a *. . . coming up . . .*

E' 9:9a *. . . coming down . . .*

F 1:10b *. . . heavens tearing open . . . 1:11 . . . voice came out of the heavens, "You are my beloved Son, in whom I am well pleased."*

F' 9:7a *. . . a cloud enveloping them . . . came a voice out of the cloud, "This is my beloved son: listen to him."*

G 1:12 *. . . Spirit drives him out into the wilderness. 1:13 . . . forty days . . . he was with the wild beasts; And the angels served him.*

G' 9:2 *And after six days . . . brings them up into a high mountain . . . 9:4 . . . Elijah with Moses: and they were talking with Jesus. 9:5 . . . let us construct three tents*

H 1:14a *. . . John was delivered up*

H' 6:17 *. . . laid hold of John, and locked him in prison . . . 6:27 . . . commanded him to bring his head. And he went and beheaded him in the prison . . . 6:29 . . . took his body, and laid it in a tomb.*

I 1:14b *. . . proclaiming the gospel of God, 1:15 and saying, "The time is complete, and the kingdom of God is at hand: repent, and believe in the gospel."*

I' 6:16 *But Herod, when he heard about it . . .*

J 1:16 *. . . Simon and Andrew . . . throwing a net in the sea . . . 1:17 . . . "Follow me . . . make you fishers of men." 1:18 . . . left the nets . . . 1:19 . . . James the son of Zebedee and John his brother and they were in the boat mending the nets. 1:20 . . . he called them: and they left their father . . .*

J' 6:7 *. . . summons the twelve . . . out two by two; and gave them power over the unclean spirits; 6:8 . . . instructed them . . . take nothing . . . 6:13 And they cast out many demons, and anointed many that were sick with oil, and healed them.*

K 1:21 *. . . go into Capernaum . . . Sabbath . . . into the synagogue and taught. 1:22 And they were astonished at his teaching . . . 1:24 . . . I know who you are, the Holy One of God." . . . 1:26 . . . came out of him. 1:27 And they were all amazed . . . they asked each other, saying, "What is this? New teaching? He commands with authority, and the unclean spirits obey him."*

K' 6:1 *. . . into his own hometown . . . 6:2 . . . Sabbath, he began to teach in the synagogue: and many hearing him were astonished, "Where have these things come from, and what wisdom has been given to him, and are such marvelous works done by his hands? 6:3 Is not this the carpenter, the son of Mary . . ." and they took umbrage at him . . . 6:5 and he could not do any marvelous work . . .*

L 1:29 . . . *out of the synagogue, they came into the house of Simon and Andrew, with James and John.* 1:30 *But Simon's mother-in-law was sick with a fever; and immediately they tell him about her.* 1:31 . . . *took her by the hand and raised her up; and the fever left her, and she served them.*

L' 5:35 . . . *they come from the house of the leader of the synagogue saying, your daughter is dead:* . . . 5:37 . . . *except Peter, and James, and John the brother of James.* 5:38 . . . *come to the house of the leader of the synagogue.* . . . 5:41 *And taking the child by the hand* . . . 5:42 *And immediately the girl arose, and walked* . . . 5:43 . . . *she should be given something to eat.*

M. 1:33 And the *entire city was gathered together at the door* . . . 1:35 . . . *went out, and departed into a deserted place* . . . 1:40 . . . *comes to him a leper, begging him, and kneeling down to him* . . . *If you will, you can make me clean."* 1:41 . . . *stretched forth his hand, and touched him* . . . 1:42 *And immediately the leprosy left him, and he was clean* . . . 1:44 . . . *go show yourself to the priest* . . .

M' 5:21 . . . *a great crowd was gathered around him;* and *he was beside the sea.* 5:22 . . . *Jairus comes; and seeing him, falls at his feet,* 5:23 and *begs him a great deal, saying, "My little daughter is at the point of death, you must come and lay your hands on her* . . . 5:27 . . . *touched his robe.* 5:28 . . . *"If I just touch his robe, I will be cured."* 5:29 *And immediately the flow of blood was dried up; and she realized in her body that her affliction was healed.* 5:30 . . . *"Who touched my robe?"* 5:31 . . . *touched me?"* . . . 5:34 . . . *Go in peace, and be free of your affliction."*

N 2:1 . . . *home.* 2:2 *And many* . . .

N' 5:3 . . . *dwelling* . . . 5:9 . . . *many."*

O 2:4 . . . *they let down the pallet* . . . 2:5 *And seeing their faith* . . . *"Child, your sins are forgiven."* . . . 2:7 *". . . He blasphemes. Who can forgive sins but one, God?"* 2:8 . . . *"Why do you debate these things in your hearts?* 2:9 . . . *pick up your pallet* . . . 2:11 . . . *pick up your pallet,* . . . 2:12 . . . *Such that they were all amazed, and began to glorify God, saying, "We never saw such a thing."*

O' 4:38 . . . *sleeping on the cushion* . . . *"Teacher, do you not care that we are going to die?"* 4:39 . . . *"Silence, be still."* . . . 4:40 . . . *"Why are you afraid? Do you not have faith yet?"* 4:41 . . . *"Who is this then, that even the wind and the sea obey him?"*

P 2:13 *And he went out again by the seaside* . . . *entire crowd came to him* . . . 2:14 . . . *"Follow me." And he arose and followed him.* 2:15 . . . *many tax collectors and sinners were reclining with Jesus and his disciples. For there were many, and they followed him.* 2:16 . . . *Why does he eat and drink with tax collectors and sinners?* 2:17 . . . *I did not come to call the righteous, but sinners.*

P' 3:31 *And his mother and brothers arrive; and standing outside they sent to him, calling him.* 3:32 *And a crowd was sitting around him* . . . *"Look, your mother, brothers and sisters are outside looking for you."* 3:33 *And answering them he says, "Who is my mother and my brothers?"* 3:34 . . . *Look, my mother and my brothers!* 3:35 *For whoever does the will of God, he is my brother, and sister, and mother.*

Q(1) 2:18 And John's disciples and the disciples of the Pharisees *were fasting*

Q'(1) 3:20 And he comes into a house. And the crowd comes together again, so that *they could not even eat bread.* 3:21 And when his family heard it, they went out to take custody of him: for they said, 'He is out of his mind.'

Q(2) And *they come and say to him, "Why do* arisees fast, but your disciples do not fast?"

Q'(2) 3:22 And the scribes who *came down from Jerusalem* said, "He is possessed by Beelzebul, and he casts out demons by the prince of the demons."

Q(3) 2:19 John's disciples and the disciples of the Pharisees And *Jesus said to them,*

Q'(3) 3:23 And he called them to him, and *said to them* in parables,

Q(4) "*Can the sons* of the bride chamber fast while the bridegroom is with them?

Q(5) As long as they have the bridegroom with them, they *cannot fast.*

Q(6) 2:20 But the days will come, when the bridegroom *will be taken away* from them.

Q(7) And then *will they fast at that time.*

Q(8) 2:21 *No one sews a piece* of unshrunken cloth on old clothing because the new patch would tear away from the old, and makes a worse tear.

Q(9) 2:22 And no one puts new wine into old wineskins because the wine will burst the wineskins. *And the wine and the wineskins are destroyed. Put new wine into new wineskins."*

R 2:23 . . . *he was going through the grain fields . . . disciples . . .* 2:25 . . . *they that were with him* 2:26 . . . *those that were with him*

Q'(4) "*How can Satan* cast out Satan?

Q'(5) 3:24 And if a kingdom be divided against itself, that kingdom *cannot stand.*

Q'(6) 3:25 And if a house be divided against itself, that house *will not be able to stand.*

Q'(7) 3:26 And if Satan has risen up against himself, and is divided, he cannot stand, but *will come to an end.*

Q'(8) 3:27 *But no one can enter* into the house of the strong man, and plunder his goods, unless he first ties up the strong man. And then he will plunder his house.

Q'(9) 3:28 Truthfully I say to you, "*All sins will be forgiven the sons of men*, and their blasphemies when ever they may blaspheme: 3:29 but whoever blasphemes against the Holy Spirit *will never have forgiveness*, but is guilty of an eternal sin:" 3:30 Because they said he has an unclean spirit.

R' 3:13 . . . *goes up into the mountain . . . those whom he wanted. . . .* 3:14 . . . *appointed twelve to be apostles, that they might be with him*

Commentary

A (1:2A), A' (9:13B)

"As it is written" begins and ends this structure. This matching element of "as it is written" is an inclusio that encompasses this structure. The first words of the structure match the last words of the structure.

B (1:2B), B' (9:12)

There are three matches in this stich:

1. "I send my messenger ahead of you" in the first hemistich matches "Elijah indeed having come first" and "Elijah has come" in the second.

2. "A voice proclaiming" in the first hemistich matches "is it written" in the second.

3. "Of the Lord" in the first hemistich matches "Son of Man" in the second.

Jesus equates Elijah and John in "Leaving the Mountain" (9:9–13). John is wearing the same costume as Elijah is described as wearing 2 Kings 1:8 (LXX). John is the subject of the first hemistich and Elijah is the subject in the second hemistich. Matthew, who thought it was his duty to explain Mark and make his point more clearly, noted this comparison by moving his version of Mark 1:2b to Jesus's discussion about John at Matt 11:10, which is not found in Mark. Luke's Gospel also contains the discussion.

C (1:4A), C' (9:11)

"John the Baptizer appeared" in the first hemistich matches "Elijah must come first" in the second. John's appearance has a magical quality to it as if he were transported there. The disciples are asking about Mal 4:5–6 which says:

> 4:5 "Behold, I am going to send you Elijah the prophet before the coming of the great and terrible day of the Lord. 6 He will restore the hearts of the fathers to their children and the hearts of the children to their fathers."

"The day of the Lord" is another description of the coming of the kingdom of God. This phrase is used several times in OT prophecy.

D (1:4B), D' (9:9B)

There are four matching elements in this stich:

1. "Proclaiming" in the first hemistich matches its opposite "tell no one" in the second.

2. "They were baptized" in the first hemistich matches "rise from the dead" in the second.

3. "Confessing" in the first hemistich matches "discussing among themselves" in the second.

4. "Baptize" found three more times in the first hemistich matches "rising from the dead" found again in the second.

Proclaiming, the act of making a public announcement, is the exact opposite of telling no one. Baptism and resurrection are inextricably linked in Christian theology: one must be baptized in order to defeat death and have everlasting life with God. The crowd confesses their sins to John, and the disciples discuss what Jesus may have meant about rising from the dead. Then baptism is mentioned again and rising from the dead is mentioned again. The four matches are in the exact same order in both hemistiches. It should also be noted that the last mention of baptism in the first hemistich is a reference to the baptism of Jesus that begins his ministry and culminates at the end of the Gospel with his rising from the dead.

E (1:10a), E' (9:9a)

"Coming up" in the first hemistich matches its opposite "coming down" in the second. This stich has opposing physical actions. Jesus came up out of the water after baptism, and Jesus and his disciples came down the mountain after his transfiguration.

F (1:10b), F' (9:7a)

There are four matching elements in this stich:

1. "Heavens tearing open" in the first hemistich matches "cloud enveloping them" in the second.
2. "A voice came out of the heavens" in the first hemistich matches "came a voice out of the cloud" in the second.
3. "Beloved son" is in both hemistiches.
4. "In whom I am well pleased" in the first hemistich matches "listen to him" in the second.

There are strange happenings in the sky in both hemistiches: the sky tears open, whatever that may mean, and a cloud envelops the disciples and presumably Jesus, Moses, and Elijah. Then a voice comes out of the heavens and out of the cloud. The word order here is notable: in the first hemistich Mark wrote "a voice came" (phonē engeneto) and in the second he wrote "came a voice" (engeneto phonē). Mark emphasizes the relationship by making a chiasmus: a voice came, came a voice.

There are also matching quotes from the OT. In the first hemistich "in whom I am well pleased" is a quote from Isa 42:1 as previously mentioned, while "listen to him" is a quote from Deut 18:15 which is about the coming prophet that Moses predicts. Mark expected his readers to be familiar with the OT passages that he quoted and their context. In the same speech from Moses at Deut 18:21–22 Moses tells the Israelites that they will know whether a person is a true prophet by whether what he says comes true. The next thing Jesus says to his disciples is that he will rise from the dead.

G (1:12–13), G' (9:2–5)

There are four matches in this stich:

1. "The spirit drives him out into the wilderness in the first hemistich matches "brings them up into a high mountain" in the second.
2. "Forty days" in the first hemistich matches "six days" in the second.
3. "He was with wild beasts" in the first hemistich matches "Elijah and Moses and they were talking with Jesus" in the second.

4. "The angels served him" in the first hemistich matches "let us construct three tents" in the second.

With the first matching elements in this hemistich there is physical movement from an outside force. The spirit drives Jesus into the wilderness in the first hemistich and in the second hemistich Jesus, presumably being driven by the spirit again, takes Peter, James, and John up the mountain.

A definite time period measured in days is mentioned in both hemistiches. The six-day time period provides evidence of a redaction that will be explained in detail below. It appears that this unnecessary detail of six days was included to make a chiastic match.

Jesus is with wild beasts in the first hemistich where Mark is equating Jesus and Adam by making a reference to Adam being with wild beasts (thēriōn) in Gen 2:19 (LXX). Equating Adam and Jesus is a Pauline theme found in Rom 5:14–19 and 1 Cor 15:20–23, 45–47. Jesus is with Moses and Elijah in the second hemistich.

Angels serving Jesus in the wilderness in the first hemistich matches Peter offering to be of service by building tents for Moses, Elijah, and Jesus in the second. Paul is said to be a tentmaker at Acts 18:3. Is this a joke by Mark comparing Peter and Paul?

There is a possible fifth match between Satan in the first hemistich and Peter in the second, both playing prominent roles in this stich. This may anticipate the confession at Caesarea Philippi where Jesus tells Peter, "Get behind me, Satan."

H (1:14A), H' (9:17–29)

There is only one match in this stich, but it is very important for Mark's story. "John was delivered up" in the first hemistich matches "laid hold of John and locked him in prison . . . commanded him to bring him his head and he went and beheaded him in prison . . . took his body, and laid it in a tomb."

In the first hemistich readers are told John the Baptizer was delivered up. In the second hemistich is the full story of how Herod killed John. The delivering up results in death and burial, just as delivering up Jesus will result in his death and burial. In order to make this match, 9:2–29 had to be repositioned to immediately follow "Return of the Twelve" (6:30–31). At first blush it may seem that passages of the Gospel are being moved wherever needed in order to create chiastic matches. But the legitimacy of this move is confirmed with nine subsequent matches. Further, textual confirmation indicates that the repositioning restores Mark's original structure.

Meagher has 1:14a as another of the clumsy constructions.[1] He opines that there is no dramatic purpose for Mark telling the reader that John has been delivered up. But there are at least two purposes. First, it makes a chiastic match with the story of John's demise. Second, in making the match Mark is foreshadowing the crucifixion of

1. Meagher, *Clumsy Constructions*, 42–43.

Jesus. Jesus is delivered up, abused by the authorities, is crucified, and laid in a tomb. Chapter 12 will demonstrate that Mark's use of the phrase "Son of Man" emphasizes Jesus being delivered up, suffering, and coming again. John, on the other hand, is delivered up, suffers, and is laid in a tomb. John does not rise from the dead, but Herod thinks he may have, foreshadowing Jesus's rising.

There is additional evidence that the repositioning 9:2–29 restores the Original Gospel. Chapter 1 notes that 9:2 in Canonical Mark seems strange:

> 9:1 And he said to them, "Truthfully I say to you, There are some standing here who will in no way taste of death, until they see the kingdom of God coming with power." 9:2 And after six days Jesus takes with him Peter, and James, and John, and brings them up into a high mountain by themselves. And he was transfigured in front of them.

Six days after what? The statement is entirely gratuitous. Meagher did not include it in his clumsy constructions, but he would have been justified in so doing. But now examine the transition after this proposed repositioning:

> 6:31 And he says to them, "Come down into the desert and rest a while." For many were coming and going, and they had no opportunity to even eat.

> 9:2 And after six days Jesus takes with him Peter, and James, and John, and brings them up into a high mountain by themselves. And he was transfigured in front of them.

Now the six-day hiatus makes sense. It is not merely a chiastic match for forty days at 1:13. While it provides that match, it now shows Jesus giving his disciples a respite after their return from the preaching and healing mission. Mark has deftly integrated a chiastic match into the story. The period of six days was probably chosen by Mark to match the six-day period in Exod 24:15–16.[2]

In addition, at Mark 9:9–10 Jesus warns his disciples not to tell anyone what they saw at the transfiguration until after he has risen from the dead, and the disciples wonder what "rising from the dead" means, as if they are hearing the concept for the first time. But in Canonical Mark they heard that he would rise from the dead at 8:31, merely sixteen verses earlier. In the reconstruction of Original Mark, 9:9–10 comes before 8:31, so it is truly the first time they have heard of the concept, and the puzzlement of the disciples is justified. Repositioning 9:2–29 to follow 6:31 smoothes out both of these narration glitches, and proves the proposition.

There is triplet evidence also. There is a triplet of Jesus being addressed by another character and what is said to Jesus is not reported. This triplet is found at 1:13, 9:4, and 8:32. In this Markan triplet Jesus is tempted by Satan at 1:13, Jesus is talking with Moses and Elijah at 9:4, and Peter chides Jesus at 8:32 after Jesus tells the disciples

---

2. Price, "Midrash."

he will be killed and rise from the dead. We know this is the correct order as it was presented in the Original Gospel because in the first and third elements Jesus is addressed by one person and in the middle element he is addressed by two persons. This follows the Markan triplet structure of the middle element being different. Therefore, it is proved that "The Transfiguration" and following pericope were located before "Peter's Confession at Caesarea" in the Original Gospel.

Albert Schweitzer came to the same conclusion over one hundred years ago, when he opined that "The Transfiguration" and "Leaving the Mountain" (9:2–13) must have come before "Peter's Confession at Caesarea Philippi" (8:27–9:1) in the Original Gospel.[3] The flow of the story and the text support the repositioning of 9:2–13 to immediately follow 6:30–31, as the chiastic structure indicated. Part II will show how this repositioning improves the dramatic effect of Mark's Gospel. Further, we may begin to suspect that the reason the redactor initially moved "The Transfiguration" and "Coming Down the Mountain" was to make Mark's Gospel more compatible with the redactor's Christology.

In relating the story of the death of John the Baptizer it appears that Mark has conflated two consecutive paragraphs of Josephus's *Antiquities of the Jews*.[4] In J.A. 18:5:1 Josephus tells about Herod's marriage to his dead brother's wife, and in J.A. 18:5:2 Josephus relates that Herod killed John because he feared that John could lead a rebellion. There is no mention by Josephus of John disapproving of Herod's marriage. On the other hand in Mark's Gospel Herod lays hold of John the Baptizer because John disapproves of Herod's marriage, beheads him, and John's disciples bury him. Josephus only relates that Herod killed John; beheading is not mentioned. Evidence will be presented that 6:14–15, 18–26, and 28 are later interpolations into the story of the presumably lascivious dance by Herodias's daughter, based on the OT book of Esther. Turton suspects the pericope has been heavily redacted because it has an unMarkan structure.[5] Eliminating this text will justified in chapter 7.

I (1:14b), I' (6:16)

"Proclaiming the gospel of God and saying 'the time is complete, and the kingdom of God is at hand: repent and believe in the gospel'" in the first hemistich matches "But Herod when he heard about it."

Jesus proclaiming and Herod hearing about it makes a humorous and ironic match. If deleting 6:14–15 properly restores the Original Gospel, it is not clear what "it" is that Herod heard in the context of "Killing John the Baptizer" in Original Mark. There are several reasons for eliminating these verses that will be presented in chapter 7 below. What Herod heard about, according to Mark's Original Gospel, is at 6:13, the

3. Schweitzer, *Mystery*, 180.

4. J.A. 18:5:1–2.

5. Turton, *HCGM,* ch 6.

disciples casting out demons and healing people on Jesus's instructions. Interestingly, Herod knows what "risen from the dead" means and assumes those in his hearing know, but Jesus's disciples do not know what it means at 9:10.

J (1:16), J' (6:7–13)

There are seven matching elements in this stich:

1. "Simon and Andrew" and "James son of Zebedee and John" in the first hemistich matches "two by two" in the second.

2. "Throwing a net in the sea" in the first hemistich matches "cast out many demons" in the second.

3. "Follow me" in the first hemistich matches "he summons the twelve" in the second.

4. "I will make you fishers of men" in the first hemistich matches "gave them powers over unclean spirits" in the second.

5. "Left the nets" and "left their father" in the first hemistich matches "take nothing" in the second.

6. "Mending the nets" in the first hemistich matches "anointed many that were sick and healed them" in the second.

7. "He called them" in the first hemistich matches "he instructed them" in the second.

At 1:14a Mark says John the Baptizer was delivered up and at 1:14b Jesus proclaims the gospel. The next event is Jesus calling his first disciples. This matches perfectly with moving 9:2–29 to follow "Return of the Twelve" because before John's death Herod hears about Jesus, and before that Jesus summons the twelve and instructs them on preaching and healing the sick.

In the first hemistich there are two sets of two brothers, Simon and Andrew and James and John, matching Jesus sending his disciples out two by two in the second hemistich.

In the first hemistich Simon and Andrew are throwing out their nets. In the second hemistich the disciples cast out demons. The same Greek verb "ballō" (to cast or throw) is used, making the match definite.

In the first hemistich Jesus says he will make them fishers of men which matches giving the apostles power over unclean spirits in the second hemistich. Jesus exerts his power in both hemistiches.

In the first hemistich he calls his disciples, which matches his instructing them in the second hemistich. While Mark often uses the historical present in his story telling both of these phrases are in the aorist past tense.

In the first hemistich Simon and Andrew leave their nets and James and John leave their father and servants This matches Jesus's instructions to take nothing with them in the second hemistich.

K (1:21–27), K' (6:1–6)

There are 9 matching elements in this stich:

1. "Into Capernaum" in the first hemistich matches "into his own hometown."

2. "Sabbath" is found in both hemistiches.

3. "Into the synagogue" in the first hemistich matches "in the synagogue" in the second.

4. "And taught" in the first hemistich matches "he began to teach" in the second.

5. "And they were astonished" in the first hemistich matches "many hearing him were astonished" in the second.

6. "I know who you are, the Holy One of God," in the first hemistich matches "is not this the carpenter, the son of Mary" in the second.

7. "Came out of him" in the first hemistich matches "could not do any marvelous work" in the second.

8. "They were all amazed" in the first hemistich matches its opposite "they took umbrage at him" in the second.

9. "They asked each other, saying, 'What is this?'" New Teaching? He commands with authority and the unclean spirits obey him'" in the first hemistich matches "Where have these things come from, and what wisdom has been given to him, and are such marvelous works done by his hands?"in the second.

With nine matching elements in this stich, it is certain that Mark intended the chiastic match, and we can be confident that the moving "The Transfiguration" and following pericopae was proper.

In the first hemistich Jesus goes into Capernaum and in the second he goes into his own hometown. Mark does not tell us the name of his hometown. At 6:4 Jesus says he got no respect from his own house, implying that this hometown is where his house is; however, at 2:1 Mark wrote that Jesus's house was in Capernaum, this means that Capernaum is the hometown into which he went at 6:1, although many assume that this hometown is Nazareth. Evidence was presented earlier that "Nazareth" might be a redaction of "Nazarene." This argument adds weight to the proposition that "Nazareth" at 1:9 was originally "Nazarene."

As noted before, the Gospel of Mark has many triplets. One of those triplets is that Jesus enters Capernaum three times, suggesting that it might be his hometown. The context of the Gospel is that Capernaum is Jesus's hometown. But Mark could not

PART I: LITERARY STRUCTURES

put that at 6:1 or he would have had Jesus entering Capernaum four times destroying the triplet. If Mark is indeed implying that Jesus's home town is Nazareth he could not have named it at 6:1 because in the first half of the Gospel Jesus enters three separate towns, Capernaum, Bethsaida, and Caesarea Philippi. Nazareth would have been the fourth town, once again destroying the triplet. Mark also relates that Jesus enters three cities in the second half of the Gospel: Jericho, Bethany, and Jerusalem, and following the pattern, he enters Jerusalem three times.

In both hemistiches Jesus enters a synagogue on the Sabbath and teaches. Following the pattern, Jesus enters three synagogues in the Gospel, and this stich contains two of the three. The first reaction to his teaching in both hemistiches is that the congregations were astonished (exeplēssonto). Everything in both hemistiches is same but Jesus is unappreciated in his hometown.

The unclean spirit in the first hemistich recognizes Jesus for who he really is, the "Holy One of God." Mark could not have had this spirit call him the "son of God" because Mark had written "son of God" in three other places. Jesus's hometown congregation recognizes him merely as the carpenter, the son of Mary. His parentage is recognized in both hemistiches, adoptive and biological.

While Jesus is able to exorcise the unclean spirit in the first hemistich, the lack of faith by his old friends in his home town results in his not being able to do any marvelous work in the second hemistich. The congregation is amazed at Jesus's teaching in the first hemistich and the congregation takes umbrage with Jesus in the second.

In the first hemistich the congregation gives three reasons why they are impressed with Jesus: new teaching, commanding with authority, and the unclean spirits obey him. To the opposite effect in his hometown the congregation is offended by three elements: where have these things come from, what wisdom has been given to him and are such marvelous works done by his hands.

L (1:29–31), Ľ (5:35–43)

There are seven matching elements in this stich:

1. "Out of the synagogue" in the first hemistich matches "leader of the synagogue" in the second hemistich.

2. "They came into the house of Simon and Andrew" in the first hemistich matches "they come to the house of the leader of the synagogue" in the second.

3. "With James and John" in the first hemistich matches "except Peter and James and John, the brother of James" in the second.

4. "But the mother-in-law of Simon was sick with a fever and immediately they tell him about her" in the first hemistich matches "they come from the house of the leader of the synagogue, saying, 'your daughter is dead'" in the second.

5. Jesus takes both Simon's mother-in-law and Jairus's daughter by the hand.

6. "Took her by the hand and raised her up and the fever left her" in the first hemistich matches "taking the child by the hand . . . and immediately the girl arose and walked" in the second.

7. "She served them" in the first hemistich matches "she should be given something to eat" in the second.

This stich matches Jesus's healing of Simon's mother-in-law with his healing of Jairus's daughter. Under the principles of form criticism similar elements should be found in all the miracle stories. However the matching elements in this stich are not just matches of form but also of specific details: synagogue, taking by the hand, serving food, Peter, James, and John being present.

In the first hemistich the mother-in-law is raised up (egeirō) and in the second Jesus tells Jairus's daughter to rise up (egeirō). In the first hemistich Simon's mother-in-law served the guests matching Jesus ordering the household to serve the girl something to eat in the second. The healing of Jairus's daughter is the only miracle story in which Jesus orders food to be served to the healed person.

M (1:32–44), M' (5:21–34)

There are eight matching elements in this stich:

1. "Entire city gathered together at the door" in the first hemistich matches "a great crowd was gathered around him" in the second.

2. "Departed into a deserted place" in the first hemistich matches "was beside the sea" in the second.

3. "Comes to him a leper, begging him and kneeling down to him" in the first hemistich matches "Jairus comes and seeing him falls at his feet and begs him a great deal" in the second.

4. "If you will you can make me clean" in the first hemistich matches "my little daughter is at the point of death you must come" in the second.

5. "He stretched forth his hand" in the first hemistich matches "and lay your hands on her" in the second hemistich.

6. "And touched him" in the first hemistich matches "touched his robe," "if I just touch his robe," "who touched my robe," and "who touched me" in the second hemistich.

7. "Immediately the leprosy left him and he was cleaned," in the first hemistich matches "immediately the flow of blood was dried up and she realized in her body that she was healed." in the second.

8. "Go show yourself to the priest" in the first hemistich matches "go in peace and be free of your affliction" in the second.

As with the prior stich several of these matching elements are typical for miracle healing stories, but the specific actions of kneeling, begging, and touching, plus the the mention of "hand" make it clear that the similarities are part of an intentional literary structure.

The Greek verbs "sunagō" and "episunagō" (epi is a prefix meaning "on") are used to show the gathering of the city and the crowd around Jesus at the seaside. Jesus actually changes venue to cure the leper and the reader does not know exactly where he is during the healing of the leper, presumably somewhere in Galilee.

A leper begs Jesus to make him clean and Jairus begs him to cure his daughter. The "to beg" (parakalei) is used in both hemistiches. The leper kneels before Jesus and Jairus falls at Jesus's feet. Different verbs are used. Both supplicate themselves and the higher-ranking person performs the greater supplication.

"Healing of Jairus's Daughter"/"Woman with Blood Flow" (5:21–43) is one of Mark's intercalations, as the curing of Jairus's daughter is interrupted to describe the healing of a woman with a flow of blood. The reader is told that the woman says to herself that she will be cured if she touches Jesus's tunic. The verb "to touch" (haptomai) is used in both hemistiches. In fact Mark uses "touch" in the second hemistich four times for emphasis. Mark uses "hand," "touch," and "daughter" to unite his intercalation of Jairus's daughter and the woman with the flow of blood. In both hemistiches, "hand" comes before "touch," and no other matching element intervenes.

N (2:1–2), N' (5:1–9)

There is a mere suggestion of a stich here with only two matches that could be coincidental. "Home" in the first hemistich matches "dwelling" in the second, and "Many" is found in both hemistiches.

"House" or "home" in 2:1 is "oikos" in Greek while "dwelling" found in 5:3 is "katoikēsin." These are related words with the same root. "Many" found in both hemistiches is "polloi." This seems to be the mere suggestion of a chiastic match, but Mark intentionally used "many" in 2:2 where fourteen verses earlier he had said "the entire city."

O (2:3–12), O' (4:37–41)

There are seven matching elements:

1. "Let down the pallet," and "pick up your pallet" twice in the first hemistich matches "sleeping on a cushion" in the second.

2. "Seeing their faith" in the first hemistich matches its opposite "do you not have faith yet" in the second.

3. "Child, your sins are forgiven" in the first hemistich matches "Teacher, do you not care that we are going to die" in the second.

4. "He blasphemes" in the first hemistich matches "Silence. Be still" in the second.

5. "Why do you debate these things in your hearts?" in the first hemistich matches "Why are you afraid" in the second.

6. "Who can forgive sins but one, God" in the first hemistich matches "Who is this that even the wind and sea obey him" in the second.

7. "Such that they were all amazed and started glorifying God, saying, we never saw such a thing" also matches "Who is this, then, that even the wind and the sea obey him?"

Reading these two miracles stories, it is easy to miss the matching elements that show Mark intended a chiastic match between them. This stich has interesting theological overtones.

The paralytic is on a pallet in the first hemistich, which matches Jesus being asleep on a cushion or pillow in the second. The Greek words for pallet and cushion are not the same, but both are lying down and the detail of Jesus on a cushion or pillow is not necessary to the story, suggesting that Mark adds this detail to underline a match. In fact, in their versions of stilling the storm neither Matthew nor Luke mention that Jesus is asleep on a cushion (Matt: 8:24, Luke 8:23). No doubt they realized that Mark used the story of Jonah as a source for this miracle. Matthew and Luke perhaps left out the cushion because there is not one mentioned in Jonah 1.

Faith is important in both halves of this stich. The paralytic and his companions have faith in the first hemistich, and this matches its opposite, the disciples not having faith, in the second. Mark is here expounding on Paul's doctrine of justification by faith.[6]

The first quotations in both hemistiches are remarkably similar to each other. Both quotations begin with a noun of address: "Child" in the first and "Teacher" in the second. The sentence spoken by Jesus in the first hemistich has five Greek words and the sentence spoken by the disciples has six Greek words, including "not," which introduces a negative question, while Jesus's statement is positive.

In the first hemistich the scribes think that Jesus should not have spoken as he did because it is blasphemy, while in the second hemistich Jesus goes one better and orders the wind and sea to be silent, reminding the reader of Ps 107:28–29, "Then they cried to the Lord in their trouble, and he brought them out from their distress; He caused the storm to be still, So that the waves of the sea were hushed."

In both hemistiches Jesus's opponents wonder who he is. With this match there can be no doubt that Mark intended a literary structure where each would be seen as

6. Rom 4–6.

theologically reflective of the other. Who but God can forgive sins? Who but God can control the wind and the seas?

In both hemistiches the observers are quoted in statements of amazement. While the observers of Jesus's miracles are always amazed at the miracle, in only three miracle stories in Original Mark are there direct quotations of amazement by the observers after Jesus performs a miracle and these are two of the three. The author intended a connection.

There is no chiastic match between the "Healing the Paralytic"/"Answering the Disciples" (9:14–29) and "Calling Levi"/"Eating with Sinners" (2:13–17) matching "The Parable Discourse" (4:1–34). Since there is no match for thirty-four verses, it appears that the redactor also moved "The Parable Discourse" from its original position to its position in Canonical Mark residing between "Who Are My Brothers" (3:31–35) and "Calming the Sea" (4:36–41). Tentatively we should consider that in Original Mark "Calming the Sea" followed immediately after "Who Are My Brothers" and "The Parable Discourse" did not intervene. In Luke's Gospel his version of "Calming the Sea" immediately follows his version of "Who Are My Brothers" at Luke 8:22. Did he know how Original Mark was organized, or is this a coincidence? See chapter 11 below. Luke's Gospel does contain "The Parable of the Sower," its explanation and Jesus's teaching to his disciples from Mark 4:21–24. Luke placed these passages before "Who Are My Brothers "at 8:5–18, so his arrangement of "Calming the Sea" immediately following "Who Are My Brothers" may be coincidental.

If the location of "The Parable Discourse" in Original Mark was in fact moved by a redactor, he had a limited number of places he could insert it without extensive editing since Jesus was sitting in a boat at the beginning of the discourse and left in a boat at the end to go "to the other side." The redactor apparently chose to place it before the boat trip involved in the "Calming of the Sea" (4:36–41), not realizing or not caring that he was interrupting a chiastic structure.

P (2:13–17), P' (3:31–35)

There are six matching elements in this stich:

1. "He went out again by the sea side" in the first hemistich matches "his mother and brothers arrive, and standing outside" in the second.

2. "Entire crowd came to him" in the first hemistich matches "a crowd was sitting around him" in the second.

3. "Follow me" in the first hemistich matches "they sent to him, calling him" in the second.

4. "And he arose and followed him" in the first hemistich matches "Look, your mother and brothers and sisters are outside looking for you. And answering them he said 'Who are my mother and my brothers?'"

5. "Why does he eat with tax collectors and sinners" in the first hemistich matches "Look, my mother and my brothers" in the second.

6. "I did not come to call the righteous but sinners" in the first hemistich matches "whoever does the will of God, he is my brother, and my sister and my mother" in the second.

Jesus calls Levi to follow him, which matches Jesus's family calling him to come with them. Levi, who is sitting, gets up and follows Jesus immediately matching the opposite, Jesus ignoring his family, continuing to sit with the crowd, and questioning, "who is my mother and my brothers." Jesus is in effect saying, "I don't know who you are talking about."

The scribes of the Pharisees ask why Jesus eats with tax collectors and sinners matching Jesus answering his own rhetorical question in the second hemistich by saying that these are my brothers and my mother.

In the first hemistich Jesus answers the scribes' question, and in the second he answers his own question. In combination Mark makes the theological point in this stich that Jesus came to call sinners to do the will of God.

Q (2:18–22), Q' (3:20–30)

This stich is a chiastic match more because of its form and less as a result of the content. The above table for this stich is designed so that the matching elements begin on the same line and the reader can appreciate the identity of the form:

1. "Fasting" matches "could not even eat bread."

2. The Pharisees match the scribes in challenging Jesus.

3. Jesus answers the challenge.

4. Jesus answers with a rhetorical question.

5. He states the principle that answers his rhetorical question. The statements end "cannot fast" (ou dyanatai nēsteuein) and "cannot stand" (ou dyanatai stathēnai).

6. A sentence follows in which Jesus tells the challengers that there will be a dire result: the bridegroom taken away in one and a house will not be able to stand in the other.

7. Next a sentence follows that tells what will happen because of the dire result, one ending "will they fast at that time" (nēsteuein en ekeinē tē hēmera) and the other ending "will come to an end" (alla telos echei).

8. Then Jesus changes the subject in further explanation: in one case to mending a tear, in the other to plundering the rich man's house.

9. Two sentences conclude to elucidate Jesus's point further, in one case about new wine in old wineskins, and in the other about blasphemies.

R (2:23–28), R' (3:13–19)

This stich has only three matching elements:

1. "Going through the grain fields" in the first hemistich matches "goes up into the mountain" in the second.

2. "Disciples" in the first hemistich matches "appointed twelve to be apostles" in the second.

3. "They that were with him" and "those that were with him" in the first hemistich matches "they might be with him" in the second.

Jesus and his disciples going through grain fields in the first hemistich matches their going up in the mountains to appoint apostles in the second. In the first hemistich Jesus talks about David and "they that were with him" reiterating it twice, which matches Jesus appointing the apostles, "that they might be with him."

Analysis of the Beginning and Transfiguration Chiastic Structure

The Beginning and Transfiguration Chiastic Structure has 18 separate stiches. In order to get these stiches to match, "The Transfiguration," "Coming Down the Mountain," "Healing of the Paralytic," and "Answering the Disciples" (9:2–29) needed to be relocated to follow "Return of the Twelve" (6:30–31). In addition, this structure has no matches with "The Parable Discourse" (4:1–35). This discourse is a very important part of Mark's Gospel and clearly original; therefore, it was relocated to follow 9:29. It appears that the redactor relocated a large block text that is sixty-three verses long: 9:2–29 and 4:1–35. The reasoning behind positioning "The Parable Discourse" to follow 9:2–29 will be discussed in chapter 9.

In the process of analyzing the text for matching stiches between the beginning of the Gospel and "The Transfiguration," there is a match at the seventh stich (G, G') between 1:12–13 and 9:2–5. Moving to the eighth stich (H, H') 1:14a says that John the Baptizer was delivered up, but there was no mention of John or his alter ego Elijah in Canonical Mark for eleven verses while up to that point in the structure there had been fourteen matches within twelve verses, a very tight structure. John the Baptizer and Elijah are mentioned at 8:28, that is a long way textually (eleven verses) from 9:2 with no matches for an important section of Mark 8 during which Peter identifies Jesus as the Christ (8:29), Jesus makes his first passion prediction (8:31), has an argument with Peter (8:32–33) and gives a sermon on discipleship (8:34–9:1). If "The Transfiguration" originally followed "Peter's Confession at Caesarea Philippi" (8:27—9:1) as it does in Canonical Mark, there would have been several chiastically matching elements between that important pericope and 1:14–28 wherein Jesus begins his ministry, calls his first disciples, and exorcises the unclean spirit in the synagogue.

The problem is that in Canonical Mark next-closest mention of John the Baptizer or Elijah is at 6:12–29, "Killing John the Baptizer." The initial analysis indicated that the structure terminates at the (G, G') stich, and it only encompasses the Prologue in the first half and "The Transfiguration" and "Coming Down the Mountain" as the second half. A structure containing two and a half chapters of text with no matching words or concepts in the middle of a chiastic structure would not fit the usual pattern of Mark's long chiastic structures. Either the structure terminated or a block of text had been moved by a redactor of Mark's Original Gospel.

As previously mentioned Koester expressed the theory that the "Bethsaida Section" (Mark 6:45–8:26) was not part of the original Gospel.[7] If that theory is correct, then the Gospel as originally written by Mark would transition from the end of "The First Feeding the Multitude" (6:32–44) to "Peter's Confession at Caesarea Philippi" (8:27—9:1). This is comparable to moving "The Transfiguration" and three subsequent pericopae (9:2–29) to follow the "Return of the Twelve" (6:30–31). Examining further, there are several matches that occur between the text subsequent to Jesus coming into Galilee proclaiming the gospel of God (1:14–15) and text before "Killing John the Baptizer" (6:12–29). In a chiastic structure the matching text runs forward in the early part of the Gospel and backwards in the later part of the Gospel. These matches include the following:

1. 1:14b matches with 6:17,

2. 1:16–19 matches with 6:7–9,

3. 1:22 matches with 6:10–12, and

4. 1:23–24 matches with 6:13.

Although a major revision of the canonical understanding of Mark's Gospel results, it is clear that the structure continues, and that either the two and a half chapters (6:29—9:1) were not part of the Original Gospel, or "The Transfiguration" and following pericopae had been repositioned by a redactor who was unaware of or decided to ignore the chiastic structure. It is inconceivable that Mark's Original Gospel does not include at least some of those two and half chapters, tentatively we should consider that pericopae have been moved by a redactor.

This is the same conclusion Albert Schweitzer reached in his 1914 book, *Mystery of the Kingdom of God*. Using a different literary analysis, Schweitzer concluded that "The Transfiguration" should be positioned after "Return Of The Twelve" and before "Peter's Confession At Caesarea Philippi."[8] Schweitzer thought that "The Transfiguration" was a much more momentous occasion than the afterthought to which the Synoptic Gospels relegate it. This makes good sense. As explained in Part II, "The Transfiguration" is a major plot point in the structure of Mark's Gospel and begins to reveal the Christology of the Original Gospel of Mark. In Canonical Mark and the other Synoptic Gospels, nothing new is learned by the reader because "The

---

7. Koester, *Ancient Christian Gospels*, 285.

8. Schweitzer, *Mystery*, 180.

Transfiguration" and "Coming Down the Mountain" follow "Peter's Confession at Caesarea Philippi" wherein Jesus reveals that he is the embodiment of Isaiah's Suffering Servant and Daniel's Son of Man.

Relocating "The Transfiguration" and "Coming Down the Mountain" is not the end of this initial major revision to the Gospel pursuant to the analysis. It is also apparent that "The Parable Discourse" in Canonical Mark is not in its original location because there is a second gap in this chiastic structure.

"Healing the Paralytic," (2:1–12) matches "Calming the Sea." (4:36–41). The clinching clue is that the paralytic is lying on a pallet and that matches Jesus lying on a cushion in the boat. The episode of Jesus calming the sea is taken from Jonah 1. In that story Jonah is on a ship when a storm comes up. Jonah is asleep below and the captain wakes him and asks why he is sleeping during a great storm. This is exactly like Mark 4:35–41, except Jonah is not asleep on a cushion. The cushion was added by Mark to chiastically match with the paralytic's pallet, although "cushion" and "pallet" are not the same word in Greek. Mark needed a pallet in the paralytic story so that others could carry it and let it down through the roof. Mark's source for the paralytic story is 2 Kings 1:2–16 LXX where King Ahaziah was laid up in bed (klinē) after falling through a lattice in his palace; yet a "klinē" would not work for the paralytic nor for use on a boat. Mark used pallet (krabatton) for the paralytic and pillow or cushion (proskephalaion) for Jesus on the boat, more suitable for use on a boat. The detail is different; however, the concept is the same.

Since "Calming the Sea" (4:36–41) appears to match with "Healing the Paralytic" (2:1–12), the analysis was continued to determine if the structure continues containing matches between "The Parable Discourse" (4:1–34), which immediately precedes "Calming the Sea," with what follows "Healing the Paralytic." Significant matches could not be detected. However, there are apparent matches between the two pericopae that follow "Healing the Paralytic," "Calling Levi" and "Eating with Sinners" (2:13–17), and "Who Are My Bothers?" (3:31–35), the pericope immediately before "The Parable Discourse." This stich contains six matches and suggests that "The Parable Discourse" has also been moved to its present location in Canonical Mark. However, that should not be considered as a viable solution unless there are subsequent matches confirming that the structure continues past Canonical 4:1–34.

There are two more stiches in the present structure. "Lesson on Fasting" (2:18–22), matches "Controversy on Beelzebul" (3:20–30) with seven matches. In this stich it is the form that matches rather than the content, although there are some similar words. Under the principles of form criticism the form of controversies should be the same or very similar. However, only these two controversies have this particular form:

1. Jesus answers a challenge with a rhetorical question,

2. He answers the rhetorical question himself in a statement ending with "cannot,"

3. He further answers the challenge using the future tense, and

4. He then changes the subject twice using aphorisms.

None of the other controversies are in this form.[9] Therefore, fortuitous placing of controversies is not a sufficient objection to these pericopae being part of the Beginning and Transfiguration Chiastic Structure.

This structure, in addition to not including "The Parable Discourse" (4:1–34), makes minimal use of the "Healing of the Gerasene Demoniac" (5:1–20). However, there is a relatively short structure overlapping the Beginning and Transfiguration Chiastic Structure, running from 2:18–3:30 for its first half, and from 5:2–6:11 for its second half. This structure demonstrates that "Healing the Gerasene Demoniac" was positioned in the Original Gospel immediately prior to the "Healing the Woman with Blood Flow," "Jairus's Daughter is Dead," and "Healing Jairus's Daughter" (5:21–43), just as it is in Canonical Mark. It almost seems as if Mark made this shorter match because he was not satisfied how "Healing the Gerasene Demoniac" fit into the Beginning and Transfiguration Chiastic Structure.

Overlapping First-Half Chiastic Structure

Below is the relatively short chiastic structure that contains only four stiches of controversies and healings. This structure demonstrates that "Healing the Gerasene Demoniac" belongs immediately before the "Healing Jairus's Daughter. The left hand column runs forward from 2:18 to 3:30 encompassing Jesus's controversies on fasting, the Sabbath, healing on the Sabbath, and on Beelzebul. The chiastically-matching right hand column runs from 6:7 to 5:2 and encompasses (in reverse Gospel order) Jesus sending out the twelve to preach, being rejected in his hometown, healing Jairus's daughter, healing the bleeding woman, and healing a demoniac.

---

9. These controversies are: "Eating with Sinners," "Healing of the Paralytic," "Plucking Grain on the Sabbath," "Healing the Man with the Withered Hand," "Looking for a Sign," "Controversy on Tradition," "Controversy on Divorce," "Questioning Jesus's Authority," "Rendering unto Caesar," and "Controversy on Resurrection."

Overlapping First-Half Chiastic Structure

A 2:18 . . . *disciples . . . disciples . . . fasting. . . .
disciples . . . disciples . . . fast, but your disciples
do not fast?* 2:19 . . . *sons of the bride chamber
fast . . . is with them . . . fast.* 2:20 . . . *fast* . . . 2:21
. . . *on old clothing . . .*

B 2:23 . . . *Sabbath . . . disciples . . .* 2:24 . . . "*Look,
why do they do what is not lawful . . . Sabbath?*"
2:25 . . . *David . . . they that were with him?* 2:26
. . . *house of God . . . those that were with him?*"
2:27 . . . *Sabbath . . . Sabbath.* 2:28 . . . *Sabbath.*"

C 3:1 . . . *synagogue; . . . hand* . . . 3:2 . . . *heal him
. . .* 3:3 . . . *hand* "*Arise.*" . . . 3:4 . . . *save a life, or
to kill*" *But they were silent* 3:5 . . . "*Stretch out
your hand* And he *stretched it out . . . hand* was
restored 3:6 . . . *they might destroy him.*

D 3:9 . . . *small boat* . . . 3:11 . . . *unclean spirits
. . . fell down before him . . . Son of God.* . . . 3:13
. . . *up into the mountain . . .* And they went to
him 3:14 . . . *they might be with him . . . send
them out to preach* 3:15 . . . *authority to cast out
demons* . . . 3:20 . . . could *not even eat bread*
3:21 And when his *family heard it . . . out of his
mind.* 3:23 *cast out Satan* . . . 3:27 . . . *into the
house of the strong man, and plunder his goods,
unless he first ties up the strong man.* . . . 3:30 . . .
unclean spirit.

A' 6:7 . . . *summons the twelve . . . them out . . .
them . . .* 6:8 . . . *them that they . . . take nothing
for their . . . no bread,* . . . 6:9 . . . *do not put on
two tunics.* 6:10 . . . *them,* "Whenever *you enter
into a house . . . you . . .* 6:11 . . . *you . . . you as
you . . . your . . .*"

B' 6:1 . . . *disciples* . . . 6:2 . . . *Sabbath* . . . 6:3 . . .
*son of Mary, and brother of James, and Joseph,
and Judas, and Simon?* . . . *sisters . . . they took
umbrage at him.* 6:4 . . . *own family,* and *in his
own house.*"

C' 5:22 . . . *synagogue . . . falls at his feet* 5:23 . . .
*lay your hands on her, that she may be cured and
live* . . . 5:27 . . . *touched his robe.* 5:28 . . . *touch
his robe . . . cured* 5:29 . . . *affliction was healed*
5:30 . . . "*Who touched my robe?*" 5:31 . . . "*Who
touched me?*" . . . 5:33 . . . *fell down in front of
him* . . . 5:35 . . . *synagogue . . . daughter is dead
. . . . . .* 5:39 . . . *make such a commotion* . . . 5:40
And they *laughed at him* . . . 5:41 . . . *hand* . . .
arise 5:42 . . . *arose* . . .

D' 5:2 . . . *boat . . . an unclean spirit* . . . 5:3 . . .
*no one could bind him any longer, not even with
a chain.* 5:4 . . . *often been tied up with shackles
and chains, and the chains had been broken by
him, and the shackles broken in pieces* . . . 5:5 . . .
in the mountains . . . 5:6 . . . *he ran and fell on his
knees in front of him* 5:7 . . . *Son of the Most High
God* . . . 5:8 . . . *unclean spirit* . . . 5:9 . . . *name . . .
name* . . . 5:10 . . . *send them out of the country*
5:11 . . . *on the mountainside* . . . 5:13 . . . *the
unclean spirits leaving him* . . . 5:14 And *those
feeding them* . . . 5:15 . . . *dressed and of sound
mind* . . . 5:18 . . . *the boat . . . he might be with
him* 5:19 . . . "*Go to your house to your family,
and tell them how much the Lord has done for
you, and that he had mercy on you.*"

Commentary

A (2:18–22), A' (6:6B–11)

There are four matching elements in this stich:

1. "Disciples" five times and "sons of the bride chamber" in the first hemistich matches "the twelve" and twelve pronouns referring to the disciples in the second.

2. Six forms of "fast" in the first hemistich matches "take nothing" and "no bread" in the second.

3. "Chamber" in the first hemistich matches "house" in the second.

4. "Old clothing" in the first hemistich matches "two tunics" in the second.

As an interesting aside, in the instructions to the twelve for their journey Mark uses a third person pronoun (they, them, their) for the first six times and second person (you, your) for the second six times. This is consistent with Mark's obsession with threes.

B (2:23–28), B' (6:1–6:6A)

There are five matching elements in this stich:

1. "Sabbath" is found in both hemistiches.

2. "Disciples," "they that were with him" and "those that were with him" in the first hemistich match "disciples" in the second.

3. "Look why do they do what is not lawful" in the first hemistich matches "they took umbrage at him" in the second.

4. "David" in the first hemistich matches "son of Mary" "brothers," "sisters" and "family" in the second.

5. "House of God" in the first hemistich matches "in his own house" in the second.

In the first hemistich Jesus mentions David, the ancestor of the Judean Messiah, while in the second hemistich the congregation knows who Jesus is because they know his family. Mark is making the ironic theological point that the congregation does not know Jesus is the Messiah. In the first hemistich Jesus says that David entered the temple when Abiathar was high priest. This is universally regarded as a Markan mistake,[10] because Ahimalech was the priest named at 1 Sam 21:1 when David took the consecrated bread for his men. Both Matthew and Luke drop the name of the priest in their versions of Mark's story. This may not have been a mistake by Mark. Mark's Jesus is making a mistake, since he is human. The author was intentionally making a reference to 2 Sam 15 wherein David flees Absolom. Abiathar is mentioned six times

---

10. Helms, *Who Wrote*, 10–11.

in 2 Sam 15. Mark typically makes at least two references to an OT passage he uses as a source. He made one reference to 2 Sam 15 in Jesus's arrest on the Mount of Olives in Mark 14 and here at 2:23–28 is his other reference. Mark is again foreshadowing Jesus's arrest on the Mount of Olives by making reference to David and Abiathar. This reference to Abiathar is immediately before the pericope in which it is narrated that the Pharisees and Herodians counseled on how they could kill Jesus.

C (3:1–6), C' (5:21–43)

There are nine matching elements in these healing miracles:

1. "Synagogue" is found in both hemistiches.

2. "Hand" is found four times and "it" referring to hand once in the first hemistich matches "hand" found twice in the second hemistich.

3. "Stretch forth your hand" and "he stretched it out" in the first hemistich match "touch" found four times in the second.

4. "They were silent" in the first hemistich matches its opposite "make such a commotion" and "they laughed at him" in the second.

5. "Arise" is in both hemistiches.

6. "Arise" in the first hemistich is also the opposite of "falls at his feet" and "fell down in front of him" in the second.

7. "To kill" and "might destroy him" in the first hemistich matches "daughter is dead" in the second.

8. "Save a life" in the first hemistich matches "child is not dead" in the second.

9. "Restored" in the first hemistich matches "affliction was healed" in the second.

One would expect that two healing miracles would have some similar aspects under the principles of form criticism. However, the specific matches of "synagogue," "hand," "touch," "kill and dead," "save a life," and "not dead" insure that Mark made intentional matches for a chiastic structure.

D (3:9–30), D' (5:2–20)

There are twelve matching elements in this stich:

1. "Boat" is in both hemistiches.

2. "Unclean spirit" is found twice in the first hemistich and three times in the second.

3. "Son of God" in the first hemistich matches "Son of the Most High God" in the second.

4. "Name" is found twice in both hemistiches.

5. "Cast out demons" and "cast out Satan" in the first hemistich matches "come out, unclean spirit, out of the man" and "the unclean spirits leaving him" in the second.

6. "Might be with him" is found in both hemistiches.

7. "Family" is found in both hemistiches.

8. "Out of his mind" in the first hemistich matches its opposite "in his right mind" in the second.

9. "Send them out to preach" in the first hemistich matches "Go to your house to your family, and tell them how much the Lord has done for you, and that he had mercy on you."

10. "Into the mountain" in the first hemistich matches "in the mountains" in the second.

11. "Ties up the strong man" in the first hemistich matches "no one could bind him any longer" in the second.

12. "Fell down before him" in the first hemistich matches "fell on his knees in front of him" in the second.

Jesus gives Simon, James, and John new names in the first hemistich, which matches his asking the unclean spirit what its name is in the second. This is the only time Jesus asks the name of a spirit in Mark's Gospel. This match ties Simon Peter, James and John to a legion of unclean spirits, a hidden Markan theme.

In the previous structure it was noted that the form of "Controversy on Beelzebul" (3:20–30) matched the form of "Lesson on Fasting" (2:18–22). In this structure the wording of "Controversy on Beelzebul" matches the wording of "Healing the Gerasene Demoniac" (5:1–20)

Jesus's family thinks that Jesus is "out of his mind" (exestē). This is the opposite of "in his right mind" (sōphronounta), the status of the demoniac that "they" observed after Jesus exorcised the unclean spirit. Usually Jesus told people to keep his healings to themselves. In this case he told the demoniac to publish the healing. This change in command may have been intended to match Jesus's instruction to the disciple to go out and preach.

Outline of Original Mark

The Beginning and Transfiguration Chiastic Structure compels the rearrangement of the Canonical Gospel of Mark as shown in Appendix 3, pericopae numbers 9–31. "The Parable Discourse" (4:1–34) has been moved from its canonical position following "Who are My Brothers" (3:31–35). "The Transfiguration," "Leaving the Mountain," "Healing the Epileptic," and "Answering the Disciples" (9:2–29) have also been repositioned to follow "The Return of the Twelve" (6:30–31). These repositionings serve to partially restore the original text of Mark's Gospel.

The next chapter analyzes another long chiastic structure that defines the contents of the middle third of the Original Gospel.

6

The Middle of the Gospel Chiastic Structure

From Feeding The Multitude To Praying At Gethsemane

THIS SIXTEEN-STICH STRUCTURE ENCOMPASSES the middle of the Gospel from the beginning of "Feeding the Multitude" at 6:34 to Jesus beginning his prayer vigil in Gethsemane at 14:32 after "The Last Supper." This first half of this structure contained in the left column meets the second half of the structure contained in the right column at "Getting a Colt for Jesus" (11:1-6) This structure contains the major Pauline teaching portion of Mark's Gospel. Chapter 16 documents the Pauline sources for this section of the Original Gospel

This structure also raises the possibility that much of the "Bethsaida Section" of Canonical Mark (6:44—8:29) was not part of Original Mark, as Koester theorizes. In addition, this structure suggests that "Controversy On Tradition" and "Eating Does Not Defile" (7:1–23) were originally located between 10:46a and 10:46b. Koester does not posit this repositioning; he eliminates these two pericope along with the rest of the "Bethsaida Section." This table again shows only the matching language.

The Middle of the Gospel Chiastic Structure

A 6:32 . . . *private desert place.* 6:33 . . . saw *them going . . . they all ran there on foot*	A' 14:32 . . . place *that was named Gethsemane . . . Sit here . . .* 14:33 . . . 14:34 . . . *stay here*, and *watch.*
B 6:34 . . . *sheep without a shepherd: and he began to teach them many things.*	B' 14:27 *And Jesus says to them . . . strike the shepherd, and the sheep will be scattered . . .*
C 6:36 . . . *buy themselves something* to eat. 6:37 . . . eat . . . *two hundred denarii for bread . . . eat* 8:5 . . . *loaves . . .* 8:6 . . . *sit down on the ground . . . loaves, and giving thanks, he broke, and gave them to his disciples, so that they might serve them; and they served them . . .* 8:7 . . . *blessed . . .* 8:8 . . . *ate . . .*	C' 14:3 . . . *reclining at dinner . . .* 14:5 . . . *might have been sold . . . three hundred denarii . . .* 14:12 . . . *bread . . . eat . . .* 14:17 . . . *with the twelve* 14:18 *And as they reclined eating . . . eating . . .* 14:22 . . . *eating, taking bread, and blessing, he broke, and gave to them . . .* 14:23 . . . *giving thanks, he gave to them:*

D 8:11 . . . *heaven* . . . 8:12 . . . *Why does this generation seek a sign* . . . *given to this generation.* 8:15 . . . *Watch out. Beware* of the *leaven of the Pharisees and the leaven of Herod.* 8:16 . . . *bread.* 8:17 . . . *bread* . . . 8:18 *Having eyes, do you not see* . . . 8:20 . . . *loaves* . . .

E 8:23 . . . *Do you see anything?* 8:24 . . . *I see men; for I see them as walking trees.* 8:25 . . . *and saw all clearly* . . .

F 8:27 . . . *Who do men say that I am?* 8:28 *And they told him, saying, John the Baptizer* . . . *Elijah* . . . *prophets.* 8:29 . . . *You are the Christ.* 8:30 . . . *tell no one about him.*

G 8:31 *And he began to teach them* . . . *the Son of Man suffer many things* . . . *rejected by the elders, and the chief priests, and the scribes* . . . *put to death, and after three days rise.*

H 8:34 . . . *take up his cross, and follow me* 8:35 . . . *life will lose it* . . *lose his life* . . . *that of the gospel* . . . 8:38 . . . *of his Father* . . . 9:1 . . . *standing here* . . .

I 9:31 . . . *The Son of Man is delivered into the hands of men, and they will kill him* . . .

J 9:35 *And sitting down, he summoned the twelve and he says to them* . . . 9:38 *John* . . . *Teacher, we saw someone who does not follow us casting out demons* . . . 9:39 . . . 9:42 *And whoever causes one of these little ones believing in me to stumble* . . . *heavy millstone* . . . *thrown into the sea.*

K 9:43 . . . *hand* . . . *two hands* . . . *into Gehenna* . . . 9:45 . . . *foot* . . . *feet* . . . *into Gehenna.* 9:47 . . . *the kingdom of God* . . . *eye,* . . . *eyes* . . . *into Gehenna;* 9:48 . . . *worm does not die and the fire is not quenched* . . . 9:50 . . . *what will you season it with* . . .

D' 13:30 . . . *this generation* . . . 13:31 *Heaven* . . . 13:32 . . . *heaven* . . . 13:33 *Take care* . . . 13:34 . . . *to keep watch* 13:35 *Watch* . . . 13:37 . . . *Watch* 14:1 . . . *unleavened bread* . . .

E' 13:28 . . . *the fig tree* . . . 13:29 . . . *you see these things* . . .

F' 13:21 . . . *if any man says to you, Look, here is the Christ* . . . *Do not believe it* 13:22 . . . *false Christs and false prophets,* . . . 13:23 . . . *I have told you all things beforehand.*

G' 13:13 *And you will be hated by all men for my name's sake* . . . *will be saved.* 13:14 . . . *abomination of desolation* . . . *let the reader understand* . . .

H' 13:10 *And the gospel must first be proclaimed* . . . 13:11 . . . *lead you away and deliver you up* . . . 13:12 . . . *deliver up* . . . *death, and the father his child* . . . *put them to death.*

I' 13:6 . . . *come in my name,* saying . . . 13:9 . . . *They will deliver you up to councils; and in synagogues you will be flogged* . . .

J' 12:41 *And sitting down* . . . *crowd threw money* . . . 12:43 *And summoning his disciples, he said to them* . . . *threw in* . . . *throwing into the treasury* 12:44 . . . *threw* . . . *she threw in all* . . . 13:1 . . . *"Teacher, look* . . . *stones* . . . 13:2 . . . *stone* . . . 13:3 *And as he is sitting on* . . . *Peter and James and John and Andrew* . . . 13:5 . . . *Be careful that no one leads you astray.*

K' 12:34 *And seeing* . . . *the kingdom of God."* . . . 12:36 . . . *right hand* . . . *a footstool for your feet.* 12:37 . . . 12:39 . . . *chief places at feasts* 12:40 *devouring widows' houses* . . . *abundant judgment.'*

L 10:1 . . . *crowds come together . . .* 10:2 . . . *divorce his wife . . .* 10:3 . . . *Moses command* you 10:4 . . . *Moses . . .* 10:5 . . . *commandment . . .* 10:7 . . . *join with his wife . . .* 10:11 . . . *divorce his wife and marry another, commits adultery against her,* 10:12 *and if a woman herself may divorce her husband and marry another, she commits adultery.* 10:13 . . . *children . . .* 10:14 . . . *children . . . kingdom of God . . .* 10:15 . . . *kingdom of God as a little child . . .* 10:17 . . . *one ran up to him* and . . . *Teacher . . . inherit eternal life.* 10:18 . . . 10:19 . . . *commandments, Do not murder, Do not commit adultery, Do not steal, Do not testify falsely, Do not defraud, Honor your father and mother* 10:20 . . . *Teacher . . .* 10:21 . . . *will have treasure in heaven . . .* 10:23 . . . *the kingdom of God* 10:24 . . . *Children . . . the kingdom of God* 10:25 . . . *enter into the kingdom of God . . .*

M 10:32 . . . *began to tell them the things that were to happen to him* 10:33 . . . *And they will condemn him to death . . .* 10:34 *And they will ridicule him, and will spit upon him, and will flog him, and will kill him . . .*

N 10:35 *And James and John, the sons of Zebedee approach him . . .* 10:37 . . . *Grant us that we may sit, one on your right hand, and one on your left hand, in your glory.* 10:38 . . . *baptized with the baptism that I am baptized with* 10:39 . . . *with the baptism that I am baptized with you will be baptized . . .* 10:42 . . . great *men exercise authority over them.*

O 7:2 . . . *disciples are eating their bread . . .* 7:3 . . . *do not eat . . .* 7:4 . . . *they do not eat . . .* cups, *and pots, and brass vessels and eating tables . . .* 7:6 . . . *This people honors me with their lips, but their heart is far away from me* 7:7 *But in vain do they worship me. Teaching as their doctrines the precepts of men.* 7:8 *You ignore the commandment of God, and observe the tradition of men.* 7:9 . . . 7:10 . . . *Honor your father and your mother . . .* 7:11 . . . *that is, a gift to God.* 7:12 *You no longer require him to do anything for his father or his mother . . .* 7:18 . . . *goes into the man . . .* 7:21 . . . *thefts . . .* 7:23 . . . *man.*

P 10:46b . . . *was sitting beside the road* 10:47 . . . *shout out . . . Jesus, son of David, have mercy on me.* 10:48 . . . shouted *out all the more, Son of David, have mercy on me . . .* 10:50 *And he, throwing away his tunic . . .* 10:52 . . . *followed him on the road . . .*

Q 11:2 . . . *find a colt tied . . .*

L' 12:18 *And Sadducees arrive . . . resurrection . . .* 12:19 *Teacher, Moses . . . leave a wife . . . leave no child . . . take his wife . . . heir* for his *brother* 12:21 . . . *took her . . . leaving no heir . . . likewise* 12:22 . . . *left no heir Last . . .* 12:23 *In the resurrection whose wife . . . wife . . .* 12:26 . . . *Moses . . .* 12:28 *And approaching one of the scribes . . . commandment . . .* 12:29 . . . *The first is, Hear, O Israel; The Lord our God, the Lord is one:* 12:30 *and you will love the Lord your God with all your heart, and with all your soul, and with all your mind, and with all your strength.* 12:31 *The second is this; you will love your neighbor as yourself. There is no other commandment greater than these.* 12:32 . . . *Teacher* 12:34 . . . *kingdom of God. . . .*

M' 12:1 *And he began to speak to them in parables . . .* 12:6 . . . *They will have respect for my son* 12:7 . . . *This is the heir. Come, let us kill him . . .* 12:8 . . . *killed him, and threw him out of the vineyard.*

N' 11:27b . . . *the chief priests and the scribes and the elders come to him.* 11:28 . . . *By what authority are you doing these things Or who gave you this authority to do these things . . .* 11:30 *The baptism of John . . .* 11:33 . . . *authority . . .*

O' 11:12 . . . *he was hungry.* 11:13 . . . *fig tree . . .* 11:14 . . . *No man may eat . . .* 11:15 . . . *tables of the moneychangers . . .* 11:17 . . . *My house will be called a house of prayer for all the nations . . . den of thieves* 11:20 . . . *fig tree . . .* 11:21 . . . *fig tree . . .*

P' 11:7 . . . *throw on him their tunics; and he sat upon him.* 11:8 And *many spread their tunics on the road; . . .* 11:9 . . . *followed cried,* "Hosanna . . . 11:10 . . . *kingdom of our father David:* Hosanna . . .

Q' 11:4 . . . *found a colt having been tied . . .* 11:5 . . . *untying the colt?"* 11:6 . . .

Commentary

A (6:32–33), A' (14:32–34)

There are three matches in this stich:

1. "Private desert place" in the first hemistich matches "a place named Gethsemane" in the second.

2. "They all ran there on foot" in the first hemistich matches "sit here" in the second.

3. "Saw them going" in the first hemistich matches "stay and watch" in the second.

As noted in an earlier structure "place" in the first hemistich is a different Greek word from "place" in the second. The match is that Jesus and his disciples go into an open area not a building or home. In the first hemistich the crowd runs to where Jesus is going to be and in the second Jesus tells Peter, James and John to stay and watch, presumably for a group coming to arrest him. "Saw them" and "watch" is an obvious match.

B (6:34), B' (14:27–28)

"Sheep without a shepherd" in the first hemistich matches "strike the shepherd and the sheep will be scattered" in the second, and "he began to teach them many things" in the first hemistich matches "Jesus says to them" in the second.

Shepherd and sheep is too much of a coincidence not to be a match. This also is evidence that the first part of the first miraculous feeding is original to the Gospel. "Sheep" comes before "shepherd" in the first hemistich and after "shepherd" in the second—a Markan reversal, common throughout his Gospel.

C (6:35–37; 8:5–9), C' (14:3–26)

In this stich there are eight matches with "Feeding the Multitude" matching "The Last Supper":

1. "Buy themselves something" in the first hemistich matches "might have been sold" in the second.

2. In the first hemistich a form of "eat" is found four times (eat, ate) matching (eat, eating, dinner) found four times in the second.

3. "Two hundred denarii" in the first hemistich matches "three hundred denarii" in the second.

4. In the first hemistich "bread" or "loaves" is found three times matching "bread" found twice in the second.

5. "Giving thanks" is found in both hemistiches.

6. "Blessing" or "having blessed" is found in both hemistiches.

7. "Sit down on the ground" is found in the first hemistich matches "reclined" found twice in the second.

8. "He broke and gave to his disciples" is found in the first hemistich matches "he broke and gave to them" (his disciples) in the second.

The second half of "First Feeding the Multitude" (6:34–44) and the first half of "Second Feeding the Multitude" (8:1–9) as found in Canonical Mark have been eliminated and everything in between, except 7:1–23. It is unmistakable that the first part of the first feeding miracle is original since "sheep and shepherd," "denarii" and "eat" found three times form chiastic matches with Mark 14. These are the only times in the Gospel that the plural of denarius is used. The singular is used at 12:15.

It is also unmistakable that the second half of the second feeding miracle found in Canonical Mark is intended to chiastically match with "The Last Supper" (14:17–25). In the second feeding miracle Jesus gives thanks for the bread and blesses the fish. In "The Last Supper" Jesus blesses the bread and gives thanks over the cup, a typical Markan reversal. This is obviously an intended match uniting "Feeding the Multitude" with "The Last Supper." On the other hand, in the second half of the first feeding miracle (the portion that has been eliminated) Jesus only "broke and blessed the loaves" and did nothing over the fish. The redactor missed the unity with the Last Supper. There are other unMarkan aspects to the portions of the feeding miracles that have been eliminated, and they will be elucidated in the analysis section below.

The theological/symbolic point Mark is making with this chiasm is unmistakable. The sacrament of the Eucharist (Last Supper) is spiritually nourishing and Christianity will spiritually nourish the world.

D (8:10–21), D' (13:30—14:2)

There are seven matches in this stich:

1. "Generation" is found twice in the first hemistich and once in the second.

2. Reversing the match in number 1, "heaven" is found once in the first hemistich and twice in the second.

3. "Leaven" in the first hemistich matches its opposite "unleavened" in the second.

4. "Bread" and "loaves" are found three times in the first hemistich and once in the second.

5. "Watch out," and "Having eyes do you not see" are found in the first hemistich matching "Watch" being found three times in the second.

6. "Beware" or "take heed" is found in the first hemistich and "take care" or "take heed" (blepete) is found in the second.

7. "Beware the leaven of the Pharisees and the leaven of Herod" in the first hemistich matches "the chief priests and the scribes looked for a way that they might take him with treachery and put him to death."

This seven-match stich confirms that collapsing the two feeding miracles found in Canonical Mark and eliminating or moving every thing in between accurately re-instates the Original Gospel. The odds would be astronomical that matching "leaven," "generation," "bread," "take heed" and "heaven" would occur by chance. "Leaven" is symbolic of insidious evil or hypocrisy and "unleavened" purity and holiness. Paul used "leaven" as a metaphor in 1 Cor 5:5–6 and Gal 5:9.

E (8:23–26), E' (13:28–29)

There are only two matches in this short stich, but the chiastic matches are clear. "Do you see anything," "I see men, for I see them," and "saw all clearly" in the first hemistich matches "when you see these things" in the second. "As walking trees" in the first hemistich matches "from the fig tree" in the second.

Jesus heals a blind man after two tries. "See" or "saw" is found four times and significantly, "he saw clearly." In the second hemistich Jesus warns his disciples "when you see these things happening know that it is near."

The blind man strangely sees men looking like trees after Jesus's first attempt at healing him in the first hemistich, and Jesus tells his disciples to learn the parable of the fig tree in the second. Scholars have puzzled over this healing, and here it is dem-onstrated that Mark was making a chiastic match with the parable of the fig tree. That is why it had to take two tries and why trees are mentioned. When Jesus says, "learn the parable of the fig tree" he could be referring back to his cursing the fig tree because it had no fruit at 11:13–21.

In "Healing the Blind Man of Bethsaida" Mark may also be making a reference to Isa 29:18 that says, "And out of their gloom and darkness the eyes of the blind will see." This quotation from Isaiah gives the impression of slowly coming out of blindness as Mark has written the healing by Jesus. This stich may also be a reference to Rom 13:11–12. In this epistle Paul mentions the season and coming out of darkness, which has elements of both hemistiches.

> Rom 13:11 And this, knowing the season, that already it is time for you to awake out of sleep: for now is salvation nearer to us than when we first be-lieved. 12 The night is far spent, and the day is at hand: let us therefore cast off the works of darkness, and let us put on the armor of light.

F (8:27–30), F' (13:21–23)

There are five matches in this short hemistich:

1. "Who do men say that I am" in the first hemistich matches "if any man says to you" in the second.

2. "They told him" and "tell no one" in the first hemistich matches "I have told you" in the second.

3. "John the Baptizer," "Elijah" and "one of the prophets" matches the opposite "false prophets" in the second.

4. "You are the Christ" in the first hemistich matches "here is the Christ" and "false Christs" in the second.

5. "You are the Christ" in the first hemistich also matches "do not believe it" in the second.

There is a very subtle match between Peter identifying Jesus as the Christ in the first hemistich and "do not believe it" in the second. This is double irony. On the surface level there is a match of opposites because Peter is correct that Jesus is the Messiah, but there is a deeper irony because Peter got it wrong. He identified Jesus as the Christ, but the astute reader can tell from Jesus's reaction to whatever Peter said that Peter intended the Jewish Messiah/Conquering King who would overthrow Rome—the Danielic Messiah. The Danielic "Son of Man" was seen as the Jewish Messiah King in pre Christian Judaism, based on 1 Enoch 37–71 and 4 Ezra 11–13.[1]

Jesus learned from Moses and Elijah on the mountain of "The Transfiguration" that God intends him to be Paul's salvation for all the world, including gentiles, based on Isaiah's Suffering Servant. In pre Christian Judaism there was no conflation of Daniel's "Son of Man" and Isaiah's "Suffering Servant."[2] It was the genius of Paul or a predessor that conflated these two differing versions of the Messiah in order to make the Christ savior of all mankind, not just the Jews. First the Messiah must die an atoning death, be raised up and then come with the clouds to institute the kingdom of God in Danielic fashion. Mark's Pauline Gospel is pointing out the error of the Jerusalem apostles, Peter, James and John, who were looking for the Danielic "Son of Man" to be the Jewish world conquering king. That is why they insisted that one must become Jewish to be a Christian, and they opposed Paul with his savior Messiah offering spiritual salvation for all nations, including gentiles, without circumcision or dietary restrictions.

The text found in this stich from "The Olivet Discourse" at 13:21–22 is a reference by Mark's Jesus directly to the Jerusalem apostles. There Jesus speaks of "false christs," "false prophets," and "men saying, 'Look here is the Christ.'" Compare that to

---

1. Cummins, *Paul And Christ*, 46.
2. Ladd, *New Tesstament*.

Paul's warnings about "another Jesus,"[3] "false apostles,"[4] "we preach Christ crucified, a stumbling block to Jews."[5] It is no coincidence that Mark 13:21–22 is in the same stich with Peter's identifying Jesus as the Christ at 8:29. This is Mark subtly pointing the finger at the disciples as being the personification of Paul's enemies, the Jerusalem apostles.

G (8:31), G' (13:13–14)

There are four matches in this stich:

1. "He began to teach them" in the first hemistich matches "let the reader understand" in the second.

2. "The son of man suffer many things" and "be put to death" in the first hemistich matches "the abomination of desolation" in the second.

3. "Rejected by the elders and the chief priests and the scribes" in the first hemistich matches "hated by all men" in the second.

4. "After three days rise" in the first hemistich matches "will be saved" in the second.

"Let the reader understand" is a strange message from the narrator of the story to the reader.[6] It conveniently provides a chiastic match. "The abomination of desolation" comes from Dan 11:31 and 12:11. Much of Mark 13 is based upon Dan 7:13–14, 11:31, 12:6–10, and 1 Thess 4:16–17.

H (8:34—9:1), H' (13:10–12)

There are five matches in this stich:

1. "Take up his cross" in the first hemistich matches "deliver you up" and "will deliver up" in the second.

2. "Follow me" in the first hemistich matches "lead you away" in the second.

3. "Lose his life" found twice in the first hemistich matches "death" found twice in the second.

4. "That of the gospel" is found in the first hemistich and "the gospel must first be proclaimed" in the second.

5. "Father" is found in both hemistiches.

---

3. 2 Cor 11:4.
4. 2 Cor 11:13.
5. 1 Cor 1:23.
6. Fowler, *Let The Reader*.

Some commentators opine that 13:10 is an interpolation into Mark. This chiastic match is evidence that it is original. In addition, with Mark's penchant for triplets, he used "gospel" (euangeliou) six times. The first two times he wrote "proclaim the gospel" and "says . . . believe in the gospel," the second two times "sake of the gospel" and the third two times "proclaim the gospel." Since "gospel" is a word in the incipit, and all the words in the incipit except "Jesus" are either found to be triplets or sextets in the text, it is inconceivable that 13:10 is a later interpolation into Mark's Original Gospel.

I (9:30–32), I' (13:6–9)

There are three matches in this stich:

1. "Son of man" in the first hemistich matches "in my name" in the second.

2. "Son of man is delivered into the hands of men" in the first hemistich matches "they will deliver you up to councils" in the second.

3. "They will kill him" in the first hemistich matches "you will be flogged" in the second.

In the first part of "The Olivet Discourse" Jesus tells his disciples what the indignities they will suffer for their faith, and Mark matches those indignities with Jesus's second prediction of the passion telling what will happen to him at his trials.

J (9:34–42), J' (12:41–13:5)

There are seven matches in this stich:

1. "Sitting down" is found in both hemistiches and "as he is sitting" is also in the second hemistich.

2. "Summoned the twelve and he says to them" in the first hemistich matches "summoning his disciples he says to them" in the second.

3. "Casting out demons" and "thrown into the sea" in the first hemistich matches "throw" used five times in the second.

4. "John" in the first hemistich matches "Peter and James and John and Andrew" in the second.

5. "Millstone" in the first hemistich matches "stone" used twice in the second.

6. "Causes one of these little one believing in me to stumble" in the first hemistich matches "Be careful that no one leads you astray" in the second.

7. "Teacher, we saw" in the first hemistich matches "Teacher, look" in the second.

We have seen the match between "throw" and "cast out" previously. "Casting out demons" matches "thrown into the sea." John son of Zebedee tells Jesus that they saw someone who is not a disciple casting out demons in Jesus's name and they made him stop. This may be another joke by Mark—having John refer to Paul. Mark has John, one of the Jerusalem apostles mentioned by Paul, telling Paul to stop doing good in Jesus' name. For those who may think this is a streatch, notice that in admonishing John, Jesus makes a backwards quote of Rom 8:31. Mark 9:40 says, "He that is not against us is for us" is the reverse of Rom 8:31, "If God is for us, who is against us." The typical Markan reversal gives this away as being an obscure reference to the dispute between Paul and the Jerusalem apostles with Jesus taking Paul's side. Of course, this is anachronistic, but Mark's Gospel is literature, not history.

In addition, the above quote from Rom 8:31 is based on Ps 118 and Jesus quotes another part of Ps 118 later in the Gospel at 12:10–11, so that the astute reader will realize the quote of Rom 8:31 was deliberate. Further, John's statement to Jesus comes three verses after Jesus has told the disciples that one who wants to be first will be last and a servant. Then later, at 10:35 Jesus reiterates that the first will be last and the last first, and three verses after that at 10:38 James and John ask to sit on Jesus's right and left hands. These sequences in Mark only make sense as a rebuke to the Jerusalem apostles and a promotion of Paul.

Finally, there is a twelve-element structure using the word "demon" in Original Mark. Twelve elements obviously refers to the disciples who Mark calls "the twelve." Plus, the final element of that structure is at 9:38 when John tells Jesus that they saw someone casting out demons. All of these incidents cannot be coincidental. Mark is referring to Paul at 9:38–40 as the unknown disciple.

K (9:43–50), K' (12:34–40)

There are seven matches in this stich:

1. "Hand" and "two hands" found in the first hemistich matches "right hand" found in the second.

2. "Into Gehenna" found three times in the first hemistich matches "receive abundant judgment" found in the second.

3. "Eye" and "two eyes" found in the first hemistich match "seeing" found in the second.

4. "Foot" and "feet" found in the first hemistich match "footstool for your feet" in the second.

5. "Kingdom of God" is found in both hemistiches.

6. "Worm does not die and fire is not quenched" in the first hemistich matches "devouring widows houses" in the second.

7. "What will you season it with" in the first hemistich matches "chief places at the feasts" in the second.

Who would have thought that Mark could arrange a chiastic matches with Jesus's sermon about cutting off one's hand and foot and plucking out his eye at 9:43–48. This sermon is better understood as an allegorical reference to 1 Cor 12:14–31 wherein Paul likens the members of a congregation to parts of the human body. Paul specifically mentions hand, foot and eye in that passage. But Jesus is using the metaphor to make the church governing point of 1 Cor 5:1–13 that the immoral members of a congregation should be expelled.

Fire, worms and insects can devour houses like Jesus says the scribes do. The "it" in "what will you season it with" is a feast.

L (10:1–27), L' (12:18–34)

There are ten matches in this long stich:

1. "The crowd comes together" in the first hemistich matches "the Sadducees arrive" in the second.

2. "Moses" is found twice in both hemistiches.

3. "Wife" is found three times in the first hemistich matching "wife" found three times and "took her" (as a wife understood) once in the second hemistich.

4. "Command," commandment" and "commandments" are all found in the first hemistich matches "commandment" found twice in the second.

5. Jesus pronounces two commandments on divorce in the first hemistich and gives a two-commandment summary of the law in the second.

6. "Children" and "child" are found three times in the first hemistich and three times in the second, although the Greek words for "child" are different.

7. "Kingdom of God" is found five times in the first hemistich and once in the second.

8. "One ran up to him" found in the first hemistich matches "approaching one of the scribes" found in the second.

9. "Teacher" is found twice in both hemistiches.

10. "Inherit eternal life" and "treasure in heaven" are found in the first hemistich match "the resurrection" found twice in the second.

Wives, children, commandments and heaven are themes in both hemistiches.

M (10:32–34), M' (12:1–8)

There are three matches in this stich:

1. "He began to tell them the things that will happen to him" found in the first hemistich matches "he began to speak to them in parables" in the second.

2. "They will condemn him to death" found in the first hemistich matches its opposite "they will have respect for my son" found in the second.

3. "They will ridicule him and will flog him and will spit upon him and will kill him" found in the first hemistich matches "come, let us kill him" and "they killed him and threw him out of the vineyard" found in the second.

It is widely recognized by exegetes that Jesus's Parable of the Wicked Tennants is his telling the crowd what is going to happen to him. It is also a chiastic match with Jesus's last prediction of the Passion as he and his disciples head to Jerusalem. It is not an accident that Jesus tells the Parable of the Wicked Tenants based on the Parable of the Vineyard at Isa 5 which starts out similarly to Jesus's parable. Jesus describes what will happen to Isaiah's Suffering Servant from Isa 53. The crowd and the reader are expected know that Jesus is talking about prophecies of Isaiah.

N (10:35–41), N' (11:27B–33)

There are three matches in this short stich:

1. "James and John, the sons of Zebedee approach him" found in the first hemistich matches "the chief priests, the scribes and the elders come to him" in the second.

2. "Grant us that we may sit, one on your right hand, and one on your left hand, in your glory" and "great men exercise authority over them" found in the first hemistich match "by what authority are you doing these things" and "or who gave you authority to do these things" found in the second.

3. "Baptism" and "baptize" found four times in the first hemistich matches "the baptism of John" found in the second.

"Authority" is found twice in both hemistiches although one of the occurences in the first hemistich is the assumption of James and John that Jesus has the authority to grant their request. The casual reader might assume that James and John are being selfish and asking Jesus to allow them to sit on his right and left hands in heaven. The careful reader will see that James and John are asking Jesus to let them sit on his right hand and left hand in an earthly glory. This pericope is another denigration of the Jerusalem apostles.

The astute reader will see that James and John are assuming that Jesus is going to use his powers to become the Messiah/King. If James and John were asking about Christ's heavenly glory, they would know he will be sitting on the right hand of God. Therefore, God will be on Christ's left hand. Therefore, if James and John are asking to sit on Jesus's right and left hand, they must be assuming the seat of glory is on Earth, not in heaven. They also should know that God dictates what happens in heaven.

James and John are assuming Jesus will have the power to grant who sits on his right and left hands. That could only mean earthly glory.

Jesus tells James and John indirectly that his glory is in heaven and not on Earth. God determines who will sit where.

O (10:46A; 7:1–23), O' (11:12–22)

In this stich there are eight matches:

1. "Eating their bread," "eat their bread," "eating tables," and "what goes into a man" is found in the first hemistich matching "he was hungry" and "fig" twice in the second.

2. "Do not eat" is found twice in the first hemistich and "no man may eat" in the second.

3. "Cups, and pots and brass vessels" in the first hemistich matches "pitcher" in the second.

4. "This people honors me with their lips, but their heart is far away from me. But in vain do they worship me. Teaching as their doctrines the precepts of men" in the first hemistich matches "My house will be called a house of prayer for all the nations" in the second.

5. "Honor your father and your mother" found in the first hemistich matches "den of thieves" found in the second.

6. "Eating tables" in the first hemistich matches "tables of the moneychangers" in the second.

7. In the first hemistich there is found "men" twice and "man" four times matching "man" in the second.

8. "Thefts" in the first hemistich matches "thieves" in the second.

The first hemistich is comprised of two pericopae, "Controversy on Tradition" and "Eating Does Not Defile" (7:1–23). These pericope have been moved from their positions in Canonical Mark to between entering and leaving Jericho at 10:46. Here the text of Canonical Mark says that they came to Jericho and they left Jericho. It appears that something has been cut out. Finding this many matching elements between 7:1–23 and "Clearing the Temple"/"Cursing the Fig Tree"/"The Withered Fig Tree" intercalation (11:11–25) demonstrates that the move was justified. Particularly telling is that there are quotes from Isaiah in both stiches. Jesus quotes Isa 29:13 in the first hemistich and Isa 56:7 in the second. Then to put the icing on the cake, Jesus follows the Isaiah quote in the first hemistich with a short quote of Deut 5:16 and Exod 20:12 and follows the Isaiah quote in the second hemistich with a short quote from Jer 7:11. It appears that Mark intended these as a chiastic match.

P (10:46B–52), P' (11:7–10)

There are six matches in this relatively short stich:

1. "Sitting beside the road" in the first hemistich matches "he sat upon him" in the second.

2. "Shout out" and "shouted all the more" in the first hemistich matches "cried" in the second.

3. "Son of David" found twice in the first hemistich matches "our father David" in the second.

4. "Throwing away his tunic" in the first hemistich matches "throw on him their tunics" and "spread their tunics" in the second.

5. "Followed him" in the first hemistich matches "those that followed" in the second.

6. "On the road" is in both hemistiches.

Note that "son of David" matches "our father David." One might wonder why the crowd would be crying about their father David, but it makes an excellent chiastic match. In addition, the unnecessary mention that Bartimaeus threw away his tunic is designed to match the throwing of tunics on the colt and the spreading of tunics on the road.

Q (11:1–3), Q' (11:4–6)

This pericope is the center of the structure as Jesus is about to enter Jerusalem. The structure encompasses the middle third of the Gospel, and as will be shown in chapters 16 and 17, the vast bulk of Mark's Pauline theology.

This stich is one pericope about the two unnamed disciples fetching a colt for Jesus to ride. This is preparatory to his entry into Jerusalem with song, praise and tunics on the road, much like entry of Simon Maccabaeus 1 Macc 13:51. Plot wise, the entry into Jerusalem shows that is not too late for Jesus to refuse to be the Suffering Servant and use his powers to become king instead.

With the demonstration of this chapter's Middle Chiastic Structure, we can now assemble the vast majority of Mark's Original Gospel. The following chapter will combine all of the tentative conclusions so far and provide further supporting evidence.

7

Removing 6:38–56 and 7:24—8:4
from Canonical Mark

CHAPTER 6 PROPOSED ELIMINATING 6:6:38–56 and 7:24—8:4 from Canonical Mark and moving 7:1–23 to between entering and leaving Jericho at 10:46. The textual support for this radical surgery on Canonical Mark is worthy of its own chapter.

Combining The Two Miracle Feedings

This Middle Chiastic Structure demonstrates with a high degree of probability that there was only one "Feeding the Multitude" in Mark's Original Gospel. All of the text between the two feedings as found in Canonical Mark has been interpolated into the Original Gospel except for 7:1–23, which was moved from 10:46 to fill in between the feedings. The motivation for this interpolation will be made clear in Part II.

The theory is that the first part of "First Feeding the Multitude" in Canonical Mark (6:32–44) and the last part of "Second Feeding the Multitude" in Canonical Mark (8:1–10) were combined in the Original Gospel. Turton helps to come to that conclusion. He states in his chapter 6:

> This pericope (Mark 6:30–44) consists of two chiastic structures. The center of the major chiastic structure is very unMarkan, and the brackets (hemistiches) do not speak to each other like typical Markan brackets. There is no reason to think that this is a construction of Mark.[1]

Turton does not think that any part of what he calls "the major chiastic structure" was part of the Original Gospel. However, as demonstrated in the Middle Chiastic Structure, "two hundred denarii," a phrase Matthew and Luke do not copy in their versions of the first feeding, was a chiastic match for "three hundred denarii" found at Mark 14:4. In addition, in the same structure "sheep without a shepherd" is a chiastic match for "I will strike the shepherd and the sheep will be scattered" at Mark 14:27. These unusual phrases show that the first part of the first feeding is indeed Markan and was part of the Original Gospel.

---

1. *Turton, HCGM,* ch 6, "Commentary to 6:30–44."

It is clear from the development of the chiastic structure that the second half of "Second Feeding of the Multitude" in Canonical Mark (8:1–9) is original. This follows from the realization that in this sequence during the miracle feeding Jesus gives thanks for the bread and blesses the fish, the reverse of his actions in "The Last Supper" wherein he blesses the bread and gives thanks for the wine. Also the tripartite action of blessing (or giving thanks), breaking, and giving to his disciples is the same at both 8:6 and 14:22. However, Jesus's actions are not the same in Canonical Mark's first feeding at 6:41 wherein the redactor has Jesus perform four actions after taking both the bread and the fish at the same time. Further, unlike the actions of Jesus during "The Last Supper," the redactor did not separate the giving of the bread and fish into two separate actions. It was noted earlier that Mark typically has his characters perform tripartite actions.

In addition, the redactor added unnecessary dialogue uncharacteristic in Mark. It is true that in Jesus's sermons Mark has Jesus saying things three times in slightly different manners, but in Mark's narrative description, or narrative dialogue the language is sparse, giving the reader only the minimum knowledge necessary to understand the action. In "First Feeding the Multitude" in Canonical Mark we find:

> 6:38 And he says to them, "How many loaves do you have? Go see." And when they found out they say, "Five, and two fish." 39 And he instructed them to sit down in groups upon the green grass. 40 And they sat down in groups, by hundreds, and by fifties.

In "Second Feeding the Multidude" in Canonical Mark, the same type of action is described as follows:

> 8:5 And he asked them, "How many loaves do you have?" And they said, "Seven." 8:6 And he instructs the multitude to sit down on the ground:

The economy of the wording in the second feeding stands out. Jesus does not tell the disciples to go see how many loaves there are. He asks and they tell him. There is unnecessary dialogue and action in the second half of the first feeding. In fact, in the second feeding the reader does not find out there are any fish until Jesus gives thanks for them. There is also unnecessary description with the crowd sitting on the "green grass." They are said to be in a desert (6:31–32), why is there green grass? Mark does not waste words. The redactor knew that Mark often made references to the OT. Therefore, he had the crowd unnecessarily sit down in ranks by fifties and one hundreds, making a reference to Exod 18:21, 25.

Similarly there are problems with the first part of the second feeding. The first problem is with the opening phrase "in those days" (en ekeinais tais hēmerais). First, in Mark's Original Gospel Jesus is almost always in a specific location when action occurs. Healing the leper is the only exception. No location is mentioned in the second feeding. Second, Mark typically uses specific important phrases three or six times.

"Kingdom of God" and "Son of Man" are very special cases used fourteen times, which will be explained in chapter 12. It is rare that a phrase is used four times. There are instances of single words being used four times, e.g., "pallet" (krabatton). If there are four uses of a phrase it is possible that one is an interpolation. The interpolated phrase can be detected by comparing all instances of the phrase. In Mark's Gospel the first and third uses of the phrase are very similar and the middle use will exhibit a different form, verb, construction, etc., as previously shown.

For example, Mark depicts the Pharisees and Herodians together three times, at 3:6, 8:15, and 12:13. At 3:6 and 12:13 the Pharisees are combined with the Herodians, but at 8:15 Jesus warns his disciples of the leaven of the Pharisees and the leaven of Herod. The word "Herodians" is used in the first and third elements, but only "Herod" is used in the middle element. This is evidence that 8:15 is original to Mark and Koester is wrong about it being interpolated.

The phrase "in those days" it is found four times in Canonical Mark:

1. 1:9 And it happened in those days, that Jesus came from Nazareth of Galilee, and was baptized by John in the Jordan.

2. 8:1 In those days there was again a large crowd, and they had nothing to eat. Summoning his disciples, he says to them,

3. 13:17 But woe to those who are pregnant and to those who are nursing in those days!

4. 13:24 But in those days after the affliction, the sun will be darkened.

In 1 and 4 "in those days" comes before the description and the sentence begins with either "and" (kai) or "but" (de or alla). In 3 the description comes before "in those days" and the sentence still begins with "but" (de). In 2 there is no "and" or "but" beginning the sentence. Number 2 is the odd man out. It is not from the hand of Mark. The other three, 1, 3, and 4, make a perfect Markan triplet. There are over eighty triplets and sextets in Mark. All of them have probably not been identified. We can safely conclude that 8:1 is not original to Mark.

The next couple of verses in the second feeding are also very curious. In every miracle story: healing, calming, or feeding, someone else always initiates the miracle. Jesus never volunteers to perform a miracle. In 8:2–3 Jesus volunteers to feed the crowd because he has pity on them. Then there is excessive explanation about the plight of the crowd: they have been with Jesus for three days; they will become weak and faint; some live far away. It is absolutely uncharacteristic of Mark's Jesus to give this much explanation unless he is sermonizing.

With regard to 8:4 the disciples say to Jesus "where can someone feed (chortasai) all these bread in this desolate place." Earlier the reader was told the crowd had "nothing to eat (phagōsin)," and Jesus has said, "They have had nothing to eat (phagōsin)." In many Markan pericopae there are triplets of important words, e.g. "rich" in 10:23–25, "daughter" in 5:21–43. Therefore, the disciples using "feed" or "satisfy" while there are two occurrences of "eat" does not fit with usual Markan construction. Mark would have reworded the sentence to have the disciples use "eat" (phagōsin). Compare 8:4 with the beginning of the first feeding 6:34–37 where a form of "to eat" (phago) is found three times. This is a more typical Markan construction.

Another suspicious aspect of the two miracle feedings in Canonical Mark is that the baskets in which the left over bread was collected are different in the two feedings. In the first feeding the disciples put the bread fragments into twelve "kophinōn" and in the second, into seven "spuridas." Both represent types of baskets, but it seems odd that there would be two different words used for them by Mark.

A further factor supporting the conclusion that the last half of the second feeding is original is that when combined with the first half of the first feeding, the center stich of the resulting pericope-level chiastic structure has a parallel structure. That means that this pericope is important for structural reasons as will be shown in chapter 13.

About the second feeding Turton says:

> Two chiastic structures make up this pericope. The structure of the first one is tricky but appears to be Markan, now that I have unraveled it. However, the opening A bracket (hemistich) is wordy and very unMarkan. In most of the pericopae where there is a serious action, the writer opens and closes with concrete location changes. Here the redactor substituted Jesus explaining a miracle to his disciples before he actually did it, quite unusual in Mark. For example, in Mark 5 he raises the dead girl but does not explain to his disciples that he will attempt such an act. Additionally, the location is not specified, and the phrase "in those days" is used, which seems to put some distance between the writer and the time of the action, something that the writer of Mark does not normally do either. In short, while the rest of the structure is Markan, the A bracket has been extensively tampered with.[2]

What Turton calls the "A bracket" is 8:1–3. It was shown that 8:4 is also unMarkan. Therefore, with the Middle Chiastic Structure, the triplet evidence, the excessive wordiness in the last half of the first feeding and the entire first half of the second feeding are atypical for Mark. These factors demonstrate that the first half of the first feeding should be married with the second half of the second feeding to result in only one "Feeding of the Multitude" in Original Mark.

This conclusion parallels that of Schweizer who wrote that there was only one feeding miracle, but that Mark copied two different versions of the same miracle into his Gospel.[3] Schweitzer also realized that "Feeding the Multitude" was a foreshadowing of "The Last Supper," and it was demonstrated above that they are chiastic matches

---

2. Ibid., ch 8, "Commentary to 8:1–13."

3. Schweitzer, *Mystery.* 168.

in the Middle Chiastic Structure. Schweitzer did not mention that the giving thanks and blessing were reversed in typical Markan fashion, but he noted the parallel.[4]

Eliminating "Walking on Water" (6:45–52)

Just because two miraculous feedings found in Canonical Mark should be combined into one feeding, that does not necessarily mean that everything in between the two should be eliminated from the Original Gospel of Mark. There needs to be further evidence before we can definitively say that a particular pericope was not part of Original Mark.

Scholars have long noted that Jesus's "Walking on Water" is a doublet for his "Calming the Storm," just as the second "Feeding the Multitude" was a doublet for the first "Feeding the Multitude." Also "Healing in the Marketplace" (6:53–56) could be said to be a doublet with "Healing the Woman with Blood Flow." With the two miracle feedings combined into one, it becomes questionable whether it is typical for Mark to double Jesus's miracles. The doubling of miracles may be a trick by the redactor to make them appear Markan. Miracles performed by Jesus in Mark's Gospel after eliminating one miracle feeding are as follows:

1. "Unclean Spirit in the Synagogue" (1:21–28)

2. "Healing Simon's Mother-in-law" (1:29–34)

3. "Healing the Leper" (1:39–45)

4. "Healing the Paralytic" (2:1–12)

5. "Healing the Man with the Withered Hand" (3:1–6)

6. "Calming the Sea" (4:36–41)

7. "Healing the Gerasene Demoniac" (5:1–20)

8. "Healing Woman with Blood Flow" (5:21–34)

9. "Healing Jairus's Daughter" (5:38–43)

10. "Feeding the Multitude" (6:34–37, 8:5–9)

11. "Walking on Water" (6:45–52)

12. "Healing the Syro-Phoenician Woman's Daughter" (7:24–30)

13. "Healing the Deaf Mute" (7:30–37)

14. "Healing the Blind Man of Bethsaida" (8:22–26)

15. "Healing the Epileptic" (9:14–29)

16. "Healing Blind Bartimaeus" (10:46–52)

17. "Withering the Fig Tree" (11:20–25)

4. Ibid., 169.

One might say that "Healing Jairus's Daughter" is a doublet with "Healing the Syro-Phoenician Woman's Daughter" in that Jairus is a Jew and the Syro-Phoenician Woman is a gentile. Other possible doublets are "Walking on Water"/"Calming the Sea," "Healing The Woman with Blood Flow"/"Healing in the Marketplace," and "Healing the Blind Man of Bethsaida"/"Healing Blind Bartimaeus."

"Walking on Water," "Healing in the Market Place," and "Healing the Syro-Phoenician Woman's Daughter" are all located between the two miracle feedings in Canonical Mark. Therefore, they are suspect as possible interpolations.

The only doublet healings that are included in long chiastic structures are "Healing the Blind Man of Bethsaida"/"Healing Blind Bartimaeus." Another factor is that the pericope-level chiastic structure of "Healing the Blind Man of Bethsaida" contains a paralleled center. Both these healings were most probably in Original Mark.

Analyzing the text of "Walking on Water" to determine if it has Markan characteristics, one notices that if this pericope has been interpolated, the redactor is very astute in that he began the pericope with "and immediately" (kai euthys) as Mark does very often. On closer inspection, however, the text says Jesus "made" or "compelled" (ēnakasen) his disciples to get into the boat. This word is used only two times in the entire NT—Mark 6:45 and Matthew's copy of it at Matt 14:22. The phrase may not be Markan.

Next Jesus "takes leave" (apotaxamenos) of his disciples. This is the only use of this word in Mark and again seems unnecessarily wordy for Mark. The next objection is the clincher. At 6:46b the text says, "he went up on the mountain to pray." There are two problems with this. The first problem is that Mark's Jesus does not go into the mountains to pray. He goes into the desert to pray. Mark's Jesus only goes up a mountains for something truly momentous. The second problem is that if this is truly by Mark, then there are four journeys up a mountain. One would expect there to be three.

The three mountain journeys in Original Mark are as follows:

1. 3:13 And he goes up (anabainai) into the mountain and summons those whom he wanted. And they went to him. 3:14 And he appointed twelve to be apostles, that they might be with him, and that he might send them out to preach,

2. 9:2 And after six days Jesus takes with him Peter, and James, and John, and brings them up (anapherai) into a high mountain by themselves. And he was transfigured in front of them.

3. 10:32 But they were on the road going up (anabainontes) to Jerusalem, and Jesus was going ahead of them: and they were amazed; and they that followed were afraid. And again he took aside the twelve, and began to tell them the things that were to happen to him.

The middle element of the triplet uses a different verb of bringing up rather than going up. Of course, Jerusalem is on Mount Zion and the reader should understand that they were going up into the mountains. All three times that Jesus goes into the mountains he takes disciples with him: to choose the twelve, to be transfigured and to a confrontation with authorities. Mark's Jesus would not go into the mountains without disciples to merely pray.

The next objection is that in this pericope about walking on water it is the seventh time Jesus gets into a boat. There are already two triplets with Jesus getting into boats. A seventh occurrence of getting into a boat would be atypical Markan construction.

BOATS AND CROWDS:

1. 4:36 And dismissing the crowd, they take him with them in the boat. And other boats were with him.

2. 5:21 And Jesus having crossed over again in the boat to the other side, a great crowd was gathered around him; and he was beside the sea.

3. 4:1 And again he began to teach by the seaside. And there is a very large crowd gathered around him, so that he entered into a boat, and sat in the sea. And all the crowd were on the land close to the sea.

In elements 1 and 3 Mark mentions the crowd once before the boat, and in the middle element the crowd is mentioned twice, before and after the boat, establishing that in Original Mark 5:21 was the middle element of the triplet and was positioned after 4:36 and before 4:1. The position of Mark 4:1 in the Original Gospel must have been subsequent to 5:21.

AWAY ALL BOATS

1. 6:32 And they went away (aplēthon) in a boat.

2. 8:10 And immediately he got into the boat with his disciples, and came (ēlthein) into the region of Dalmanutha.

3. 8:13 And sending them away, and again embarking into the boat he went away (aplēthon) to the other side.

In the first and third elements Jesus and his disciples "went away" in the middle element they "came."

At 6:51 in "Walking on Water" in Canonical Mark, Jesus climbs into the boat with the struggling disciples. There is no crowd, no going away or coming. This is an interpolated pericope by a redactor that did not understand Mark's triplets.

At 6:52 the redactor gratuitously tells the reader that the disciples "did not understand about the loaves but their hearts were hardened." It appears to me as if the redactor is foreshadowing another of his interpolations at 8:19 in "Leaven of the Pharisees."

The clincher is that there is already a "hard of heart" triplet in Original Mark at 3:5, 8:17 and 10:5. In this triplet Mark uses three different words to indicate hardness of heart, but the middle element is a question and the first and third elements are declarative statements. The redactor was unaware of this, and in his interpolated "hardness" the redactor used the same word as Mark did at 8:17, confirming suspicions that the redactor was trying foreshadow 8:17 at 6:52 by using a Markan phrase.

With all of the unMarkan attributes found in "Walking on Water" (6:45–52) in Canonical Mark in addition to not being a part of a long chiastic structure, we can safely conclude that this pericope has been interpolated by a redactor.

Eliminating "Healing in the Marketplace" (6:53–56)

There are two words found in this short pericope (6:53–56) that are found nowhere else in Mark. The first is "anchored" (prosōrmisthēsan). In Original Mark the boats Jesus travels in never anchor. Jesus just gets out of the boat or they come to a region. The anchoring is superfluous colorful detail and does not comport with Mark's sparse style. The second unusual word is "fringe" (kraspedou). Once again a superfluous detail mentioning that the people could touch the fringe of Jesus's robe to be cured. In "Healing of the Woman with Blood Flow" (5:21–34) she touched his robe or clothing (himatiou). Touching the fringe is an unnecessary colorful detail. The real Mark will have colorful detail if he needs it to make a chiastic match, but there is not "fringe" match or "anchoring" match in the structures.

There is also a disrupted triplet in this pericope. Without counting 6:54 there is a "recognizing" (epiginōskō) triplet found at 2:8, 5:30, and 6:33. In the first and third elements the person recognizing something (Jesus, many) is named after the word "recognize." In the middle element "Jesus" comes before "recognized." The redactor did not realize that there was a triplet using the word "recognize" and disrupted Mark's structure. It also appears that the redactor was using Mark 6:33 as a template. The redacted passage at 6:54 says, "54 And when they got out of the boat, immediately the people are recognizing him, 55 and running around the whole region . . ." While Original Mark has at 6:33, "And many saw them going, and recognized them. And they all ran there on foot from all the cities." Both passages have "recognizing" and "running," although the verb for "running" is different (preritrechō vs. suntrechō) in the different passage.

Turton wrote that this pericope might have been original to Mark, but that the chiastic structure has been tampered with.[5] He had no comment on the unusual words or the disrupted triplet.

The unusual words, the disrupted triplet and the poor chiastic structure of this pericope lead to the conclusion that the Middle Chiastic Structure correctly identifies this pericope as having been interpolated by the redactor.

5. Turton, HCGM, ch 6, "Bethsaida by Pericope: Analysis."

Moving "Controversy on Tradition" and "Eating Does Not Defile" (7:1–23)

Moving 7:1–23 from its location in Canonical Mark to between entering and leaving Jericho at 10:46 results in seven chiastic matches with 11:12–22, establishing that these pericopae were originally in that location in the text. The next structure analyzed in the following chapter also confirms this placement for the "Controversy on Tradition" and "Eating Does Not Defile."

Turton mentions that 7:1–23 might belong at 10:46:

> There's absolutely no question that this (Mark 10:46) is unMarkan. The standard Markan A bracket (hemistich) has a location change that is both singular and concrete. Thus, I join with those who say that something has been removed here. In my own view it is most likely to be Mark 7:1–23, in which the scribes come down from Jerusalem. That is easy to see if Jesus is in Jericho on his way to the big city, but difficult to imagine if Jesus is in Galilee.[6]

Eliminating Healing The Syro-Phoenician Woman's Daughter (7:24–30)

This is a strange pericope and Turton is adamant that this was not written by Mark. He says:

> This pericope is non-Markan and has been created and inserted as unit. My rules for analyzing structures in Mark will create a chiastic structure for this pericope, but not a Markan one. . . . The non-Markan nature of this pericope is signaled by several things, but for our purposes the central structure—or lack thereof—is the key:
>
> > E And he said to her, "Let the children first be fed, for it is not right to take the children's bread and throw it to the dogs."
> >
> > D But she answered him, "Yes, Lord; yet even the dogs under the table eat the children's crumbs."
> >
> > C And he said to her, "For this saying you may go your way; the demon has left your daughter."
>
> This is a tripartite exchange, and there is nothing else like it in Mark. There is no way to bracket it to yield a proper Markan chiasm with a prolix/pithy center. Nor do ask/answered questions typically occur in Markan centers.[7] The chiasm here is simply a pleasing ordering of the verses, but it is not a real Markan structure. Hence, this pericope is non-Markan.

6. Ibid., "Analysis: Recovering the Original Structure of Mark."

7. Turton is wrong here. There are asked and answered questions in Markan chiastic centers but they are invariably paralleled centers: Mark 8:22–26, 10:35–41, 12:12b–17.

In this pericope Jesus at first refuses to help cure a gentile woman's daughter, and the reference to "dogs" is a reference to gentiles. However, Jesus did not refuse to help the Gerasene demoniac who must have been gentile since he spread Jesus's fame around the Decapolis. Refusing to help anyone who asked is not characteristic of Mark's Jesus.

The redactor was extremely clever in attempting to copy Mark's style. The redactor realized than much of Mark's Gospel was based upon OT stories. "Healing the Syro-Phoenician Woman's Daughter" appears to be based upon Elisha healing the Shunammite woman's son at 2 Kings 4:8–37. In both there is an exchange where the woman has the upper hand in the exchange. In addition, both victims are found lying in bed. "Healing Jairus's Daughter" (5:38–43) and "Healing the Epileptic" (9:14–27) are also based on this story from 2 Kgs 4.

The redactor uses the Markan style of using the word "daughter" three times. He also mentions "children" three times, but he uses two different words for "children" (teknōn and paidiōn), which is not Mark's style. In addition, he only mentions "dogs" (kynaria) twice, and one would expect "dogs" to be mentioned three times, assuming "dogs" represents the gentiles and further assuming spreading the Gospel to gentiles is being authorized by this periocope. The most egregious mistake made by the redactor is that the woman calls Jesus "Lord." In Mark's Original Gospel Jesus calls himself "Lord" indirectly at 2:28 and 11:3, but other characters call him "Rabbi" or "Teacher" never "Lord."

Another reason to suspect that this pericope is not original to Mark is that it starts out:

> 7:24 And rising from there, he went away into the region of Tyre and Sidon. And he entered into a house, and did not want it to be known; and he was not able to hide.

This is the same beginning to a pericope as found at 10:1:

> 10:1 And rising from there he comes into the region of Judea and beyond the Jordan. And again crowds come together around him. And as he was accustomed to, he taught them again.

I find the similarity to be too close for them both to be original. While Mark has similar ideas expressed in different places, he never uses the exact same words, unless it is part of a triplet such as "in those days" or "all things are possible." There is no "rising from there" triplet. One or two significant words will be the same so that the reader will recognize the pattern, but the framework around the pattern is different. At 10:1 Jesus is leaving Capernaum and Galilee to start towards Jerusalem. This begins the turning point of Mark's story and "rising" used there (anastas) can have the connotation of rising from the dead and is foreshadowing 16:6 when the young man tells the women he is risen, although the Greek there is "ēgerthē" which may also connote "awakened." At 7:24 the redactor has also used "anastas." It seems inappropriate. Since there is no "rising from there" (ekeithen anastas) triplet, this increases the suspicion that 7:24 has been interpolated.

Further, the redactor once again gives the reader too much information. He writes, "and he was not able to hide." The second sentence of 7:24 is similar to 9:30, "Leaving there, they passed through Galilee; and he did not want that anyone should know it." But the real Mark leaves out that Jesus could not hide. Presumably the redactor added this to make it reasonable that the Syro-Phoenician woman found him, but taciturn Mark would not have added that. If Mark had written this pericope, he would have let the fact that the woman found Jesus speak for itself.

All of the evidence, the unMarkan chiasm with the tripartite exchange, the woman calling Jesus "Lord," "rising from there," the failed triplets of "children" and "dogs," and "he was not able to hide" lead to the conclusion that "Healing the Syro-Phoenician Woman's Daughter" was not in the Original Gospel. This conclusion confirms the lack of chiasitic matches with this pericope.

Eliminating Healing the Deaf Mute (7:31–37)

Turton is skeptical that this pericope belongs in Original Mark. He states:

> This pericope is also non-Markan, although it has a superficially Markan feel that may indicate simply very heavy redaction. . . . Note how each bracket (hemistich) consists of verses that are simple statements. The writer of Mark typically varies the length of his brackets (hemistiches), and the centers usually have a nice rhythm. Note also how the A' bracket (hemistich) does not signal a concrete change of location, but simply announces that the scene is over and has shifted. The writer of Mark likes to use concrete locations when he shifts to a new pericope. None of those is definite, but the non-Markan pattern and habits signal that this one is probably not from the writer of Mark either.[8]

I have more concrete evidence of the non-Markan creation of this pericope. The most obvious is the use of an Aramaic phrase. The redactor did not realize that there were already three Aramaic phrases in the Gospel and this fourth one would prove the interpolation. The other three are at 5:41, 15:22, and 15:34. Once again the middle one is different from the first and third elements in that Jesus speaks the first and third, while the middle one is in the narration.

"Healing of the Deaf Mute" includes Jesus saying an Aramaic phrase. Why is it spurious? With the other three Aramaic phrases Mark uses the word "translated" or "interpreted" (methermēneuomenon). In this interpolated pericope the redactor wrote "ho estin" (that is). Jesus praying to God in Gethsemane saying "Abba, Father"

---

8. Turton, *HCGM*, ch 6, "Analysis: Recovering the Original Structure of Mark."

does not count as an Aramaic phrase because it is part of another triplet, using the addressee's name, a very important triplet to be explained later. Plus Mark does not say he is translating "Abba." He expects the reader to know this use of "Abba, Father" from Rom 8:15 and Gal 4:6, where Paul uses the same phrase.

Other non-Markan construction in this pericope is that Jesus looks to heaven only at 6:41 and 7:34 in Canonical Mark, both of which are suspected interpolations. In 7:34 Jesus sighs. The only other time Jesus sighs is when the Pharisees ask him for a sign from heaven and he is exasperated. Sighing, an indication of defeat, in a healing situation is not consistent with the character of Mark's Jesus, a man of action.

Verse 7:36 says, "And he instructed them that they should tell no one, but the more he instructed them, the more greatly they proclaimed it." This does not make sense. How many times would Jesus have instructed "them" to tell no one? The language makes this admonition seem like an on going process, unlike any thing else in Mark.

In verse 7:37 the redactor wrote, "And they were exceedingly astonished, saying, 'He has done all things well. And he makes the deaf to hear, and the mute to speak.'" While it is typical for the witnesses to a miraculous healing to be amazed or astonished, this is the only time that they reiterate what Jesus has done. The redactor knew that Isaiah had prophesied at 35:5–6 that the deaf would hear and the mute would speak. The redactor is reiterating this prophecy. In Original Mark "Healing the Epileptic" (9:14–27) is the casting out of a deaf and mute unclean spirit, but there are two healings of the blind. Perhaps the redactor thought there should also be two healings of the deaf. In addition, the phrase, "he has done all things well" is singularly unMarkan. The phrase is too general to have been written by Mark. He is usually very specific.

Conclusion

Koester theorized that the entire "Bethsaida Section" or "Great Omission" (Mark 6:45–8:26) was not in UrMarcus because Luke does not include it in his Gospel and because some peculiar language appears in the section. Koester would keep the entire first feeding as being original, and he would eliminate the second. It is clear that Luke copied the first feeding and eliminated the second. That is why Koester does the same. This analysis agrees with Koester as far as Mark 6:45–56, and 7:24–8:4 are concerned. Also, 7:1–23 is not located between Mark 6:32 and 8:27 in the Original Gospel. Koester is incorrect to state that 8:5–27 was not in the Original Gospel, although it is probable that verses 8:14 and 8:19 are not original and were added by the redactor.

Based on this analysis, Luke's copy of Mark did have the Bethsaida Section in it, because he clearly copied Mark 6:38–44 (the last half of "First Feeding the Multitude"). Luke also mentions the "Leaven of the Pharisees" saying at Luke 12:1 and condemns the Pharisees about washing dishes at Luke 11:39. It is possible under the

Farrar-Goulder theory that he could have seen those in Matthew; however, in Luke's "Feeding the Multitude," Luke 9:14–16 could only have come from Mark 6:39–40, since Matthew did not include that in his Gospel. Turton's analysis also eliminates many of these same pericopae based on the pericopae-level chiastic structures.

Based on the analysis so far, we can set out the vast majority of Mark's Original Gospel, adding pericopae numbers 32–69 shown in Appendix 3. We now are only missing the placement of "Healing the Epileptic" (9:14–27), "Answering the Disciples" (9:28–29) and "The Parable Discourse" (4:1–35).

Before positioning "The Parable Discourse," "Healing the Epileptic" and "Answering the Disciples," the repositioning of 7:1–23 will be emphasized with another chiastic structure that encompasses the entire second half of the Gospel from 10:32 to 16:8. The next structure also confirms the placement most of the pericopae numbered 32–73.

8

The Jerusalem Chiastic Structure

THE NEXT STRUCTURE IS called "The Jerusalem Chiastic Structure" because it covers the entire second half of the Original Gospel from Jesus heading to Jerusalem to the women fleeing the empty tomb. This structure begins at the turning point of the Original Gospel (10:32). It overlaps the just-discussed Middle Chiastic Structure from 10:32—14:32. This structure terminates at the end of the Original Gospel (16:8) with the women fleeing the empty tomb. The midpoint of this structure is the end of Jesus's teaching in the temple "The Widows Mite" (12:41–44) and "Wonderful Buildings" (13:1–2), the introduction to "The Olivet Discourse." This structure provides additional proof that 7:1–23 belongs between entering and leaving Jericho at 10:46.

The Jerusalem Chiastic Structure

A 10:32 . . . *on the road going up to Jerusalem, and Jesus was going ahead of them: . . . amazed; and they that followed were afraid . . . the twelve, and began to tell them . . .*

A' 16:7 . . . *tell his disciples . . . he goes ahead of you into Galilee. . . he told you." 16:8 . . . trembling and astonishment . . . told no one anything for they were afraid.*

B 10:33 . . . *death . . . 10:34 And they will ridicule him, and will spit upon him, and will flog him, and* will *kill him . . . three days he will rise.*

B' . . . 15:43 . . . *Pilate . . . 15:44 And Pilate . . . dead . . . centurion, . . . dead 15:45 . . . centurion, . . . the corpse . . . 15:46 . . . he wrapped him in the linen cloth . . . 16:1 . . . that they might come and anoint him . . . 16:6 . . . crucified. He is risen . . .*

C 10:35 *And James . . . approach . . . do for us . . .*

C' 15:40 . . . *looking on from a distance . . . James . . . served him . . .*

D 10:38 . . . *Can you drink the cup that I drink? Or be baptized . . . baptism . . . baptized with? 10:39 . . . The cup that I drink, you will drink . . . baptism . . . baptized . . . baptized.*

D' 15:36 . . . *gave it to him to drink, . . . Elijah . . .*

E 10:40 . . . *right hand or on my left hand . . .*

E' 15:27 . . . *two robbers, one on his right hand, and one on his left.*

F 10:42 . . . *gentiles lord it over them; and those powerful men exercise authority over them.*

F' 15:12 *And Pilate . . . "Crucify him." 15:14 And Pilate . . . 15:15 But Pilate . . . having flogged Jesus, delivered him to be crucified.*

G 7:2 ... *hands* ... 7:3 ... *hands* ... *hands* ... 7:20 ... *Things that proceed out of the man are what defiles the man. 7:21 For from within, out of the heart of men, evil thoughts proceed* ... 7:22 ... *deceit,* ... *slander,* ... 7:23 ... *proceed from within, go out and defile the man.*

H 10:50 *And he, throwing away his tunic, leaped up* ... 10:52 ... *followed him on the road.*

I 11:1 ... *he sends two of the disciples* 11:2 ... *Go into the village* ... *will find a colt tied, that no man ever yet sat upon* ... 11:3 ... *'The Lord has need of him,' and immediately he will send him back* ... 11:6 *But they said to them what Jesus had told them, and they let them go* ...

J 12:12 *And they wanted to take him; For they realized that he spoke the parable against them* ... *they went away.*

K 12:13 ... *send to him some of the Pharisees and of the Herodians* ... 12:14 ... *they say to him* ... 12:15 *Should we pay, or should we not pay* ... *Why do you test me? Bring me a denarius* ... 12:16 ... *Whose is this image and inscription?* ...

L 12:19 ... *brother die* ... *wife* ... *leave no child* ... *brother* ... *wife,* ... 12:21 ... *died, leaving no heir* ... *likewise* 12:22 ... *heir* ... *died.* 12:23 *In the resurrection whose wife* ... 12:24 ... *the power of God* 12:25 ... *rise from the dead* ...

M 12:35 ... *the temple* ... *Christ is the son of David* 12:36 ... *Sit on my right hand* ... 12:39 ... *seats in the synagogues* 12:40 ... *devouring widows' houses* ... 12:41 *And sitting down over in front of the treasury* ...

G' 14:58 ... *hands* ... 14:68 *But he denied, saying, "I neither know nor understand what you are saying."* ... 14:70 *But he again denied it* ... 14:71 *But he began to curse and swear, "I do not know this man you are talking about."* ...

H' 14:50 *And leaving him, they all fled.* 14:51 ... *following him, having a linen cloth thrown* ... 14:52 *but leaving the linen cloth he fled naked.*

I' 14:13 *And he sends out two of his disciples* ... *Go into the city, and you will meet a man carrying a pitcher* ... 14:14 ... *'The Teacher says, "Where is my guest room, where I might eat the Passover with my disciples?"* 14:15 *And he will show you a large upstairs room furnished and ready.* ...

J' 14:10 ... *that he might deliver him to them.* 14:11 *But when they heard it, they were glad* ... *conveniently deliver him.*

K' 14:3 ... *there came a woman* ... 14:4 ... *saying to each other* ... 14:5 *For this oil might have been sold* ... *three hundred denarii* ... 14:6 ... *Why do you bother her?* ... 14:9 ... *woman has done will be told in memory of her.*

L' 13:11 ... *but the Holy Spirit.* 13:12 *And brother will deliver up brother to death* ... *father his child; and children* ... *put them to death* 13:13 ... *will be saved* ... 13:17 ... *who are pregnant and to those who are nursing in those days* ...

M' 13:1 ... *the temple* ... *what wonderful buildings* 13:2 ... *great buildings that will not be torn down* ... 13:3 *And as he is sitting on the mount of Olives in front of the temple* ... 13:6 *Many will come in my name* ...

Commentary

A (10:32), A' (16:7–8)

There are six matches in this stich that only has one verse in the first hemistich and two verses in the second:

1. "On the road going up to Jerusalem" in the first hemistich matches "goes ahead of you into Galilee in the second.

2. "Jesus going ahead of them" in the first hemistich matches "he goes ahead of you" in the second.

3. "Trembling and astonishment" in the first hemistich matches "astonished" in the second.

4. "They that followed" in the first hemistich matches "the disciples and Peter" in the second.

5. "They . . . were afraid" in the first hemistich matches "they were afraid" in the second.

6. "Tell them" in the first hemistich matches "tell the disciples," "he told you" and "they told no one" found in the second.

Different Greek words for "astonished" or "amazed" are used in the separate hemistiches (ethambounto and exethambēthēsan).

"They were afraid" is found in both hemistiches. This is two-thirds of a very important triplet. "They were afraid" is found at 10:32, 11:18, and 16:8. This triplet is built around (ephobounto, the third person plural imperfect indicative middle or passive). All three elements occur in the second half of the Original Gospel: at the turning point when Jesus heads to Jerusalem to confront his fate, as Jesus is clearing the temple, and the women fleeing Jesus's tomb. All three instances are combined with a word of amazement (ethambounto, exeplēsseto, or ekstasis). In the middle element the word of amazement follows "they were afraid" while in the first and third elements the word of amazement precedes "they were afraid."

The significance of this triplet is that it unifies the turning point, angering the Jerusalem authorities, and the end of the Gospel. "Heading to Jerusalem, Third Passion Prediction" (10:32–34) is the turning point of the Gospel as Jesus has decided to go to Jerusalem for Passover where his fate awaits. "Clearing The Temple" (11:15–19) seals Jesus's fate as far as the authorities are concerned, and "The Women at the Tomb" (16:2–8) is the result of those actions. The stich beginning this chiastic structure contains the first and third elements of that triplet.

B (10:33–34), B' (15:42–16:6)

There are five matches in this stich:

1. "Death" in the first hemistich matches "dead" in the second.

2. "Gentiles" in the first hemistich matches "Pilate" found twice and "centurion" found twice in the second.

3. "They will ridicule him and will spit upon him and will flog him" found in the first hemistich matches its opposite "he wrapped him in the linen cloth" and "they might come and anoint him" in the second.

4. "Will kill him" in the first hemistich matches "the corpse" in the second.

5. "After three days he will rise" in the first hemistich matches "He is risen" in the second.

Jesus's third and final prediction of the Passion matches his burial and rising from the dead. Other predictions of the Passion have chiastically matched The Parable of the Wicked Tennants and "Peter's Confession at Caesrea Philippi."

C (10:35), C' (15:40–41)

There are three matches in this stich:

1. "James" is found in both hemistiches.
2. "Approach" in the first hemistich matches its opposite "from a distance" in the second.
3. "Do for us" in the first hemistich matches its opposite "served him" in the second.

This stich has the opposites of "approach" (prosporeuontai) and "from afar (makrothen). James and John ask Jesus to serve them by granting a request, and the women served Jesus when he was in Galilee. The irony is palpable. James and John approach Jesus physically, but they are far from understanding his message. The women are at a distance from Jesus at his crucifixion, but they served him as he said he came to do for others. The women understood; his disciples did not.

D (10:36–39), D' (15:36)

This stich has two matches. "The cup that I drink" is found twice in the first hemistich and "gave it to him to drink" is found in the second. "Baptized" is found four times in the first hemistich and "Elijah" is found in the second.

This stich presents another irony with James and John saying they could drink the cup Jesus drank and Jesus is offered a sponge full of vinegar. Baptism matches Elijah because Mark equates Elijah and John the Baptizer throughout the Gospel.

E (10:40), E' (15:27)

There is only one match here when James and John ask to be on Jesus's right and left hand and then ironically two robbers are crucified with Jesus on his right and left hand.

Scholars have noted the irony of James and John asking to be on Jesus's right and left hands and then as he dies he is crucified between two criminals. Mark making the two incidents a stich in a chiastic structure shows that these scholars were correctly interpreting Mark.

F (10:42), F' (15:12–15)

There are two matches in this stich. "Gentiles" in the first hemistich matches "Pilate" found twice in the second. "Exercise authority over them" in the first hemistich matches "having flogged Jesus, delivered him to be crucified."

Just as in the (B, B') stich "gentiles" matches "Pilate," confirming that the matches were intentional. Pilate orders Jesus to be crucified. The power of life and death is the ultimate authority.

G (7:1–23), G' (14:58–72)

This stich has an interesting set of matches. "Hands" is found three times in the first hemistich and twice in the second. In the first hemistich Jesus condemns the Pharisees by saying three times that evil comes from within. These three phrases match Peter denying that he knows Jesus three times:

a. "Things that proceed out of the man are what defiles the man" matches "But he denied saying 'I neither know nor understand what you are saying.'"

b. "For from within, out of the heart of men evil thoughts proceed . . . deceit . . . slander" matches "but he denied it again."

c. "All these evil things proceed, go out and defile the man" matches "but he began to curse and swear, 'I do not know this man you are talking about.'"

The match of three iterations by Jesus that evil comes from within with Peter's three denials of Jesus leaves no room for doubt that 7:1–23 was originally placed between entering and leaving Jericho at 10:46 by the author. Mark has chiastically matched a pair of triplets, and once again disparaged Peter and by extension the Jerusalem apostles.

As is usual in Markan triplet construction the triplet about evil proceeding out of a man, the word "proceed" or "go forth" (ekporeuetai) comes before "defile the man" (koion ton anthrōpon) in the first and third elements, while "from the heart of men" (ek tes kardias ton anthrōpon) comes before "proceed" in the middle element. In Peter's denials he is directly quoted in the first and third elements, and the denial is narrated for the middle element.

H (10:50–52), H' (14:50–52)

There are three matches in this stich:

1. "Throwing away his tunic" in the first hemistich matches "linen cloth thrown around his naked body" and "leaving the linen cloth" in the second.

2. "Leaped up" in the first hemistich matches "they all fled" and "he fled" in the second.

3. "Followed him" in the first hemistich matches "following him" and "leaving him" in the second.

In "Curing Blind Bartimaeus" Bartimaeus throws his clothes around, which is a chiastic match for the young man running away naked at Jesus's arrest. The naked young man was deleted by Matthew and Luke in their versions.

I (11:1–7), I' (14:12–15)

There are five matches in this stich:

1. "Sends two of his disciples" is found in both hemistiches.

2. "Go into the village" in the first hemistich matches "go into the city" in the second.

3. "Find a colt no man ever sat upon" in the first hemistich matches "meet a man with a pitcher."

4. "The Lord has need of him and immediately he will send him back" in the first hemistich matches "The Teacher says, 'where is my guest room that I might eat the Passover with my disciples'" in the second.

5. "But they said to them what Jesus had told them and they let them go" in the first hemistich matches "and he will show you a large upstairs room that is furnished and ready" in the second.

This is a stich where the two hemistiches have parallel stories with Jesus sending two unnamed disciples to either get a colt for him to ride into Jerusalem or find a room in Jerusalem in which to eat the Passover meal. Both have a supernatural feel of Jesus being able to predict the future. Many scholars have noted that these pericopae have parallel elements. That they are matching pericopae in a chiastic structure encompassing the last half of the Gospel confirms their analysis.

At 11:3 Jesus indirectly refers to himself as "Lord." He has not done that since 2:28 when he said that the Son of Man was Lord of the Sabbath. This second use of "Lord" by Jesus is immediately before his triumphal entry into Jerusalem, based upon the triumphal entry into Jerusalem by Simon Maccabeus at 1 Macc 13:51. Perhaps this is a hint by Mark that Jesus has not totally accepted his role as "Suffering Servant" and he might still foment a revolution.

J (12:12), J' (14:10–11)

There are three matching elements:

1. "They wanted to take him" in the first hemistich matches "he might deliver him to them" in the second.

2. "They realized he spoke the parable against them" in the first hemistich matches the ironic opposite "and when they heard it they were glad" in the second.

3. "They went away" in the first hemistich matches "conveniently deliver him" in the second.

This is another stich with an obviously parallel subject matter. In the first hemistich, the elders, scribes and chief priests want to take Jesus. In the second Judas, somehow knowing the desires of the chief priests, offers to deliver him up.

K (12:13–17), K' (14:3–9)

There are six matches in this stich:

1. "They send to him some of the Pharisees and the Herodians" found in the first hemistich matches "There came a woman" in the second.

2. "They say to him" in the first hemistich matches "saying to each other" in the second.

3. "Should we pay or not pay" in the first hemistich matches "this oil might have been sold" in the second.

4. "Why do you test me" in the first hemistich matches "Why do you bother her" in the second.

5. "Bring me a denarius" in the first hemistich matches "for more than three hundred denarii" in the second.

6. "Whose is this image and inscription" in the first hemistich matches "what this woman has done will be told in memory of her."

In the second matching element selling is the opposite of paying. This is the third time in the Gospel that Roman money has been mentioned, another Markan triplet. This phrase was also a match for the two hundred denarii in "Feeding the Multitude." The middle element of the triplet is at 12:15 and it is singular whereas the other two were plural. This solidifies that the "First Feeding the Multitude" in Canonical Mark is original at least to the point of mentioning the denarii.

There is an ironic match in that the whole world knows Caesar, and Jesus says the whole world will remember this woman, yet her name is not revealed to the reader. It is true we are still reading about her two thousand years later. The woman has annointed Jesus at dinner as Samuel annointed Saul as first king of Israel in 1 Sam 9:22—10:1. The symbolism is clear that she is annointing him Messiah. Is this the signature of the author, and "Mark" was a woman who wrote the first Gospel about the Messiah? Perhaps Jesus's statement, "What this woman has done" refers to writing the Gospel.

L (12:19–25), L' (13:11–18)

There are six matches in this hemistich:

1. "Die" is found or referred to four times in the first hemistich matching "death" found twice in the second.

2. "Wife" in the first hemistich matches "who are pregnant and those who are nursing" in the second.

3. "Brother" is found twice in both hemistiches.

4. "Child" and "heir" mentioned twice in the first hemistich matches "child" and "children" in the second.

5. "Resurrection" and "rise from the dead" in the first hemistich matches "will be saved" in the second.

6. "Power of God" in the first hemistich matches "Holy Spirit" in the second.

Both of these hemistiches are full of family members and death. The final days and the resurrection are also mentioned.

M (12:35), M' (13:1–7)

There are five matches in this stich:

1. "Temple" is found once in the first hemistich and twice in the second.

2. "Christ, the son of David" is found in the first hemistich matches "many will come in my name" in the second.

3. "Sitting on my right hand" and "seats in the synagogue" found in the first hemistich matches "sitting on the Mount of Olives" is in the second.

4. "In the synagogues" "widows' houses" and "the treasury" found in the first hemistich matches "wonderful buildings" and "great buildings" are found in the second.

5. "Devouring widow's houses" found in the first hemistich matches "that will not be torn down" found in the second.

This stich has a building theme tying it together. It consists of the end of Mark 12 and the beginning of Mark 13.

Analysis Of The Jerusalem Chiastic Structure

This thirteen-stich structure covers the entire last half of the Gospel from the turning point as Jesus and his entourage head to Jerusalem to the three women fleeing the empty tomb. This is the last half of Act II, Act III and the Epilogue. This structure confirms that 7:1–23 should, indeed, be placed between entering and leaving Jericho at 10:46. It also demonstrates that Jesus turning to head to Jerusalem is an important division point in the Gospel.

The discussion to this point has not dealt with the location of "The Parable Discourse" (4:1–35), "Healing the Epileptic" (9:14–27) or "Answering the Disciples" (9:28–29) in Mark's Original Gospel. The next chapter discusses the structure and function of "The Parable Discourse" and "The Olivet Discourse."

The Discourses

The Parable Discourse

THIS DISCOURSE IS ONE large chiastic structure in and of itself. It is possible that Mark copied it from another source and inserted it into his Gospel, but it does have the markings of a Mark written piece. The twinned center has the Markan trait of being succinct, containing a long hemistich and a short one.

While the matching hemistiches in other large structures are a mix of identical words, parallel concepts and opposite concepts, the matching elements in "The Parable Discourse" structure are predominantly matching words. A small number of opposites and parallel concepts are found.

The Parable Discourse Chiastic Structure

A 4:1 . . . *by the seaside . . . boat . . . by the sea . . .*

A' 4:35 . . . *other side.* 6:32 . . . *boat . . .*

B 4:2 . . . *taught . . . parables, and said . . . teaching*

B' 4:33 . . . *spoke the word . . . parables . . .* 4:34 . . . *parable . . . explained everything.*

C 4:3 . . . *sower . . . sow* 4:4 . . . *sowed some . . . birds . . .* 4:5 *And other . . . ground . . . earth . . . sprang up . . . soil* 4:6. . . . *root . . .* 4:7 *And others . . . yielded no fruit* 4:8. *And others . . . soil, and yielded fruit, growing . . . bore . . .*

C' 4:31 . . . *seed . . . earth . . . seeds . . . earth* 4:32 . . . *sown, grows . . . garden plants, and puts out great branches . . . birds of the heavens . . .*

D 4:10 . . . *parables.* 4:11 . . . *kingdom of God . . . parables . . .* 4:13 . . . *parable . . . parables*

D' 4:30 . . . *kingdom of God . . . parable . . .*

E 4:14 *The sower sows . . .* 4:15 . . . *sown . . . sown . . .* 4:16 . . . *sown . . . rocky places, . . .* 4:17 . . . *root . . .* 4:18 . . . *sown . . .* 4:19 . . . *unfruitful* 4:20 . . . *soil . . . bear fruit . . .*

E' 4:26 . . . *a man should throw seed . . . earth* 4:27 . . . *seed . . . sprout up and grow . . .* 4:28 *The earth bears fruit . . . the blade, then the head . . . full grain in the head* 4:29 . . . *ripe . . . harvest . . .*

F 4:21 . . . *bushel. . . .* 4:22 . . . *hidden . . . made manifest. . . . secret . . . coming to light.*

F' 4:24b . . . *measure you measure . . . measured . . .* 4:25 . . . *that has . . . will be given . . . that has not . . . will be taken away . . . which he has.*

G 4:23 . . . *ears to hear . . . hear."*

G' 4:24a . . . *hear*

Commentary

A (4:1), A' (4:35, 6:32)

In this stich there are two matches. "By the seaside," "in the sea" and "by the sea" in the first hemistich matches "other side" in the second, "of the sea" being understood after "other side." Both hemistiches contain "boat" with the second hemistich having it twice.

If the redactor wanted to retain 4:35, it could only be located immediately before 4:36, 5:1, 5:21, or 6:32 where Jesus is in a boat or gets out of a boat. Because all of those except 6:32 are in the middle of chiastic structures that do not allow for a thirty-five-verse insert without any matches, immediately preceding 6:32 is the only place "The Parable Discourse" could have been in the Original Gospel.

Placing "The Parable Discourse" before "Feeding the Multitude" also makes sense in the theological structure of the Gospel, as will be shown in chapter 17.

B (4:2), B' (4:33–34)

There are three matches in this stich:

1. "Taught," and "teaching" are found in the first hemistich matching "explained" in the second.

2. "Said" in the first hemistich matches "spoke," "speak" in the second.

3. "Parables" found in the first hemistich matches "parable" and "parables" found in the second.

The word "parable" is found a number of times in this structure. This stich is about speaking in parables.

C (4:3–9), C' (4:31–32)

There are seven matches in this stich:

1. "Sow," "sowed," and "sower" found in the first hemistich match "sown" found twice in the second.

2. "Some," "other" and "others" found twice in the first hemistich match "seed" and "seeds" found in the second.

3. "Ground," "earth" and "soil" found in the first hemistich match "earth" and "heavens" found in the second.

4. "Sprang up," "growing," "bore" and "yielded" found twice in the first hemistich match "puts out, and "grows" found in the second.

5. "Birds" are found in both hemistiches.

6. "Root" found in the first hemistich matches "branches" found in the second.

7. "Fruit" found twice in the first hemistich matches "garden plants" found in the second.

The beginning and ending of the first hemistich are signaled by "Listen" and "let him hear." There is no match for this in the second hemistich, but it does foreshadow the center bracket of the structure as will be seen below.

One can see how Mark contrived to use the "birds" parallel by having Jesus say that birds can make a nest in the shade of mustard plants, when he could have said they reach the height of a man or a cow or something else. "Birds" appears to be contrived to make a chiastic match.

D (4:10–13), D' (4:30)

In this stich there are only two matches. "Parable" is found four times in the first hemistich and once in the second. "Kingdom of God" is found once in both hemistiches.

More "parables" are combined in this stich with "kingdom of God." This stich is telling the reader that "The Parable Discourse" is about the coming kingdom of God, a centerpiece of Pauline theology.

E (4:14–20), E' (4:26–29)

This stich has four matches:

1. "Sower" "sow" and "sown" four times are found in the first hemistich and "if a man should throw seed" is found in the second.

2. "Rocky places" and "soil" are found in the first hemistich and "earth" is found twice in the second.

3. "Root" is found in the first hemistich and matches "blade," "head" and "full grain in the head" found in the second.

4. "Unfruitful" and "bear fruit" are found in the first hemistich and "grow," "ripe and "harvest" are found in the second.

Scholars have noted that the use of "rocky soil" in this parable could well be a Markan anti-Petrine comment.[1] This adds weight to the conclusion that the Gospel of Mark is Paulinist.

---

1. Tolbert, *Sowing the Gospel*; Goodacre, "Rock on Rocky Ground," 63.

F (4:21–22), F' (4:24B–25)

This stich has three matches:

1. "Bushel" found in the first hemistich matches "measure" found twice and "measured" once in the second.

2. "Hidden" and "secret" found in the first hemistich match "taken away" and "has not" found in the second.

3. "Made manifest" and "coming to light" found in the first hemistich match "shall be given," "that has" and "that which he has" in the second.

Mark seems to be emphasizing "measure." Many translations have "bushel basket" in v. 21. The Greek work used is "modion" meaning "bushel." The translators assume that Jesus is saying that no one puts a lamp under a basket. That is a logical assumption. The New American Standard Bible translates the Greek as "basket" but footnotes the word and informs the reader "or peck-measure." The analysis shows that Mark, in fact, meant "bushel" or "peck" as a measure of grain to match chiastically with "measure" found in the second half of the stich.

G (4:23), G' (4:24A)

"Hear" is in both hemistiches and "ear" is also in the first hemistich.

This is the center of the structure and the essence of "The Parable Discourse." Words of hearing and listening are used throughout the discourse.

Analysis Of "The Parable Discourse" Chiastic Structure

The (C, C') stich begins with the word "listen" and ends with "let him hear" in this translation. The initial "listen" spoken by Mark's Jesus seems entirely gratuitous, but there is method to Mark's madness. The Greek is "akouete" at the beginning and "akoueto" for the end, the first being the present imperative second person and the last being the present imperative third person of "listen." This introduction to the first parable in the discourse tells the reader that this discourse is about listening to the word and foreshadows and emphasizes the twinned center.

"Ears to hear" at 4:23 ends one quote of Jesus and "Pay attention to what you hear" at 4:24 begins a new quote. Verses 23 and 24a mark the middle of the chiastic structure. Mark is telling the reader to seek the deeper meaning and it will be revealed to him. Mark knew that when one makes his own discovery through working at it, the lesson is much more satisfying and ingrained.

"The Parable Discourse" begins the Pauline section of the theological structure of Original Gospel as will be explained in chapter 17. Paul wrote that he was revealing mysteries that had been secret in ages past.[2] The center section of "The Parable Discourse" is about Christianity revealing past mysteries.

Textual Relationship Of The Discourses

"The Parable Discourse" and "The Olivet Discourse" (13:3–37) are related. Both are long sermons by Jesus dealing with the kingdom of God. At a surface level the reader of the Gospel can see that "The Parable Discourse" emphasizes hearing the word. That is what the first parable is about. In the thirty-four verses of "The Parable Discourse" are found: "he taught," "said to them," "listen," "Who has ears to hear, let him hear," "the twelve asked," "and he said to them," "hearing they might hear," "sows the word," "takes away the word," "of the word," "have heard the word," "the word," "such as hear the word," "he said to them," "if any man has ears to hear, let him hear," "be careful what you hear," "he said to them in his teaching, " "he spoke the word to them," "as they were able to hear it," "he did not speak without a parable," and "he explained everything."

Contrast that with "The Olivet Discourse" where the emphasis is seeing. In the thirty-seven verses of "The Olivet Discourse" and the introductory "Wonderful Buildings" is found: "Teacher, look," "See these great buildings," "what is the sign," "watch out for yourselves," "when you see," "look, here is the Christ," "look there," "give signs and wonders," "the sun will be darkened," "the moon will not giver her light," "they will see the Son of Man," "when you see these things happening," "stay awake," "porter to keep watch" and "be vigilant" twice.

There are other interesting parallels between the two discourses. At the beginning of both discourses the reader is told Jesus is sitting: in a boat for "The Parable Discourse," and on the Mount of Olives for "The Olivet Discourse." One says, "be careful what you hear;" the other says, "watch out for yourselves." In one Jesus blurts out "who has ears to hear, let him hear" in the other the narrator blurts out "let the reader understand." The reader, of course, is seeing the page of the Gospel.

"Understand" is used three times in "The Parable Discourse" with Jesus asking his disciples "do you not understand" or "how will you understand." "Understand" is used only once in "The Olivet Discourse" when the narrator addresses the reader, "let the reader understand." To the opposite effect "Look" is used once in "The Parable Discourse" and three times in "The Olivet Discourse." This is another typical Markan reversal. Both "understand" and "look" are used in both discourses with "understand" three times as much in "The Parable Discourse" and "Look" three times as much in "The Olivet Discourse." If it is assumed that "understand" means to hear and understand, and that is how it is used in "The Parable Discourse," then the uses of "understand" and "look" are parallel in the two discourses. In "The Parable Discourse"

---

2. Rom 16:25–26; 1 Cor 4:5.

"heaven" is found one time and "earth" is found five times. In "The Olivet Discourse" "earth" is found one time in the nominative case and "heaven" is found five times.

The central relationship between the discourses is that at 4:21–25 "The Parable Discourse" says that mysteries, meaning the mystery of the kingdom of God, will be revealed. The revelation of mysteries is a Pauline concept from Rom 16:25–26 and 1 Cor 4:5. Then in "The Olivet Discourse" Jesus reveals to his disciples what will happen at the coming of the kingdom of God.

In "The Parable Discourse" there is a triplet using "kingdom of God." At 4:11 is found "kingdom of God . . . parables," at 4:26 is found "kingdom of God" immediately followed by the parable of "The Seed Growing Secretly," and at 4:31 is found "parable . . . kingdom of God" at the end of the parable of "The Seed Growing Secretly." So the triplet is: 1. "kingdom of God, parable;" 2. "kingdom of God;" 3. "parable, kingdom of God." With typical Markan construction the middle element is different from the first and third elements and the construction of the triplet is chiastic. On the other hand, "The Olivet Discourse" is about what his disciples can expect at the coming of the kingdom of God, but amazingly the phrase "kingdom of God" is not used in that discourse.

It appears that Mark has created a mystery of his own: why would the author not use the phrase "kingdom of God" in a long discourse about the coming of the kingdom of God? Mark may have left us clues to the solution of this mystery. There are two triplets suggesting the kingdom of God: "kingdom," "kingdom" and "king" (basileia, basileian, basileōn) found at 13:8–9 and "God," "Lord" and "Father" (Theos, Kyrios, Patēr) found at 13:19, 13:20, and 13:32. In addition, there is another triplet located between "Kyrios" and "Patēr" consisting of "Christ," "Son of Man" and "son" found at 13:21, 13:26 and 13:32. The solution to the mystery will be revealed in chapter 12.

Both "The Parable Discourse" and "The Olivet Discourse" are about the kingdom of God. "The Parable Discourse" consists of parables regarding the process in realizing the kingdom of God. The "Parable of the Sower" is Paul preaching his gospel of the crucified and risen Christ Jesus, the word. "The Seed Growing Secretly" is God sending his son as an atonement sacrifice. "The Parable of the Mustard Seed" is the coming of the kingdom of God with the birds of heaven being the elect joining Christ coming with the clouds of heaven and making their home in the kingdom of God.

The three parables contained in "The Parable Discourse" are about the coming of the kingdom of God. Jesus explains the first parable to his disciples so that the reader will understand that the seed represents the word. The word is the Christology of Paul as presented in the epistles. Therefore, the first parable is about Paul's ministry and writings. Paul envisioned himself as the sower of seeds at 1 Cor 3:6, "I planted, Apollos watered, but God gave the increase." He also implies that at 2 Cor 9:10, "He that supplies the seed to the sower and bread for food shall supply and multiply your seed for sowing." Naturally, the disciples do not understand Paul's gospel, and the insult to Peter with the seed falling on rocky ground goes over their heads. The Pauline nature of "The Parable of the Sower" is also signaled by the Pauline section on revealed mysteries at 4:21–25 that immediately follows Jesus's explanation of the first parable to the disciples.

The second parable, "The Parable Of The Seed Growing Secretly," is about God sending Jesus into the world. This parable has a chiastic structure:

A And he said, "So is the kingdom of God,

   B as if a man should throw seed upon the earth,

      C and should sleep and rise night and day.

         D And the seed should sprout up and grow,

            E he does not know how.

            E' The Earth bears fruit by herself;

         D' first the blade, then the head, then the full grain in the head.

      C' But when the grain is ripe,

   B' immediately he sends the sickle, because the harvest is come."

A' And he said, "How can we picture the kingdom of God?

The (A, A') stich both contain "and he said" and "kingdom of God." The (B, B') stich has the man sowing and harvesting. The (C, C') stich has the man sleeping and waking and the grain becoming ripe. The (D, D') stich has "the seed should sprout up and grow" and a description of the seeds growing. The (E, E') stich is the twinned center saying that the man does not know how it grows and the Earth grows it by herself.

God throws seed (man) on the Earth and waits. Finally, a man worthy of being adopted by God is born and springs from the earth. Then God can harvest what he has sown for the salvation of mankind. The hint by Mark is that the crop when ready for harvest "delivered itself" using the aorist subjunctive active third person singular of the Greek "paradidōmi," which means "to deliver." That is the verb that most NT translations translate as "betray" but Mark means "deliver up." Mark uses it a number of times to indicate the "Son of Man" would be delivered up to the authorities. Jesus delivers himself up to be the ransom for many. At Rom 8:32 Paul said that God delivered up his son for us all. Certainly Paul did not mean that God "betrayed" his son.

When the grain is to be harvested, the man who planted the seed is said to "send out the sickle." "Send out" (apostellei) seems to be an odd way to say one is going to harvest, but it does bring to mind apostles that are sent out to preach the word. In addition the harvester in the parable is said to use a "drepanon" which can be a sickle but is usually a grape vine cutter for harvesting grapes. At "The Last Supper" Jesus says at 14:25 he "will not drink of the fruit of the vine until I "drink it anew in the kingdom of God." In that phrase" Mark used "genēmatos" for "fruit" that can mean "fruit" but usually means more like "offspring" or "child."[3] Jesus is the child of God that delivers

---

3. Strong, *Concordance*, 1081.

himself for harvest. Verse 14:25 is a "kingdom of God" passage and the parable at 4:26–28 is about the coming of the kingdom of God. These passages are related.

Then "The Parable Of The Mustard Seed" is the coming of the kingdom of God as Jesus says at 4:30. The kingdom of God is small at first, just an idea, a prophecy in Daniel 7, but when it comes, it will grow larger than all the other garden plants, that is, the other kingdoms on Earth. The birds of heaven are the elect who will make their homes in the shade of the branches of kingdom of God.

I have interpreted "The Parable Of The Seed Growing Secretly" as being Adoptionist in that God waits for a man that is worthy of being adopted. Mathew and Luke did not like Mark's Adoptionism and wrote their Gospels to eliminate Adoptionism. Matthew eliminated Mark's "Parable Of The Seed Growing Secretly" and replaced it with "The Parable Of The Tares" at Matt 13:24–30 and 13:36–43. In it Matthew made the parable about separating the Christians from the non-Christians and sending the non-believers to hell. Luke also eliminated Mark's parable, but did not replace it. It seems that both of them realized the parable was about Adoptionism and rejected it.

"The Olivet Discourse" is a visual description of the coming of the kingdom of God Jesus describes to his disciples. It is the interim between Jesus's crucifixion and rising and his coming with the clouds of heaven. It seems to fit into "The Parable Discourse" between "The Seed Growing Secretly" and "The Mustard Seed," where Jesus says, "How can we picture (Pōs homoiōsōmen) the kingdom of God?" In "The Olivet Discourse" Jesus gives his disciples a picture of the coming of the kingdom of God; once again drawing attention to the hearing/looking dichotomy of the two discourses, but showing their interrelationship.

Locating "The Parable Discourse" in Original Mark

In locating the original position of "Healing the Epileptic," (9:14–27) the smooth transition from "The Transfiguration" and "Leaving the Mountain" to the healing is persuasive that "Healing the Epileptic" follows "Coming Down the Mountain" in Original Mark. In addition, both Matthew and Luke have their versions of "Healing the Epileptic" immediately following their versions of the transfiguration. Since they both were apparently using Canonical Mark as their source, that would not be persuasive, but it is some evidence. A chiastic or parallel structure containing "Healing the Epileptic," "Answering the Disciples" or "The Parable Discourse" has not yet revealed itself.

The logical place to locate "Healing the Epileptic," "Answering the Disciples" and "The Parable Discourse" is between the end of "The Transfiguration" and "Coming Down the Mountain" at 9:13 and the beginning of "Running Ahead of Jesus" at 6:32. That theory will be tested by looking at what the redactor found after he had moved "The Transfiguration," "Coming Down the Mountain," "Healing the Epileptic," and "Answering the Disciples."

The redactor split "Feeding the Multitude" in order to retain the transition from the miraculous feeding to Jesus going by boat to Dalmanutha (8:10) and confronting the Pharisees. Then he could design his own pericopae to add in between the two feedings. With moving "The Transfiguration," "Coming Down the Mountain," "Healing the Epileptic," and "Answering The Disciples" (9:2–29) away from the location immediately following "Return of the Twelve" (6:30–31), the redactor was faced with a difficult transition. He now had 4:1 immediately following 6:31. It looked like this:

> 6:31 And he says to them, "Come down into the desert and rest a while." For many were coming and going, and they had no opportunity to even eat.

> 4:1 And again he began to teach by the seaside.

If he kept "The Parable Discourse" where it was, he had to get Jesus from the desert to the seaside smoothly. Rather than do unnecessary redaction and maybe confuse something else, he moved "The Parable Discourse" (4:1–35) to a position after "Who Are My Brothers" (3:31–35) where there the pericope ends and Jesus and his disciples go on a boat trip. Since 4:35 ending "The Parable Discourse" has Jesus saying, "let us go over to the other side." The redactor chose to place "The Parable Discourse" immediately before "Calming the Sea" (4:36–41).

After the redactor moved "The Transfiguration," "Coming Down the Mountain," "Healing the Paralytic," and "Answering the Disciples," to follow "Peter's Confession at Caesarea Philippi." He then moved "The Parable Discourse" to follow "Who Are My Brothers." It worked out well. Now he needed to get Jesus from "Return of the Twelve" to "Feeding the Multitude." This was not difficult. At the end of "Return of the Twelve" Jesus tells his disciples to come out to the desert (6:31), and immediately before "Feeding the Multitude" in Original Mark Jesus decides to leave in a boat (4:35). All the redactor had to do was add "to their private desert place" (eis erēmon topon kat' idian). The problem is that in the redactor's version (Canonical Mark) the reader is told three times that they are in the desert at 6:31, 6:32 and 6:35—a sure sign of redaction. Mark's Original Gospel only tells the reader once at 6:35 when the disciples complain to Jesus that the place is desolate. That is the style of the actual author of the Original Gospel of Mark.

Since "The Parable Discourse" is a self-contained unit, the redactor's repositioning of it made little apparent difference. It did change the theological structure. Chapter 17 will show how positioning "The Parable Discourse" immediately before "Feeding the Multitude" makes good sense in the theological structure.

I have found that the word "twelve" was used twelve times in Original Mark—not a surprising finding. Mark structured these twelve occurrences of "twelve" into three quartets, each with an a, b, b, a structure. Interestingly, the structure does not work unless 4:10 in "The Parable Discourse" comes after 5:25, 5:42, and 6:7 in the Original

Gospel. This is additional evidence that "The Parable Discourse" (4:1–34) was not located before "Calming the Sea" (4:36–41) in Mark's Original Gospel.

The redactor padded the text between "First Feeding the Multitude" and "Second Feeding the Multitude." The redactor added several pericopae (6:38–56, 7:24–37)) and moved "Controversy on Tradition" and "Eating Does Not Defile" (7:1–23) from its original location after the turning point designed by the author to before "Peter's Confession at Caesarea Philippi" (8:27–9:1). By doing this, Peter's confession is repositioned to be approximately at the middle of the Gospel. In Canonical Mark 47.6% of the words of the Gospel come before "Peter's Confession at Caesrea Philippi" and 51.4% of the words after it. This makes it likely to be mistaken for the turning point and satisfying Aristotle's idea of a recognition, which typically occurs near the center of a play. The redactor deceived many exegetes who opine that Peter's confession is the turning point in Canonical Mark. And it is. It is just not the turning point Mark designed in his Original Gospel.

Now the outline for Original Gospel of Mark is complete. There are seventy-eight pericopae as numbered by chiastic structure starting and ending with movement or a change in cast.

In this reconstruction of Mark's Original Gospel 9:2–29 has been moved to be located two chapters earlier than in Canonical Mark. "The Parable Discourse" has been moved to be three chapters later than in Canonical Mark, and 7:1–23 was moved to be three chapters later than in Canonical Mark. This may seem like radical surgery to a document that has been accepted by Christians for over nineteen hundred years. There is an early Christian writing that suggests that the Gospel of Mark may have been or may need to be revised.

Eusebius of Caesarea, known as the father of church history wrote in 340 CE that Papias of Hieropolis had written about the Gospel of Mark. Papias lived about 70 CE to 163 CE, some two hundred years before Eusebius. Papias was Bishop of Hieropolis, but none of his writings have survived. Eusebius wrote about Papias:

> But now we must add to the words of his, which we have already quoted the tradition that he gives in regard to Mark, the author of the Gospel. It is in the following words: "This also the presbyter said: Mark, having become the interpreter of Peter, wrote down accurately, though not indeed in order, whatsoever he remembered of the things said or done by Christ. For he neither heard the Lord nor followed him, but afterward, as I said, he followed Peter, who adapted his teaching to the needs of his hearers, but with no intention of giving a connected account of the Lord's discourses, so that Mark committed no error while he thus wrote some things as he remembered them. For he was careful of one thing, not to omit any of the things which he had heard, and not to state any of them falsely." These things are related by Papias concerning Mark.[4]

4. Eusebius, *Ecclesiastic History*, 3:39:1.

What we have here is a triple hearsay. Eusebius said that Papias said that the Presbyter said. The reliability of the statement is anyone's guess. There is considerable doubt that the author of the Gospel of Mark was a follower of Peter, as copiously documented herein. Mark is very definitely Pauline and expresses Paul's teachings. He is consistently antagonistic to Peter. Chapter 16 will demonstrate that the middle half of the Original Gospel is based on Paul's epistles. But assuming Eusebius quoted Papias correctly, there is a suggestion by Papias that Mark's Gospel gets the events out of order. Which events we are not told. Is Papias suggesting that the Presbyter was suggesting that the order of events in Canonical Mark has been changed from the Original Gospel or was the Presbyter suggesting that Original Mark needed to be changed? Perhaps neither, but it is intriguing. Perhaps this analysis has put the events back in the correct order to the Presbyter's liking.

The Literary Structures Found In Original Mark

With the demonstration of The Jerusalem Chiastic Structure, it can be seen that the author of the Original Gospel of Mark, included the beginning of the Gospel and the end of the Gospel in three separate literary structures: another triplet. Interestingly, two are chiastic structures and one is a parallel structure, maintaining the tradition that the middle element of at triplet is slightly different from the first and third elements. In this case the parallel structure described in chapter 3, encompasses only the prologue and epilogue.

I have found six total multi-pericopae chiastic or parallel structures. This is consistent with Mark's triplet mindset. Two chiastic structures come before "The Parable Discourse," two come after "The Parable Discourse" and two involve both the beginning and the end of the Gospel, one being the parallel structure and one being the chiastic structure. Therefore, before "The Parable Discourse" there are two complete chiastic structures, the first half of a parallel structure, and the first half of a chiastic structure. Then after "The Parable Discourse" there are two complete chiastic structures, the second half of a parallel structure and the second half of a chiastic structure. Mark loved symmetry, although there is certainly no guarantee that all of Mark's large chiastic structures have been discovered. There should be one that includes "The Parable Discourse" and "Healing the Epileptic."

10

Textual Revisions and Answering Questions

Now that the content and positioning of the pericopae in Original Mark are set, textural revisions and questions can be dealt with. Two pericopae have obviously been redacted: "Killing John the Baptizer" (6:13–29) and "Leaven of the Pharisees" (8:13–21). Answers to the questions about odd constructions that were posed in chapter 1 can also be provided.

"Killing John the Baptizer" (6:13–29)

The story of the death of John the Baptizer found in Canonical Mark is too long for the entire story to be part of the Beginning and Transfiguration Chiastic Structure. If Mark wrote the entire story (6:12–29) as found in Canonical Mark, there would be more chiastic matches between that story in the second half of the structure and the pericope about Jesus coming into Galilee (1:14–15). Turton argues that there has been a major interpolation into Mark's original passage on the death of John the Baptizer. Turton gives five reasons why he believes that the passage has been heavily redacted:

1. The author of Mark nowhere else mentions the Book of Esther, which is odd because he has a habit of citing a book that he parallels elsewhere in the Gospel. 6:14–29 is big, and it would be unusual for a structure of this size not to pop up somewhere else . . .

2. The story is intercalated between the two halves of the sending of the disciples but not in the writer's usual deft way in which one story comments on the other when they are sandwiched together. A good example of the typical style is Peter's denial, in the A, B, A' format. While Jesus affirms who he is Peter is out in the courtyard, denying who Jesus is. Then even as the soldiers mock Jesus and tell him to "Prophesy!" as if he can't, his prophecy of Peter's denial is coming true out in the courtyard . . .

3. Another strike here is that while Mark often writes off the OT, and sometimes off Jewish legends and stories, it is rare that a passage of such length is entirely without allusions to OT verses in the details. For example, in the Cleansing of the Temple, the story frame is Jehu's cleansing of the Temple of Ba'al, but the verses themselves are not taken from 2 Kings, but from Zechariah, Nehemiah, and Jeremiah . . .

4. The writer of Mark does not use the novelistic Jewish literature like Esther at all, except perhaps a bit of Tobit in Mark 16.

5. Mark 6 is an inverted parallel of Mark 3 . . . Guess what story is not paralleled in Mark 3? You guessed it: JBap's death.[1]

Turton seems to be suggesting that the entire killing of John the Baptizer is in the wrong place. If this indeed is his suggestion, he cannot be correct on that point since it fits with the Beginning and Transfiguration Chiastic Structure. It is the Herod birthday party and the interchange between Herodias and her daughter (6:18–26) that is the bulk of the interpolation

After the reconstruction "Killing John the Baptizer" in Original Mark is shorter than in Canonical Mark. Turton states that he believes that the beginning of the pericope about the killing of John is original to Mark, but that a redactor has added material and the original can no longer be discerned.[2] Seeing that the Beginning and Transfiguration Chiastic Structure had a match for killing John, but that there were no matches for the long middle of the story about Herodias and her daughter, the redactor must have added material to the story based on the Book of Esther. The redactor is aware that Mark uses OT stories as the basis for the narrative about Jesus. The redactor wanted to add material to the portion of Mark's Gospel before "Peter's Confession at Caesarea Philippi" (8:27—9:1) in order to make that the midpoint of the Gospel. So in his desire to pad the first half of the Gospel, he added material to "Killing John the Baptizer" based on Esther. The reconstruction of "Killing John the Baptizer" in the Original Gospel is as follows:

A 6:12 And going out they preached that all should repent.

  B 6:13 And they cast out many demons, and anointed many that were sick with oil, and healed them.

    C 6:16 But Herod, when he heard about it, said, "John, whom I beheaded, is risen."

      D 6:17 For Herod himself sent out men who laid hold of John, and locked him in prison on account of Herodias, the wife of his brother Philip because he had married her.

      D' 6:27 And immediately the king sent an executioner and commanded him to bring his head.

    C' And he went and beheaded him in the prison, 6:29 And hearing about it, his disciples came and took his body,

  B' and laid it in a tomb.

A' 6:30 And the apostles gather together with Jesus; and they told him about every thing, what they had done, and what they had taught.

---

1. Turton, HCGM, ch 6, "Historical Commentary."

2. Ibid.

This chiastic structure now makes immanent sense. The wordy, unMarkan beginning with its redundancies is gone and the dancing of Herodias' daughter based upon the Book of Esther has been eliminated. The center (D, D') stich is Markan with the long version of Herod imprisoning John because he opposed Herod's marriage and the short version of ordering his death. This center matches J.A. 18:5:1–2, Mark's probable source, with the D hemistich summarizing Josephus's paragraph 1 and the D' hemistich summarizing paragraph 2. Josephus does not say that John disapproved of Herod's marriage or that John was beheaded by Herod. Josephus only says that Herod slew John. Josephus also says that Herod killed John for political reasons.[3]

The (B, B') stich matches, with the disciples of Jesus healing people and the disciples of John laying his body in a tomb, ironic opposites so common in Mark. The (C, C') stich matches, with Herod hearing about the healings of Jesus's disciples and John's disciples hearing about John's death, plus "beheaded" is found in both hemistiches. The pericope now meets Turton's objection about the intercalations commenting on each other. Herod hears about Jesus's disciples healing and preaching and John's disciples hear that Herod had killed John. Now 6:12–30 is a satisfactory, much shorter, Markan chiastic pericope.

Several textural clues lead to the conclusion that 6:14–15 of Canonical Mark is an interpolation. First, the passage is reiterative of 6:16 telling the reader twice that John "is risen." As pointed out before, Mark does not repeat himself with respect to narrative facts. Second, it is reiterative of telling the reader that Herod heard about it. Third, it is reiterative of what the disciples say about Jesus at 8:28. The redactor had the habit of copying Markan phrases and inserting them into his interpolations to make the interpolations sound Markan, a clever trick, but it actually violates Mark's style because he did not repeat long phrases. Fourth, there is a triplet of "risen" in the sense of rising from the dead outside of Jesus's three predictions of the Passion wherein he says he will rise from the dead. The "risen" triplet is at 6:16, 9:9, and 16:6. At 6:16 the Greek word is "ēgerthē;" At 9:9 the Greek is "anastē;" and at 16:6 the Greek is "ēgerthē" again. The pattern of the middle element of the triplet being slightly different is typical. At 6:14 the text has "ēgegertai," the same verb as elements one and three of the actual triplet, but a different tense. Verse 6:14 is the one that does not belong and is therefore the interpolation.

If 6:18–26 is an interpolation, then 6:28 must also be an interpolation since it refers back to 6:18–26.

---

3. Josephus states, "Herod, who feared lest the great influence John had over the people might put it into his power and inclination to raise a rebellion, (for they seemed ready to do any thing he should advise,) thought it best, by putting him to death, to prevent any mischief he might cause," J.A. 18:5:2.

"Leaven of the Pharisees" (8:13–21)

It is definite that "Leaven of the Pharisees" is part of Mark's Original Gospel because it provides chiastic matches with Mark 14. In addition, one of Mark's triplets involves the Pharisees and the Herodians as mentioned above. This is the middle element of the triplet and Mark wrote "Herod" in conjunction with the Pharisees while in the first and third elements he wrote, "Herodians," once again conforming to the pattern, and clearly establishing that the pericope is original. Further, there is another triplet about "hard of heart" found 3:5, 8:17 and 10:5. The middle element is at 8:17 where Jesus included "hard of heart" in a question, whereas in the first and third elements it is in a declaration. These three attributes of "Leaven of the Pharisees" demonstrate that it is original to Mark's Gospel. However, in the Canonical Mark version of this pericope Jesus reminds his disciples of two miracle feedings, and there is only one in Original Mark. Therefore, some of the text must have been interpolated.

Turton thinks that the whole pericope is interpolated. He is wrong about this. Here is the Markan original:

A 8:13 And sending them away, and again embarking into the boat he departed to the other side.

B 8:15 And he admonished them, saying, "Watch out. Beware of the leaven of the Pharisees and the leaven of Herod."

C 8:16 And they discussed among themselves saying, "We have no bread."

D 8:17 And realizing it he says to them, "Why do you discuss about having no bread? Do you not yet perceive nor understand? Are your hearts hardened?

D' 8:18 Having eyes, do you not see? And having ears, do you not hear?

C' And do you not remember 8:20 when I broke the loaves among the four thousand, how many basketfuls of broken pieces were left over?" And they say to him, "Seven."

B' 8:21 And he said to them, "Do you still not understand?"

A' 8:22 And they come to Bethsaida. And they bring to him a blind man, and beg him to touch him.

Verse 8:14 in Canonical Mark wherein the narrator tells the reader that the disciples forgot to take bread is one of those explicative verses that the redactor likes to add, but is unMarkan. Mark would not tell the reader that the disciples forgot bread. When the disciples discuss having no bread among themselves, the reader knows all he needs to know. Then, at 8:19 Jesus reminds his disciples of the second half of the first feeding. This must have been interpolated. The redactor probably inserted

the five loaves among the five thousand, how many baskets full of broken pieces were left over? They say to him, Twelve. The time

between "broke" and "the" in verse 8:20. Also it appears that the redactor changed "loaves" (artous) to "seven" (hepta) in 8:20. But he forgot to add "and" (kai) at the beginning of 8:20. Only one of the eight primary Markan manuscripts has "kai" as the second word of 8:20. It looks as if the redactor may have forgotten to stick in "and" when he added the verse about the five loaves.

The evidence for his changing "loaves" to "seven" in 8:20 is two-fold. In Canonical Mark the word "loaves" is found eight times, but with eliminating one feeding miracle and "Walking On Water," the number of time "loaves" occurs is only two. However, if "seven" is changed to "loaves" in 8:20 then "loaves" is found three times, and it makes a perfect Markan triplet at 8:5, 8:6 and 8:20 with the triplet being "loaves . . . seven," "seven loaves" and "loaves . . . seven," conforming to the middle element is different pattern. In addition, with "loaves" changed to "seven" by the redactor, who must do that in order to distinguish it from the five-loaf feeding, there are eight occurrences of "seven." There are twelve occurrences of "twelve," four occurrences of "four," and nine (three times three) occurrences of "three." The normal expectation would be that the author of the Original Gospel had written the word "seven" seven times. Changing "seven" to "loaves" at 8:20 restores Markan sensibilities.

In Canonical Mark's "Leaven Of The Pharisees" the redactor used two different words for "basket" just as two different words were used in the separate miracle feedings. He also telegraphed this interpolation when he wrote "Walking On Water" and wrote that the disciples did not understand about the loaves but their hearts were hardened. "Are your hearts hardened" in 8:17 appears to be original because there are three questions in the D hemistich, followed by three more questions.

As stated above, in Original Mark the word "twelve" is used twelve times, what one would expect from Mark. If the second half of the "First Feeding the Multitude" and the entire "Leaven Of The Pharisees" were original to Mark, there would be fourteen uses of the word "twelve." Since twelve has significance with the twelve tribes of Israel and the twelve disciples, it would be uncharacteristic for Mark to use that word fourteen times. The fourteen occurrences of the phrases "Son of Man," and "kingdom of God," and the fourteen miracles performed by Jesus in Original Mark are special cases explained in chapter 12.

Moving the Boat Trips

In Original Mark "The Parable Discourse" (4:1–34) precedes "Feeding the Multitude" (6:34–37, 8:5–9), so that Jesus tells his disciples they should go to the other side of the sea at 4:35 and they go away in a boat at 6:32. Also in Original Mark Jesus leaves the house where he had the controversy with the scribes from Jerusalem about casting out Satan and gets into a boat with his disciples before the storm comes up. When the redactor moved "The Transfiguration," "Coming Down the Mountain" and "Healing the Epileptic" (9:2–27) to follow "Peter's Confession at Caesarea Philippi" (8:27–9:1), he found that "The Parable Discourse" (4:1–35) now followed "Return of the Twelve" (6:30–31) which quotes Jesus as saying, "Come out to the desert." Then suddenly he is in a boat by the sea. Apparently the redactor did not like that transition and so he decided to move "The Parable Discourse." However, he wanted to maintain its general location in the text preceding "Peter's Confession at Caesarea Philippi," and he had to place it before a boat trip unless he wanted to write an extensive transition. The only place available was before "Calming the Sea" 4:36–41. The redactor added "since he was in" (hōs ēn en) to 4:36. This seems like another unnecessary explanation of motive that is unMarkan.

By moving "The Parable Discourse" to be located immediately before "Calming the Sea," the redactor inadvertently destroyed the design of the triplet about Jesus entering boats in the presence of crowds. In Canonical Mark the first and second elements of the triplet have the crowd before the boat and the third element has the boat before the crowd, not a Markan pattern. See chapter 7, section "Boats and Crowds" above. This establishes conclusively that in Original Mark 5:21 was located before 4:1.

Questions Answered by the Revised Gospel

Now the questions posed in the chapter 1 can be answered:

1. Why would Mark write a long episode about the killing of John the Baptizer? It seems odd since it incorporates two ancient sources: J.A. 18:5:1–2 and Esth 1:10–11, 7:2, 6.

   The answer is, he did not. The portion of the episode taken from Esther was interpolated later. Mark used the OT as the source for the narrative portion of his Gospel; however, he did not typically pile two narrative sources on top of each other. In addition, he usually used an OT source more than once for emphasis. The Esther story is never used again after it serves as a motivation for the killing of John in Canonical Mark.

2. Why at Mark 6:45–53 does Jesus order his disciples to Bethsaida, but they go to Gennesaret?

   The answer is, they did not go to Gennesaret. In the Original Gospel of Mark Gennesaret is not mentioned, and Jesus did not order his disciples to go to Bethsaida. It seems the redactor got confused. Jesus gets out of a boat in Bethsaida and never gets in a boat again. The redactor, knowing that Jesus ends up in Bethsaida healing a blind man, writes a miracle story of Jesus walking on water and has Jesus order his disciples to go to Bethsaida. He then wrote additional miracles and added them after Walking On Water. He probably intended that the intervening pericopae have no certain location, as he wrote for the "Second Feeding of the Multitude." "Controversy on Tradition" and "Eating Does Not Defile" also have no certain location after the redactor removed them their original

Jericho location. The command to go to Bethsaida may have become lost in the interpolation.

3. At the beginning of "The Transfiguration" (9:2–8) pericope, Mark wrote "After six days." The question, "six days after what?" immediately comes to mind. Here is Canonical Mark:

> 9:1 And he said to them, "Truthfully I say to you, There are some standing here who will in no way taste of death, until they see the kingdom of God coming with power." 9:2 And after six days Jesus takes with him Peter, and James, and John, and brings them up into a high mountain by themselves.

After a sermon by Jesus the reader is told that six days later Jesus takes Peter, James and John up the mountain. He did not leave the crowd, he did not dismiss the crowd, and he did not tell his disciples to leave the crowd.

Here is the beginning of "The Transfiguration" in the Original Gospel as reconstructed based on literary structures:

> 6:30 And the apostles gather together with Jesus; and they told him about every thing, what they had done, and what they had taught. 6:31 And he says to them, "Come down into the desert and rest a while." For many were coming and going, and they had no opportunity to even eat. 9:2 And after six days Jesus takes with him Peter, and James, and John, and brings them up into a high mountain by themselves.

Now the reader can see that Jesus allowed his disciples to rest up from their journey for six days before taking Peter, James and John up the Mountain of the Transfiguration. It makes sense. There is a reason for the six-day interregnum.

As pointed out by Bowman[4] the six days is probably taken from Exod 24:12–18 where Moses and Joshua go up Mount Sinai to get the ten commandments and are enveloped in a cloud for six days before God gives them the stone tablets. Jesus takes Peter, James and John up the mountain with him and they get enveloped in a cloud, while Moses only takes Joshua, but he leaves Aaron and Hur in charge of the camp while they are gone. In each case three disciples are mentioned.

4. Why at Mark 7:1–23 would scribes and Pharisees go all the way from Jerusalem to Gennesaret to visit Jesus?

The answer again is, that they did not. Gennesaret is not mentioned in Original Mark and the scribes and Pharisees only had to go to Jericho to meet Jesus. The redactor moved 7:1–23 from a position after "Peter's Confession at Caesarea" (8:27—9:1) to before that pericope, thereby nudging "Peter's Confession" closer to the center of Canonical Mark. When deciding where to place 7:1–23

---

4. Bowman, "The Gospel of Mark," 190.

the redactor chose to insert it in the middle of his interpolation (last half of "First Feeding the Multitude," "Walking on Water," "Healing in the Marketplace," "Healing the Syro-Phoenician Woman's Daughter," "Healing the Deaf Mute," and first half of "Second Feeding the Multitude"). The redactor may have chosen that particular spot so that his interpolation would be broken with authentic Markan material, making the interpolation less obvious.

5. Why did Mark include a strange healing of a blind man that took two tries with the blind man seeing men "as walking trees" at 8:23–26?

In all of Jesus's miracles in Mark Jesus either performs the miracle immediately or tells the afflicted persons that their faith has cured them. This is the only time Jesus must do the healing twice. It appears Mark wrote the story of the blind man in this particular manner so that the text would make a chiastic match with his "parable of the fig tree" in "The Olivet Discourse." It is also reminiscent of Rom 13:12 and Isa 16:18, as the blind slowly come out of the dark into the light.

6. Why does it appear that the disciples are hearing "rise from the dead" for the first time at 9:10 when they heard it at 8:31?

By relocating "The Transfiguration" and "Coming Down the Mountain" (9:2–13) to their original positions immediately following "Return of the Twelve," (6:30–31), no longer does the first passion prediction occur before "The Transfiguration." In the reconstruction, when Jesus and the three disciples are leaving the mountain after his transfiguration, Jesus tells them for the first time that he will rise from the dead. Therefore, when the narrator tells the reader that the disciples question what "rising from the dead should mean" at 9:10, they have not heard it before, and it is reasonable for the disciples to question what the term meant. In Canonical Mark, Jesus tells them he will rise from the dead at 8:31 and his disciples do not question what rising from the dead means, but Peter rebukes Jesus. With the rearrangement it makes more sense to have the disciples questioning what "rising from the dead" means during "Coming Down the Mountain" (9:9–13). Subsequently, there is the confession at Caesarea Philippi and Peter rebukes Jesus, having had time to think over what rising from the dead means. In "Second Passion Prediction (9:30–32), the disciples still do not understand, but they are afraid to ask because Peter was admonished when he objected at the previous prediction. The narrative makes more sense.

7. What happened in Jericho at 10:46?

Jesus had a controversy with the Pharisees about washing dishes and following the tradition of elders rather than following God's commandments. The redactor moved this controversy two chapters earlier to be located between the two feeding miracles in order to pad the text before "Peter's Confession at Caesarea Philippi" (8:27—(9:1) and to reduce the text after it.

8. Why does Mark report that Jesus goes into Jerusalem at 11:11 and turn around and leave?

This is one element of a triplet. Jesus enters Jerusalem and the temple three times parallel to his entering Capernaum three times in the first half of the Gospel. The three times he enters Jerusalem are at 11:11, 11:15, and 11:27. Since a woman anoints him with oil in Bethany in Mark 14 and presumably the Passover meal was eaten in Jerusalem, Jesus must have entered Jerusalem at least four times, but Mark only specifies three in the text. The middle element of the triplet has "having entered" (eiselthōn) between "Jerusalem" and "Temple," while the first and third elements do not.

At 11:15 Jesus clears the Temple and at 11:27 the authorities confront him. The 11:11 incident provides the first element of the triplet that builds the conflict: Jesus looks around getting a sense of what goes on in the temple, then he disrupts the temple routine, then the authorities confront him. After hearing the Parable of the Vinyard they decided to kill him.

The Original Gospel Of Mark

I have provided my translation of the Original Gospel of Mark set out with its pericope-level chiastic structures in Appendix 1. At this point the reader is urged to turn to Appendix 1 and read that reconstruction of Mark's Gospel. Answer these questions: Does this reconstruction of Mark's Original Gospel read more smoothly than Canonical Mark? Does it make more sense? Is there more drama? Is the character of the protagonist Jesus more completely drawn? See for yourself how it reads in its original form. A description of moving this pericope here and that pericope there will not give you the sense of The Original Gospel of Mark as the author intended it.

11

Luke—Redactor of Mark

IN ORDER TO WREST the Original Gospel of Mark out of Canonical Mark, this analysis has eliminated about eight per cent of the text of Canonical Mark: 6:14–15, 6:18–26, 6:28, 6:38–56, 7:24—8:4, 8:14, and 8:19. Comparing this eliminated text with the style of the writing of Original Mark reveals an interesting stylistic difference between the two sets. The author of Original Mark was succinct and sparse, providing few details and even less motivation of the characters. He concentrated on the action, enticing the reader to fill out the picture and discern motivation from the action. On the other hand, in the eliminated text the narrative gives duplicative information, motivation of the characters, and unnecessary but colorful detail. In other words, the style of the eliminated eight per cent is much different from the retained ninety-two per cent. This stylistic dichotomy supports the chiastic structure analysis.

The writer who tells the reader of Canonical Mark twice within two verses (6:14–16) that Herod think Jesus is John the Baptizer risen from the dead, tells the reader twice in two verses (8:1–2) that the crowd has had nothing to eat, and tells the reader four times within three verses (8:14–17) that the disciples forgot to take bread on a boat voyage is not the same writer who tells the reader Jesus was tempted by Satan in the wilderness (1:12–13) with no description whatsoever of the temptation. It is also not the same writer who tells the reader that Peter rebukes Jesus at Caesarea Philippi after Jesus makes his first Passion prediction (8–32–33) but leaves the reader in the dark as to what Peter said. The reader only knows that Jesus calls Peter "Satan" and accuses him of not being concerned about God's will. It is also not the same writer who gives the reader no hint why Jesus tells unclean spirits, demons and some of the afflicted he healed not to tell by whom they were cast out or healed. It is also not the same writer who tells the reader that the cock crowed the second time (14:72), but never tells the reader that the cock crowed the first time. Finally, the verbose, detail loving writer of the eliminated passages cannot be the same writer who ended the Gospel having frightened women fleeing from an empty tomb and never telling anyone what they saw.

The above examples are not the only instances of less than full explanations to the reader. The Original Gospel of Mark is replete with enigmatic passages in addition to those above:

1. What does faith have to do with sins being forgiven (2:5)?

2. What does patching old clothes or putting wine into wineskins have to do with not fasting (2:21–22)?

3. Why does Jesus not want those outside who hear his parables to be forgiven (4:12)?

4. What was hidden and is now coming to light (4:22–23)?

5. How can someone who has nothing have something taken away from him (4:25)?

6. Why does Mark not tell the reader the name of Jesus's hometown (6:1)?

7. What does Jesus mean by "leaven of the Pharisees" and "the leaven of Herod" (8:21)?

8. How can one cast out an unclean spirit by prayer (9:29)?

9. What does "salted with fire" mean (9:49)?

10. What does "salt become unsalty" mean (9:50)?

11. What does "have salt in yourselves" mean (9:50)?

12. Why did Jesus stop a man from carrying a pitcher in the temple (11:16)?

13. What is the name of the woman who will be remembered (14:9)?

14. What is it that was written about the fate of the Son of Man (14:21)?

15. Who is the young man who fled away naked from Jesus's arrest (14:50–51)?

16. Who are Rufus and Alexander (15:21)?

17. Why did Joseph of Arimathea vote to have Jesus crucified (14:55, 64, 15:43)?

18. Who is the young man in Jesus's tomb (16:5)?

The writings that engender these questions are not from the same hand that presented the following to the reader: The words in *italics* are the redundant, unusual, unMarkan phrases:

1. 6:14 And king Herod heard of him *for his name had become known*. And he said, "John the Baptizer is risen from the dead, *and this is why these powers work in him*."

2. 6:25 And she came in immediately *with haste* to the king, and asked, saying, "I wish that you *at once* give me on a platter the head of John the Baptizer." 6:26 And the king was exceedingly sorry. *Because of his oaths and of those that reclined at dinner with him, he could not refuse her.*

3. 6:28 And brought his head on a platter, *and gave it to the girl; and the girl gave it to her mother.*

4. 6:38 And he says to them, "How many loaves do you have? *Go see.*" *And when they found out* they say, "Five, and two fish."

5. 6:39 And he instructed them to sit down in groups upon *the green grass*. 6:40 And they sat down *in groups, by hundreds, and by fifties*.

135

6. 6:49 and seeing him walking on the sea, they thought that it was a ghost, and cried out; 6:50 *for they all saw him, and were troubled.* But immediately *he spoke to them*, and says to them, "Take heart. *It is I*; do not be afraid."

7. 6:53 And crossing over, they came to *the land in* Gennesaret, *and anchored.*

8. 6:56 And wherever he entered, into villages, *or into cities, or into fields*, they laid the sick in the marketplaces, and begged him that they might touch *only the fringe of* his clothing. And those who touched him were healed.

9. 7:24 And rising from there, and went away into the region of Tyre and Sidon. And he entered into a house, and did not want it to be known; *and he was not able to hide.*

10. 7:25 But immediately a woman *having heard of him*, whose young daughter had an unclean spirit, came and fell down at his feet. 7:26 Now the woman was a *Greek, a Syro-Phoenician by descent.* And she begged him that he would cast the demon out of her daughter.

11. 7:29 And he said to her, "*Because of what you said*, go; the demon is gone out of your daughter." 7:30 And she went away to her home, *and found the child lying on the bed, and the demon was gone.*

12. 7:33 And he took him aside from the crowd *privately*, and put his fingers into his ears, and he spat, and touched his tongue; 7:34 and *looking up to heaven, he sighed*, and says to him, "Ephphasa," *that is*, "Be opened."

13. 7:36 And he instructed them that they should tell no one, *but the more he instructed them, the more greatly they proclaimed it.* 7:37 And they were exceedingly astonished, saying, "*He has done all things well. And he makes the deaf to hear, and the mute to speak.*"

14. 8:1 *In those days* there was again a large crowd, *and they had nothing to eat.* Summoning his disciples, he says to them,

15. 8:2 *I have pity on the crowd, because they have been with me now three days, and have nothing to eat. 8:3 And if I send them away to their homes without food, they will become weak on the way; and some of them have come from far away.*"

16. 8:4 And his disciples answered him, "Where can *someone feed all these bread in this desolate place?*"

17. 8:14 *And they forgot to take bread; and they only had one loaf in the boat with them.*

It is interesting that all seventeen of these examples are located in the first half of Canonical Mark, before "Peter's Confession at Caesarea Philippi" (8:27–9:1). The redactor was deliberately padding the first half of Mark's Gospel to make Peter's confession the center of the Gospel. Chapter 17 reveals the motivation for this.

One can see in these seventeen unMarkan examples above that the redactor is wordier than Mark and given to over-explaining situations, especially the motivation of characters. In Original Mark the motivation of Jesus is never given. He is said to get angry, frustrated, and indignant. He loves the rich man, he has compassion for the leper and the crowd, but he is a man of action and few words. The only pericope in Original Mark in which a character's motivation is specifically described to the reader is "Healing the Woman with Blood Flow."

After the interpolated passages of Canonical Mark were identified, they were analyzed in order to attempt to confirm that these passages were indeed unMarkan. During the process of this analysis, it became evident that the suspected interpolated passages were similar to the manner in which the author of The Gospel of Luke edited Mark's Gospel in creating his Gospel. Luke is given to explaining ambiguities found in Mark, adding detail for color, and explaining motivation. This penchant of Luke to add colorful detail is one of the reasons his parables (The Good Samaritan, The Prodigal Son, The Lost Coin, etc.) are the most memorable of all the evangelists. Therefore, Luke was analyzed with respect to the passages wherein Luke had edited Mark by adding detail, showing character motivation and explaining Mark's ambiguities.

Edits Of Mark In The Gospel Of Luke

An analysis of Luke's edits to Mark as found in The Gospel of Luke demonstrates that the author of Luke has the same style of edits of Mark as the redactor has in creating Canonical Mark from Original Mark. In this analysis sixty-nine passages in the Gospel of Luke were found, listed in Appendix 5, wherein Luke has edited Mark by adding detail, showing character motivation, or clearing up ambiguities. There are some nine or ten additional instances, but they appear to be passages wherein Luke is merely copying Matthew's editing of Mark. Those are not included.

Below are some examples comparing Mark's original language and Luke's version of it found in The Gospel of Luke along with commentary describing the nature of Luke's editing of Mark's Gospel.

> Mark 1:26 And having thrown the man into convulsions the unclean spirit shouted with a loud voice and came out of him.

> Luke 4:35 And when the demon had thrown him down in the midst, he came out of him, having done no harm.

For some reason Luke feels like he needs to tell the reader that the convulsions of the unclean spirit did not harm the man who had been possessed. This is certainly unnecessary detail. It may be that Luke is following the principle known to good story tellers that the addition of detail gives a story more credibility and makes it more believable. For example, where Mark says that Jesus healed a man with a withered hand, Luke specifies that it was his right hand. Also Mark says that at Jesus's arrest the servant of the high priest had his ear cut off, but Luke says it was his right ear.

Mark 2:3 And they come bringing him a paralytic being carried by four. 2:4 And not being able to come near to him because of the crowd, they removed the roof where he was: and after they had opened it up, they let down the pallet that the paralytic lay on.

Luke 5.18 And behold, men were bringing on a bed a man who was paralyzed, and they sought to bring him in and lay him before Jesus; 5.19 but finding no way to bring him in, because of the crowd, they went up on the roof and let him down with his bed through the tiles into the midst before Jesus.

In his "Healing the Paralytic" Luke tells the reader that the paralytic's friends want to lay him before Jesus. Of course they did. Mark led the reader to that conclusion by showing all the trouble they encounter in order to get the paralytic into Jesus's presence. Then, after expressing their motivation, Luke adds to the detail by telling the reader that the bed went through the tiles to get to Jesus. Luke beats the reader over the head with the desperation of the paralytic and his friends. That is not Mark's style, but it is similar to the redactor's style.

Interestingly, in his version of "Healing the Paralytic" Luke has the paralyzed man on a bed (klinēs) instead of a pallet (krabatton) as Mark does. Luke probably realized that this story was based on 2 Kgs 1:12–16 and that Ahaziah was laid up in a bed.

Mark 2:14 And passing by he saw Levi the son of Alphaeus sitting at the tax collector's booth,

Luke 5.27 After this he went out, and saw a tax collector, named Levi, sitting at the tax office;

It was mentioned that Mark's redactor told the reader three times that the "First Feeding the Multitude" was in the desert, twice in "Second Feeding the Multitude" that the crowd had nothing to eat, and four times that the disciples forgot bread on their boat trip to Bethsaida. Here, in Luke's edit of one of Mark's shorter pericopae, Luke tells his readers twice that Levi was a tax collector. Mark did not feel that it was necessary.

Mark 2:23 . . . and his disciples began to pluck the ears as they went

Luke 6:1 . . . his disciples plucked and ate some heads of grain, rubbing them in their hands.

Mark says that the disciples plucked the ears of grain. Luke adds that they ate them and the colorful detail that they rubbed the heads of the grain in their hands to get the kernels off the heads. Colorful indeed, but it is not Mark's style of minimal narrative. This is similar to the colorful detail of telling the reader that in "First Feeding

Of The Multitude" that the crowd sat on the green grass, and that they sat down in groups by fifties and hundreds.

> Mark 3:6 And the Pharisees went out and immediately consulted with the Herodians against him, how they might destroy him.

> Luke 6.11 But they were filled with fury and discussed with one another what they might do to Jesus.

Here is another instance of Luke adding character motivation to Mark's story. Mark thought it was sufficient to tell the readers that the Pharisees and Herodians discussed killing Jesus. Luke adds that they were filled with fury. In the first half of "Second Feeding the Multitude" in Canonical Mark, the redactor tells the reader Jesus's motivation for performing the miracle. Describing Jesus's motivation is not a characteristic of Original Mark.

> Mark 4:25 For he that has, to him will be given: and he that has not, from him will be taken away even that which he has.

> Luke 8.18 Take heed then how you hear; for to him who has will more be given, and from him who has not, even what he thinks that he has will be taken away.

Luke saw the non sequitur in Mark 4:25 that says those who have nothing will lose what they have. Perhaps Luke did not understand or felt his readers would not understand that Jesus was parabolically saying that those who have no faith will lose their lives, but in any case he felt the need to explain that those who have nothing will lose what they think they have. Mark wrote a parable and if the reader understood it, he understood it. If he did not understand it, he did not understand it.

> Mark 4:37 And there arises a large windstorm, and the waves washed into the boat, so that the boat was already filling.

> Luke 8.23 And as they sailed he fell asleep. And a storm of wind came down on the lake, and they were filling with water, and were in danger.

Mark tells the reader that the boat was filling with water. Luke feels the need to add that they were in danger. The desperate situation is communicated by Mark in the disciples' impertinent question to their teacher. Luke guilds the lily like the redactor did when he told the reader that Herod could not refuse the request of Herodias' daughter to kill John the Baptizer because his guests had heard him promise her she could have what ever she wanted.

> Mark 5:27 Having heard things about Jesus, she came in the crowd behind and touched his robe. 5:28 For she said, "If I just touch his robe, I will be cured."

5:29 And immediately the flow of blood was dried up; and she realized in her body that her affliction was healed.

Luke 8.43 And a woman who had had a flow of blood for twelve years and could not be healed by any one, 8.44 came up behind him, and touched the fringe of his garment; and immediately her flow of blood ceased.

This is the smoking gun evidence of Luke being the redactor. Luke edits Mark's "Healing the Woman with Blood Flow" (5:21–34) by adding a detail that she touched the fringe (kraspedou) of Jesus's garment. In the redactor's interpolated pericope of "Healing in the Market Place," the redactor wrote that the sick begged Jesus that they might touch the fringe (kraspedou) of Jesus's garment (6:56). That is the only occurrence of that word in Canonical Mark. It is not listed as one of Koester's peculiarities in Mark's Bethsaida Section,[1] that led him to postulate that the entire section had been interpolated, but it qualified.

Mark 5:33 But the woman fearing and trembling, seeing what had been done to her, came and fell down in front of him, and told him the truth. 5:34 And he said to her, "Daughter, your faith has cured you. Go in peace, and be free of your affliction."

Luke 8.47 And when the woman saw that she was not hidden, she came trembling, and falling down before him declared in the presence of all the people why she had touched him, and how she had been immediately healed. 8.48 And he said to her, "Daughter, your faith has made you well; go in peace."

Continuing on with "Healing the Woman with Blood Flow," Luke felt it necessary to explain to the reader that the woman could not hide from Jesus's accusing eyes and that she declared to all present her motivation and the result. Mark only writes that "she told him the truth." Luke could not help himself from adding colorful detail to his stories, just like Mark's redactor. The redactor was clever enough to copy Mark's "and immediately" (kai euthys). He was clever enough to copy Markan phrases into his interpolations. He was clever enough to use OT stories as the basis for some of his interpolations. But he could not restrain his story-telling talent for adding realistic detail to his interpolations. No doubt he was proud of himself for improving the quality of Mark's writing.

Mark 10:47 And hearing that it is Jesus the Nazarene, he began to shout out, and to say, "Jesus, son of David, have mercy on me."

Luke 18.36 And hearing a multitude going by, he inquired what this meant. 18.37 They told him, "Jesus of Nazareth is passing by." 18.38 And he cried, "Jesus, Son of David, have mercy on me!"

1. Koester, *Ancient Christian Gospels*, 285.

One can sympathize with Luke as he was copying Mark's "Healing Blind Bartimaeus" (10:46b–52) into his Gospel wondering how a blind man could know Jesus the Nazarene and his entourage were passing by. Perhaps Luke's logical mind was bothered by a blind man somehow knowing who is passing by, in any case Luke added a few words to Mark's version to say that the blind man inquired of a passerby as to what was going on, putting Luke's sensibilities to rest, but giving exegetes a clue to who might have interpolated "John the Baptizer is risen from the dead and this is why these powers work in him" into "Killing John The Baptizer" and "they forgot to take bread and they only had one loaf in the boat with them" into "Leaven Of The Pharisees." In addition, Luke changes Mark's "Nazarēnos" to "Nazōraios" in his version of "Healing Blind Bartimaeus." This is the same version of "Nazarene" that Matthew uses in his Gospel at 2:23.

> Mark 14:54 And Peter had followed him at a distance up to inside the court of the high priest. And he was sitting with the servants, and warming himself at the fire.

> Luke 22:54 . . . Peter followed at a distance; 22.55 and when they had kindled a fire in the middle of the courtyard and sat down together, Peter sat among them.

Apparently Luke was bothered by a fire appearing out of nowhere in Mark's version of Peter's denials; therefore, he adds the colorful detail of having "them" kindle a fire to sit around while Peter denies to the assembled that he knows Jesus. Luke was a storyteller par excellence. He must have shuttered at Mark's sparse style. Mark designed his Gospel to get the reader and hearer involved in the story by stimulating their imaginations to add the detail themselves. Luke, on the other hand, designed his Gospel to get the reader and hearer involved by imparting the colorful detail, making the story more real and worthy of belief. Luke's problem was that when he ventured to redact Mark's Gospel to hide the Adoptionist Christology, he could not bring himself to faithfully copy Mark's style.

Luke's Failure To Copy The Redactor

There is a curious aspect to Luke's Gospel. While Luke included the vast majority of Canonical Mark in his Gospel he omitted a large continuous portion some times called "The Great Omission" or "The Bethsaida Section." In Canonical Mark it runs from 6:45—8:26, from the end of "First Feeding the Multitude" to "Peter's Confession at Caesarea Philippi." It is called the Bethsaida Section because at the beginning of the section Jesus tells his disciples to take a boat to Bethsaida while he goes to pray, and although they actually go to Gennasaret and Dalmanutha in the interim, they finally end up in Bethsaida just before Peter's Confession.

I mentioned previously that Koester theorizes that Luke's copy of Mark did not contain the Bethsaida Section and that it was interpolated later into Mark. Matthew copied most of the Bethsaida Section into his Gospel. Actually, it is not strictly true that none of the Bethsaida Section finds its way into Luke. In Luke's Gospel Jesus warns his disciples to beware the leaven of the Pharisees although the full pericope (Mark 8:13–21) with his disciples forgetting to take bread in the boat is missing. Also according to Luke, Jesus tells "the crowd" instead of the Pharisees that no sign will be given, after Luke splits up Mark's pericope (Mark 8:10–12). Matthew and Luke both add that the sign of Jonah will be given. In addition, Luke does mention eating without washing and that Pharisees wash their dishes and cups. This is a small portion of Mark's "Controversy on Tradition" (Mark 7:1–15). Therefore, it appears that Luke's copy of Mark did have the Bethsaida Section whether or not Luke has been correctly identified as the redactor of Mark.

A redactor interpolated 6:38–56, and 7:24–8:4 into Original Mark and moved 7:1–23 from its original location just before the "Healing of Blind Bartimaeus" (10:46b–54) to its location in the middle of the interpolation. Only seven verses, 6:38–44, of that theorized interpolation find their way into Luke's Gospel. In addition, the redactor greatly expanded "Killing John the Baptizer" (6:14–29), and only four verses out of the fifteen-verse pericope are found in Luke. Further, the redactor added two verses to "Leaven of the Pharisees" (8:13–21) and only nine words out of the entire pericope are in Luke's Gospel. It looks like Luke was consciously avoiding including the interpolations into his Gospel. Can this be merely coincidence?

If Luke is not the redactor of Mark, why would he have failed to copy those pericopae that appear to be total interpolations, substantial interpolations and the two pericopae that were moved into the interpolated group? To be sure, there are several other pericopae found in Original Mark that Luke also failed to use in his Gospel. "Calling the First Disciples" (1:14–20) has been so heavily edited by Luke that it is almost unrecognizable, except for a few phrases. Likewise only a few phases of "The Withered Fig Tree" (11:20–25) and "Anointing with Oil in Bethany" (14:3–9) show up in Luke. "Healing the Blind Man of Bethsaida" (8:22–26), "Request of James and John" (10:35–41) and "Cursing the Fig Tree" (11:13–14) are completely missing from Luke.

In writing his Gospel, Luke edited Mark to eliminate Jesus's human emotions and much of the dullness of the disciples. So it is not surprising that Luke eliminated the cursing of the fig tree by Jesus and also eliminated James and John asking Jesus to let them sit at his right and left hand. One can also see that Luke may have felt that healing one blind man (Bartimaeus) was sufficient to fulfill Isaiah's prophecies (Isa 29:18, 35:5), so that "Healing the Blind Man of Bethsaida" could be ignored. But that does not answer why Luke failed to include the interpolated pericopae and those with substantial interpolations in them in his Gospel.

Luke redacted Mark to obscure Mark's Adoptionism and to at least partially re-habilitate Jesus's disciples. He later decided to do a complete rewrite of the gospel story, eliminating completely any Adoptionism, human emotions of Jesus, and completely rehabilitating the disciples, much like Matthew had done. However, in Matthew's rewrite of Mark's Gospel, Matthew had made it too Jewish, reinstating Jewish law that Mark's Jesus had repealed. Luke's Gospel is much less Jewish than Matthew's Gospel. In addition, Luke's Gospel is more revolutionary. Meaning that the poor and downtrodden are idealized in Luke, while the rich and powerful are denigrated. The heroes in the parables of Matthew's Jesus are kings and rich people, while the heroes in the parables of Luke's Jesus are the poor and afflicted.

Luke decided that Matthew's rewrite, while it eliminated Mark's Adoptionism, eliminated the human emotions of Jesus and rehabilitated his disciples, was basically written to convince Jews to become Christians and was not appropriate for the vast gentile world outside of Palestine. Luke did not completely reject Matthew because it had a plethora of good teaching in it. In creating his own Gospel Luke had to decide whether to use the portions of Mark that he had interpolated or leave them out of his Gospel. Perhaps he felt that his writings were already preserved as part of Mark and he did not need to preserve them again, or perhaps he thought that if he included them in his Gospel others would see that the interpolated passages were much like his writing style and not as much like Mark's style, exposing his redaction of Mark. Or maybe it just did not feel right to copy one's own redactions.

In any case it is a very interesting phenomenon that little of the interpolated text into Mark that was identified by using chiastic structures, triplets, and style differences found its way into Luke's Gospel. This cannot be a coincidence. It must have been a conscious decision by the author of Luke's Gospel.

There are two exceptions. The major exception is that Luke included in his Gospel "First Feeding Of The Multitude" from Canonical Mark, of which only the first half is original, the second half having been interpolated by the redactor. It would have been impossible for Luke to have failed to include both miracle feedings. First, there is the symbolism of Jesus feeding the multitude as a symbol of Christianity spiritually feeding the world. The metaphor is too good to pass up. All three Synoptic gospels say that the crowd was filled or satisfied (echortasthēsan). Second, both Canonical Mark and Matthew had two feedings, Luke surely needed at least one. So what was Luke to do, since he had redacted both feedings? It appears to me that what he did was to use Matthew as his template and edited that a bit.

There are a number of words and phrases in the "First Feeding The Multitude" found in both Matthew's Gospel and Luke's Gospel that are not found in Mark:

1. "Followed him" – Luke 9:11, Matt 14:13

2. Jesus healed the sick – Luke 9:11, Matt 14:14. These are not worded exactly the same in Greek, but the concept of healing is not found in this pericope of Mark at all.

3. "Dismiss the multitudes" – Luke 9:12, Matt 14:15. Mark has "dismiss them."

4. Disciples saying the word "loaves" – Luke 9:13, Matt 14:17. In Mark Jesus asks his disciples how many loaves they have and they say "five."

5. The disciples give the loaves to "the multitudes" – Luke 9:16, Matt 14:19. Once again Mark has the disciples giving the loaves "to them."

6. "About" five thousand men – Luke 9:14, Matt 14:21. Mark says there were "five thousand men."

The overall pericope of Matthew is closer to the wording and meaning of Mark than Luke is to Mark. It appears to me that Luke is one generation further away from Mark than is Matthew. This leads me to the conclusion that Luke edited Matthew's version of the pericope rather than Mark's version.

There are only eight verses in Luke's version of the first feeding and yet there are six instances where he and Matthew have the same or similar wording not found at all in Mark. Therefore, the conclusion is that Luke used Matthew as his guide for creating his version of "First Feeding the Multitude" rather than Mark, thereby including a feeding in his Gospel but not using his redaction of Mark as a template.

The second minor exception is a small portion of "Killing John the Baptizer" (Mark 6:14–29). It was shown that 6:14–15, 18–26, and 28 were interpolated by the redactor. Luke's version is only three verses in his Gospel and he used portions of Canonical Mark (6:14, 15 and 20), shown in italics.

> Luke 9:7 *Now Herod* the tetrarch *heard* of all that was done: and he was *perplexed*, because that it was said by some, that *John was risen from the dead*; 9:8 and by some, that *Elijah* had appeared; and by *others*, that *one of* the ancient *prophets* was risen again. 9:9 And Herod said, John *I beheaded*: but who is this, about whom I hear such things? And he sought to see him.

Luke changes the story so that it is not Herod who thinks Jesus is John risen from the dead, but others think Jesus is the risen John. Luke must have felt it necessary to include the beheading of John in his Gospel, and he did it using a minimum of his interpolations into Mark. He added "ancient" (archaiōn) to prophets and moved "perplexed" (diēporei) from Herod being perplexed about John's preaching in Canonical Mark to Herod being perplexed as to why some would say Jesus was John risen from the dead. The redactor had called Herod "king" going along with Original Mark 6:27, but Matthew had more correctly called Herod "Tetrarch" and Luke copies that in his abbreviated pericope.

It appears that Luke felt he needed to include the killing of John the Baptizer in his Gospel, but he decided to minimally utilize the redacted version in Mark's Gospel, totally avoiding any of the interpolated portion concerning Herodias and her daughter.

The redactor added "Healing the Deaf Mute" (7:31–34) to Original Mark presumably because in addition to pushing "Peter's Confession at Caesarea Philippi" (8:27–9:1) closer to the center of the Gospel, he thought that since Mark's Jesus healed two blind men, he should heal two deaf persons. Luke added Jesus healing a mute (Luke 11:14–15) to his Gospel and passed up including "Healing the Deaf Mute" from Canonical Mark, it being one of the presumed interpolated pericopae. In addition, in Original Mark "Healing the Epileptic" (9:14–29) is the casting out of a deaf and mute unclean spirit, and Luke copied Matthew in changing that to healing an epileptic. As a side note: how did the deaf and mute spirit in Mark 9:25 hear Jesus's command to come out of the man's son? Maybe Matthew and Luke had the same question.

Matthew also did not copy "Healing the Deaf Mute" from Canonical Mark into his Gospel but he did include Jesus healing another deaf mute at Matt 9:32–34. Luke appears to have copied that healing (Luke 11:14–15), although editing it heavily.

Conclusion

There are so many stylistic parallels between the redactor of Mark and the author of Luke that they must be one and the same person. They both liked to tell their readers the motivation of the characters. They both liked to include colorful details in their descriptions of the action. They both liked to tell their reader important facts more than once, so that the reader would not miss them. Finally, they both eschewed ambiguity, wanting to make the story as clear as possible.

After redacting Mark to obscure the original Adoptionist outlook, apparently Luke was not satisfied. He wanted a Gospel that clearly pictured Jesus as being the Son of God from birth. Matthew's Gospel had a virgin birth story, a genealogy from David, and post resurrection appearances of Jesus, but it was designed for Jews. Luke wanted a non-Adoptionist gentile Gospel, and so he wrote one.

Appendix 5 is a table of sixty-eight passages found in Canonical Mark and their counterparts in The Gospel of Luke. Comparing those passages will give the reader a sense of how Luke adapted Mark to his Gospel and how he changed Mark's original text into his style of writing.

Part II

Style, Plot, Purpose, Sources, and Structure of the Original Gospel of Mark

12

Markan Structure Puzzles

THROUGHOUT HIS BOOK *LET The Reader Understand* Fowler refers to Markan puzzles. He is referring to puzzling and ambiguous text, such as 4:11–12 and 8:21. But there seem to be other puzzles, structural puzzles, that once appreciated lead the curious reader into a deeper message from the author of Mark. It seems like Mark included secret knowledge in his Gospel, and he wanted the curious, perceptive reader to solve imbedded puzzles to attain that secret knowledge. A redactor, unaware of the puzzles and the clues thereto, inadvertently destroyed the clues by using Markan phrases and words that Mark uses a particular number of times in order to pose the puzzle.

After reading Mark's Original Gospel several times even the casual reader will notice that a number of things happen in threes—three predictions of the Passion, three predictions of the Parousia, three favorite disciples, three denials by Peter, three women at Jesus's tomb. A more careful reader might also notice that throughout the Gospel actions happen in threes. Once that realization dawns then the reader might start noticing that important words, actions, and phrases occur in threes—"prophet," "in those days," Pharisees connected with Herod, entering synagogues. Next, one might be curious enough to count that "Satan" is found six times, but "gospel" and "Christ" are found seven and "beginning" and "son of God" are found four. However, it is curious that "beginning," "gospel," "Christ" and "son of God" are all found in 1:1. So if 1:1 is not counted as part of the text, there are six "gospels," six "Christs" three "beginnings" and three "son of Gods." The Markan pattern of threes is restored. But if he is inclined to go deeper, the curious reader will encounter vexing structural puzzles Mark included in his Gospel.

Mark 1:1 is not part of the text that contains triplets and sextets. That is, Mark apparently considers 1:1 the title or incipit and not part of the text. This conclusion was reached because there is a triplet of "beginning" (archē) found at 10:6, 13:8 and 13:19; there is a triplet of "Son of God" (huiou Theou) found at 3:11, 5:7 and 15:39; there is a sextet of "gospel" (euangeliou) found at 1:14, 1:15, 8:35, 10:29, 13:10 and 14:9; and finally there is a sextet of "Christ" (Christos) at 8:29, 9:41, 12:35, 13:21, 14:61 and 15:52. With regard to the sextet of "Christ," at 13:22 is found "false Christs," making it appear that there are seven "Christs," but "false Christs" is a different word in Greek (pseudochristoi) from Christ (Christos).

All of the words in the incipit, except Jesus, are found in either triplets or sextets, and the order is triplet, sextet, sextet, triplet, a chiasmus. For the record there are seventy-nine occurrences of the word "Jesus" in the text of the Original Gospel, not including the incipit, with the middle, fortieth occurrence at the turning point at 10:32. Interestingly, in Canonical Mark there are no occurrences of the word "Jesus" between 6:37 and 8:27, where all of the interpolated text by the redactor is found, except for the interpolations into "Killing John the Baptizer."

Scholars have argued that Mark is not Adoptionist because "Son of God" is found at 1:1.[1] Ehrman argues that it is Adoptionist and that "Son of God" was not in the Original Gospel. It will be shown below that it is definite that "Son of God" was in the original, but Ehrman is certainly correct that Mark's Original Gospel is Adoptionist. In any case, if one is adopted is he not still a son? Mark 1:1 does not say "Jesus Christ, the natural born Son of God." The argument that the occurrence of "Son of God" in the incipit negates Mark's Adoptionism is specious.

There are other sextets in addition to the incipit phrases: "Satan," Jesus entering a boat (two triplets), "Power" (two triplets), and "forgiveness of sins." Original Mark contains several larger structures wherein the word or phrase is used a number of times and the number is evenly divisible by three. There is one nonet wherein the word "three" is used nine times There are two dodekets: the word "twelve" is found twelve times (three quartets), and the word "demon" (diamonion) is found twelve times. There is one structure of fifteen using the word "way" or "path" or "journey" (hodos). Appendix 2 sets out the triplets and sextets discovered in the Original Gospel of Mark, showing chapter and verse of their location and how the middle element of each triplet differs from the other two elements.

Mark seems to be playing a game with the reader regarding numbers. Numbers he considers important (twice, three, four, seven and twelve) he used a particular number of times. It almost seems as if he is testing the reader to see if he notices the pattern.

A Number Of Numbers

Twice Two

"Twice" (dis) is found two times in Mark's Original Gospel (14:30, 14:72) as Jesus tells Peter he will deny knowing Jesus three times before the cock crows twice.

Three Times Three Threes

"Three" is used by Mark nine times, 9:5, 8:31, 9:31, 10:34, 14:5, 14:30, 14:58, 14:72, and 15:29. There are three triplets. There are three "after three days rise," at 8:31, 9:31

---

1. Ehrman, *Corruption of Scripture,* 85–88.

and 10:34. The first and third elements have the words "chief priests and scribes" before "after three days rise" and the middle element has "men" before "after three days rise." There are three buildings or constructions. Peter offering to make three tents and the false witnesses saying twice that Jesus said he would rebuild the temple in three days. In the first and third elements "construct" or "build" comes before "three" and in the middle element "build" comes after "three." The third triplet of threes combines "three" with another number. It is mentioned two times that Peter will deny knowing Jesus three times before the cock crows twice, and the expensive nard the unnamed woman poured over Jesus could be sold for three hundred denarii, combining three and a hundred (triakosioi). In the first and third elements there is a short dramatic sentence coming after the "three": "And they made noises against her," and "and breaking down he wept." In the middle element Peter vehemently protests Jesus's prophecy.

FOUR FOURS

The word "four" is found four times, at 2:3, 8:9, 8:20 and 13:27. These four are in an (A, B, B′, A′) structure. "Come bringing him . . . four," "four thousand," "four thousand," "he will send the angels . . . four."

SEVEN SEVENS

After concluding that the redactor changed Mark's "loaves" to "seven" at 8:20, we find that in the Original Gospel Mark used the word "seven" seven times paralleling four "fours" and twelve "twelves." The "sevens" are found at 8:5, 8:6, 8:8, 8:20, 12:20, 12:22, and 12:23. There seems to be two triplets (8:5 loaves . . . seven, 8:6 seven loaves, 8:20 loaves . . . seven) and (12:20 seven . . . wife, 12:22 seven . . . no heir, 12:23 seven . . . wife). The last element of the first triplet also forms a chiasm with the remaining "seven"—(8:8 seven . . . baskets (spyridas) . . . four thousand and 8:20 four thousand . . . baskets . . . seven), wherein the words "seven" "baskets" and "four thousand" are reversed.

TWELVE TWELVES

In Mark's Original Gospel "twelve" is found twelve times, and one might think Mark made four triplets, but instead he made three quartets. The twelve occurrences of the word "twelve" are as follows:

1. 3:14 And he appointed *twelve* to be apostles, that they might be with him, and that he might *send them out* to preach.

2. 5:25 And a woman, who had an issue of blood *twelve years*.

3. 5:42 And immediately the girl arose, and walked, for she was *twelve years* old.

4. 6:7 And he summons the *twelve*, and began to *send them out* two by two; and gave them power over the unclean spirits.

5. 4:10 And when he was alone, those that were around him *with the twelve* asked him about the parables.

6. 9:35 And sitting down, he summoned the *twelve* and he *says to them*.

7. 10:32 . . . And again he took aside the *twelve*, and began *to say to them* the things that were to happen to him.

8. 11:11 . . . since it was late, he went out to Bethany *with the twelve*.

9. 14:10 And *Judas Iscariot*, one of the *twelve*.

10. 14:17 And evening having arrived, he comes with the *twelve*. 14:18 And as they *reclined eating*.

11. 14:20 But he said to them, "It is one of the *twelve* who *dips with me in the bowl*.

12. 14:43 And immediately, while speaking of him, *Judas*, one of the *twelve*, comes . . .

The first quartet is: A. send out (apostellē), B years, B' years, A' send out. The second quartet is: A with the twelve (syn tois dōdeka), B tells them (legei autois), B' to tell them, A' with the twelve. The third quartet is: A Judas B eating B' dips in the bowl A' Judas. All three quartets are structured (A, B, B', A'). This is parallel to the structure of the four "fours" that is also (A, B, B', A')

There is a textual dispute with regard to 3:14–16. Some manuscripts have "twelve" in 3:14, some have it in 3:16 and some have it in both. It cannot be in both. That would mean one too many "twelves" in the Original Gospel and would destroy the structure. It is most likely that the Original Gospel had "twelve" at 3:14 because in that case "send them out" follows "twelve" making it parallel to 6:7. Also notice that to make the three (A, B, B', A') quartets, 4:10 must be located after 6:7 and before 9:35. This is additional evidence that the redactor moved "The Parable Discourse" (4:1–35) from after "The Transfiguration," "Coming Down the Mountain," "Healing the Epileptic," and "Answering the Diciples" (that originally followed 6:31) to before "Calming The Sea" (4:36–41).

NO FIVES

"Five" is not found in Mark's Original Gospel. However, in Canonical Mark there are four fives all in connection with the "First Feeding of the Multitude." Two of them are found in the feeding itself with five loaves and five thousand men and two are found in "Leaven Of The Pharisees" where Jesus reminds his disciples of dividing the five loaves among the five thousand. It would have been unusual for Mark to have used the number "five" four times and not five times, if he considered it an important number.

This is further evidence justifying the elimination of the second half of the first feeding miracle and the elimination of 8:19 from "Leaven Of The Pharisees."

The Puzzling Non-Triplets

Original Mark contains many triplets, several sextets, and longer structures evenly divisible by three. These structures are important phrases and actions such as "son of David," "Satan," entering Jerusalem, going to a synagogue, "demon," "twelve." and "way." But there is an odd happenstance. Some very important phrases and actions are found in the Original Gospel in a group not evenly divisible by three. There are five uses of the phrase "Jesus the Nazarene," eight uses of both "Moses" and "Elijah" and the odd trio of fourteen occurrences of "Son of Man," "kingdom of God" and Jesus performing miracles. These words, phrases, or events need one more occurrence to be evenly divisible by three. If it were random one would think that in at least one of the six instances listed above the number of elements would be one more than an amount evenly divisible by three. But instead all are one short of an amount evenly divisible by three. Plus all of these odd structures are extremely important to the author of Mark's Gospel. It appears that Mark has laid out puzzles for his readers – find the unwritten occurrence, learn the secret knowledge that only the most diligent readers will learn.

The Nazarene Triplet Plus Two

Mark uses the phrase "Jesus the Nazarene" five times and that assumes that "Jesus came from Nazareth of Galilee" found at 1:9 in Canonical Mark was originally "Jesus the Nazarene came from Galilee."

Not only does "Jesus the Nazarene" seem to be important because of its limited use, there appears to be a hidden message involved with the five uses of "Nazarene." Examining the five instances of "Jesus the Nazarene," one gets a summary of Jesus's ministry:

- 1:9 And it happened in those days, that Jesus the Nazarene came from Galilee, and was baptized by John in the Jordan.

- 1:24 (unclean spirit) saying, "What are we to you, Jesus, the Nazarene? Have you come to destroy us? I know who you are, the Holy One of God."

- 10:47 And hearing that it is Jesus the Nazarene, he (Blind Bartimaeus) began to shout out, and to say, "Jesus, son of David, have mercy on me." . . . 10:49 . . . And they call the blind man, saying to him, "Cheer up. Arise; he calls you."

- 14:67 and seeing Peter warming himself, she (the servant girl) looked at him, and says, "You also were with the Nazarene, Jesus." 14:68 But he denied, saying, "I neither know, nor understand what you are saying."

- 16:6 And he says to them, "Do not be astonished. You are looking for Jesus, the Nazarene, who was crucified. He is risen. He is not here.

These passages tell the reader: a. Jesus came and was baptized. b. Why did Jesus, the Holy one of God, come to Earth? c. Arise. He calls you d. Peter and the disciples do not understand Jesus's message e. He was crucified and is risen. Perhaps the author of The Gospel of Matthew noticed this summary of Jesus's ministry and edited "the Nazarene" out when writing his Gospel because he wanted to rehabilitate Peter and the disciples.

With all the triplets and sextets in Mark, one would expect there to be six occurrences of "Jesus the Nazarene." The sixth element is missing. It appears that Mark intended that the reader puzzle out the sixth element for himself. Where is the missing element of the sextet? Where one would not expect to look: the sixth element is in the incipit. The incipit does not call Jesus "the Nazarene," but "Jesus Christ"—the only place in the Gospel he is called "Jesus Christ." If this is correct, then it violates Mark's usual pattern of forming triplets and sextets without consideration of the content of the incipit. This instance is an exception because it is the solution to a Markan puzzle and there is a hidden message of Jesus's ministry associated with "Nazarene." The incipit is the only other place in the Gospel where Jesus has an epithet other than "Nazarene."

The sextet is not of "Jesus Nazarene" but "Jesus (epithet)," five times he is called "Nazarene" and once "Christ." This is additional proof that Mark's Original Gospel did not contain "from Nazareth," which would not be an epithet in this particular use, but mere information to the reader. Mark increased the difficulty of the puzzle by using "Nazarene" five times and by using the incipit as the solution to the structural puzzle. This is consistent with the incipit being something special and not part of the regular text.

What about Jesus's ministry in connection with the sixth element "Christ"? Mark has laid another puzzle for the reader. The first word of the Gospel is "archē" in Greek, meaning "beginning." But it has a double meaning. "Archē" also means "rule." The sixth element of the sextet describing Jesus's career is the prediction that Jesus will rule Earth when he comes as the Christ. However, there is a problem. This element logically should be located at the end of the Gospel, so that Christ's rule on his return follows "he is risen." Perhaps Mark intended for the incipit also to be an unwritten ending. Or perhaps with his enigmatic ending, he anticipated that as the reader finished reading the Gospel, he would say, huh?, and go back to the beginning and start reading again to see what he had missed. The first thing he would get to is the incipit.

Mark left another hint. The last three uses of "Nazarene" form a triplet: Jesus the Nazarene; the Nazarene Jesus; Jesus the Nazarene with the middle element being different from the first and third elements. This should entice the reader to look for similarities with the other two and see if there may be another triplet. There is a similarity with the first two uses of "Nazarene" being associated with the aorist (past) tense of the verb "to come" (ēlthen). Another use of "to come" would cement a triplet. However, there is no verb in the incipit. On the other hand, the reader has been told three times that "the Son of Man" will come with the clouds of heaven and this phrase is associated with "came to serve." Perhaps Mark intended that the reader supply the verb, the future tense of "to come," to complete a triplet of "Jesus Nazarene/Christ will come to rule." Jesus was "the Nazarene" before his crucifixion and rising. Afterwards he is "the Christ."

This possible solution to the puzzle seems very speculative. Such a strange literary construction should not be accepted unless there are other similar instances in the Original Gospel.

THE NINTH ELIJAH AND THE NINTH MOSES

Both Elijah and Moses are mentioned eight times in the Original Gospel. One mention of Elijah was eliminated from Canonical Mark found at 6:15 in the redaction to "Killing John the Baptizer," and the analysis found in this section proves that it was correct to do so. With Mark's penchant for triplets one would expect these prophets to be mentioned nine times. This appears to be another Markan puzzle.

Moses is found eight times in Mark's Original Gospel:

1. 1:44 "Moses commanded"

2. 9:4 "Elijah and Moses"

3. 9:5 "Moses and Elijah"

4. 10:3 "Moses command"

5. 10:4 "Moses permitted a man to write"

6. 7:10 "Moses said"

7. 12:19 "Moses wrote"

8. 12:26 "did you not read in the book of Moses"

There are two triplets a. commanded, command, said and b. write, wrote, read. Then there is a doublet of Moses and Elijah. Before finding the ninth "Moses" let us look at the Elijah sequence.

In Canonical Mark "Elijah" is found nine times, but one was eliminated at 6:15 as being an interpolation. The interpolation at 6:15 seems to be the redactor copying 8:28 from Original Mark in order to give a Markan feel to his interpolation into "Killing John the Baptizer." The following logic proves the assessment about 6:15 to be correct. Like Moses, Elijah is also found eight times in Mark's Original Gospel:

1. 9:4 Elijah and Moses

2. 9:5 Moses and Elijah

3. 9:11 "Elijah must come first"

4. 9:12 "Elijah indeed having come first"

5. 9:13 "Elijah has come"

6. 8:28 "John the Baptizer, and others, Elijah, but others, one of the prophets"

7. 15:35 "he calls Elijah"

8. 15:36 "see if Elijah comes and take him down."

There does not seem to be a discernible triplet with regard to Elijah. There is the triplet within "Coming Down the Mountain" (9:9–13) about Elijah coming but then there is another "Elijah comes" during the crucifixion. There is no set of triplets associated with Elijah in Mark's Original Gospel.

The clue to solving this puzzle is the realization that Mark has linked Elijah and John the Baptizer implying that John is the coming of Elijah as prophesied by Malachi. Mark did this at 1:6 by copying the LXX version of the description of Elijah at 2 Kgs 1:8 word for word. He also linked them at 9:13 implying that the killing of John was the killing of Elijah. This is one of the reasons Mark placed "The Transfiguration" almost immediately after "Killing John the Baptizer" in the Original Gospel. Mark also links John and Elijah at 8:28 as referenced above.

At 11:32 the narrator tells the reader, "Everyone truly held John to be a prophet." This is the ninth Elijah in the structure. The structure, then, is an uncharacteristic four "prophets," four "comings" and one "calls." The association of Elijah with Moses twice at 9:4–5, with other prophets at 8:28 and John being called a prophet at 11:32 constitute the four-prophet structure. There is a hint at 8:28 where John is named along with "other prophets." The three Elijah "comings" in "Coming Down the Mountain" and the one at "The Crucifixion" constitute the four-comings structure.

This also may seem a little far-fetched, but there is more. The ninth mention of Moses still needs a solution. The key here is Mark 9:7 in "The Transfiguration." At 9:7 Mark quotes Deut 18:15 where Moses says to the Israelites, "The Lord your God will raise up for you a prophet like me from among you, from your countrymen, you shall listen to him."[2]

At Mark 9:7 the voice in the cloud tells the three disciples that Jesus is his beloved son and that they should listen to him. The alert reader of Mark will know that Mark has quoted Deut 18:15 which indicates that Jesus is a prophet like Moses. But the ninth mention of Moses in Mark's Original Gospel comes at 6:4 where Jesus implies that he is a prophet. Note that at 6:4 Mark specifically uses "Jesus" rather than "he." This is not very remarkable in an of itself, but Mark made the specific choice to use "Jesus"

2. NASB.

instead of a pronoun. 6:4 "And Jesus said to them, 'A prophet is not without honor, except in his own hometown, and among his own family, and in his own house.'"

In Greek there are three words between "Jesus" and "prophet" (Iēsous hoti ouk estin prophētēs). This parallels 11:32 where the reader is told that John the Baptizer is a prophet and there are two Greek words between "John" and "prophet" (Iōannēs ontōs hoti prophētēs). These passages are the only passages in Mark where either Jesus or John is specifically said to be a prophet.

Therefore, the ninth mention of Moses is Jesus identifying himself as a prophet like Moses and the ninth mention of Elijah is the narrator telling the reader that everyone held John to be a prophet like Elijah. The reader who solves these puzzles will get the hidden message that Jesus is a prophet and John the Baptizer is a prophet.

THE RULE OF FIFTEEN

The three structures included this section each have fourteen elements, and it appears that Mark has constructed a puzzle challenging the reader to discover the fifteenth element. Fifteen is evenly divided by three, and the theory is that Mark would not have had three important phrases and events with only fourteen elements. The puzzles with fourteen elements concern: "Son of Man," "kingdom of God" and miracles. These are extremely important phrases and events in Mark's Original Gospel.

Everyone who has read the Gospel of Mark will agree that "Son of Man" and "kingdom of God" are important phrases in the Gospel. In addition, miracles performed by Jesus are important events in the Gospel. Seeing that so much in Mark's Original Gospel is done in threes: triplets, intercalations, the structure of the Gospel as will be seen in chapter 17, it seems that there should be fifteen of these important events and phrases.

Mark provided a clue that this theory is correct. This clue is revealed by one structure. There is one structure that contains fifteen elements, five separate triplets. This structure points to Mark's mindset of a satisfactory, completed structure. This structure with fifteen elements is one containing the Greek word "hodos." This means "way," "road," "journey," or "path." The five separate triplets are not easy to discern and they are not consecutive. The elements are found at 1:2, 1:3, 2:23, 6:8, 4:4, 4:15, 8:27, 9:33, 9:34, 10:17, 10:32, 10:46, 10:52, 11:8, and 12:14. The five triplets are documented in Appendix 2. It cannot be a coincidence that the only fifteen-element structure in the Gospel involves the word meaning "the way." Mark seems to have left a clue for those who were curious about the fourteen incidences of the theologically important phrases "Son of Man," and "kingdom of God" and the fourteen miracles performed by Jesus.

The Son of Man—Five Quartets Plus Two

Scholars have been struggling with Mark's use of the Danielic title "Son of Man" since the early days of Christianity.[3] What did Mark mean? Is Mark's Jesus referring to himself? Is he speaking about mankind in general? Most agree that the source of the phrase used by Mark's Jesus is Dan 7:13. The title "Son of Man" in connection with Jesus rarely occurs outside the Gospels. It is not found in any NT epistle. In other words, Mark did not get this title for Jesus from Paul. It was the genius of Mark that appropriated the title from Daniel. Mark, being the first written Gospel, is no doubt the source of the phrase for the other Gospels. The other Gospel writers, of course, were aware that the phrase came from Dan 7:13, but it works well as a literary device with Jesus using it to refer to himself as a man and perhaps also a divine being. Dan 7:13 says:

> 13 I kept looking in the night visions, And behold, with the clouds of heaven One like a Son of Man was coming, And He came up to the Ancient of Days And was presented before Him. 14 And to Him was given dominion, Glory and a kingdom, That all the peoples, nations and men of every language Might serve Him. His dominion is an everlasting dominion Which will not pass away; And His kingdom is one Which will not be destroyed.

Daniel says "one like a Son of Man." Is that a man? Is it a divine being? It is not clear. Notice also other phrases common to Mark: "shall not pass away," "with the clouds of heaven." It is no wonder that the other Gospel writers kept the phrase in their Gospels.

Debate has raged about whether the historical Jesus actually used the phrase about himself, or it was interpolated into the Gospels later.[4] It will be shown herein that it is a literary construct of Mark, and he used it to reinforce a major point. Certainly Mark got the concept of the Son of Man from Dan 7:13. Chapter 15 below provides evidence that Mark wrote his Gospel to promote the Christology of Paul. Part of Paul's Christology was that the Parousia was coming soon and that Christ would descend from heaven with the clouds to establish the kingdom of God on Earth.

> 1 Cor 7:29 I mean, brothers and sisters, the appointed time has grown short; from now on . . . 31 . . . For the present form of this world is passing away.

> 1 Thess 4:16 For the Lord himself shall descend from heaven, with a shout, with the voice of the archangel, and with the trump of God: and the dead in Christ shall rise first; 17 then we that are alive, that are left, shall together with

---

3. Tertullian, "*Against Marcion*," 4:10.

4. Burkett, *Son of Man*.

them be caught up in the clouds, to meet the Lord in the air: and so shall we ever be with the Lord.[5]

1 Cor 15:24 Then comes the end, when he shall deliver up the kingdom to God, even the Father; when he shall have abolished all rule and all authority and power. 25 For he must reign, till he has put all his enemies under his feet.[6] 26 The last enemy that shall be abolished is death.

Paul developed his Christology from what he interpreted as revelation from the OT. This is evident from his references above to Psalm 110:1 and Dan 7:13–14. There are hundreds of other OT references in his epistles. If Paul's Christ Jesus is to descend from heaven with the clouds to initiate the end of the present world and establish the kingdom of God, what better way for Mark to imply that to readers than to have Jesus identify himself as "the Son of Man," making immediate reference to Dan 7:13. In addition, when Mark's Jesus speaks of the kingdom of God, he is simultaneously making reference to Paul[7] and Daniel.

While Daniel uses the term "Son of Man," he does not use the exact phrase "kingdom of God," but it is clear that the kingdom that the one like a Son of Man is given dominion over is of God, whom he calls "Ancient of Days." Paul uses the term "kingdom of God" but does not use the term "Son of Man," but it is clear that he is referencing Dan 7 in his epistles.

As stated before Mark uses triplets and sextets to enhance plot connections and make theological points. The structure of his "Son of Man" phrases, like the "Jesus the Nazarene" phrases, is more complicated. There are fourteen instances of Jesus using the phrase "Son of Man." Fourteen is not divisible by three evenly. It was shown above that Mark seems to have structured a sextet using the incipit with "Jesus Christ/the Nazarene." He did the same with the "Son of Man" phrase. Both of these are references to Jesus himself. He refers to himself as "the Son of Man," while others refer to him as "Jesus the Nazarene," or "Teacher," or "Rabbi."

Here are the fourteen quotes (two indirect) of Jesus using the phrase "Son of Man" with reference to himself:

1. 2:10 Just so you know that the Son of Man has authority on Earth to forgive sins.

2. 2:28 The Sabbath was made for man, and not man for the Sabbath. So that the Son of Man is even lord of the Sabbath.

3. 9:9 And as they were coming down from the mountain, he instructed them that they should tell no one what things they had seen, until the Son of Man had risen from the dead. 9:10 And they pondered the words.

---

5. Dan 7:13–14.

6. Ps 110:1; Mark 12:36.

7. Rom 14:17; 1 Cor 4:20, 6:9, 15:50; Gal 5:21.

4. 9:12 And he said to them, "Elijah indeed coming first restores all things. And why it is written of the Son of Man, that he should suffer many things and be despised."

5. 8:31 And he began to teach them, that it is necessary that the Son of Man suffer many things, and be rejected by the elders, and the chief priests, and the scribes, and be killed, and after three days rise.

6. 8:38 For whoever might have been ashamed of me and of my words in this adulterous and sinful generation, the Son of Man also will be ashamed of him, when he comes in the glory of his Father with the holy angels.

7. 9:31 For teaching his disciples he said to them, "The Son of Man is delivered into the hands of men, and they will kill him; and when he is killed, after three days he will rise."

8. 10:33 "Look, we are going up to Jerusalem; and the Son of Man will be delivered to the chief priests and the scribes. And they will condemn him to death, and will deliver him to the gentiles. 10:34 And they will ridicule him, and will spit upon him, and will flog him, and will kill him; and after three days he will rise."

9. 10:42 And summoning them to him Jesus says to them, "You know that they who seem to rule over the gentiles lord it over them; and those great men exercise authority over them. . . . 45 For the Son of Man also did not come to be served, but to serve, and to give his life as a ransom for many."

10. 13:26 And then they will see the Son of Man coming in clouds with great power and glory.

11. 14:21a For the Son of Man goes as it has been written of him. But woe to the man by . . .

12. 14:21b whom the Son of Man is delivered! It would be better for that man if he had not been born.

13. 14:41 . . . The hour is at hand. Look, the Son of Man is delivered into the hands of sinners. 42 Wake up; let us be going. Look, he that delivers me is coming."

14. 14:62 And Jesus said, "I am. And you will see the Son of Man sitting at the right hand of Power, and coming with the clouds of heaven."

The first two times Jesus refers to himself as the "Son of Man" (2:12 and 2:28) are fundamentally different from the other twelve times he so refers to himself. It is worth noting that at 10:42, long after the nature of the "Son of Man" references has changed, Jesus refers back to those first two mentions of the "Son of Man." At 10:42 "lord" and "authority" are repeated from 2:12 and 2:28. They are also in the reverse order of how they are found at 2:12 and 2:28, demonstrating that the reference is typically Markan and intentional. After referring back to 2:12 and 2:28 at 10:45, Jesus instructs his disciples about why the Son of Man came.

Theodore Weeden theorized that there was a dichotomy and a paradox with respect to the "Son of Man" between the first half of Canonical Mark (chapters 1–8) and the last half (chapters 9–16).[8] The first half/second half demarcation is correct with respect to Canonical Mark since "The Transfiguration" and "Coming Down the Mountain" (9:9–13) are in the second half in Canonical Mark, but they are located in the first third of Original Mark. Nevertheless, Weeden correctly discerned that a fundamental change occurs when Jesus begins telling his disciples that the Son of Man will be killed. In Original Mark that change occurs at 9:9 soon after "The Return of the Twelve" (6:30–31). In Canonical Mark the fundamental change occurs at 8:31 during "Peter's Confession at Caesarea Philippi." "The Transfiguration" is a major plot point with Jesus discovering that in addition to Daniel's Son of Man, he is also Isaiah's Suffering Servant. The change in usage of "Son of Man" confirms that plot point.

In the text of the Gospel prior to "The Transfiguration" it would seem that Jesus as the Son of Man was invincible. He had authority to forgive sins and was lord of the Sabbath. He could calm the wind and the seas. Unclean spirits and demons know him and obey him. A chink in his armor does appear soon before "The Transfiguration" when he could not heal the people in his own hometown (6:1–6a). After "The Transfiguration" his disciples and the reader learn that the Son of Man will die. A fundamental change in the nature of the Son of Man has occurred at "The Transfiguration," just as Weeden discerned. Through no fault of his own, Weeden assumes it occurs at 8:31 because the redactor had moved "The Transfiguration" and three following pericopae to a location subsequent to "Peter's Confession at Caesarea Philippi."

The twelve occasions of "Son of Man" occurring after Jesus's transfiguration, form five intertwined quartets. And each quartet is two doublets. In those twelve occurrences of "Son of Man" the reader is told:

a. Four times that the Son of Man has been predicted (it is written, teach, teach, it is written).

b. Four times that the Son of Man will be delivered (delivered into the hands of men, delivered (no object), delivered (no object), delivered into the hands of sinners);

c. Four times that he will suffer (despised, rejected, killed, killed);

d. Four times that he will rise from the dead the difference being the tense of "to rise" (anistēnai) (aorist, aorist, future, future); and

e. Four times that he came or will come again (with angels, to serve, in clouds, with clouds).

These quartets are either (A, B, B', A') or (A, A', B, B'). It is interesting to note that if "The Transfiguration" and "Coming Down the Mountain" were originally in the text subsequent to "Peter's Confession at Caesarea Philippi" as found in Canonical Mark, then the four predictions of the Son of Man would be teach, it is written, teach, it is

---

8. Weeden, *Conflict*.

written; that is, (A, B, A', B') not the symmetry one would expect from Mark who loves the twinned center of a chiastic structure. This is additional evidence confirming the reconstruction of Mark's Original Gospel.

The last twelve "Son of Man" passages begin at The Transfiguration approximately thirty percent of the way in to the Gospel. These passages tell the reader four times that:

a. It is written that the Son of Man

b. Will be delivered to authorities,

c. Abused and killed,

d. Will rise from the dead, and

e. Come to Earth.

These are the five quartets, that is, these above five statements are each made four times in connection with the twelve times that Jesus refers to himself as the "Son of Man" after "The Transfiguration" in Mark's Original Gospel.

The above five quartets do not explain or utilize the first two times Jesus refers to himself as the "Son of Man" (2:12 and 2:28). Mark's Gospel never tells the reader what will happen on Earth after the Son of Man comes in the clouds. One reasonable solution might be that Mark created a puzzle in the Gospel text that disclosed to the curious, diligent reader that the Son of Man is lord, has authority, and will come in the clouds to Earth to rule—a triplet. In fact, Mark gives the reader a hint for this solution in the "Son of Man" phrase at 10:45 using the aorist (past tense) of "to come" (ēlthen) and prior to that at 10:42 referring to "lord" and "authority." In the past tense the Son of Man "came" to serve, to be a ransom for many, but in the future he will rule. The story will be complete when the Son of Man comes with the clouds to rule Earth.

There is another hint of this in the incipit. (Archē tou euangeliou Iēsou Christou huiou Theou.) "The beginning of the good news of Jesus Christ, Son of God." As discussed earlier "archē" not only means "beginning;" it also means "rule." "Monarch" is the rule of one (mono + archē). One of Mark's main points that he wants the reader to grasp from reading his Gospel is Paul's Christology that Christ is coming to Earth soon to establish the kingdom of God.

If "archē" in the incipit is determined to mean "rule" in conjunction with "Son of God" also found in the incipit, that combination is the triplet Mark wants the reader to discover. The Son of Man has authority (2:12); the Son of Man is lord (2:28); the Son of God will rule (1:1). Changing the order of the words of the incipit slightly, it would be, "The good news of the rule of Jesus Christ, Son of God." This is not a "Son of Man" triplet; it is a "Son" triplet. Like the Nazarene/Christ sextet was an epithet sextet. Mark has thrown the reader another curve. It cannot be a coincidence that the only place in Mark's Original Gospel one finds the word "archē" meaning "to rule" (archein) is at 10:42, which also contains "authority" and "lord" referring back to 2:12 and 2:28.

This confirms the proposed theory. Mark was making an intentional reference that Jesus Christ, as the Son of God, will rule. While Mark's Jesus the Nazarene is on Earth he is the Son of Man, a human. When he comes with the clouds, it will be as the Son of God. Like the Nazarene/Christ sextet, this triplet also has a better design if the incipit (1:1) comes after the women flee the tomb at 16:8. The discovery of this "Son" triplet also demonstrates that Bart Ehrman is incorrect when he opines that the Original Gospel did not have the words "Son of God" at 1:1.[9]

The Kingdom Of God—Three Triplets Plus Five

Like "Son of Man" the phrase "kingdom of God" is also found in the text of the Original Gospel fourteen times. These occurrences seem to be a series of triplets. There is a "kingdom of God" triplet in "The Parable Discourse" at 4:11, 4:26, and 4:30 that was previously analyzed. In this triplet the word "parable" occurs before the first element and after the last element.

There is a second triplet occurring at 9:47, 10:14, and 10:15. This triplet tells the reader how to lead his life in order to attain the kingdom of God. In "Teaching the Disciples, Millstone Award" 9:33–50 Mark's Jesus sermonizes that Christians should excommunicate immoral persons from their congregations, repeating Paul's lesson from 1 Cor 5:1–13. Mark 9:47 is the culmination of that sermon. Then at 10:14 and 10:15 Jesus says that one must be childlike to enter the kingdom of God. The triplet can be seen with "enter into the kingdom of God," "the kingdom of God belongs to . . . these" and "kingdom of God . . . enter into it." Once again the middle element is different by not containing "enter into" and the words "enter into" bracket the triplet.

The third triplet follows close on the heels of the second one with Jesus teaching that it is difficult for a rich person to enter the kingdom of God at 10:23, 10:24, and 10:25. The wording is "those who have riches enter the kingdom of God," "trust in riches to enter the kingdom of God," and "a rich man to enter the kingdom of God." The first and third elements involve *having* riches and the middle element *trusting* riches. In addition, in the Greek construction the "trust in riches" follows "kingdom of God" whereas the "having riches" and "rich man" come before "kingdom of God."

There is an incomplete "kingdom of God" sextet scattered through the Gospel at 1:15, 9:1, 12:34, 14:25 and 15:43. Naturally, the words surrounding the target phrase "kingdom of God" provide clues to the missing element of the sextet. Below the wording around "kingdom of God" is shown in italics. The following is those times the phrase "kingdom of God" is used and are not part of the three triplets analyzed above:

---

9. Ehrman, *Coruption of Scripture*, 87.

1:14 And after John was delivered up Jesus came into Galilee, *proclaiming the gospel of God*, 1:15 and saying, "*The time is complete*, and the kingdom of God is at hand: repent, and believe in the gospel."

9:1 And he said to them, "*Truthfully I say to you*, There are some standing here who *will in no way taste of death*, until they see the kingdom of God coming with power."

12:34 And seeing that he replied wisely, Jesus said to him, "*You are not far from the* kingdom of God." And after that *no one dared question him*.

14:25 *Truthfully I say to you*, I *will not drink of the fruit of the vine*, until that day when I drink it anew in the kingdom of God."

15:43 Joseph from Arimathea, a prominent Council member, *who also himself was expecting* the kingdom of God; arrived and he *boldly went in to Pilate, and petitioned for the body of Jesus.*

At the first time "kingdom of God" is used (1:14–15) Jesus proclaims the gospel and says, "*the time is complete*." That language is not used again in conjunction with a "kingdom of God" phrase. In the second occurrence Jesus says, "*truthfully I say to you*" and "*will no way taste of death*." This second occurrence (9:1) matches the fourth occurrence (14:25) where Jesus uses the same phrase, "*truthfully I say to you*" and then says that he "*will not drink of the fruit of the vine*." "*Taste of death*" and "*drink of the fruit*" are opposites especially since "taste" (geusōntai) also means "eat." The relationship is eat and drink. In the third occurrence (12:34) has Jesus tells a scribe that the scribe is "*not far from* the kingdom of God" and *no one dared question him after that*. In the fifth occurrence (15:43) Joseph of Arimathea is "*expecting (or waiting for) the kingdom of God*," and then *he boldy goes in to Pilate* to ask for Jesus's body. So the similar relationship with the kingdom of God (*not far, expecting*) is followed by an opposite of *no one dared to question* and *boldly going in to Pilate and asking*.

Similar language found in the second and fourth occurrences (*truthfully I say to you*) is followed by opposing concepts (*eat and drink*). The same pattern is found in the third and fifth occurrences with similar language (*not far, expecting*) being followed by opposing concepts (*no one dared question, boldly asking Pilate*). This pattern provides the clue on how to complete the sextet: find a passage where similar language to "*proclaiming the kingdom of God*" as occurs at 1:14 is followed by a concept opposite to "*the time is complete*" as occurs at 1:15. Such a discovery will satisfactorily complete the sextet. In addition, if we have correctly gauged the mind of the author of the Original Gospel of Mark, it should be located between 12:34 and 14:26. This is because the pattern we have discovered is (A, B, C, B', C'). If Mark actually did create this "kingdom of God" puzzle, we would expect the solution to be found between the

C occurrence at 12:34 and the B' occurrence at 14:26. That would satisfactorily make the pattern (A, B, C, A', B', C')—a Markan style sextet. It so happens that "The Olivet Discourse" (13:3–37) fits the bill exactly.

In "The Olivet Discourse" Jesus tells his disciples about the coming of the kingdom of God, but as noted earlier the phrase "kingdom of God" is not found in that discourse. It was also pointed out that there are triplets located in "The Olivet Discourse" of "kingdom," "kingdom," "king" and "God," "Lord," "Father." We are looking for two sets of text (similar to *proclaiming the gospel* and opposite of *time is complete*) in order to complete the sextet, and this text should be found near the "kindom" triplet and the "God" triplet. There is such text. Near the beginning of the discourse is found:

> 13:8 For nation will rise against nation, and *kingdom* against *kingdom*. There will be earthquakes in various places. There will be famines. These things are the beginning of birth pains. 13:9 But watch out for yourselves. They will deliver you up to councils; and in synagogues you will be flogged. And you will stand before governors and *kings* for my sake, as a witness to them. 13:10 And the *gospel must first be proclaimed* to all the nations.

The text of *proclaiming the gospel* is in the verse immediately following the completion of the "kingdom, kingdom, kings" triplet. Near the end of the discourse is found:

> 13:19 For those days will be an affliction such as there has never been since the beginning of the creation that *God* created until the present. And never will be. 13:20 And if the *Lord* had not shortened the days, no flesh would have been saved. But because of the elect, whom he chose, he shortened the days . . .
> 13:32 But *when that day or that hour comes no one knows*, not even the angels in heaven, nor the son, but the *Father*. 13:33 Take care, stay awake: for *you do not know when the time is.*

Just after the final element of the "kingdom" triplet there is the similar language of "the gospel must be proclaimed." And immediately after the "God, Lord, Father" triplet is completed we find in the text "you do not know when the time is," the opposite of "the time is complete." Mark uses the same word for time (kairos) in both places. All of the criteria set out for the sixth element of the "kingdom of God" sextet are satisfied.

Mark designed "The Olivet Discourse," the description of the coming of the kingdom of God, to be the sixth element of the sextet, with "kingdom" and "God" being triplets in the discourse. Mark may have also intended "lord of house" (kyrious tēs oikias) found at 13:35 to be a further hint to the solution of this puzzle.

As with the "Son of Man" structure, the "kingdom of God" structure has fourteen elements and is incomplete. The fifteenth element of the "Son of Man" structure is in the incipit where we find "Son of God," as was the sixth element of the "Jesus Nazarene" structure where we find "Jesus Christ." With the "kingdom of God" structure the fifteenth element is "The Olivet Discourse," a discription of the coming of the kingdom of God.

A Triplet, a Sextet And Three Nonets in Miracles

The previous sections explained why there were fourteen occurrences of "the Son of Man" and "kingdom of God" instead of a number that was divisible by three as expected. There is another set of fourteen in Original Mark. Those are miracles performed by Jesus. There are nineteen miracles in Canonical Mark. The analysis utilizing chiastic structures, triplets, and stylistic differences eliminates five miracles performed by Jesus: one miraculous feeding, "Walking On Water," "Healing in the Marketplace," "Healing the Syro-Phoenician Woman's Daughter," and "Healing the Deaf Mute." Those generalized healing sessions at 1:34 or 3:10 are not included in the miracles.

In the fourteen miracles Jesus performs in Original Mark there are five words or phrases that are found as either a triplet, a sextet, or importantly, a set of nine. Below are the fourteen miracles performed by Jesus in Original Mark. The repeated phrases have been counted for the benefit of the reader by placing the number in parentheses after each time it is found in the text. The repeated phrases are:

- *Silence/say nothing/no one should know* (phimoō, siōpaō)

- *Raised up/Arise* (egeirō)

- *Go to/home/ house/priest/on your way* (hupagō)

- *Faith* (pistis)

- *Taking by the hand* (krateō)

The fourteen miracles performed by Jesus in Original Mark with the repeated phrases counted and in *italics* are:

1. 1:25 And Jesus admonished him, saying, "*Be silent* (1) and come out of him."

2. 1:31 and he came and *took her by the hand* (1) and *raised her up*; (1) and the fever left her, and she served them.

3. 1:41 . . . he stretched forth his hand, and touched him, and says to him, "I will; be clean." . . . 1:44 And says to him, "*Say nothing to any one* (2) but *go show yourself to the priest.* (1)

4. 2:5 And seeing *their faith* (1) Jesus says . . . 2:9 Which is easier, to say to the paralytic, 'Your sins are forgiven.' or to say, '*Arise,* (2) and pick up your pallet, and walk? 2:11 I say to you, *Arise,* (3) pick up your pallet, and *go to your home.*" (2) 2:12 And he *arose,* (4) and immediately picked up the pallet, and went out in front of all of them.

5. 3:3 And he says to the man who had the withered hand, "*Arise.*" (5) 3:4 And he says to them, "Is it lawful to do good, or to do harm on the Sabbath? To save a life, or to kill?"

But they were *silent*. (3) 3:5 . . . he says to the man, "Stretch out your hand." And he stretched it out; and his hand was restored.

6. 4:39 And awakening and admonishing the wind, he said to the sea, "*Silence*, (4) *be still*." (5) And the wind ceased, and there was a great calm. 4:40 And he said to them, "Why are you afraid? Do *you not have faith* (2) yet?"

7. 5:8 For he said to him, "Come out, unclean spirit, out of the man." . . . 5:19 And he did not permit him, but says to him, "*Go to your house* (3) to your family . . ."

8. 5:29 And immediately the flow of blood was dried up; and she realized in her body that her affliction was healed . . . 5:34 And he said to her, "Daughter, *your faith* (3) has cured you. *Go in peace*, (4) and be free of your affliction."

9. 5:41 And *taking the child by the hand*, (2) he says to her, "Talitha cumi;" which is translated, "Little girl, I say to you, *arise*." (6) . . . 5:43 And he admonished them strongly that *no one should know this*. (6)

10. 9:25 . . . saying to him, "You mute and deaf spirit, I order you, come out of him, and do not enter him again." . . . 9:27 But Jesus *taking him by the hand* (3) *raised him up*; (7) and he arose.

11. 8:5 And he asked them, "How many loaves do you have?" And they said, "Seven." 8:6 And he instructs the multitude to sit down on the ground: and taking the seven loaves, and giving thanks, he broke, and gave them to his disciples, so that they might serve them; and they served them to the crowd.

12. 8:25 Then again he laid his hands upon his eyes; and he opened them, and was restored, and saw all clearly. 8:26 And he sent him home, saying, "Neither enter the village *nor tell anyone in the village*." (7)

13. 10:48 And many admonished him, that *he should be silent*, (8) but he shouted out all the more, . . . And they call the blind man, saying to him, "Cheer up. *Arise*; (8) he calls you." "10:51 And answering him Jesus said, "What do you want me to do for you?" But the blind man said to him, "Rabbi, that I might see." 10:52 And Jesus said to him, "Go on *your way*; (5) *your faith* (4) has cured you. And immediately he could see, and followed him on the road."

14. 11:20 And passing by the next morning, they saw the fig tree had been withered away from the roots. 11:21 And remembering Peter says to him, "Rabbi, look, the fig tree that you cursed is withered away." 11:22 And answering Jesus says to them, "*Have faith* (5) in God."

In counting the number of commands of silence, in "Calming the Sea" (4:36–41) Jesus uses two different words for silence. There is a textual controversy as to whether at Mark 8:26 Jesus tells the blind man not to tell anyone what has happened, "nor may tell it to anyone in the village" (mēde eipēs tini en tē kōmē). The analysis is that the command to the blind man to keep silent was written by Mark so that his Gospel would contain eight silence commands in the fourteen miracles.

Within the miracle stories there is a triplet of "taking by the hand" using the verb "krateō." Jesus takes the loaves of bread and the hand of the blind man, but those are different verbs. In taking the loaves Mark used the same verb as in the Last Supper, and in taking the hand of the blind man, Mark used a verb he never used in any other place in the Gospel, indicating this is not part of the structure.

The fourteen miracle stories also contain an incomplete sextet of "faith." The first half is found at 2:5, 4:40 and 5:34 with "their faith," (pistin autōn) "have faith" (echete pistin) and "your faith" (pistis sou). At 4:40 Jesus questions his disciples about whether they "do not have faith yet." The second half of the sextet is incomplete and is in reverse order from the first one. At 10:52 and 11:22 there is "your faith" (pistis sou) and "have faith" (eschete pistin) with the "have faith" phrase in a command by Jesus to his disciples, just as the other "have faith" phrase was said to his disciples. The pattern suggests that there should be a "their faith" phrase after 11:22, but there is no miracle performed by Jesus after 11:22. If the "faith" sextet were complete it would have a chiastic structure: (A) their faith, (B) have faith, (C) your faith, (C') your faith, (B') have faith, (A') their faith.

There are only eight instances of "silence," "raised up" and "go." These are three incomplete nonets, or sets of nine. With the expected Markan pattern there should be a fifteenth miracle containing the phrase "their faith" to complete the sextet, the ninth occurrence of "silence," to complete the nonet, the ninth occurrence of "raised up" to complete the nonet and, finally, the ninth occurrence of "go" to complete the nonet.

Perhaps it was a mistake to eliminate some of the other miracles. Perhaps one of the eliminated miracles is the fifteenth miracle and contains the missing phrases of "their faith," "silence," "raised up" and "go." None of the five miracles in Canonical Mark that have been removed contain all of them. Neither "First Feeding the Multitude," "Second Feeding the Multitude," "Healing in the Marketplace," nor "Walking on Water" has any of the phrases. "Healing the Deaf Mute" contains "tell no one," but none of the other three. Finally, "Healing the Syro-Phoenician Woman's Daughter" contains "go" but not as a transitive verb. In the other miracles Jesus tells the healed person to "go home," or "go to your house," or "go on your way," or "go in peace." In "Healing The Syro-Phoenician Woman's Daughter" there is just a command "go." None of the other phrases are found in this miracle. However, there is a fifteenth miracle with the ninth "risen," the ninth "go," and the ninth "say nothing." It is Jesus's resurrection, a miracle that Jesus does not perform and the reader is only told about after the fact.

> 16:6 And he says to them, "Do not be astonished. You are looking for Jesus, the Nazarene, who was crucified. He is *risen*. (9) He is not here. Look at the place where they laid him! 16:7 But *go, tell his disciples* (9) and Peter, he goes ahead of you into Galilee. . . . " 16:8 And going out they fled from the tomb

for trembling and astonishment had came over them: and *they told no one anything* (9) for they were afraid.

"Risen" (ēgerthē) used by the young man is the same verb as in the other five miracles. "Go" (hypagate) is the same verb as in the other miracles except that at 16:7 it is in the second person plural since there are three women. The women tell no one anything (oudeni ouden eipan) and when Jesus healed the leper he instructed him, "tell no one anything" (medeni meden eipes).

This points up the extreme irony of Jesus telling demons and healed persons to stay quiet, and then, at the crucial point of the Gospel the women do not tell anyone when the young man urges them to. In "Coming Down the Mountain" after "The Transfiguration" Jesus told Peter, James, and John not to tell anyone what they had seen until after he had risen from the dead. After he is risen is the time to tell. The further irony is that the leper told everyone about his cure even though Jesus told him to keep quiet. The leper telling everyone about his healing is the only time in Original Mark that the healed person disobeyed Jesus's command to be silent, a further irony.

Having the Original Gospel and being able to analyze what Mark intended to be read without the confusion engendered by interpolation and misplaced pericopae, puts a new spin on the "Messianic Secret." In the Original Gospel Mark's intention to have the women's silence be a tragic ironic counterpoint to Jesus's desire for silence about him becomes clearer. Perhaps that is all Mark intended the Messianic Secret to be—an ironic counterpoint to the women's unwanted silence.

But wait! While all of this word play is consistent with Jesus's resurrection being the fifteenth miracle in the Gospel, evenly divisible by three; and these phrases found in the miracles are nonets, also evenly divisible by three, one of the phrases is missing—faith. Mark left "faith" out of Jesus's resurrection. The women apparently did not have faith. They did not abandon Jesus as his disciples had. The disciples apparently fled to Galilee while the women stayed and watched the crucifixion and the burial, but their faith was lacking.

Mark wants the reader to supply the faith. Since there are three women, it is "their faith" that is lacking from the text, which, if included, would have been the sixth element of the sextet—"their faith," (2:5) "have faith," (4:40) "your faith," (5:29) "your faith," (10:52) "have faith," (11:20) "their faith" (16:_) The second half is a mirror image of the first half and chiastic, obviously Markan. Additionally, the first half of the structure occurs before the turning point (10:32) and the second half occurs after the turning point.

The most puzzling aspect to Mark's Gospel is the ending. The women run out of the tomb and tell no one anything "for they were afraid" (ephobounto gar). We saw in chapter 3 that this is the same phrase used to end a sentence at Gen 18:15 (LXX). Mark is directly referencing that sentence in Genesis. At Gen 18:14 God says to Abraham,

"Shall anything be impossible with the Lord?"[10] "All things are possible" is a triplet in Mark's Original Gospel located at 9:23, 10:27, 14:36. Gen 18:14 is also referred to by Paul when he tells the Romans the story of Abraham and Sarah. At Rom 4:19–21 Paul says:

> 19 And without being weakened in faith he considered his own body now as good as dead (being about a hundred years old), and the deadness of Sarah's womb; 20 yet, looking to the promise of God, he did not waver through unbelief, but waxed strong through faith, giving glory to God, 21 and being fully assured that what he (God) had promised, he (God) was able also to perform.

At Rom 4:21 Paul is reiterating that all things are possible with God from Gen 18:14. At Rom 4:19–20 Paul is explaining Abraham's faith. Here is the sixth "faith" to complete the sextet. Romans 3:19—5:20 contains Paul's doctrine of justification by faith in which he mentions Abraham seven times. Abraham is Paul's prime example of justification by faith because Abraham came before Moses and the law. With the last two enigmatic words of the Gospel Mark supplies the sixth faith by referring to Gen 18:15, Sarah's fear, and to Rom 4:19–21, Abraham's faith.

The final "their faith" is the faith that the women lacked. Like Sarah at Gen 18:15 the woman at Jesus's tomb failed to understand that with God all things are possible. God can make a hundred year old woman bear children and can raise a person from the dead. Sarah lacked faith but Abraham had faith. With the final "ephobounto gar" Mark points to Sarah's lack of faith and ascribes it to the three women. If the reader is familiar with Paul's Epistle to the Romans, he will understand that he needs to have faith like Abraham.

THE DOUBLET AND THE QUARTET—"IT IS WRITTEN" IN ISAIAH

An extremely difficult puzzle to solve is, where is Mark's third mention of Isaiah? Isaiah is mentioned twice in the Original Gospel and the phrases seem to be chiastic. The first line of the Gospel after the incipit at 1:2 is "as it is written in Isaiah the prophet." The second mention of Isaiah occurs just after Jesus and his entourage start the trek toward Jerusalem while they are in Jericho. At 7:6 Jesus says to the Pharisees, "rightly prophesied Isaiah about you hypocrites as it has been written." In 7:6 "written," "Isaiah," and "prophet" are in reverse order from 1:2. It is in the same in Greek. Most English translations of Mark place "Isaiah" before "prophesied" at 7:6, and their readers miss the chiasm.

Not only is there a missing third reference to "Isaiah," there is a fourth, extra instance of "as it is written" (kathōs gegraptai). Both mentions of Isaiah contain the phrase "as it is written." It is possible that they are connected. The first three times "as it is written" occurs in the Original Gospel form a triplet:

10. LXX.

1. 1:2 "As it is written in Isaiah the prophet"

2. 9:13 "But I say to you that Elijah has come, and they did to him what they wanted to, just as it is written of him."

3. 7:6 "Rightly prophesied Isaiah about you hypocrites. As it is written . . . "

Both 9:2–29 and 7:1–23 have been moved so that in Original Mark 9:13 occurs before 7:6. So the "as it is written" triplet is Isaiah, Elijah, Isaiah, with the middle element being different from the first and third as is typical in Mark. This is further proof that 9:13 is located before 7:6 in Original Mark.

Isaiah is mentioned in the first line of the Gospel and at 7:6 just after the turning point (10:32). With Mark's love of symmetry one might expect the third mention to be near the end of the Gospel. The fourth, extra "as it is written" concerns the Son of Man: 14:21 "For the Son of Man goes as it is written of him." Isaiah is associated with "as it is written" at 1:2 and 7:6. Mark used Isaiah as a source at least twenty times. Paul referenced Isaiah eighty-six times in his epistles. Perhaps we can find written in Isaiah a prophecy of what is to happen to the Son of Man. We can. Isaiah's "Song Of The Suffering Servant" (52:13–53:12) fills the bill.

Before getting to the Suffering Servant look at Isa 51:12:

> I, I am he who comforts you; who are you that you are afraid of man who dies, of the *Son of Man* who is made like grass.[11]

Isaiah 51:12 (LXX) uses the phrase "huiou anthrōpou" (Son of Man). Isaiah is not writing about Daniel's "one like a Son of Man," who is given dominion over Earth, but never-the-less, the only time the phrase "Son of Man" is used in Isaiah is within three hundred fifty words of the beginning of his "Song Of The Suffering Servant" (52:13–53:12), an interesting coincidence, if it is one.

Now let us look at Isaiah's Suffering Servant in detail:

> 52:15 so shall he startle many nations; kings shall shut their mouths because of him; for that which has not been told them they see, and that which they have not heard they understand.

Mark's Jesus chastised his disciples because even though they had eyes, they could not see and even though they had ears they could not understand.[12] In Isa 52:15 the Suffering Servant will make it so even those who have not been told will see and they will understand that which they have not heard.

> 53:3 He was despised and rejected by men; a man of sorrows, and acquainted with grief; and as one from whom men hide their faces he was despised, and we esteemed him not.

---

11. LXX.

12. Mark 8:18.

Jesus predicted at 9:12 that he would be despised and at 8:31 that he would be rejected.

> 53:5 But he was pierced for our transgressions; he was crushed for our iniquities; upon him was the chastisement that brought us peace, and with his wounds we are healed.

This translation of the Masoretic text says that the Suffering Servant was "pierced for our transgressions." The Septuagint uses "traumatizō" (wound). "Pierced for our transgressions" and "with his wounds we are healed" recalls Mark 10:45 wherein Jesus said that the Son of Man came to be a ransom for many.

> 53:6 All we like sheep have gone astray; we have turned—every one—to his own way; and the Lord has laid on him the iniquity of us all.

Isaiah 53:6 is paraphased by Jesus at Mark 14:27 by quoting Zech 13:7 about striking the shepherd and the sheep being scattered. This quotation comes six verses after Jesus says that the Son of Man goes as it is written of him apparently referencing Isaiah.

> 53:7 He was oppressed, and he was afflicted, yet he opened not his mouth; like a lamb that is led to the slaughter, and like a sheep that before its shearers is silent, so he opened not his mouth.

Jesus remains silent under the questioning of the high priest at Mark 14:61 and under the questioning of Pilate at Mark 15:5.

> 53:8 By oppression and judgment he was taken away; and as for his generation, who considered that he was cut off out of the land of the living, stricken for the transgression of my people?

This recalls Mark 10:45 again, Jesus saying that the Son of Man came to be a ransom for many.

> 53:9 And they made his grave with the wicked and with a rich man in his death, although he had done no violence, and there was no deceit in his mouth.

This seems to be the source of Mark's story of a rich man, Joseph from Arimathea, putting Jesus's body in Joseph's tomb.

> 53:11 Out of his anguish he shall see light; he shall find satisfaction through his knowledge. The righteous one, my servant, shall make many righteous, and he shall bear their iniquities. Therefore I will allot him a portion with the great, and he shall divide the spoil with the strong; because he poured out himself to death, and was numbered with the transgressors; yet he bore the sin of many, and made intercession for the transgressors.

The above set of verses of Isaiah seem to be the basis of Pauline Christology of the atonement. At 14:20 when Mark's Jesus says, "the Son of Man goes as it is written of him" Mark is making reference to Isaiah's Suffering Servant, without specifically naming Isaiah. So the extra "it is written" becomes the missing third time Isaiah is mentioned. Mark could easily have written "as prophesied by Isaiah" instead of "as it is written of him" but Mark apparently wanted the reader to puzzle it out for himself, as Fowler said.

One implication to the solution of this Markan puzzle is that Mark is not making a mistake at 1:2 in writing "as it is written in Isaiah the prophet" and then quoting Malachi. He was intentionally making a chiastic match with 7:6 and at the same time setting up his missing element of the Isaiah triplet puzzle. Mark intentionally limits the naming of OT prophets to Moses, Elijah and Isaiah (three, of course). This means that the Original Gospel could not mention Malachi and did not mention Daniel at 13:14 as some disputed manuscripts have. Daniel's Son of Man plays a large role in Mark's Original Gospel, but Daniel's name is not mentioned. If Mark had mentioned Daniel, he probably would have done so three times, or made another puzzle out of it.

Conclusion

Mark created many triplets in his Gospel, and Appendix 2 documents the ones found to this point. In addition to two "twices" nine "threes," four "fours," seven "sevens" and twelve "twelves," there are eight special structures, which at first glance appear to have missing/added pieces: the "Nazarene/Christ" sextet, the ninth Elijah, the ninth Moses, the fifteenth "Son of Man/son of God," the fifteenth "kingdom of God," the fifteenth miracle, the third Isaiah, and the extra "it is written." This may not be an exhaustive list of Mark's puzzles. One would not expect eight puzzles. There may be a ninth one that has not been identified.

13

Pericope-Level Chiasms with Parallel Centers

IT WAS NOTED EARLIER that some of Mark's pericope-level chiastic structures have parallel centers. The author uses these pericopae to signal the beginning or end of major divisions or sections in his Gospel. Not all parallel centered pericopae are created equal by Mark. Three of them (another triplet) have three parallel stiches each. All others have two parallel stiches. "The Crucifixion," (15:20b–39) has two separate parallel structures within that one pericope, the two-stich parallel center (GA–GB') structure wherein Jesus is taunted while on the cross, and the three-stich (CA–CC') structure wherein the soldiers' crucifying process matches Jesus's dying.

The following are the pericopae having parallel stiches:

1:2–3	"Messenger to Prepare the Way"
1:14–20	"Calling the First Four Disciples"—Three parallel stiches
2:1–12	"Healing the Paralytic"
2:23–28	"Plucking Grain on the Sabbath"
4:36–41	"Calming the Sea"
5:1–20	"Healing the Gerasene Demoniac"
6:34–37, 8:5–9	"Feeding the Multitude"
8:22–26	"Healing the Blind Man of Bethsaida"
10:17–31	"Entering the Kingdom of God"
10:35–41	"Request of James and John"
10:46a—7:15	"Controversy on Tradition"—Three parallel stiches
12:12b–17	"Rendering Unto Caesar"
14:53–72	"The Sanhedrin Trial, Peter's Denials"
15:20b–39	"The Crucifixion" —Parallel (C, C') Stich—Three parallel stiches

Three Parallel Stiches

Three of the parallel centered pericopae have three parallel stiches while all others have two. These must be the special of the special. The first one ends the prologue and begins Jesus's ministry as he calls his first four disciples. The last one is very unusual in that it is contained in "The Crucifixion," and the three stiches are not at the center of the pericope. Atypically the three-stich parallel structure is in the (CA–CC') stich, whereas (GA – GB') is the center parallel structure, with only two stiches.

Jesus dies at the end of the (CA–CC') stich. This momentous event must be the reason for the parallel structure:

CB' 15:37 And Jesus uttered a loud sound, and the spirit departed from him.
CC' 15:38 And the curtain of the temple was torn in two from the top to the bottom.

The three stich parallel structures that are found at 1:14–20, 10:46a—7:15, and 15:20b–39 mark Jesus's ministry. The middle element of this threesome is "Controversy on Tradition." This pericope was relocated from its position in Canonical Mark so that in Original Mark it is located between entering and leaving Jericho at 10:46. This is in a cluster of three pericopae with paralleled centers The cluster signals the turning point Mark constructed in his Original Gospel.

There is also a dichotomy within the "Controversy on Tradition" pericope. With the three-stiched parallel center, the first half (CA–CC) is about what Isaiah said, and the second half (CA'–CC') is about what Moses said. Jesus uses these prophets to excoriate the Pharisees, saying they have lost sight of God's will. Then the (B') hemistich of this pericope is Pauline with Jesus saying that nothing going into a man can defile him, it is what comes out. The Pauline lesson is explained more fully in the next pericope "Eating Does Not Defile" (7:16–23) where Jesus explains his saying to his disciples, and the narrator adds the comment that Jesus "made all foods clean," (katharizōn panta ta brōmata), a Pauline teaching reiterating Rom 14:20 "all things are clean" (panta men kathara).

The three parallel-stiched pericopae mark the beginning, middle and end of Jesus's ministry. Also they are doing double duty. In addition to showing the beginning, middle and end of Jesus's ministry, they are marking the end of the prologue, the turning point and the beginning of the epilogue.

The Physical Divisions Of Original Mark

The parallel centered pericopae are located at strategic places in the Gospel:

a. The first pericope, beginning of the prologue at 1:2–3,

b. The first pericope after the end of the prologue and the beginning of Jesus's ministry at 1:16–20,

c. There are two consecutive pericopae at 4:35—5:20 with parallel centers. This marks the end of Act I and beginning of Act II. Act I ends with the disciples asking, "Who is this then, that even the wind and the sea obey him?" This is a perfect dramatic ending for Act I.

d. There are three pericopae with parallel centers from 10:17—7:15. This is a signal that something important occurs here. It is the turning point of the Gospel as Jesus heads to Jerusalem and his destiny. As mentioned in the previous section "Controversy on Tradition" marks the midpoint of Jesus's ministry.

e. The last pericope of Act II, 14:53–72 "The Sanhedrin Trial, Peter's Denials " has a parallel center. Act II ends with Peter hearing the cock crow for the second time and breaking down. Another perfect ending for an act with dramatic effect.

f. "The Crucifixion" (15:20b–39) does double duty and contains two parallel constructions. The death of Jesus/end of his ministry is marked by the three parallel stiches of (CA–CC'). The further purpose of the parallel center (GA–GB') is to mark the last pericope before the beginning of the epilogue, just as the first pericope after the end of the prologue had a paralleled center.

g. "Healing The Paralytic" (2:1–12) and "Plucking Grain on The Sabbath" (2:23–28) are in a section near the middle of Act I. This is a four pericopae section on Pauline teaching. This section expounds on justification by faith, eating, fasting and the Sabbath based on Rom 3:19—5:20, Gal 2:11–15 and Rom 14:2–6. In "Healing The Paralytic" the paralyzed young man was told by Jesus that his sins were forgiven after Jesus saw the faith of him and his companions. This reiterates Rom 3:19—5:20 wherein Paul sets out his doctrine of justification by faith, in opposition to the justification by the law advocated by the Jerusalem apostles. At Mark 2:15–17 Jesus eats with "sinners" as Paul reports in Gal 2:11–15 that Peter refused to do in Antioch. At Mark 2:18–22 Jesus's disciples are criticized for not fasting, reminding the reader of Rom 14:3–4 where Paul writes, "Let not him who does not eat judge him who eats. Who are you to judge the servant of another?" "Plucking Grain on the Sabbath" is based on Rom 14:5–6:

> One man esteems one day above the others another esteems every day
> alike. Let each man be fully assured in his own mind. He that regards
> the day regards it to the Lord.

h. "Rendering Unto Caesar" (12:12b–17) marks another Pauline section. This section runs from 11:22 to 12:44, and "Rendering Unto Caesar" is at the center of this section. The section begins with Jesus referencing to 1 Cor 13:2 about having faith to move mountains and ends with "The Widow's Mite" (12:41–44) based on 2 Cor 9:7 where Paul says, "Let each man do as he sets his heart not out of regret or necessity for God loves a cheerful giver." The center of this section is from Rom 13:6–7:

6 For this cause you pay tribute also; for they are ministers of God's service, attending continually upon this very thing. 7 Render to all what they are due: tribute to whom tribute is due; custom to whom custom; fear to whom fear; honor to whom honor.

Paul and Mark use the same word "render" (apodote).

i. "Feeding the Multitude" (6:34–37, 8:5–9) is at the beginning of the large Pauline section that extends from "The Parable Discourse" to "The Olivet Discourse." "Feeding the Multitude" is a foreshadowing of "The Last Supper" (14:17–25) based upon 1 Cor 11:23–25. "Feeding the Multitude" is an allegorical spiritual feeding of the world by Christianity.

j. "Healing the Blind Man of Bethsaida" (8:22–26), "Request of James and John" (10:35–41), and "The Sanhedrin Trial, Peter's Denials " (14:53–72) mark Jesus's three predictions of the Passion and three predictions of the Parousia. The first two enclose all three predictions of the Passion and the first and third enclose all three predictions of the Parousia. The coming of the Parousia is a primary theme of Pauline theology and a primary theme of the Original Gospel.

Mark uses a literary technique to get his point across. He has Jesus make three predictions of his death on the cross and rising from the dead. In his Gospel story these predictions of Jesus come to fruition. This sets up the reader to believe that Jesus is a prophet (Deut 18:15) like Moses, and his prophecies will come true. Mark has Jesus make three predictions of the Parousia. Since Mark has written that the Passion predictions of Jesus came true, the reader should readily accept that the Parousia predictions will also come true.

Mark used a chiastic structure for every one of his seventy-eight pericopae. In fourteen of those pericopae he constructed fifteen parallel stitches to signal important points in the Original Gospel. These paralleled centered pericopae confirm the reconstruction.

14

The Plot and Drama of the Original Gospel of Mark

Plot Summary

WITH SEVERAL PERICOPAE ELIMINATED and others repositioned, the plot of Mark's Original Gospel becomes very different from Canonical Mark, Matthew and Luke.

In Original Mark "The Transfiguration" and "Coming Down the Mountain" (9:2–13) happen before "Peter's Confession at Caesarea Philippi" (8:27—9:1). This makes a difference in the plot and Christology. In Canonical Mark Jesus appears to know at least from baptism, and arguably his whole life, that he was the Christ/Atonement Suffering Servant. The reader learns this when Peter recognizes Jesus as the Christ. At that point Jesus immediately tells his disciples that he will be put to death and rise again. At this point in Canonical Mark he has not yet been transfigured. However, in Original Mark with "The Transfiguration" and "Coming Down the Mountain" happening before Peter's confession, the text suggests that Jesus only learned he was the Isaiac Suffering Servant, the atonement sacrifice for mankind, from Moses and Elijah. Why else would Mark tell the reader that Jesus was talking to Moses and Elijah? Mark rarely gives useless information. The astute reader can infer what they told Jesus by what Mark tells him immediately after "The Transfiguration." As Jesus, Peter, James and John are coming down the mountain, Jesus instructs the three not to tell what they saw on the mountain until the Son of Man rises from the dead. The narrator tells the reader that the three do not know what that means. Jesus never mentioned rising from the dead before "The Transfiguration" in Original Mark.

In addition, on the way down the mountain the disciples ask Jesus about Elijah coming first (9:11). That is an obvious reference to prophecies of the Messiah. The disciples bring up that subject up because they had heard the discussion among Jesus, Moses and Elijah. Mark tells the reader that the disciples know who the other two people on the mountain are. Peter suggests building a tent for Moses and Elijah. The three disciples must have heard the discussion wherein Moses and Elijah tell Jesus who they are and a discussion about the Messiah, the Christ. Mark has cleverly implied what Jesus, Moses and Elijah were talking about—his mission as Messiah.

Mark, as a writer and an observer of human nature, knew that people talk about what is going on in their lives, what they have experienced, what is causing them emotional pain, what puzzles them. Therefore, he has the disciples bring up the subject of what they just experienced—a discussion among two revered Jewish prophets, who reportedly did not die but were taken up to heaven, and the disciples' teacher who refers to himself in Daniel's language as "the Son of Man."

At 9:9–11 Mark tells the reader that the Son of Man will rise from the dead and that Elijah will precede the coming of the Messiah. He has included messianic prophecies of Daniel, Isaiah and Malachi. In Dan 7 the one like a Son of Man is given dominion over the Earth that shall not pass away.[1] That implies that the Son of Man is immortal and cannot die, but then Jesus says the Son of Man will rise from the dead. Isaiah's Suffering Servant is killed. No wonder the disciples are puzzled. How can one who is immortal die, much less rise from the dead? Then the disciples bring up what Mal 4:5–6 says about Elijah. Here for the first time in the Gospel, Mark has combined Daniel, Isaiah and Malachi. To make it clear, Mark combines the prophecies of Isaiah and Daniel in Jesus's prediction of the passion at 8:31, 9:31 and 10:33–34 by using Daniel's "Son of Man" title with indignities to be endured by Isaiah's Suffering Servant.

With that insight the reader can see at his baptism, with the spirit going into him, Jesus knew he was the Danielic Son of Man. He thought his mission was to proclaim the kingdom of God and be its earthly king (1:14, 1:38, 2:10 [having authority], 2:17, 2:28 [being Lord], 3:35). Jesus did not realize that there was an Isaiac Suffering Servant component to God's mission for him. After Moses and Elijah inform him about the full mission, Jesus has a moral dilemma. He possesses extraordinary powers, presumably acquired at baptism with the spirit. He could use these powers to become the Jewish Messiah King prophesied in Dan 7. He has been calling himself the "Son of Man," a Danielic expression. The downside is at this point he is still a man and will die.

With "The Transfiguration" happening before "Peter's Confession at Caesarea Philippi," in "Coming Down the Mountain" Jesus calls himself "the Son of Man" for the third time. First, he said the Son of Man had authority to forgive sins (2:10). Second, he said the Son of Man was Lord of the Sabbath (2:28). The third time he tells his disciples that he will conquer death (at 9:9, immediately after 6:31 in Original Mark). He also says for the first time that the Son of Man will suffer many things and be rejected (9:12). Telling his disciples about his suffering, dying, and rising at this point implies that he had just learned it from Moses and Elijah. There is no reason why the Suffering Servant of Isaiah should be necessarily connected to the Son of Man of Daniel. The evidence is that first century Messianic Judaism did not consider Isaiah's Suffering Servant to be the Messiah.[2] Jesus could use his powers acquired at baptism to become king and lead a revolt against Herod and Rome, just as Josephus wrote that

---

1. Dan 7:14.
2. Ladd, *New Testament*, 154.

Herod feared from John the Baptizer.[3] On the other hand, Jesus could follow God's plan as revealed to him by Moses and Elijah on the mountain and become the Christ of atonement for mankind. This requires that Jesus rise from the dead and come with the clouds to establish the kingdom of God on Earth as preached by Paul.

"Peter's Confession at Caesarea Philippi" (8:27—9:1) has Jesus telling his disciples that he will be rejected, killed and rise from the dead after three days. Peter admonishes him, but the reader is not told what Peter said. Mark has designed this as the second temptation of Jesus. With so much in the Original Gospel coming in threes, it is absolutely impossible that Jesus could only be tempted once. There must be three temptations. Although the reader is not told what Peter says, just as the reader is not told how Satan tempted Jesus in the wilderness, Peter must be tempting Jesus to use his powers to become king. The reader can discern that because it prompts Jesus's response of calling Peter "Satan." Mark intended this to recall to the reader Jesus's temptation by Satan in the wilderness after Jesus's baptism. The third temptation comes in Gethsemane, with Jesus using the word "temptation" in connection with Simon Peter (14:38).

Mark gives the reader a clincher that Peter is tempting Jesus at 8:32. The word "Satan" appears six times in Mark's Gospel.

1. 1:13 ". . . he was *tempted* by *Satan*."

2. 3:23a ". . . in *parables*, how can *Satan* . . ."

3. 3:23b " . . . *cast out Satan*."

4. 3:26 "if *Satan* has risen up against himself and is divided he *cannot stand*."

5. 4:13b, "And how will you understand all the *parables*? 4:14 . . . and when they have heard it, immediately *Satan* comes"

6. 8:33, "Get behind me *Satan* because you are minding not the things of God, but the things of men." In other words, "Do not tempt me, Satan."

Six occurences of the word "Satan" make a sextet that is chiastic: tempt – parables – cast out – cannot stand – parables – a temptation. Being tempted is the motivation for Jesus to call Peter "Satan." Jesus turns and looks at the other disciples before chiding Peter. He can see that they agree with Peter. The reader knows that Jesus can tell what is in someone's heart. Mark provided a chiastic sextet clue that Peter's so-called confession is actually a temptation. This means that Peter's confession is not "a recognition" as defined by Aristotle in his *Poetics*. Mark did not design Peter's confession as the turning point in the Original Gospel. Peter's confession is another and major instance of the disciples not understanding Jesus. Not only do they misunderstand, they actively try to undermine God's plan, tempting Jesus to become king.

---

3. J.A. 18:5:3.

Jesus does not fully understand his mission until he talks with Moses and Elijah; therefore, according to Mark, Jesus is only human, an adopted Son of God. Adopted at baptism. An additional clue for this conclusion is that Jesus says, "Abba, Father" in Gethsemane (14:36), confirming what Paul wrote at Gal 4:6 and Rom 8:15 that adopted sons of God will say when they fully accept their adoption.

With this new perspective Jesus's sermon at 8:35–37 immediately after this second temptation takes on a new meaning:

> 8:35 For whoever would preserve his life will lose it; and whoever will lose his life for my sake and that of the gospel will preserve it. 8:36 For what does it benefit a man, to gain the whole world, and forfeit his soul? 8:37 For what should a man give in exchange for his soul?

Jesus could be wrestling within himself whether to follow God's plan or become a king on Earth. This part of the sermon has a Hamletesque quality to it.

In the Original Gospel of Mark Jesus is a righteous human, a Nazarene, one set apart, who has been adopted by God to become the atonement sacrifice for mankind as preached by Paul. He has a moral dilemma whether to follow God's plan or use his powers to gather the people and rebel against Herod and Rome, becoming king with all its glory. The turning point in the Original Gospel occurs when Jesus heads to Jerusalem. He could foment a revolution there or be rejected and killed by the authorities. He heads to his destiny.

At the Last Supper it appears that Jesus is resigned to his fate to be killed as he predicts he will be handed over to authorities and that Peter will deny him three times. But he says that, "for the Son of Man it goes as it has been written of him." Jesus does not say what writing that is. Is it Isa 53:5 "He was pierced through for our transgressions, he was crushed for our iniquities." Or is it Dan 7:14, "And his kingdom is one that will not be destroyed." The reader does not know. Perhaps Jesus might still become Messiah/King.

In Gethsemane the third temptation occurs. Jesus has impressed the crowds at the temple and they are on his side. There is a triplet at 11:32, 12:12, and 14:2 which sets up how the crowd favors Jesus over the high priests, elders and scribes. Jesus tells Peter, James and John to watch for the high priests' gang. With his rhetorical skills he could turn the gang against the high priests, and start the revolution right there during Passover with the crowds behind him. He goes into Gethsemane to pray for guidance and comes back three times to find Peter and the others sleeping each time. When Judas and the authorities find Jesus, he says, "let the scriptures be fulfilled" (14:49). In the end Jesus submits himself to God's plan and "give(s) his life as a ransom for many.[4]"

There is also a triplet uniting the three temptations: Jesus addresses a person by a proper name three times in Mark's Gospel. He calls Peter "Satan," at 8:29, God "Abba"

---

4. Mark 10:45.

at 14:36, and Peter "Simon" at 14:37: Satan – God – Simon (Satan). Satan and Simon both begin with a sigma in Greek. Jesus also tells Peter not to enter into temptation at 14:38. Jesus uses "Simon" and "temptation" in the same speech. Even though Jesus renamed Simon "Peter" at 3:16, and the narrator calls him "Peter" starting at that point, Jesus calls him "Simon" at 14:37 to emphasize the connection with Satan. The sextet of "Satan" unites the first and second temptations, and the personal addresses triplet unites those two temptations with the third.

The author of the Original Gospel of Mark probably knew Aristotle's *Poetics* and the importance of plot. As Aristotle said:

> For by plot I here mean the arrangement of the incidents . . . Every play contains spectacular elements as well as character, plot, diction, song, and thought. But most important of all is the structure of the incidents.[5]

If the plot is not good, no one will read or perform your play or Gospel. Mark knew that and wrote an exciting plot. An anti-Adoptionist redactor spoiled that plot by moving "The Transfiguration" and "Coming Down the Mountain" to follow Peter's confession so that it appeared that Jesus always knew what his mission was and doggedly followed it. This redaction, of course, makes the two references to the Son of Man at 2:10 and 2:28 unintelligible. The actual author of Mark does not give useless information. The two early references to the Son of Man have an important part to play in the plot. They must mean that the human Jesus misunderstood his mission. The nature of the Son of Man changes at "The Transfiguration."

The redactor then padded the Gospel text before 8:27 by adding another feeding, several miracles and moving a controversy in Jericho to before the second feeding to make it appear that Peter's confession was an Aristotelian recognition. The redactor was extremely clever. The full extent of his editing has escaped detection for some nineteen hundred years.

The Turning Point

A number of scholars have theorized that Canonical Mark has a geographical structure.[6] Jesus is in Galilee and environs until Mark 10 and then he heads to Jerusalem and is in Jerusalem for the remainder of the Gospel, Mark 11—16. Even with a clear geographic dichotomy, Jesus's heading toward Jerusalem is not generally thought to be the turning point of the Gospel. There is almost unanimity that the turning point of Canonical Mark is 8:27–28 when Peter identifies Jesus as "the Christ."[7] As Larsen says:

5. Aristotle, *Poetics*, 6.

6. Larsen, "Structure of Mark," 146.

7. Ibid. 145.

Many Markan scholars would consider the Caesarea Philippi episode as the central pericope and turning point of the Gospel. Juel calls Peter's confession 'the great transitional scene', and Stock calls Peter's confession 'the decisive turning point in Mark's Gospel'. Thus in the broadest and simplest of proposed divisions, scholars have divided the Gospel into two sections: 1.1–8.26 and 8.27–16.8.[8]

The pericope of Peter's confession is essentially at the center of the Canonical Gospel, where the turning point is typically located in ancient literature. Aristotle called the turning point "the recognition" in his work on the structure of drama.[9] At the recognition the protagonist is recognized for who he really is either by other characters or by himself. Therefore, "Peter's Confession at Caesarea Philippi" (8:27—9:1) fits perfectly with ancient ideas of the recognition/turning point. However, that is not what was intended by the author. While Peter correctly identifies Jesus as "The Christ," he is fundamentally wrong. Peter thinks that Jesus is the Jewish Messiah-King of Dan 7 who will lead Israel to break free of Rome and become a world power. The evidence that Peter's belief is erroneous is in the pericope as written by Mark.

A 8:27 And Jesus and his disciples went into the villages of Caesarea Philippi: and on the way he questioned his disciples, saying to them, "Who do men say that I am?"

B 8:28 And they told him, saying, "John the Baptizer and others, Elijah; but others, one of the prophets."

C 8:29 And he asked them, "But who do you say I am?"

D Peter answers and says to him, "You are the Christ."

E 8:30 And he admonished them that they should tell no one about him.

F 8:31 And he began to teach them that it is necessary that the Son of Man suffer many things, and be rejected by the elders, and the chief priests, and the scribes, and be put to death, and after three days rise.

F' 8:32 And he spoke these words plainly.

E' And taking him, Peter began to admonish him.

D' 8:33 And turning around and seeing his disciples, he admonished Peter, and says, "Get behind me, Satan; because you are minding not the things of God, but the things of men."

C' 8:34 And summoning the crowd with his disciples, he said to them, "If any man wishes to come after me, he must deny himself, and take up his cross, and follow me. 8:35 For whoever would preserve his life will lose it; and whoever will lose his life for my sake and that of the gospel will preserve it. 8:36 For what does it benefit a man, to gain the whole world, and forfeit his soul? 8:37 For what should a man give in exchange for his soul? 8:38 For whoever might have been ashamed of me and of my words in this adulterous and sinful generation,

8. Ibid.

9. Aristotle, *Poetics*, 16.

the Son of Man also will be ashamed of him, when he comes in the glory of his Father with the holy angels."

B' 9:1 And he said to them, "Truthfully I say to you, There are some standing here who will in no way taste of death, until they see the kingdom of God coming with power."

A' 9:30 Leaving there, they passed through Galilee; and he did not want that anyone should know it.

Jesus asks his disciples who they think he is and Peter says that he is the Christ. Jesus is no doubt is relieved that they finally understand. After all, three of them heard the discussion at "The Transfiguration." So Jesus tells them that as the Christ he must be killed by the authorities and then he will rise from the dead. Peter apparently disagrees with Jesus. Mark does not tell us what Peter says, but the reader should infer from Peter's tone and Jesus's response that Peter said something like, "You cannot die; you will be king of all the world and beloved of men." The Greek word used by Mark for Peter's tone to Jesus is "epitiman" meaning to rebuke, admonish, chide or warn. Jesus looks at the other disciples and presumably sees that they agree with Peter (why else would Mark tell the reader that Jesus looked at them). The disciples still do not understand—none of them. So Jesus tells Peter he is wrong in no uncertain terms, "Get behind me Satan, because you are minding not the things of God, but the things of men." In other words, "Don't tempt me to use these powers I have to become king, that is not what God wants me to do."

Peter's recognition is a false recognition. Aristotle describes a false recognition that can take place in especially good drama:

> Again, there is a composite kind of recognition involving false inference on the part of one of the characters, as in the Odysseus Disguised as a Messenger. "A" said that no one else was able to bend the bow; . . . hence "B" (the disguised Odysseus) imagined that "A" would recognize the bow which, in fact, he had not seen; and to bring about a recognition by this means–the expectation that "A" would recognize the bow–is false inference.[10]

There may be a double false inference in this pericope. The first one is that Peter fails to understand who Jesus is at 8:29b then the second one is at 8:30 where Jesus's infers that his disciples finally understand who Jesus is. They do not.

Observe how Mark's chiastic structure of this pericope enhances the meaning he intends for the reader to grasp. Naturally the (A, A') stich is movement into and out of the pericope. In the (B, B') stich the disciples tell Jesus that men say he is one of the prophets and Jesus makes his prophecy of the Parousia, telling them who he really is, the one who will bring the kingdom of God. In the (C, C') stich Jesus asks the disciples who they think he is, and he tells them and the crowd what he requires from his

10. Ibid.

disciples, impliedly answering the question of who he is. In the (D, D') stich Peter says, "you are the Christ" and "Jesus calls Peter "Satan." Clearly Peter is wrong. Mark is telling the reader that Peter has the wrong Christ, the false Christ, the "pseudochristos" of 13:22 and "another Jesus" of 2 Cor 11:4. Jesus tells Peter that he is minding the things of men rather than God. That tells the perceptive reader that Peter has said something to Jesus about earthly glory or fame or riches. Peter and the disciples are thinking that Jesus is the Danielic Son of Man, Daniel's Messiah, whereas Jesus knows he has to be the Isaiaic Suffering Servant while on Earth. He will become the Danielic Son of Man after his resurrection. The (E, E') stich is Peter admonishing and Jesus admonishing. Finally the (F, F') center stich is Jesus plainly revealing that he is the Isaiaic Suffering Servant.

In Original Mark, but not in Canonical Mark, Peter, James and John were told this coming down the mountain from the transfiguration when Jesus said he would rise from the dead. The very clever and talented redactor objected to the Adoptionism of Original Mark. He also objected to Mark's deprecation of the disciples. He blunted the Adoptionism by moving "The Transfiguration" and "Coming Down the Mountain" to follow Peter's confession. This renders irrelevant any conversation Jesus had with Moses and Elijah. It is now interesting color—Jesus talking with the sages of the OT who were taken directly into heaven and did not die. In Canonical Mark it appears that Jesus is the Son of God who knows all along who he is. In Original Mark Jesus is a man who does not fully understand what God wants him to do until Moses and Elijah tell him. After moving "The Transfiguration" and "Coming Down the Mountain" to follow "Peter's Confession at Caesarea Philippi," the redactor split "Feeding the Multitude" into two parts and put in new pericopae between them including one from after the Original turning point in order to move Peter's confession closer to the center of the Gospel and render it a likely turning point in the revised story.

Mark wrote a Pauline Gospel putting Paul's teachings in Jesus's mouth. Along the way he took Paul's side in the dispute between Paul and the Jerusalem leaders, James, Peter and John. Paul wrote about this dispute in Galatians. This is reason the disciples seem like such dunderheads throughout Mark's Gospel. They never understand Jesus's message. It is inconceivable that Mark would write in one of the most important parts of his Gospel—the turning point—that Peter did something right. According to Mark, Paul had the real message of Christ. The Jerusalem apostles had misinterpreted it, according to Paul, and Mark took Paul's side of the dispute.

Some scholars give the disciples the benefit of the doubt and theorize that at Caesarea Philippi there is a shift in the disciples' attitude but from lack of understanding to misunderstanding.[11] I do not think Mark was being so charitable in the Original Gospel. The upshot is, given the basis for Mark's Gospel, "Peter's Confession at Caesarea Philippi" cannot be the recognition/turning point; it is an Aristotelian false recognition. The actual turning point must come later in the Gospel. And it does,

11. Rhoads, *Mark as Story.*

when Jesus recognizes that he must go to Jerusalem for the Passover and his destiny. He cannot stay in Galilee teaching and healing. Jesus's Passion Predictions get more detailed as the Gospel progresses from 8:31 to 9:31 to 10:33–34. The turning point comes at the third passion prediction in "Heading to Jerusalem, Third Passion Prediction" (10:32–34). Jesus leads his entourage toward Jerusalem and the group is afraid. But James and John still do not understand and ask Jesus if they can sit on his right and left hand in his glory (10:35–41).

One might think that the disciples have finally understood Jesus' message and are asking for glorification in heaven. But there is another possibility. It makes more sense that James and John still think Jesus will be the Jewish Messiah-King and will be all-powerful on Earth. After all, if Jesus is in his glory in heaven, is not God on his left hand? If there are spaces on Jesus's left and right hand, it must be on Earth where the Son of Man is ruling the kingdom without end. Therefore, he would have the power to grant that they sit at his right and left hands in his kingly glory or splendor on Earth.

Peter shows his lack of understanding at Caesarea Philippi immediately before Jesus's first prediction of his Passion, and James and John show their lack of understanding on the road to Jerusalem immediately after his third prediction of his Passion. All three of the Jerusalem apostles mentioned by Paul get embarrassed by their lack of understanding of Jesus's message. Mark's message to his readers is that the Jerusalem apostles never understood Jesus's message—only Paul understood it.

15

Promoting Paul

IT HAS BEEN STATED previously herein that one of the main purposes of Mark for writing his Gospel was to promote Pauline Christianity. However, only limited evidence has been offered. Koester agreed that Mark was promoting Paul, writing:

> Its (The Gospel of Mark) primary purpose, therefore, was to present a narrative account of the individual topics of the Pauline kerygma which is quoted as "gospel" in 1 Cor 15:1–5.[1]

While it is nice to know that this theory is agreed with by a respected NT scholar like Koester, in order to make an informed judgment with respect to the claim, one must compare the salient principles of both Paul's Christianity and Mark's Christianity.

The book *Matthew, Mark, Luke, and Paul* documents that Mark used Pauline sources in his Gospel over seventy-five times.[2] Some may argue that just because Mark's Jesus has the same message as Paul, does not mean that Mark used Paul as the source of the message. Tradition holds that Paul learned Jesus's message from his disciples and then repeated it to his congregations. Let us examine the facts.

1. Paul's epistles were written before Mark wrote his Gospel.[3] Therefore, it is historically possible that Mark had copies of Paul's epistles.

2. Paul writes that he learned his gospel from no man.[4]

3. Based on Paul's letters, it is evident that Peter, James and John, the Jerusalem apostles, were actual people and colleagues/opponents of Paul. But there is no suggestion in the epistles that they were members of an original group of disciples of an earthly Jesus. While 1 Cor 15:3–11 is probably a later interpolation,[5] 1 Cor 15:5–7 speaks of Peter and James as if they are not part of "the twelve." Assuming 1 Cor 15:3–11 is a later interpolation, the likely scenario is that Mark invented "the twelve," using that term to describe

---

1. Koester, *Ancient Gospels*, 26; Dykstra, *Canonizer*, 23.
2. Smith, *MMLP.*
3. Koester, *Ancient Gospels*, 4.
4. Gal 1:12.
5. Price, "1 Corinthians."

the disciples ten times in the Original Gospel. Therefore, the use of the phrase "the twelve" in the interpolation to 1 Cor 15:5 is probably based on Mark's name for them.

4. Paul writes that he learned his gospel through revelation.[6]

5. In Paul's teachings he virtually never credits Jesus with being the author of the teaching. There are two exceptions and they are likely interpolations.[7]

6. Paul only tells his congregations seven facts about Jesus. That is the sum total of what Paul seemed to know about the life of Jesus. Those are:

   a. He was crucified[8]

   b. He was resurrected from the dead[9]

   c. He was born[10]

   d. He was Jewish[11]

   e. David was an ancestor[12]

   f. He was poor[13]

   g. He had a last supper[14]

Paul does not seem to be some one who has any information on an earthly life of Jesus. This tends to negate Paul learning about Jesus from Jesus's disciples.

Christian historians and theologians have assumed with no proof other than Christian tradition that there was an earthly Jesus and that Paul learned about his life and teachings from his disciples. Nothing in Paul's epistles indicates that he knew anything about an earthly Jesus. In fact, he specifically denies learning anything about Jesus from any man.

---

6. Rom 16:25; 1 Cor 11:23.

7. 1 Cor 7:10, 9:14. The Lord's Supper, also in 1 Cor seems to quote Jesus, but Paul says that the Lord gave it to him, presumably through revelation. It is interesting that the only epistle containing attributions to Jesus is 1 Cor. A number of scholars think 1 Cor has been heavily redacted.

8. 1 Cor 2:8. Notice in this passage of Paul's about Christ's crucifixion, Paul apparently does not know when the crucifixion occurred or who was responsible.

9. 1 Cor 15:12.

10. Gal 4:4. This is probaby an anti-Marcionite interpolation. It makes little sense in the epistle.

11. Ibid.

12. Rom 1:1–3. This appears to also be an interpolation since it interrupts the flow of the sentence.

13. 2 Cor 8:9.

14. 1 Cor 11:23–25. This is obviously Paul adapting the Greek custom of a communal religious meal to Christianity. So many of the Jewish dietary restrictions deal with forbidding Jews to touch, eat or drink blood, and human blood causes uncleanliness, it is absolutely impossible that any Jewish preacher would institute a sacrament of drinking blood, even using wine as a substitute. While the Last Supper stories in the gospels have Jesus eating with the disciples, Paul does not mention who is with Jesus at the Last Supper and who Jesus passes the bread and wine to.

The first written Gospel is Mark. Chapter 16 below demonstrates that Mark created his stories of Jesus by adapting OT stories. In essence Jesus's life was revealed to Mark through his reading of the OT, just as Paul learned about Jesus from the OT. Mark was a Pauline Christian. It is possible that Mark knew Paul and understood that Paul got his facts about Jesus through revelation.

Coming Of The Kingdom of God

Paul uses the phrase "kingdom of God" six times in his seven authentic epistles.[15] The phrase is not used in the OT except for Wis 10:10.[16] The concept of God being a king is certainly an OT concept, and the concept is very clear in Dan 7. Paul's use of the term "gospel" is the first use in Christian literature.[17] It is quite likely that Mark got both concepts from Paul's epistles.[18] Koester speculates that a later scribe inserted "gospel" into Mark because Matthew failed to copy the word in his version of some of the Markan passages; however, chapter 12 and Appendix 2 document that Mark's use of "gospel" is a sextet (proclaim the gospel twice, sake of the gospel twice and proclaim the gospel twice) disposes of that idea. The fourteen-element structure of "kingdom of God" also explained in chapter 12 testifies to its occurrence in Mark's Original Gospel.

Paul's concept of the kingdom of God is a bit vague in his epistles. Scholars are fond of saying with no proof whatsoever that the concept was so familiar to the people of the first century that it did not need to be defined.[19] Paul purposefully used the concept to cover a number of different situations. "Kingdom of God" as used by Paul could mean a present earthly environment of Christian brotherhood,[20] a future kingdom on Earth ruled by Christ, or an eternal heavenly kingdom.[21] In any case it was coming soon according to Paul.[22] Likewise the kingdom of God of Mark's Jesus was a bit vague, but Mark was clearer than Paul with regard to when it might happen.[23] As chapter 16 points out, Mark obtained a number of Olivet Discourse metaphors from 1 Thess 5—pregnancy, a thief (or master) coming suddenly in the night, staying awake/be vigilant, sparing the elect.

The coming of the kingdom of God is a major theme of Mark. He believed Paul's gospel and wanted to convince his readers that the kingdom of God was coming soon.

15. Most NT scholars consider Romans, 1 Corinthians, 2 Corinthians, Galatians, Philippians, 1 Thessalonians and Philemon to be authentically written by Paul. The others are later pseudapigraphica.

16. Vivano, *Kingdom of God,* 17.

17. Koester, Ancient Gospels, 4.

18. Ibid. 13, as to "gospel," citing Stuhlmacher, *Das paulinsche Evangeliumz.*

19. Vivano, *Kingdom of God,* 18.

20. Rom 14:18; 1 Cor 4:20.

21. 1 Cor 15:50.

22. 1 Cor 7:29–31; 1 Thess 14:15, 5:2.

23. Mark 1:15, 9:1, 13:3–37.

One of the literary devices Mark uses to convince the reader of the coming of the kingdom of God was to have Jesus predict three times that he would be abused and killed by the authorities and that he would rise from the dead. These predictions proved to be true in his narrative. Parallel to those predictions, Mark's Jesus predicted that the kingdom of God was coming soon after his death and resurrection. This device was designed to persuade the reader that since Jesus was correct in his predictions about his death and resurrection, he could be trusted to be correct in his predictions about the coming kingdom of God.

Note the placement of these predictions in the narrative. The first Passion Prediction is at 8:31. The first Parousia Prediction follows closely in the same pericope at 9:1. Almost immediately Jesus makes his second Passion Prediction at 9:31, which is in the following pericope in the reconstructed Original Gospel. Then Jesus makes his third Passion Prediction at the turning point at 10:33–34 as the entourage heads to Jerusalem to confront the authorities. The second Parousia Prediction (coming of the kingdom of God) does not come until "The Olivet Discourse" (13:3–37) as Jesus tells his disciples what to expect. And the third Parousia Prediction is made to the Council at Jesus's first trial, when he has nothing to gain by lying, as the reader sees that Jesus's Passion Predictions are coming true.

Mark skillfully plants in the reader the inevitability of Paul's coming of the kingdom of God. And it will be coming soon.

Controversies

In Mark's Original Gospel Jesus has nine controversies with the Pharisees, three with unaffiliated scribes, one with the Sadducees, and one with the high priests. All of Jesus's controversies with the Pharisees, the Sadducees and the high priests are based on controversies Paul had with the Jerusalem apostles or factions in his congregations. One of the controversies with a scribe, "The Greatest Commandment," (12:28–34) is not really a controversy but provides Mark with an opportunity to have Jesus reiterate Paul's teaching of the golden rule based on Rom 13:8 and Gal 5:14. The other two controversies with unaffiliated scribes, Healing the Paralytic (2:1–12) and "Controversy on Beelzebul" (3:20–30) are both based on 2 Kgs 1:2–16 and are about faith and forgiveness of sins.

On the surface these two latter controversies do not seem to have a Pauline component, but they do. There is a triplet of pericopae on forgiveness of sins in Mark. The elements are found at "John the Baptizer at the Jordan" (1:4–8), "Healing the Paralytic" (2:1–12), and "Controversy on Beelzebul" (3:20–30), evenly spaced throughout Act I of the Gospel. John is baptizing for the forgiveness of sins at 1:4; Jesus tells the paralytic his sins are forgiven at 2:5 and Jesus says all sins will be forgiven the sons of men at 3:28. Within this triplet of pericopae, the term "forgiveness of sins" (aphesin hamartiōn or variations) is used six times, four times in the "Healing the

Paralytic" and one each in the other two pericopae. With Mark's use of this phrase he always placed "forgive" before "sins."

All three of these pericopae make reference to 2 Kgs 1:2–16. The description of John's clothes at 1:6 is word-for-word copied from 2 Kgs 1:8 (LXX); "Beelzebub" is only found in the OT at 2 Kgs 1:2, 1:4, 1:6, and 1:16, and the story of the paralytic with faith being lowered down through the roof to Jesus for healing is a reversal of the story of Ahaziah falling through a lattice. Ahaziah was confined to bed and sought the help of the god of Ekron, Beelzebub, instead of Yahweh. In "Healing the Paralytic" "arise" is found three times, and in the story of Ahaziah "come down" is found seven times.

Clearly these three pericopae make references to 2 Kgs 1:2–16, with the first and third elements using distinctive words from the OT story and the middle element being a complete reversal of the OT story. "Healing the Paralytic" is forgiveness of sins, but faith engendered the forgiveness. The people John baptized came to him in faith. The paralytic and his friends who came to Jesus had faith, but the scribes from Jerusalem had no faith, and they were not forgiven because they blasphemed the Holy Spirit. Mark is advocating Paul's justification by faith (Rom 3:19—5:20, 1 Cor 15:17, Gal 2:16) without directly refering to the epistles.

Paul used Psalm 32 to get his point across at Rom 4:3–8:

> 3 Abraham believed God, and it was counted to him as righteousness. 4 Now to the one who works, his wages are not counted as a gift but as his due. 5 And to the one who does not work but believes in him who justifies the ungodly, his faith is counted as righteousness, 6 Even as David also pronounced blessing upon the man, unto whom God reckons righteousness apart from works, 7 saying, Blessed are they whose iniquities are forgiven, And whose sins are covered. 8 Blessed is the man to whom, the Lord will not reckon sin.

Mark created a triplet of pericopae about forgiveness of sins and used a form of "forgive sins" six times, but linked them to the OT story of a king who died because he did not have faith in Yahweh. The key to solving this puzzle is to realize that in the middle pericope faith is the main subject. Look what happened to the paralytic. He had faith and his sins were forgiven and he walked. Look what happened to Ahaziah. He had no faith, he never walked again and he died. It is the juxtaposition of faith and forgiveness of sins in Mark that leads the reader to Paul's doctrine of justification by faith.

At 2:16 the Pharisees object to Jesus's eating with tax collectors and sinners. This controversy recalls Paul's disagreement with Peter recounted in Gal 2:11–15 when Peter refused to eat with gentiles, Paul noting that in the eyes of Jews all gentiles are sinners. At Mark 2:18 Jesus is confronted because his disciples are not fasting. This controversy reiterates Paul's teaching at Rom 14:3–4 even to the detail of the disciples of the Pharisees accusing Jesus's disciples:

14:3 Let not him that eats set at naught him that eats not; and let not him that eats not judge him that eats: for God has received him. 4 Who are you to judge the servant of another?

The two controversies of "Plucking Grain on the Sabbath" (2:23–28) and "Healing the Man with a Withered Hand" (3:1–6) are Mark's version of Paul's teaching at Rom 14:5 that it does not matter which day one considers holy. These also have OT overtones with Jesus justifying his disciples by referenceing what David did at 1 Sam 21:1 and the man with the withered hand being based upon 1 Kgs 13:1–6.

The controversy of "Seeking a Sign" (8:10–12) is based on 1 Cor 1:22 where Paul says, "Jews ask for signs" and then responds, "but we preach Christ crucified, to Jews a stumbling block." Which Jews is Paul referring to? The Jews with whom he has been having disputes—the Jerusalem apostles. They do not recognize a crucified Christ. They preach another Jesus.[24] A Danielic Messiah who was not crucified. The Jerusalem apostles know nothing of a crucified Jesus. Jesus tells the Pharisees that this generation will not get a sign, in other words, there was no earthly crucifixion of an earthly Jesus. Matthew and Luke understood what Mark was saying here and tried to negate it by adding "but the sign of Jonah"[25] making a reference to the three days between Jesus's crucifixion and his rising.

"Leaven of the Pharisees" (8:13–21) is a controversy between Jesus and his disciples about the Pharisees. Mark uses the metaphor of leaven as a spreading evil based upon Paul's use of leaven as a metaphor at 1 Cor 5:6–7 and Gal 5:9. The disciples do not understand because they do not understand Paul's message.

"Controversy on Divorce" and Jesus teaching his disciples that "Remarriage Is Adultery" (10:1–12) is Jesus repeating Paul's teaching from 1 Cor 7:10–11. Paul's "not I, but the Lord" (ouk egō alla ho Kyrios) at 1 Cor 7:10 is an obvious interpolation.

"Controversy on Tradition" (7:1–15) is also taken from 1 Corinthians. Mark quotes Isa 29:13 while excoriating the Pharisees, and Paul quotes Isa 29:14 excoriating the Jewish scribes and wise men at 1 Cor 1:19. Then in the next pericope Mark's Jesus repeats Paul's lesson from Rom 14:14–17 that all foods are clean.

The high priests and elders ask Jesus for his authority in "Questioning Jesus's Authority" (11:27–12:12a). Paul tells the Galatians that his authority comes from God at Gal 1:1 and specifically says it does not come from men. This is echoed by Jesus's question to the high priests at 11:30 on whether John's baptism came from God or from man. While Paul says that his authority comes from God, he makes a point of telling the Galatians that James, Peter and John approved of it at Gal 2:9. At 2 Cor 3:1–3 Paul implies that other apostles have letters of recommendation but that he does not. Likewise Mark's Jesus refuses to tell the high priests from where his authority comes.

24. 2 Cor 11:4.

25. Matt 12:39, 16:4; Luke 11:29.

The last set of controversies takes place in three pericopae at Mark 12:13–34 in "Rendering unto Caesar," "Controversy on Resurrection" and "The Greatest Commandment." In "Rendering unto Caesar" Jesus repeats Paul's lesson from Rom 13:1–7 wherein Paul specifically mentions rulers, tribute and rendering. This is followed by Jesus's only controversy with the Sadducees about the resurrection. Mark reiterates Paul's lesson on resurrection found at 1 Cor 15:12–54. Some in the congregation at Corinth questioned the resurrection, and Mark puts their question into the mouths of the Sadducees. Josephus explained that the Sadducees did not believe in resurrection of the dead.[26] Mark used Paul's spiritual body concept from 1 Cor 15:44 to have Jesus say that the resurrected dead are like angels.[27] In Jesus's final controversy a scribe asks him what is the greatest commandment and Jesus replies from Rom 13:9 and Gal 5:14 that one should love his neighbor as himself.

As Paul was always battling Judaisers, immoral congregants, and skeptics, Mark turned these into controversies in the ministry of Jesus. Mark used the controversies as a plot device to provide an impetus for the authorities to want to get rid of Jesus. Mark adapted Paul's Christianity and Paul's struggles to create the story of Jesus, his message and his crucifixion as preached by Paul.

Disciple Bashing

Paul had disagreements with the Jerusalem Christian leadership, James, Peter and John. The crux of the disagreement was whether one had to convert to Judaism and follow Jewish law in order to be a Christian.[28] Paul said that faith in God and Jesus as Savior was sufficient. Naturally, Paul did not want conversion to Judaism to be a requirement for Christians. He would have had a much harder time making converts of gentiles if that were a requirement. The Pauline view eventually won out, but it is unclear how long this dispute lasted between the Pauline Christians and the Jerusalem Christians. The dispute must have still been rife at the time Mark wrote his Original Gospel. Mark's Original Gospel would not have been so anti disciple if the dispute had been settled. One does not write a polemical book against a non-existent enemy.

The conventional theory is that Mark wrote his Gospel soon after 70 CE. This date is based upon Mark knowing about the destruction of the temple that took place in 70 CE No Gospel is mentioned in patristic literature until about 120 CE in the writings of Justin Martyr, and by that time at least all three synoptic Gospels had been written. Mark probably wrote his Gospel about 100 CE give or take a few years, since

---

26. J.A.18:1:4.

27. Mark 12:25.

28. 1 Cor 1:22–23, 7:18–19, 9:1–5; 2 Cor 11:3–4, 11:13–15, 11:22–23; Gal 2:1–14, 3:1–15, 3:24–28, 5:1–6, 6:12–16; Phil 3:2–10.

he seems to know Josephus's *Antiquities of the Jews*. Josephus is thought to have written *Antiquities* in 93–94 CE.[29]

Taking Paul's side in his dispute with the Jerusalem apostles, Mark's Gospel takes every opportunity to belittle the disciples, especially Peter. There are thirty instances of Mark disparaging the disciples:

1. 2:15 And it happened, that he was reclining at dinner in his house, and many tax collectors and sinners were reclining with Jesus and his disciples. For there were many, and they followed him. 16 And the scribes of the Pharisees, seeing that he was eating with the sinners and tax collectors, said to his disciples, "Why does he eat and drink with tax collectors and sinners?" 17 And having heard this Jesus says to them, "Those that are healthy do not need a physician, but those that are sick. I did not come to call the righteous, but sinners."

2. 4:40 And he said to them, "Why are you afraid? Do you not have faith yet?"

3. 5:31 And his disciples said to him, "You see the crowd pressing on you, and you ask, Who touched me?

4. 9:5–6 And Peter answers and says to Jesus, "Rabbi, it is good for us to be here, and let us construct three tents: one for you, and one for Moses, and one for Elijah." For he knew not what to answer; for they became afraid.

5. 9:10 And they pondered the words, discussing among themselves what "rising from the dead" is.

6. 9:18–19 And when it seizes him, it throws him down: and he foams, and grinds his teeth, and he is pining away. And I spoke to your disciples that they might cast it out; but they were not able to." And answering them he says, "Oh faithless generation, how long must I be with you? How long must I endure you? Bring him to me."

7. 9:28–2 And entering into a house, his disciples asked him privately, "Why were we not able to cast it out?" And he said to them, "This kind can come out by only by prayer."

8. 4:5–6 And other fell on the rocky ground, where it did not have much Earth; and immediately it sprang up. Because it had no depth of soil 6 and when the sun rose, it was scorched. And because it had no root, it withered away. ("Rocky" in Greek is "petrōdēs." This may be a word play on "Peter.[30])

9. 4:13 And he says to them, "Do you not understand this parable? And how will you understand all the parables?

10. 4:16–17 And these likewise are those that are sown upon the rocky places, who, when they have heard the word, immediately receive it with joy; And they have no root within themselves, but are only temporary. Then when tribulation or persecution comes because of the word, immediately they stumble.

29. Feldman, "Josephus," ABD, 981–82.
30. Tolbert, *Sowing the Gospel*.

11. 6:37 But he answered and said to them, "You give them something to eat." And they say to him, "Should we go and pay two hundred denarii for bread, to give them to eat?"

12. 8:18–21 ". . . Having eyes, do you not see? And having ears, do you not hear? And do you not remember? 8:20 When I broke the loaves among the four thousand, how many basketfuls of broken pieces were left over?" And they say to him, "Seven." And he said to them, "Do you still not understand?"

13. 8:33 And turning around and seeing his disciples, he chided Peter, and says, "Get behind me, Satan; because you are minding not the things of God, but the things of men."

14. 9:32 But they did not understand the saying, and were afraid to ask him

15. 9:33–34 And they came to Capernaum. And coming into the house he asked them, "What were you discussing on the road?" But they were silent: for they had arguing with each other on the road about who was the greatest.

16. 9:39 But Jesus said, "Do not forbid him. For no man who does a mighty work in my name, will be able easily to speak evil of me."

17. 10:10 And in the house the disciples asked him again about this.

18. 10:13–14 And they were bringing to him little children so that he would touch them. And the disciples admonished them. But Jesus seeing it became indignant, and said to them, "Allow the little children to come to me; do not forbid them. For the kingdom of God belongs to such as these."

19. 10:32 But they were on the road going up to Jerusalem, and Jesus was going ahead of them: and they were amazed; and they that followed were afraid. And again he took aside the twelve, and began to tell them the things that were to happen to him.

20. 10:37–38 And they said to him, "Grant us that we may sit, one on your right hand, and one on your left hand, in your glory." But Jesus said to them, "You do not know what you are asking. Can you drink the cup that I drink? Or be baptized with the baptism that I am baptized with?"

21. 10:41 And hearing this the ten became indignant toward James and John.

22. 7:17–18 And when he went into the house away from the crowd, his disciples asked him about the parable. And he says to them, "Are you so without understanding also? Do you not realize, that whatever goes into the man from outside cannot defile him."

23. 10:48 And many admonished him, that he should be silent: but he shouted out all the more, "Son of David, have mercy on me."

24. 14:4 But there were some that were indignant saying to each other, "Why has there been a waste of the anointing oil?"

25. 14:27 And Jesus says to them, "All you will stumble for it is written, I will strike the shepherd, and the sheep will be scattered."

26. 14:31 But he spoke vehemently, "If it is necessary that I die with you, I will not deny you." And likewise they all spoke. (This in itself is not denigrating to the disciples, but it sets them up to show them to be hypocrites or cowards.)

27. 14:32–42 And they come to a place that was named Gethsemane: and he says to his disciples, "Sit here while I pray." And he takes with him Peter and James and John, and became greatly awe struck, and deeply troubled. And he says to them, "My soul is extremely sorrowful even to death: you stay here, and watch." And going on a little farther he fell on the ground, and prayed that, if possible, the hour might pass by him. And he said, "Abba, Father, all things are possible for you. Remove this cup from me. But not what I desire, but your will." And he comes, and finds them sleeping, and says to Peter, "Simon, are you asleep? Could you not watch one hour? Watch and pray that you do not enter into temptation. The spirit indeed is willing, but the flesh is weak." And again going away, he prayed, saying the same words. And again coming he found them sleeping for their eyes were very heavy; and they did not know what to answer him. And he comes the third time, and says to them, "Are you still sleeping and taking your rest? Enough. The hour is at hand. Look, the Son of Man is delivered into the hands of sinners. Wake up; let us be going. Look, he that delivers me is coming."

28. 14:50 And leaving him, they all fled

29. 14:66–72 And Peter was below in the court yard there comes one of the servant girls of the high priest; and seeing Peter warming himself, she looked at him, and says, "You also were with the Nazarene, Jesus." But he denied, saying, "I neither know, nor understand what you are saying." And he went out into the porch. And the servant girl seeing him again began to say to them that standing there, "This is one of them." But he again denied it. And after a little while again those standing there said to Peter, "Truly you are one of them; for you are a Galilean." But he began to curse and swear, "I do not know this man you are talking about." And immediately the second time the cock crowed. And Peter remembered the words, that Jesus said to him, "Before the cock crows twice, you will deny me three times." And breaking down, he wept.

30. The thirtieth instance of disciple bashing is not obvious from the text. There is a twelve-element structure using the word "demon" (diamonion). The other twelve-element structure is one using the word "twelve." Significantly Mark refers to the disciples as "the twelve" ten times in the Gospel. A further significant fact is that the twelve occurrences of the word "demon" culminate at 9:38 when John tells Jesus that a man who does not follow Jesus was casting out demons in Jesus's name. Chapter 6 explains that 9:38–40 was a denigration of the disciples and a praise of Paul. This twelve-element structure using "demon" confirms that assessment.

The first instance of maligning the disciples at 2:15–17 is not obvious at first glance. The reader must realize that this is a controversy based on Paul's disagreement with Peter in Antioch as related by Paul at Gal 2:11–15. In these thirty passages Mark has told the reader that the disciples are infuriating, exasperating, dumb, hypocrites, uncaring, disrespectful, petty, arrogant, faithless and cowards. These people are not worth listening to because they did not understand Jesus's message. Mark accuses the disciples of not understanding Jesus's message twelve times, specifically using the word "understand" five times.

It is very clear that Mark's Gospel is attempting to destroy the credibility of Peter, James and John. Chapter 4 above contains a discussion regarding the evidence that James son of Zebedee is the same person as James the Just who was the leader of the Jerusalem Christians.

Paul, Mark and Adoptionism

There is no indication in Paul's epistles that Paul was an Adoptionist. Paul's Christ Jesus was a celestial being and not an earthly human,[31] though later interpolations into Paul made it seem that his references to Jesus might be references to a human.[32] Mark's Original Gospel, on the other hand, is clearly Adoptionist. According to Paul, Christians become adopted children of God at baptism.[33] Here in Paul's epistles Mark finds a device that he can use to concretize Paul's heavenly Jesus and bring him to Earth. Paul's Christianity was abstract in nature, and many people understand concrete concepts better. In order to make Paul's abstract Christianity more understandable, Mark needed to put Jesus on Earth in a historical context that average people could grasp. Paul wrote in both Romans and Galatians that adopted sons of God would cry out, "Abba, Father" as the spirit of God's son enters them. Mark has Jesus do just that at his third temptation when he finally, fully accepts God's plan.[34] Paul also says that adopted sons of God would be transfigured[35] and Mark makes the transfiguration of Jesus a pivotal scene in his Gospel.

Since Paul's epistles contain no details of what led up to Jesus's crucifixion, Mark had to create them using the OT as a guide. For his historical context he used Josephus's *Antiquities* 18:1–5. He may have already known about them, but more than likely he got his historical characters, John the Baptizer, Herod Antipas, and Pontius Pilate from Josephus.

Paul's theology was that man's soul was not worthy of living an everlasting life with God in heaven because of Adam's original sin, but God made a plan to redeem mankind. God delivered a blameless son for crucifixion to atone for man's sinful nature. Those who accepted the sacrifice of God's son as atonement for their sinful

31. Doherty, *Jesus Neither*, 15.

32. Rom 1:3; Gal 4:3.

33. Rom 8:15; Gal 4:5. Is it just a coincidence that the two passages in Paul that imply Jesus was a human are in the same epistles as the two mentions of Christians being adopted sons of God?

34. Mark 14:36.

35. 2 Cor 3:18.

nature, having faith in God and Jesus's sacrifice, were justified to God and would receive everlasting life in heaven with God. But before Christians joined God in heaven, Jesus would come to Earth with the clouds as prophesied by Daniel and after the day of the Lord[36] create the kingdom of God on Earth. All of the elect would join God in heaven.

Paul combined the Messianic prophecies of Isaiah's Suffering Servant with those of Daniel's one like a Son of Man to create a crucified being who would establish the kingdom of God on Earth and redeem all mankind, not just Jews. The Jerusalem apostles on the other hand, must have based their messiah solely on Dan 7–12 and did not synthesize their Messiah with Isaiah's Suffering Servant.[37] In 2 Cor 11:4 Paul says that if others come preaching a Jesus that Paul did not preach, they should be rejected. What would be another Jesus that Paul did not preach? Paul tells the Corinthians at 1 Cor 1:23 "We preach Christ crucified, a stumbling block to Jews." The Jews Paul is speaking of here who do not recognize that Christ was crucified are the Jerusalem pillars, James, Peter, and John who reject Paul's Christ, a synthesis of Isaiah's Suffering Servant with Daniel's Son of Man.

Mark followed Paul's synthesized Christ, and to create an interesting plot, he developed a conflict between Jesus being solely the Danielic Messiah and being the combined Paulinist Isaiaic and Danielic Messiah. A Danielic Messiah could save the Jews, but a combined Isaiaic and Danielic Messiah could save all mankind. What this means is that the Jerusalem apostles were unaware of a Jesus who was crucified by the Romans and rose from the dead. They were waiting on their king to come to Earth from heaven with the clouds for the first time.

In order to put his Jesus into a historical context, Mark used the device of having a worthy man be adopted by God at his baptism and being infused with a god-like spirit. Paul's Christianity had baptism as an initiation rite, mentioned in his epistles, and Josephus had mentioned a respected itinerant preacher, John the Baptizer, as having been killed by Herod. Therefore, Mark could use the respected John as Malachi's coming of Elijah as a precursor to the Messiah.[38] Mark was not an Adoptionist that believed an actual human Jesus was adopted by God as his son. Rather Mark used adoption at baptism as a literary device to historicize Paul's celestial Christ Jesus. Mark's Original Gospel may have engendered the Adoptionist branch of early Christianity.

At some point early on an anti-Adoptionist redactor edited Mark to make it less Adoptionist. At the same time he partially rehabilitated Peter and the disciples by making it appear that "Peter's Confession at Caesarea Philippi" was the turning point of the Gospel with the disciples finally understanding who Jesus was. Matthew and Luke, then, did the redactor one better, and in their Gospels completely obliterated

---

36. 1 Thess 5:2; Mal 4:5.

37. Ladd, *New Testament*, 77.

38. Mal 4:5.

Mark's Adoptionism by adding a virgin birth, rearranging the teaching sections, and adding their own material to skew the story toward their particular points of view. They also added post resurrection appearances of Jesus to change Mark's puzzling ending to a more hopeful and satisfying ending for Christians who missed Mark's message.

Conclusion

Mark used the same "gospel" and "kingdom of God" terminology as Paul. He adapted Paul's adoption of Christians by God to bring Jesus to Earth. Mark wrote that Jesus predicted the Parousia a magical three times, as he had predicted the Passion three times. Mark used Paul's epistles as a source for Jesus's teachings, and denigrated the disciples, especially the Jerusalem apostles that Paul identified by name, Peter, James and John. It is a safe conclusion that one of Mark's main objectives in writing his Gospel was the promotion of Pauline Christianity.

16

Sources of the Original Gospel of Mark

THIS CHAPTER WILL ANALYZE the Original Gospel and document the sources of each pericope and some subpericopae. Very often one could say text in Mark's Original Gospel was sourced from either a Pauline epistle or the OT. Paul referenced the OT hundreds of times in his epistles. There are over three hundred and eighty references to the OT in six epistles of Paul: Romans, 1 Corinthians, 2 Corinthians, Galatians, Philippians and 1 Thessalonians. So in some cases it is difficult to know whether Mark might have been referencing text from an epistle or the OT passage Paul was using.

In the instances where Mark is using an OT or Pauline source, he invariably uses it at least twice and sometimes three times. Not only that, the diligent reader who goes to the source and reads it will find additional relevant text around it. The experience of reading Mark's Gospel is enhanced by checking Mark's sources. For example, Mark's source for Mark 1:10–11 is Isa 42:1:

Mark	Isaiah
1:10 And immediately coming up out of the water, he saw the heavens tearing open, and *the Spirit like a dove descending into him*: 1:11 And a voice came out of the heavens, "You are my beloved Son, *in whom I am well pleased.*"	42:1 Behold, my servant, whom I uphold; my chosen, *in whom my soul delights*: I have put my *Spirit upon him*; he will bring forth justice to the nations. 2 He will not cry, nor lift up his voice, nor cause it to be heard in the street.

Mark 1:10–1:11 has used language from Isa 42:1, in reverse order, of course, as Mark is wont to do. Notice that in Isa 42:1, if one takes this as a prophecy of the Messiah, he can use this to claim that Isaiah is saying that the Messiah is for all nations not just Israel. It is perfect for justifying Paul's ministry to gentiles.

Josephus As A Source For Mark

The evidence points to Mark's use of Josephus's *Antiquities Of The Jews, Wars Of The Jews,* and *Life of Flavius Josephus* as sources in order to place Jesus in a historical context. There are a number of facts mentioned by Mark that are also mentioned in the first five chapters of Book 18 of *Antiquities of the Jews, The Wars of the Jews* Book 2, chapters 8 and 9, and *Life of Flavius Josephus,* 76:

1. John the Baptizer baptized the people with water. (Mark 1:5; J.A.18:5:2)

2. Jesus tells the apostles to "take nothing for their journey" but a staff. (Mark 6:8) Essenes "carry nothing at all with them when they travel" except weapons. (J.W 2:8:4). The Greek is considerably different in the two constructions, but the concept is the same.

3. Herod Antipas married his brother's wife, Herodias. (Mark 6:17; J.A. 18:5:1)

4. Herod Antipas killed John the Baptizer. (Mark 6:27, J.A.18:5:2)

5. "Corban" is money given to the temple treasury. (Mark 7:11; J.W 2:9:4)

6. Essenes numbered four thousand. Coincidentally this is the same number that Jesus fed with seven loaves and a few fishes. (Mark 8:9; J.A. 18:1:5)

7. Sadducees deny the resurrection of souls after death. (Mark 12:18; J.A. 18:1:4; J.W. 2:8:14)

8. Sadducees argue with teachers of philosophy. (Mark 12:18–23; J.A. 18:1:4)

9. Mark identifies Passover as "the Passover and the (feast of) Unleavened Bread" (pascha kai ta azyma) Josephus identifies it as "the feast of Unleavened Bread, that we call Passover" (azymon heortē tes agomenes en pascha). Notice Mark reversed Josephus's order, a sure signal of source. (Mark 14:1; J.A. 18:2:2)

10. Pontius Pilate was the procurator of Judea in the first half of the first century CE. (Mark 15:1; J.A. 18:3:4, J.W. 2:9:2–4)

11. Pilate releases Barabbas at Passover. Vitellius, President of Syria and Pilate's superior, comes to Judea at Passover and releases the inhabitants of Jerusalem from paying taxes on fruits and vegetables sold. (Mark 15:15; J.A. 18:2:3)

12. Jesus is crucified with two thieves. Joseph from Arimathea goes into Pilate and asks for Jesus's body. Jesus is resurrected. Josephus sees three of his friends that Titus is crucifying and he goes into Titus and asks that he be allowed to take them down. Titus agrees and Josephus gets them medical help, but two die and one lives. (Mark 15:27–45; J.L. 76).

"Joseph Arimathea" (Iōsēph Harimathaiasis) is very close phonetically to Josephus's name in Greek "Joseph bar Matthias" (Iōsēph bar Matthaios). The name "Joseph from Arimathea" could be an homage to Josephus by Mark.

Wars of the Jews was written about 78 CE and *Antiquities of the Jews* was written in 93 or 94 CE. The publication date of *Life of Flavius Josephus* is unknown, but it is assumed to be after *Antiquities*.[1] It is possible that Mark got his historical context from the sources other than Josephus, but if Mark used Josephus, then the Original Gospel of Mark was not written until the last few years of the first century or the very early second century. Matthew and Luke wrote their Gospels after Mark, meaning that those Gospels were not written until the early second century. This also means that the dispute between the Pauline faction and the Jerusalem apostles was still boiling at the end of the first century. Otherwise there is no point in Mark writing his Gospel in its

1. Goldberg, *Flavius Josephus.*

present form. If every dispute between the two factions had been settled, Mark would have written a Gospel expounding the settled Christianity.

It seems too much of a coincidence that eight facts that Mark states in the Original Gospel are found in J.A. 18:1–5, unless Mark used *Antiquities* as a source. It also appears that Mark combined paragraphs 1 and 2 of J.A. 18:5 to create the story that Herod killed John because John disapproved of Herod's marriage to Herodias. Josephus does not say that Herod imprisoned John because John disapproved of Herod's marriage. Josephus says nothing about John condemning or approving or even knowing of Herod's marriage. Josephus only relates the circumstances of Herod's marriage in paragraph 1, and in paragraph 2 writes that Herod killed John because he thought John might lead a rebellion. Josephus does connect Herod's marriage to the killing of John by saying that some Jews thought that Herod's defeat by Aretas was God's punishment of Herod for killing John. Aretas went to war against Herod because Herod sent his first wife, Aretas' daughter, away so that he could marry Herodias. It appears that Mark invented John's condemnation of Herod's marriage based on Josephus's presentation of the two separate events in Herod's life as contiguous paragraphs.

Josephus also specifically says that John's baptism was not for the remission of sins. This is the traditional meaning of baptism or tevilah, the Jewish ritual washing. Before Mark wrote his Original Gospel, Paul had instituted baptism as a sacrament/initiation rite into Christianity, transforming the Jewish tevilah into a one-time initiation event.[2] Paul connects baptism with becoming an adopted son of God.[3] Therefore, Josephus's John the Baptizer becomes the perfect literary vehicle to engender Jesus's adoption by God. In the process Mark changes the nature of John's baptism to become the symbolic remission of sins that Paul preached.[4]

Mark could not have determined a historical context for Jesus from Paul's epistles. The epistles only contain seven facts about Jesus and provide no historical setting for Jesus. Paul's epistles do not mention John the Baptizer, Herod Antipas or Pilate. Paul apparently did not know when or by whom Jesus was crucified. In 1 Cor 2:8 Paul says Jesus was crucified by "the rulers (archontōn) of this age (aiōnos)."[5]

Mark needed to put Jesus into a historical context so that the Jerusalem apostles living at the same time as Paul and who opposed him could reasonably be the same disiples who were Jesus's companions and misunderstood his message. It seems to be a pretty good bet that Mark used *Antiquities* as a source for his historical context of Jesus, placing Jesus's ministry about seventy years before Mark was writing. That way there would be no person living who could contradict the story, and Paul's opponents could reasonably have been alive at that point.

2. Rom 6:3; 1 Cor 1:13–16, 12:13; Gal 3:27.

3. Gal 3:27—4:6; Rom 8:15–16.

4. Rom 6:1–8.

5. Scholars are divided over whether "archontōn" means earthly rulers or demonic rulers.

OT, Pauline, And Josephus Sources Of Mark

This section analyzes every pericope in the Original Gospel of Mark and demonstrates the sources Mark used in creating his Gospel. He used the OT, Josephus and the epistles of Paul.

"Messenger to Prepare the Way" (1:2–3)

Mark's sources are:

- Malachi 3:1, "I am sending my messenger to prepare a way before me."

- Exodus 23:20, "I am going to send an angel [messenger] in front of you . . . to bring you to the place I have prepared."

- Isaiah 40:3, "A voice cries out in the wilderness, 'prepare the way of the Lord. Make straight in the desert a highway for our God.'"

While Mark writes that the quote is from Isaiah, the first half of the quote is Malachi's adaptation of Exod 23:20. The second half is from Isaiah. Many exegetes think that Mark made a mistake in writing that the quote was from Isaiah. In fact, Mark merely left out a reference to Malachi. Mark did many things in threes. In his Gospel he only mentions three OT prophets: Moses, Elijah and Isaiah. If he had mentioned Malachi that would have been four. In addition Mark was making a chiastic match with 7:6 and creating a puzzle of the missing third mention of Isaiah at 14:21.

"John the Baptizer at the Jordan" (1:4–8)

Mark's sources are:

- *Antiquities* 18:5:2, "John, that was called the Baptizer: . . . baptism; . . . not in order to the putting away of some sins, but for the purification of the body."

- 2 Kings 1:8, "'A hairy man with a leather belt around his waist.' He said, 'It is Elijah the Tishbite.'"

In *Antiquities* Josephus reports that there was a preacher, John the Baptizer, who lived at the time of Herod Antipas and was killed by Herod. The description of John's clothes at Mark 1:6 is identical to the description of Elijah's clothes in 2 Kgs 1:8 (LXX). This is the first hint by Mark that John is the return of Elijah as prophesied by Malachi.[6] It is also Mark's signal that the reader needs to be familiar with the OT in order to fully understand his Gospel.

---

6. Mal 4:5.

"Baptism of Jesus" (1:9–11)

Mark's sources of are:

- Genesis 22:12, "your beloved son."[7]

- Psalms 2:7, "You are my son, today I have begotten you."

- Isaiah 42:1, "Here is my servant whom I uphold, my chosen in whom my soul delights, I have put my spirit upon him, he will bring forth justice to the nations."

- 2 Kings 2:6–13,[8] wherein Elisha asks Elijah for a double portion of his spirit, they go to the Jordan River, Elijah parts the river and is taken away. Elisha picks up the mantle and also parts the river.

Mark deliberately misquotes Isaiah to have the spirit go "into" Jesus rather than "onto" him. This forms a chiastic match with the spirit departing from him as he dies on the cross. It also implies God adopted Jesus at his baptism. With the spirit going into Jesus, he apparently gains some divine powers not available to other men. In 2 Kgs 2:7–12 Elijah puts a double portion of his spirit onto Elisha at the Jordan. Some of the miracles performed by Jesus in Mark's Gospel are copies of miracles performed by Elijah or Elisha. While at his baptism Jesus comes up out of the water and the sky parts. At the death of Elijah the water of the Jordan parts, and Elijah goes up into the sky. Jesus's baptism is the reverse of Elijah's death. This is the first reversal of a source in the Gospel.

In a number of places throughout his Gospel Mark reverses the order of his sources. That is, he uses OT stories in reverse order from that found in the OT. The reversal of the order of stories is a signal by Mark to the observant reader that the reversed OT story is the source of the story found in his Gospel. In other words, Mark is deliberately signaling to the reader from where he got his story. For centuries exegetes have assumed that Mark collected oral stories about Jesus from disciples or other witnesses. In fact, Mark had left clues in his Gospel that he created the stories about Jesus based upon OT stories. The conclusion must be that if Mark used the OT as a source for creating the events in Jesus's life, then Mark did not gather the stories from Jesus's disciples or other witnesses. The further conclusion is that the OT stories are not prophecies of the Messiah that Mark is reporting as having come true.

"Temptation Of Jesus" (1:12–13)

The source of this pericope is 1 Kgs 19:4–8.[9] Elijah, fleeing Jezebel and Ahab, goes into the wilderness and an angel brings him food. After Elijah's encounter with the

---

7. LXX.
8. Price, "Midrash."
9. Ibid.

angel he stays forty days in the wilderness. This is again the reverse order of Mark's Gospel wherein Jesus is in the wilderness for forty days and then angels come and serve him. This is the second occasion of Mark reversing an OT story he used as a source.

"Calling The First Four Disciples" (1:14–20)

Mark's sources for this pericope are:

- *Antiquities* 18:5:2, wherein Josephus reports that Herod imprisoned John.
- 1 Kings 19:19–21,[10] wherein Elijah recruits Elisha to be his disciple.

Following his forty days in the wilderness, God tells Elijah to recruit Elisha to be his disciple. Mark uses a similar time line for Jesus recruiting his first four disciples. When Elijah throws his mantle over Elisha, Elisha does not join Elijah immediately, but goes back to his home to make a farewell feast for his parents before joining Elijah. Whereas, when Jesus calls Simon and Andrew, they drop their fishing nets and follow Jesus immediately. James and John also immediately leave their father in the boat to follow Jesus.

"Unclean Spirit in the Synagogue" 1:21–28

The sources for this pericope are:

- Nahum 1:15,[11] "Look! On the mountains the feet of one who brings good tidings, who proclaims peace!"
- 1 Kings 17:18,[12] "What have I to do with you, O man of God, . . . have you come to destroy my son?"

Nahum 1:15 is the only place in the LXX where the word "gospel" (euangiliou) is used meaning a theological "good tidings." "Capernaum" means "village of Nahum." Mark chose this village to be Jesus's home because of the LXX reference to "gospel." This is consistent with the conclusion that Jesus was not from Nazareth, according to Mark but was "a Nazarene."

In Jesus's first healing miracle at Mark 1:24, the unclean spirit paraphrases what the widow of Zaraphath says to Elijah at 1 Kgs 17:18. Elijah healing the widow's son is his only healing miracle.

---

10. Ibid.
11. Ibid.
12. Price, "Midrash."

"HEALING SIMON'S MOTHER-IN-LAW" (1:29–34)

The source of this pericope is 1 Kg 17:19–24 wherein Elijah raises the widow of Zaraphath's son. The widow's son died and Elijah laid him on Elijah's bed just as Simon's mother-in-law is lying in bed with a fever. Elijah revives the son by lying on top of him and praying. Jesus revives Simon's mother-in-law by taking her hand and raising her up.

"DESERT TO PRAY" 1:35–38

This pericope is a foreshadowing of Jesus's arrest at 14:43–49. Simon and others find Jesus praying in the desert paralleling Judas and others finding Jesus praying in Gethsemane. Simon tells Jesus prophetically, "Everyone is looking for you." Jesus's arrest on the Mount of Olives is based on David's flight from Absolom at 2 Sam 15–17.

"HEALING THE LEPER" (1:39–45)

The sources for this pericope are:

- Exodus 4:6–7,[13] wherein God gives Moses leprosy and then cures it.
- Leviticus 14:1–32, the Mosaic law of leprosy.

In Exod 4:6–7 Moses takes his hand out of his robe and it is cured. This parallels the leper in Mark 1:41 streatching out his hand and it is healed. At 1:44 Jesus tells the leper to do what Moses commanded. This reference to Moses is Mark's signal that "Healing the Leper" is based on the healing of Moses's leprosy. Lev 14:1–32 is the law of leprosy to which Jesus referred.

"HEALING THE PARALYTIC" (2:1–12)

The sources of this pericope are:

- 2 Kings 1:2–16, the story of Elijah and King Ahaziah who did not have faith.
- Romans 3:19—5:20, wherein Paul espouses his doctrine of justification by faith.

Mark created Jesus's healing of the paralytic by adapting 2 Kgs 1:2–16 wherein Ahaziah falls through a lattice and breaks his leg. Elijah condemns Ahaziah because he sought the counsel of the priests of Beelzebub, the god of Ekron rather than Yahweh. Ahaziah did not have faith in Yahweh and he died. The paralytic and his friends had faith that Jesus could see, and he was healed. The paralytic's sins were forgiven. Jesus says, "Arise" twice, and the narration says the paralytic arose. In the Elijah and Ahaziah story

---

13. Ibid.

"come down" is stated seven times, four times in reference to Ahaziah coming down from his bed and three times in reference to fire coming down from heaven. This is a Markan clue that "Healing the Paralytic" concerns the opposite of Elijah and Ahaziah.

Jesus tells the paralytic that his sins are forgiven after seeing his faith and that of his friends. This is Mark's pronouncement on Paul's doctrine of justification by faith as set forth in Rom 3:19—5:20. Ahaziah has no faith and dies,[14] whereas the paralytic has faith and his sins are forgiven, and presumably will have eternal life. This pericope begins a short Pauline section in Mark's Gospel.

"CALLING LEVI" (2:13–14)

The source of this short pericope is 1 Kgs 19:19–21. This is Mark's third use of 1 Kgs 19, and second use of 1 Kgs 19:19–21. Just as with his first four disciples, Jesus asks Levi to follow him, and Levi immediately leaves his tax-collecting booth to follow Jesus. In both 1 Kgs 19:21 (LXX) and Mark 2:14 the disciple "arose" (anastas) and then followed.

"EATING WITH SINNERS" (2:15–17)

The source of this pericope is Gal 2:11–15 as Mark continues his Pauline section in the early part of the Gospel. Mark's Jesus is challenged by the scribes of the Pharisees because he is eating and drinking with sinners (hamartōlōn) and tax collectors. This is similar to Gal 2:11–15 wherein Paul recounts an occasion when Peter refuses to eat with gentile sinners (hamartōloi), and Paul calls Peter a hypocrite. In this pericope Mark is drawing an analogy between Peter with the scribes of the Pharisees and Paul with Jesus. At Gal 2:16 Paul reiterates his doctrine of justification by faith that began this Pauline section in Mark's Gospel.

"LESSON ON FASTING" (2:18–22)

Mark continues his Pauline section in this pericope by having Jesus express Paul's view on eating and fasting from Rom 14:2–6. At Rom 14:4 Paul asks "Who are you to judge the servant of another." In "Lesson on Fasting" Mark constructs the story such that "they" are judging Jesus's disciples for not fasting as the disciples of John and the disciples of the Pharisees do. This detail of Paul condemning those who judge another's servant and Jesus's challengers condemning his disciples for not fasting is powerful evidence that Mark used this passage from Romans as a basis for his story about Jesus. At Rom 14:3 Paul writes, "Let not him that eats disparage him who eats not; and let not him that eats not disparage him who eats." At Mark 2:19–20 Jesus tells his challengers that there is a time to eat and a time to fast.

---

14. 2 Kgs 1:17.

"Plucking Grain on the Sabbath" (2:23–28)

The lesson of this pericope comes from Rom 14:5–6 while Jesus makes reference to 1 Sam 21:1 and 2 Sam 15. At Rom 14:5–6 Paul says it does not matter which day you set aside for God. When the Pharisees condemn Jesus's disciples for plucking grain on the Sabbath, Jesus reminds the Pharisees of 1 Sam 21. In this pericope Mark gets the name of the priest wrong. He has Jesus say that Abiathar was the priest in 1 Sam 21 when in fact it was Ahimelech. Many think this is a mistake by Mark, including the authors of The Gospel of Matthew and the Gospel of Luke, both of whom omit the name of the priest in their versions of the story. Mark was deliberately making a reference to 2 Sam 15 where Abiathar is mentioned during David's flight from Absolom. Mark typically uses an OT section as a source at least twice and some times three times. "Plucking Grain on the Sabbath" is his one of his two references to 2 Sam 15, 16. The other is at Jesus's arrest in Gethsemane.

"Healing the Man with a Withered Hand" (3:1–6)

Mark uses 1 Kgs 13:4–6[15] as a source for this healing on the Sabbath. In 1 Kgs 13:4–6 (LXX) a mysterious "man of God" causes Jeroboam's hand to wither when he stretches (ekteinon) it out to touch the man of God. Jesus tells the man with the withered hand to "stretch out (ekteinon) your hand." At 1 Kgs 13:6 Jeroboam's withered hand is restored when the man of God entreats Yahweh to cure him. Jesus restores the man's hand to the consternation of the Pharisees.

"Crowd at the Sea; Demons Know the Son of God" (3:7–12)

Isaiah 9:1–7 provides the inspiration for this pericope. The passage in Isaiah is basically a hymn about the coming Messiah from the house of David. In the introduction to the hymn Isaiah mentions coming by sea, Galilee, and beyond the Jordan. The LXX version of Isa 9:1–7 also mentions Judea which does not appear in translations of the Masoretic text of the OT. Mark says that Jesus and his disciples withdraw to the sea. He also mentions where the crowd gathering around Jesus comes from: Judea, Galilee, beyond the Jordan. Mark also has Jesus ask that a boat wait on him. At Mark 3:10 Jesus cures the infirm. Isaiah 9:2 says, "the people that walked in darkness have seen a great light." At Mark 3:11 the demons identify Jesus as the Son of God. At Isa 9:6 it reads, "unto us a son is given" and at Isa 9:7 "upon the throne of David." It is almost as if Mark is telling the reader that Isa 9:1–7 lets him know who Jesus is.

---

15. Price, "Midrash."

"APPOINTING THE TWELVE" (3:13–19)

The source of this pericope is Exod 18:19–26 wherein Jethro, Moses' father-in-law, recommends to Moses that he appoint lesser judges to rule in the lesser cases, rather than judging all cases himself. Moses follows his advice. In Mark Jesus chooses twelve of his disciples to be apostles as his representatives who he can send out to preach and cast out demons. Mark has Jesus following in Moses' footsteps in ministering to the twelve tribes of Israel.

"CONTROVERSY ON BEELZEBUL," "WHO ARE MY BROTHERS" (3:20–34)

The sources of these two pericopae are:

- Exodus 18:1–14 wherein Moses's family come to visit him
- 2 Kings 1:1–16 wherein Elijah condemns Ahaziah for consulting with Beelzebub rather than Yahweh about his injury.
- 1 Corinthians 7:12–17, Paul's discourse on the family.

These pericopae contain one of Mark's intercalations where one story is interrupted by another story and then the first story is completed. These tripartite constructions are sometimes called "Markan Sandwiches."

In Exod 18:1–14, Jethro, Moses's father-in-law, brings Moses' wife and children back to him. Jethro sends word to Moses that he is coming with Moses' wife and sons. Moses goes out to meet them, bows down and kisses Jethro. In one of Mark's ironic opposites Jesus's family come to get him because they think he is crazy, presumably for traveling around Galilee claiming to be the "Son of Man." They call to Jesus and he ignores them, the opposite of Moses's reaction to Jethro and his family. This is the second use of Exod 18 by Mark. As we have seen happen before, Mark put the stories of Exod 18 in reverse order in his Gospel, first appointing the twelve apostles and then describing the visit of Jesus's family. In Exodus 18 the visit of the family comes first and then the appointment of judges. This is the third reversal of an OT story by Mark

In the interrupting story the scribes from Jerusalem accuse Jesus of casting out demons by Beelzebul. This is the third use by Mark of an element of 2 Kgs 1:2–16, the only passage in the OT that mentions Beelzebub. In 2 Kgs 1 Beelzebub is not another name for Satan, but is the God of Ekron. As stated in chapter 15 all three pericopae in Mark that reference 2 Kgs 1:2–16 contain the phrase "forgiveness of sins."

At 1 Cor 7:12–17 Paul explains that a Christian's true family is his fellow Christians and a Christian should not worry if an unbelieving spouse leaves him. In Mark 3:33–34 Jesus rejects his family because they think he is crazy. Jesus says that those who do God's will are his true family.

"CALMING THE SEA" (4:36–41)

The sources of this story about Jesus are:

- Jonah 1:4–15, wherein the sea is calmed by throwing Jonah into the sea.
- Psalms 107:29–30,[16] which says that God calms the sea.

The story of Jonah is remarkably similar to Jesus calming the storm. Jonah is asleep when the captain awakens him to ask him about the storm. In Mark Jesus is asleep when the disciples awaken Jesus to tell him about the storm. Jonah tells the sailors to throw him overboard and the sea is calmed. Jesus tells the sea to be quiet and it is calmed. Psalms 107:28–29 says, "Then they cried out to the Lord in their trouble, and he brought them out from their distress. He made the storm be still and the waves of the sea were hushed."

"HEALING THE GERASENE DEMONIAC" (5:1–20)

The source for this healing is Ps 107:10–16. This passage of Psalms has many of the same elements as "Healing of the Gerasene Demoniac:" living in the tombs, bound with shackles, falling down, crying out, going to family, and praising God for wonderful works. This is the second reference to Ps 107 and again, Mark puts it in reverse order from the OT. This is the fourth reversal of an OT source in Mark's Gospel. In both Mark and the OT these reversed sourced pericopae are consecutive. That is, when Mark bases two events in Jesus's life on consecutive OT stories, he typically puts the them consecutively in his Gospel but in reverse order from the OT. We can be assured that Mark did this intentionally and was signaling to the astute reader what he was doing.

"WOMAN WITH BLOOD FLOW," "JAIRUS'S DAUGHTER IS DEAD," "HEALING JAIRUS'S DAUGHTER" (5:21–43)

The sources of these pericopae, another intercalation, are:

- 2 Kings 4: 8–37,[17] wherein Elisha heals the Shunammite woman's son.
- Leviticus 15:19–33, concerning the law on menstruation.
- Isaiah 4:4, containing a prophesy about women and blood.

The first and third parts of this intercalation, "Jairus's Daughter Is Dead" and "Healing Jairus's Daughter are very similar to Elisha healing the Shunammite woman's son. Jairus is the leader of the synagogue, and the Shunammite woman is rich. Jairus

16. Ibid.

17. Price, "Midrash."

seeks Jesus out as he comes ashore from a boat, and the Shunammite woman rides on a donkey to find Elisha. Jairus falls at Jesus's feet, and the Shunammite woman falls at Elisha's feet. Jairus tells Jesus his daughter is at the point of death, and the Shunammite woman tells Elisha her son is dead. Jairus's daughter is in a bed in the house, and the Shunammite woman's son is in a bed. Jairus asks Jesus to lay his hands on his daughter to cure her, Elisha lies on top of the Shunammite woman's son and puts his hands on the son's hands to cure him. Jesus takes Peter, James and John in with him when he cures the daughter, and Elisha sends his disciple Gehazi to the boy's bed to lay Elisha's staff on the boy. Jesus tells the daughter to arise and she does, and after the boy awakens Elisha tells the Sunammite woman to take her son and she does.

In Act I of Mark's Gospel some of the events in Jesus's life are based on events in Elijah's life. Beginning in Act II events in Jesus's life are no longer based on Elijah, but on events in Elisha's life. References to Elisha cease after "Feeding the Multidude" (6:34–37, 8:5–9).

The woman with the flow of blood is unclean according to Lev 15:19–33. Isaiah 4:4 says, "Once the Lord has washed away the filth of the daughters of Zion and cleansed the bloodstains of Jerusalem from its midst by a spirit of judgment and by a spirit of burning." Instead of being cleansed by burning, Mark's Jesus cures the woman by her touching his robe, and he tells her that her faith has cured her. The blood flow for twelve years symbolizes the twelve tribes of Israel, which have become unclean. Mark is metaphorically saying that Judaism will become clean with faith.

"JESUS REJECTED IN HIS OWN COUNTRY" (6:1–6)

This pericope is base on 1 Sam 10:10–13[18] wherein Saul is given the gift of prophecy, and his old friends ask derisively whether Saul is now one of the prophets and what has come over the son of Kish. This is parallel to Jesus's rejection in his hometown wherein the congregation asks who Jesus thinks he is, what mighty works has he done, and is this not the carpenter, the son of Mary.

"SENDING OUT THE TWELVE" (6:7–11)

This pericope is based on another Elisha story from 2 Kgs 5:22[19] wherein Elisha refuses a gift from Naaman after Elisha cures Naaman of his leprosy. However, Elisha's disciple Gehazi runs after Naaman and asks for money and two changes of clothes. Naaman gives him two bags of silver and two changes of clothes. When Jesus sends out the apostles to preach, he tells them not to take a bag or money or a change of clothes.

---

18. Price, "Midrash."
19. Ibid.

"Killing John the Baptizer" (6:12–29)

The pericope as found in The Original Gospel of Mark is based entirely on J. A. 18:5:1–2 The redactor added material from Esther. In Book 18 of *Antiquities* Josephus writes in paragraph 2 about Herod killing John the Baptizer because he feared John might foment a revolution. In paragraph 1 Josephus writes that Herod married the wife of his dead brother Philip, and divorced his previous wife who was the daughter of King Aretas, but Josephus says nothing about John disapproving of the second marriage. The fact that Mark connected the two events and that Josephus reports them consecutively in *Antiquities* is a strong indication that Mark used *Antiquities* as a source for this story.

"Return of the Twelve" (6:30–31)

This is another pericope based on an event in Elisha's life found at 2 Kgs 5:15–19.[20] Elisha heals Naaman's leprosy and Naaman returns to Elijah to thank him and offer gifts in exchange for the healing. After Jesus sends the twelve out to preach and heal the sick, they return to Jesus and tell him about the success they had. This intercaltion of sending out the twelve and their return is the fifth occasion that Mark has written his story of Jesus in the reverse order from his OT source. If one considers the first and third elements of an intercalation as one story, this OT reversal is also consecutive as were the previous OT reversals. This pericope also follows the pattern of being based upon an event in Elisha's life after concluding events based on Elijah's life.

"The Transfiguration," "Coming Down the Mountain" (9:2–13)

These pivotal pericopae are based on:

- 2 Corinthians 3:18 wherein Paul says Christians will be transfigured.
- Malachi 3:2, "He is like . . . the fuller's soap."
- Malachi 4:5, "Lo, I will send you Elijah, before the great and terrible day of the Lord comes."
- Exodus 24:12–18, wherein Moses goes up on the mountain with Joshua and waits six days in a cloud for God to give him the law.
- Exodus 34:29–30, wherein Moses's face is shining after being in God's presence on the mountain.
- Deuteronomy 18:15, wherein Moses tells the Israelites that God will raise up a prophet like him and that the Israelites should listen to him.

20. Ibid.

In 2 Cor 3:18 Paul says that Christians will be transfigured into the image of the Lord. The same word "metamorphoō" is used by both Mark and Paul. In Mal 3:2 "fuller's soap" is mentioned, and Mark says that Jesus's clothes become whiter than any fuller (launderer). As Jesus and the disciples are coming down the mountain Jesus refers to Mal 4:5 with the coming of Elijah before the day of the Lord. This reference also hearkens back to the beginning of the Gospel at Mark 1:2 that says "I send my messenger before you" from Mal 3:1.

The six-day period of rest Jesus gives the disciples derives from the six-day period Moses waited for God on the mountain in Exod 24:12–18 before God gives Moses the law. At Exod 34:29–30 Moses' face began to shine from being in God's presence. This is probably Paul's source for his statement at 2 Cor 3:18 about Christians being transfigured, since earlier in that chapter of 2 Corinthians Paul wrote about the veil of Moses. In Deut 18:15 Moses tells the Israelites that God will raise up a prophet like him and that they should listen to him. At "The Transfiguration" the voice from the cloud tells Jesus's disciples they should listen to him.

"Healing The Epileptic" (9:14–27)

This miracle healing of a boy possessed by a deaf and mute spirit is based on:

- Isaiah 29:18, "On that day the deaf will hear"

- Isaiah 35:5–6, "The ears of the deaf unstopped . . . the tongue of the speechless sing for joy."

- 2 Kings 4:31 wherein Elisha's disciple Gehazi fails to heal the Shunammite woman's son.

This pericope is the third use by Mark of 2 Kgs 4:18–37 about Elisha and the Shunammite woman. Elisha sends Gehazi ahead with Elisha's staff to try to heal the woman's son, but he fails. After Jesus, Peter, James and John come down the mountain of the transfiguration they find a crowd with the rest of the disciples and a father tells Jesus that the disciples tried to cast an unclean spirit out of his son but they failed.

Isaiah 29 and 35 are part of Deutero-Isaiah that foretells of the Messiah being sent by God to restore Israel. In the two passages referenced above Isaiah prophesies that the deaf will hear. The unclean spirit that has possessed the boy in this pericope is a deaf and mute spirit. Jesus exorcises the spirit.

"The Parable Discourse" (4:1–34)

The sources of this discourse are:

- Isaiah 6:9, "Go and say to this people, 'keep listening but do not comprehend, keep looking but do not understand.'"

- Isaiah 40:18; "To whom then would you liken God, or what likeness compare with him."

- Romans 2:6, "For he will repay according to each one's deeds."

- Romans 16:25, ". . . according to the mystery that was kept secret for long ages."

- 1 Corinthians 2:7, "But we speak God's wisdom, secret and hidden, which was decreed before the ages for our glory."

- 1 Corinthians 3:6, "I planted, Apollos watered, but God gave the growth."

- 1 Corinthians 4:5, ". . . before the Lord comes, who will bring to light the things now hidden in darkness . . ."

- 1 Corinthians 11:31–32, "If we judged ourselves, we would not be judged."

The Parable Discourse is an important demarcation in Mark's Original Gospel. It ends the first section based primarily on the OT and starts the section based primarily on Paul's epistles. Mark may have got the idea of parables about sowing seed and growing from 1 Cor 3:6. The middle of the discourse, 4:21–25, is the most important point that Mark is attempting to get across to his reader. It tells the reader that what has been kept from mankind is now being revealed. Romans 16:25 says, ". . . according to the mystery that was kept secret for long ages." First Corinthians 4:5 says, ". . . before the Lord comes, who will bring to light the things hidden in darkness, . . ." Both Paul and Mark use the Greek "kruptos" (hidden, secret) and "phaneroō" (made manifest, come to light). Mark is deliberately making reference to Paul. Mark also makes the Pauline points that one will be judged as he judges others and shall receive as he gives.

Mark's Jesus quotes Isa 6:9 at 4:11–12 when Jesus tells his disciples, "all things are done in parables so that seeing they might see, and not perceive; and hearing they might hear, and not understand; they might never turn again, and it be forgiven them." Is Jesus being sarcastic at 4:11–12 just as God is being sarcastic with Isaiah at Isa 6:8–10? It is a puzzling statement. It may have something to do with the disciples failure to understand Jesus's message. Jesus quotes Isa 40:18 at Mark 4:30, "How can we picture the kingdom of God? Or in what parable can we present it?" All five direct references to Paul in "The Parable Discourse" are located between the two quotes of Isaiah: Isaiah–Paul–Isaiah. This is the same basic structure of the Gospel: OT–Paul–OT as will be seen in the next chapter.

"Feeding the Multitude" (6:34–37, 8:5–9)

The reconstituted single "Feeding the Multitude" in Original Mark is based upon the following:

- 2 Kings 4:42–44 wherein Elisha feeds one hundred prophets.

- Jeremiah 23:1–5 wherein God is lamenting that Israel is like a flock of sheep without a shepherd.

- 1 Corinthians 11:23–26 wherein Paul institutes the Eucharist.

"Feeding the Multitude" is constructed as are several pericope in Mark where the overall story is an adaptation of a particular OT story and then Mark sprinkles in quotes from other scripture. This is another miracle based upon the life of Elisha. In 2 Kgs 4:42–44 Elisha feeds a hundred prophets during a drought with twenty loaves of barley and fresh ears of grain. His servant complains that this amount of food is not enough for one hundred prophets. When Jesus feeds the multitude his disciples complain that there is not enough food for the multitude. In 2 Kgs 4 the prophets' hunger is satisfied and there is food left over. In Jesus's feeding the crowd's hunger is satisfied and the disciples gather seven baskets of scraps. This is the last event in Jesus's life Mark bases on events in Elisha's life.

Jesus's miracle is more spectacular than Elisha's miracle, of course, as he feeds four thousand with only seven loaves and a few fish. Mark may have got the number of the crowd, four thousand, from *Antiquities*, 18:1:5 where Josephus writes that four thousand belonged to the Essene sect. Jeremiah 23:1–5 is referred to regarding shepherds feeding sheep, and Jesus has compassion for the crowd because they are like sheep without a shepherd.

The blessing of the bread and fish is based on Paul's institution of the Eucharist at 1 Cor 11:23–26 and reprised in "The Last Supper" (14:22–24.) In a typical Markan reversal Jesus here gives thanks for the bread and blesses the fish, whereas in "The Last Supper" he blesses the bread and gives thanks for the cup. The alert reader can see that this miraculous feeding at the beginning of the main Pauline section of the Gospel symbolically portrays Jesus spiritually nourishing the world. Mark telegraphs this with the reference to Jer 23:1–5 at the beginning of the pericope. This symbolic feeding is positioned in the Original Gospel immediately after Jesus tells his disciples that secrets hidden from mankind for ages will be revealed.

"SEEKING A SIGN" (8:10–12)

Mark based "Seeking a Sign" upon 1 Cor 1:22–23 wherein Paul says, "Seeing that Jews ask for signs, and Greeks seek after wisdom, but we preach Christ crucified." Mark's Jesus tells the Pharisees that there will be no sign given to this generation after they have asked him for a sign from heaven. Paul is saying that his Judaising opponets, the Jerusalem apostles, are unaware of a crucifixion of Jesus. Paul reports that he has disputes with Jews, these same disputes show up in Mark's Gospel as Jesus disputing with Pharisees.

"LEAVEN OF THE PHARISEES" (8:13–21)

In "Leaven of the Pharisees," Mark is making reference to one of Paul's metaphors: leaven. The main source for this pericope is 1 Cor 5:6–8, but Paul also mentions leaven at Gal 5:9. First Corinthians 5:6–8 says:

> 5:6 Your glorying is not good. Do you not know that a little leaven leavens the whole lump? 7 Purge out the old leaven, that you may be a new lump, even as you are unleavened. For our Passover also has been sacrificed, even Christ. 8 Therefore, let us keep the feast, not with old leaven, neither with the leaven of malice and wickedness, but with the unleavened bread of sincerity and truth.

Heretofore in Mark's Original Gospel the author has demonstrated that the Pharisees and Herodians are wicked and full of malice. At Mark 3:6 the Pharisees and Herodians consulted on how to kill Jesus. The Herodians killed John the Baptizer (6:27). The Pharisees complained about the disciples picking grain on the Sabbath (2:24). At this point in the Gospel the reader knows that the Pharisees and Herodians are Jesus's opponents. When Jesus tells his disciples to beware the leaven of the Pharisees, the reader knows Jesus is referring to malice and wickedness.

Paul's opponents were the Jerusalem apostles and Paul referred to them using the leaven metaphor. Gal 5:2–10 says:

> 5:2 Listen! I, Paul, am telling you that if you let yourselves be circumcised, Christ will be of no benefit to you. 3 Once again I testify to every man who lets himself be circumcised that he is obliged to obey the entire law. 4 You who want to be justified by the law have cut yourselves off from Christ; you have fallen away from grace. 5 For through the Spirit, by faith, we eagerly wait for the hope of righteousness. 6 For in Christ Jesus neither circumcision nor uncircumcision counts for anything; the only thing that counts is faith working through love. 7 You were running well; who prevented you from obeying the truth? 8 Such persuasion does not come from the one who calls you. 9 A little yeast leavens the whole batch of dough. 10 I am confident about you in the Lord that you will not think otherwise. But whoever it is that is confusing you will pay the penalty.

Mark's Jesus is referring to Paul's leaven of malice and wickedness from 1 Cor 5:8 and he is referring to the Judaising opponents of Paul who the reader knows from Gal 2:9 are Peter, James and John. At Mark 8:18 Jesus refers back to Mark 4:12 and indirectly to Isa 9:16 accusing his disciples of not seeing and not hearing, of being dense.

Mark is telling his readers that the disciples do not understand Paul's Christology. They do not understand Paul's leaven of malice and wickedness. They do not understand Paul's justification by faith and insist that Paul's Greek converts get circumcised.

Meagher thought that Mark obtained an incomplete story about Jesus that he did not understand, but passed it on anyway.[21] As with the disciples, Meagher fails to grasp Mark's reference to Paul. After all, it does not make sense that Jesus could have been referring to documents that were written more than twenty years after Jesus died. Mark's purpose was to convince his readers that the Jerusalem apostles misunderstood Paul's Christianity. But he could not have blatantly said as much without disrupting the drama of his Gospel. He left it up to the reader to reach the desired conclusion.

"Healing the Blind Man of Bethsaida" (8:22–26)

The sources of this healing of a blind man are:

- Isaiah 29:18, ". . . and out of the gloom and darkness the eyes of the blind shall see."

- Isaiah 35:5, "Then the eyes of the blind shall be opened."

- Isaiah 42:7, "to open the eyes of the blind . . ."

- 2 Corinthians 4:4 "In whom the god of this age (Satan) has blinded the minds of the unbelieving, that the light of the gospel of the glory of Christ, who is the image of God, should not dawn upon them."

The blind man of Bethsaida does not get his blindness cured instantly. As Jesus works with him, he slowly comes out of a fog reminiscent of 2 Cor 4:4 and Isa 29:18. In both Paul and Isaiah the reader gets the feeling of coming out of a fog, rather than an instantaneous cure. Isaiah prophesied that the Messiah would make the blind see. Isaiah was not being literal, but metaphorical, and he meant that the Messiah would make the unbelievers see the wonders of God's work. Mark understood that and was also being metaphorical.

"Peter's Confession at Caesarea Philippi" (8:27–37)

Jesus's prediction of his death and resurrection, the Passion, is discussed in the next section. The remainder of this pericope, consisting of Peter's identification of Jesus as the Christ, Jesus's rebuke of Peter and Jesus's sermon on discipleship, is derived from Paul's epistles:

- 2 Corinthians 11:13–14, wherein Paul compares the Jerusalem apostles to Satan.

- Romans 1:16, "For I am not ashamed of the gospel."

- Philippians 3:10–11, wherein Paul expresses his willingness to suffer as Jesus did.

21. Meagher, *Clumsy*, 79.

After Peter has identified Jesus as being the Christ, Jesus makes his first prediction of his Passion. Peter says something to Jesus. Mark only tells the reader that it is a rebuke. Jesus responds by admonishing Peter and addresses him as "Satan" for not minding the things of God. Mark has Jesus repeating Paul's comparison of the Jerusalem apostles with Satan at 2 Cor 11:13–14:

> 13 For such men are false apostles, deceitful workers, fashioning themselves into apostles of Christ. 14 And no marvel; for even Satan masquerades as an angel of light.

In this passage from 2 Cor 11, Paul excoriates the Judaisers, those who want to impose Jewish law on Christians, the Jerusalem apostles, which includes Peter. Mark joins Paul in calling Peter "Satan."

Paul also writes about shame and the gospel at Rom 1:16. Mark and Paul both use the verb "I am ashamed" (epaischunomai). Mark's Jesus says at 8:38, "For whoever might have been ashamed of me and of my words in this adulterous and sinful generation, the Son of Man also will be ashamed of him." Mark has told the reader at 1:1, the incipit, that this is the "gospel of Jesus." Therefore, when Jesus says "me and my words" it is synonymous with "gospel." At Rom 1:16 Paul says that he is not ashamed of the gospel. Mark's Jesus is telling the crowd to be like Paul.

Jesus tells the crowd that they need to take up their crosses at Mark 8:34. Paul does not specifically say that he is ready to "take up his cross" but he expresses the same idea at Phil 3:10–11, "10 That I may know him, and the power of his resurrection, and the fellowship of his sufferings, becoming conformed with his death 11 if by any means I may attain the resurrection of the dead."

JESUS'S PREDICTIONS OF THE PASSION (8:31–33), (9:30–32), (10:32–34)

In Paul's theology derived from Isaiah's Suffering Servant, Jesus was crucified buried and raised from the dead in propitiation for the sins of mankind. Mark used Paul's expressions of that theology to have Jesus predict his Passion.

- 1 Corinthians 1:23, "We preach Christ crucified . . ."

- 1 Corinthians 15:3–4, Wherein Paul expresses his creed.

- 2 Corinthians 13:4, "For he was crucified through weakness, yet he lives through the power of God . . ."

- Isaiah 53:3, "He was despised and rejected by others, a man of suffering."

- Isaiah 53:12, ". . . he poured himself out to death . . ."

- Hosea 6:2, ". . . on the third day he will raise us up."

At 1 Cor 15:3–4 Paul sets out his creed:

> For I delivered unto you first of all that which also I received: that Christ died
> for our sins according to the scriptures; 4 and that he was buried; and that he
> has been raised on the third day according to the scriptures.

"According to the scriptures" (kata tas graphas) in this context means that what happened to Jesus was revealed to Paul through the scriptures, the OT. This is what Paul means at Gal 3:1 when he writes, "Oh foolish Galatians who did bewitch you, before whose eyes Jesus Christ was crucified as written before hand (proegraphē)." "Written before hand" is Paul's reference to the OT.

Mark's Jesus predicts three times that he will be killed and raised from the dead.

Jesus's Predictions of the Parousia (8:38—9:1, 13:26–27, 14:62)

One of Mark's objectives in writing his Gospel was to convince Christians and prospective Christians that Christ would be coming to Earth soon to establish the kingdom of God. This is the part of Paul's theology with which the Jerusalem apostles agreed. Mark's Jesus makes three predictions that the Parousia (coming of the kingdom of God) will happen soon. Paul's theology is based upon Dan 7:13–14. Mark's Jesus repeats Paul's theology on the coming of the kingdom of God:

- 1 Thessalonians 3:13, ". . . at the coming of our Lord Jesus with all his saints."

- 1 Thessalonians 4:16–17, wherein Paul tells the Thessalonians how the kingdom of God will be initiated.

- Daniel 7:13–14, that contains the source of Jesus's "Son of Man."

Paul writes to the Thessalonians his theology on the coming of the kingdom of God at 1 Thess 4:16–17:

> 16 For the Lord himself, with a cry of command, with the archangel's call and
> with the sound of God's trumpet, will descend from heaven, and the dead in
> Christ will rise first. 17 Then we who are alive, who are left, will be caught up
> in the clouds together with them to meet the Lord in the air; and so we will be
> with the Lord forever.

It is evident that Paul got his theology from Dan 7:13–14 even though Paul never uses the term "Son of Man":

> 13 I saw one like a son of man coming with the clouds of heaven. And he came
> to the Ancient of Days and was presented before him. 14 To him was given do-
> minion and glory and kingship, that all people, nations, and languages should
> serve him. His dominion is an everlasting dominion that shall not pass away,
> and his kingship is one that shall never be destroyed.

"TEACHING THE DISCIPLES" (9:33–35) (10:31) (10:33–45)

Jesus tells his disciples that they must be servants to be great; that the first will be last and the last first, reiterating Paul who wrote at Phil 2:5–8:

> 5 Have this in your mind, which was also in Christ Jesus: 6 who, existing in the form of God, did not depend upon being equal with God something to take advantage of, 7 but emptied himself, taking the form of a slave, being made in the likeness of men; 8 and being found in fashion as a man, he humbled himself, becoming obedient even unto death, yes, the death of the cross. 9 Therefore, God highly exalted him, and gave him a name which is above every name.

At 9:35 Mark uses a different word for being in servitude from Paul. Mark uses "diakonos" meaning "servant," while Paul uses "doulou" which means "slave." But at 10:34 Mark, in having Jesus stating his point again, uses Paul's "doulou" from Phil 2:7.

"ANSWERING JOHN" (9:36–41)

When John tells Jesus they forbid a man from casting out demons in Jesus's name, Jesus tells John not to do that, because "he that is not against us is for us." This is a reversal of Rom 8:31 where Paul says, "If God is for us, who can be against us?" Paul's quote is taken from Ps 118:6.

The unnamed man who did a mighty work in Jesus's name that the disciples stopped is Paul. The alert reader will notice that Jesus makes a reverse quote of Rom 8:31 and realize that Mark's Jesus is admonishing the Jerusalem apostles for opposing Paul.

"MILLSTONE AWARD" (9:42–50)

The sources of "The Millstone Award" are:

- 1 Corinthians 5:1–13, wherein Paul writes that the congregation should excommunicate evildoers.
- 1 Corinthians 12:12–20, wherein Paul compares the congregation to parts of a human body.
- Isaiah 66:24, ". . . for their worm shall not die, their fire shall not be quenched, and they shall be an abhorrence to all flesh."

Jesus's gives a strange sermon at Mark 9:42–50 that seems to advocate cutting off offending body parts. In reality this sermon is a lesson on excommunicating immoral members from the congregation based upon 1 Cor 5:1–13, using Paul's metaphor of church members being separate body parts of the congregation from 1 Cor 12:12–20.

This interpretation is confirmed by the observation that Paul at 1 Cor 12:12–20 and Jesus at Mark 9:42–47 both use the words "hand," "eye" and "foot" twice.

First Corinthians 5:11–13 says:

> 11 But as it is, I wrote to you not to keep company, if any man that is named a brother be a fornicator, or covetous, or an idolater, or a reviler, or a drunkard, or an extortioner; with such a one do not even eat. 12 For what have I to do with judging them that are outside? Do not you judge them that are inside? 13 But they that are ouside God judges. Send away the wicked man from among you.

The main part of Paul's metaphor on body parts is at 1 Cor 12:14–17:

> 14 For the body is not one member, but many. 15 If the foot shall say, "Because I am not the hand, I am not of the body;" it is not, therefore, not part of the body. 16 And if the ear shall say, "Because I am not the eye, I am not of the body;" it is not, therefore, not part of the body. 17 If the whole body were an eye, where is the hearing? If the whole were hearing, where is the smelling?

Notice how cleverly Mark has combined two passages from Paul into a memorable sermon by Jesus. Jesus begins this sermon at 9:46 by saying, "And whoever causes one of these little ones believing in me to stumble, it would be better for him if a heavy millstone were put around his neck, and he were thrown into the sea." Telling the reader that if one causes another to stumble it would be better if they were thrown into the sea rather than somewhere else. Then Jesus goes into a foot causing one to stumble, a hand causing one to stumble, and an eye causing one to stumble. Therefore, the reader should be aware that the sermon is about evil influences and throwing them away, i.e., excommunicating them, as Paul advised the Corinthians.

"CONTROVERSY ON DIVORCE" AND "REMARRIAGE IS ADULTERY" (10:1–12)

The Christian doctrine on divorce was first expressed by Paul at Rom 7:2–3 and 1 Cor 7:10–11, 39. Mark's Jesus repeals Jewish law on divorce and says that once a husband and wife are married, they commit adultery if they divorce and marry others. Jesus's new rule is reiterative of Paul's doctrine.

Paul set out the basic commandment at Rom 7:2:

> 2 For the woman who has a husband is bound by law to the husband as long as he lives; but if the husband die, she is discharged from the law of the husband. 3 Therefore, then, if while the husband lives, she be joined to another man, she shall be called an adulteress. But if the husband dies, she is free from the law, so that she is no adulteress, though she be joined to another man.

Paul restates the commandment at 1 Cor 7:10–11 and 7:39:

> 10 But to the married I give this charge, not I, but the Lord, That a wife not leave her husband 11 (but if she leaves, let her remain unmarried, or else be reconciled to her husband); and that a husband not leave his wife . . . 39 A wife is bound for so long time as her husband lives; but if the husband is dead, she is free to marry to whom she will.

The above quotation is from a long passage wherein Paul deals with a number of questions on marriage and divorce. It is obvious that a redactor added "not I, but the Lord" to 1 Cor 7:10. Paul never gives Jesus credit for any of the teachings Paul expresses. Other redactions have been noted to 1 Cor by exegetes.[22]

"Entering The Kingdom of God" (10:13–16)

Jesus's lesson that one must be like a child to enter the kingdom of God is based on Phil 2:14–15:

> 14 Do all things without murmuring and questioning: that you may become innocent and harmless, children of God without blemish in the midst of a crooked and perverse generation, among whom you are seen as lights in the world.

"The Rich Man" (10:17–31)

The sources of this pericope are:

- 2 Corinthians 6:10, wherein Paul recounts his virtues
- 2 Corinthians 8:9, wherein Paul tell the Corinthians they will be rich in heaven.
- Romans 4:21, "and (Abraham) being fully assured that what he (God) had promised, he was able also to perform."
- Genesis 18:14, "Is anything impossible for the Lord?"

Jesus echoes Paul's teaching that spiritual riches are more important than earthly ones. Paul recounts his virtues in 2 Cor 6:10, "As sorrowful, yet always rejoicing; as poor, yet making many rich; as having nothing, and possessing all things." Then Paul tell the Corinthians that they will become rich in heaven at 2 Cor 8:9, "For you know the grace of our Lord Jesus Christ, that, though he was rich, yet for your sakes he became poor, that through his poverty you might become rich."

Paul explains his doctrine of justification by faith by giving the example of Abraham in Rom 4. Paul says that nothing is impossible for God, which is based on Gen 18:14, and the story of Abraham and Sarah having a child at an advanced age. Mark's Jesus also says nothing is impossible with God.

22. Price, "1 Corinthians."

"Request of James and John" (10:35–41)

James and John ask Jesus that they sit at his right and left hands in his glory. Jesus tells James and John metaphorically that they will suffer persecution because they are Christians as Paul writes about the persecutions he has suffered at 2 Cor 11:23–27:

> 23 Are they ministers of Christ? (I speak as a madman) I am better; with more labor, in more prisons, receiving more stripes, often at the point of death. 24 From the Jews five times I received forty stripes save one. 25 Three times was I beaten with rods, once was I stoned, three times I suffered shipwreck, a night and a day have I been in the sea; 26 journeying often, perils of rivers, perils of robbers, perils from my countrymen, perils from the gentiles, perils in the city, perils in the wilderness, perils in the sea, perils from false brothers; 27 in labor and travail, in watching often, in hunger and thirst, in fasting often, in cold and nakedness.

It is not clear that James and John understand Jesus's metaphor. He is telling them they will suffer instead of being associated with a glorious earthly king as they are assuming. The reader knows that James and John are asking about earthly glory and not heavenly glory, because in heaven Jesus would have God on his left hand.[23] Therefore, James and John are not asking about heavenly glory.

"Controversy on Tradition" (10:46a, 7:1–7:15)

This pericope is based on 1 Cor 1:19–20 wherein Paul is excoriating the Jews and the legalistic arguments of the scribes:

> 19 For it is written, I will destroy the wisdom of the wise, and the discernment of the discerning will I bring to nought. 20 Where is the wise? Where is the scribe? Where is the disputer of this world? Has not God made foolish the wisdom of the world?

Paul here quotes Isa 29:14. To indicate his source, Mark's Jesus quotes Isa 29:13 in excoriating the Pharisees:

> 13 Because these people draw near with their mouths and honor me with their lips, while their hearts are far from me, and their worship of me is a human commandment learned by rote.

After quoting Isaiah Jesus then gives an example of a legalistic argument in support of breaking the commandment to honor your father and mother, accusing the Pharisees of making such arguments, echoing Paul's objection to the legalistic arguments of the scribes at 1 Cor 1:19–20.

---

23. Mark 14:62; Rom 8:34.

"EATING DOES NOT DEFILE" (7:17–23)

This pericope wherein Jesus repeals Jewish dietary laws is based on Rom 14:14–20:

> 14 I know, and am persuaded in the Lord Jesus, that nothing is unclean of itself: save that to him who accounts anything to be unclean. To him it is unclean. 15 For if because of food your brother is grieved, you are no longer walking in love. Do not destroy with your food one for whom Christ died. 16 Let not then your good be spoken of as evil, 17 for the kingdom of God is not eating and drinking, but righteousness and peace and joy in the Holy Spirit. 18 For he that serves Christ is pleasing to God, and approved of men. 19 So then let us follow after things that make for peace, and things whereby we may edify one another. 20 Do not overthrow the work of God for the sake of food. All things indeed are clean; however, it is evil for a man who eats with offence.

Jesus says that evil comes from the heart of men and all food is clean. Both Paul and Mark use the word "katharizōn" (to make clean). Both are saying that Jewish dietary restrictions are not necessary for Christians. Paul is defying the Jerusalem apostles who want to impose Jewish law on his converts. Mark is supporting Paul.

"HEALING BLIND BARTIMAEUS" (10:46B–52)

"Healing Blind Bartimaeus" begins a section of Mark's Original Gospel about the replacement of Judaism with Christianity. It is based on:

- Romans 2:19, "And are you confident that you yourself are a guide of the blind, a light for them that are in darkness."
- 2 Corinthians 3:19, 4:3–4, wherein Paul writes about the mind of the Jews being veiled so that they cannot see the glory of Christ.

Jesus heals the blind man and he follows Jesus. Paul accuses the Jews of being blind at Rom 2:17–24 and refers to the veil of Moses at 2 Cor 3:19, 4:3–4:

> 3:19 But their minds were hardened: for until this very day at the reading of the old covenant the same veil remains, it not being revealed to them that it is done away in Christ . . . 4:3 And even if our gospel is veiled, it is veiled in them that perish. 4 In whom the god of this age (Satan) has blinded the minds of the unbelieving, that the light of the gospel of the glory of Christ, who is the image of God, should not dawn upon them.

Mark uses Blind Bartimaeus as a metaphor for all Jews who he believes should begin to follow Jesus.

"GETTING A COLT FOR JESUS" (11:1–6)

In "Getting a Colt for Jesus" Jesus sends two disciples into a town to get a colt for Jesus to ride upon. This pericope is based on 1 Sam 9:3–10[24] wherein Saul and a servant attempt to locate three donkeys belonging to Saul's father and they go into a town and ask the seer Samuel where the donkeys are. This pericope ends a Pauline section of the Original Gospel and begins an OT section.

"ENTERING JERUSALEM" (11:2–10)

"Entering Jerusalem" is based upon:

- Zechariah 9:9, "Rejoice greatly, O daughter Zion! Shout aloud, O daughter Jerusalem! Lo, your king comes to you; triumphant and victorious is he, humble and riding on a donkey, on a colt, the foal of a donkey."
- Psalms 118:26 "Blessed is the one who comes in the name of the Lord. We bless you from the house of the Lord.
- 1 Maccabees 13:51, wherein Simon Maccabeus triumphantly enters Jerusalem.

Jesus triumphantly rides into Jerusalem with the crowd spreading branches before him and singing praises. In 1 Macc 13:51 Simon Maccabeus triumphantly comes into Jerusalem:

> 51 On the twenty-third day of the second month, in the one hundred and seventy-first year, the Jews entered the citadel with shouts of praise, the waving of palm branches, the playing of harps and cymbals and lyres, and the singing of hymns and canticles, because a great enemy of Israel had been crushed.[25]

This pericope is another where Mark uses a particular OT story as the framework for his pericope and then utilizes quotations from other books of the OT. Here the story is from 1 Macc 13, but the quotations are from Zech 9 and Ps 118.

"CURSING THE FIG TREE" (11:11–14)

Jesus's cursing of a fig tree because it had no fruit is based on the comparison of Israel to a fig tree found in Hosea 9:9,[26] "Like grapes in the wilderness, I found Israel. Like the first fruit on the fig tree, in its first season." The comparison becomes more obvious in the second part of this intercalation when the fig tree is withered.

---

24. Price, "Midrash."
25. NAB.
26. Price, "Midrash."

"Clearing the Temple" (11:15–18)

"Clearing the Temple" is based on:

- 1 Maccabees 13:47–50 wherein Simon Maccabeus clears the citadel in Jerusalem.

- Isaiah 56:7, ". . . For my house shall be called a house of prayer for all peoples."

- Jeremiah 7:11, "Has this house, which is called by my name, become a den of robbers in your sight? . . ."

Simon Maccabeus cleaned the citadel at 1 Macc 13:47–50:

> 47 So Simon came to terms with them and did not attack them. He expelled them from the city, however, and he purified the houses in which there were idols. Then he entered the city with hymns and songs of praise. 48 After removing from it everything that was impure, he settled there people who observed the law. He improved its fortifications and built himself a residence. 49 The people in the citadel in Jerusalem were prevented from going out into the country and back to buy or sell; they suffered greatly from hunger, and many of them died of starvation. 50 They finally cried out to Simon, and he gave them terms of peace. He expelled them from the citadel and cleansed it of impurities.[27]

This is the second reference by Mark to 1 Macc 13. For the sixth time Mark puts the source in reverse order in his Gospel. These stories are almost consecutive with only the first half of an intercalation dividing the two references to Simon Maccabeus. Again Mark uses 1 Macc 13 as the framework and quotes from Isa 56 and Jer 7.

Simon would not let men come out of the citadel to get food, and Jesus would not let a man carry a pitcher through the temple. Jesus cleansing the temple of its profanities is another metaphor for the replacement of Judaism with Christianity.

In typical Markan fashion, this intercalation of cleansing the temple with the withering of the fig tree are two aspects of the replacement of Judaism by Christianity. This entire section of the Original Gospel began with Jesus healing Blind Bartimaeus, a metaphor for the blind Jews seeing the light and following Jesus.

"The Withered Fig Tree" (11:19–25)

"The Withered Fig Tree" ends an OT section of the Gospel and begins a Pauline section. It is based on:

- Hosea 9:16, "Ephraim is stricken, their root is dried up, they shall bear no fruit."

- Amos 2:9, ". . . I destroyed his fruit above, and his roots beneath."

---

27. NAB.

- 1 Corinthians 13:2, ". . . And if I have all faith, so as to remove mountains, but have not love, I am nothing."

- Romans 8:26, "And in like manner the Spirit also helps our infirmity. For we know not how to pray as we ought . . ."

Mark completes the intercalated metaphors for Israel's demise and the ascendancy of Christianity and returns to Pauline lessons. The first is from 1 Cor 13:2 about having faith to move mountains. The second Pauline lesson is from Rom 8:26 wherein Paul writes that we do not know how to pray. Mark's Jesus supplies that deficiency by advising his disciples to ask their Father in heaven to forgive their trespasses. Matthew turns Mark's outline of a prayer into "The Lord's Prayer." This beautiful prayer could not have been composed by Jesus and handed down by his disciples because Paul wrote to the Romans that "we do not know how to pray." If Paul knew anything about an earthly Jesus, he would have known "The Lord's Prayer."

"Questioning Jesus's Authority" (11:27–33)

"Questioning Jesus's Authority" is based upon three sources:

- 1 Maccabees 10:6–8, wherein Demitrius gives Jonathan Maccabeus authority.

- 2 Corinthians 3:1, wherein Paul complains that his authority is being questioned.

- Galatians 1:1, wherein Paul writes that his authority is not from men.

Jesus is in the temple when chief priests, scribes and elders ask him for his authority to do the things he has done. Jesus asks them if John's baptism was from men or from heaven. Jonathan Maccabeus is given authority in the citadel at 1 Macc 10:6–8:

> 6 So Demetrius authorized him to gather an army and procure arms as his ally; and he ordered that the hostages in the citadel be released to him. 7 accordingly Jonathan went to Jerusalem and read the letter to all the people and to those who were in the citadel. 8 They were struck with fear when they heard that the king had given him authority to gather an army.

At 2 Cor 3:1 Paul sarcastically reacts to his authority being questioned because he does not have a letter of recommendation as others do, "Are we beginning again to commend ourselves? Or do we need, as do some, letters of commendation to you or from you?" At Gal 1:1 Paul says his authority is not from men, "Paul, an apostle (not from men, neither through man, but through Jesus Christ, and God the Father, who raised him from the dead)."

"PARABLE OF THE WICKED TENANTS" (12:1–12A)

This parable of Jesus is based on Isa 5:1–7. Jesus also quotes Ps 118 that Paul quoted at Rom 8:31.

Isaiah's "Parable of the Vineyard" is about God's destruction of Israel and Judah. Mark's Jesus turns it into a parable about Judaism's rejection of the prophets and ultimately the Messiah. Mark's Original Gospel contains a theme of the Jerusalem apostles rejecting the Suffering Servant of Isaiah. This parable metaphorically makes that point.

Jesus quotes Ps 118:22–23, "The stone that the builders rejected has become the chief cornerstone. 23 This is the Lord's doing; it is marvelous in our eyes." This is the third time Ps 118 has been quoted by Mark.

"RENDERING UNTO CAESAR" (12:12B–17)

"Rendering unto Caesar" is derived from Rom 13:1–7. The subject of this pericope and Rom 13:1–7 is paying taxes. Both Mark and Paul use the verb "render" (apodidōmi). Paul writes that Christians should pay honor and respect to those to whom it is due. In like fashion Jesus says to pay to Caesar the things that are Caesar's.

"CONTROVERSY ON RESURRECTION" (12:18–27)

"Controversy on Resurrection" is based on:

- *Antiquities* 18:1:4, about the doctrines of the Sadducees.
- *War* 2:8:14, also about the doctrine of the Sadducees.
- 1 Corinthians 15:12–14, wherein Paul argues against those who deny resurrection of the dead.
- 1 Corinthians 15:35–52, wherein Paul explains heavenly flesh as opposed to earthly flesh.

Josephus and Mark both write that the Sadducees do not believe in resurrection of the dead. Mark again turns a controversy Paul reports as having with some faction into a controversy of Jesus, this time with the Sadducees about resurrection of the dead. Apparently there were some in Corinth who denied resurrection after death. Paul writes at 1 Cor 15:12–14:

> 12 Now if Christ is preached that he has been raised from the dead, why do some among you say that there is no resurrection of the dead? 13 But if there is no resurrection of the dead, neither has Christ been raised. 14 And if Christ has not been raised, then is our preaching vain, your faith also is vain.

Mark's Jesus explains to the Sadducees that in the resurrection humans will have a spiritual flesh, just as Paul explains in 1 Cor 15:50–52.

> 50 Now this I say, brothers, flesh and blood cannot inherit the kingdom of God; neither does corruption inherit incorruption. 51 Behold, I tell you a mystery. We shall not sleep, but we shall be changed, 52 in a moment, in the twinkling of an eye, at the last trumpet. He will sound the trumpet, and the dead shall be raised incorruptible, and we shall be changed.

"THE GREATEST COMMANDMENT" (12:28–34)

Jesus's "Love your neighbor as yourself" is based on:

- Romans 13:9, ". . . You shall love your neigbor as yourself."
- Galatians 5:14, "For the whole law is fulfilled in one word, even in this: you shall love your neighbor as yourself."
- Leviticus 19:18, "You shall not take vengeance or bear a grudge against any of your people, but you shall love your neighbor as yourself: I am the Lord."

Mark's Jesus copies Paul, and Paul copies Leviticus.

"BEWARE THE SCRIBES" (12:35–40)

"Beware the Scribes" is based upon:

- Psalms 110:1, "The Lord says to my lord, Sit at my right hand until I make your enemies your footstool."
- 1 Corinthians 15:25, "For he must reign, until he has put all his enemies under his feet."
- Malachi 3:5, "Then I will draw near to you for judgment; I will be swift to bear witness against . . . those who oppress . . . the widow and the orphan . . ."

Mark's Jesus quotes Psalm 110, just as Paul did at 1 Cor 15:25. Jesus excoriates the scribes for oppressing widows, among other things as Malachi wrote that God will render judgment to those who oppress widows and orphans among other things. Mark's Jesus says that the scribes will receive abundant judgment.

"THE WIDOW'S MITE" (12:41–44)

"The Widow's Mite" is about financially supporting the church and is based upon:

- Malachi 3:8, "Will anyone rob God? Yet you are robbing me! But you say, 'How are we robbing you?' In your tithes and offerings!"

- 2 Corinthians 9:6–7, wherein Paul urges the Corinthians to give what they promised to the church in Macedonia.

Mark's Jesus admires the widow who gave all she had to the Temple as Paul urges at 2 Cor 9:6–7:

> Moreover, he that sows sparingly shall also reap sparingly; and he that sows bountifully shall reap bountifully. Each man should do according as in his heart proposes: not grudgingly, or of necessity, for God loves a cheerful giver.

Malachi 3:8 says that his readers should give more to the temple. Jesus implies that the rich should give more than they are giving.

"THE OLIVET DISCOURSE" (13:3–37)

"The Olivet Discourse" is based on both OT and Pauline writings:

- Daniel 7:13, the prophecy of the "Son of Man."

- Daniel 11:31, "Forces sent by him shall occupy and profane the temple and fortress. They shall abolish the regular burnt offering and set up the abomination of desolation."

- Daniel 12:6, " One of them said to the man clothed in linen, who was upstream, 'How long shall it be until the end of these wonders?'"

- Daniel 12:10, " . . . None of the wicked shall understand, but those who are wise shall understand."

- Isaiah 13:6, "Wail, for the day of the Lord is near; it will come like destruction from the Almighty!"

- Isaiah 13:8, ". . . Pangs and agony will seize them; they will be in anguish like a woman in labor."

- Isaiah 13:10, "For the stars of the heavens and their constellations will not give their light; the sun will be dark at its rising, and the moon will not shed its light."

- Isaiah 13:13, "Therefore I will make the heavens tremble, and the Earth will be shaken out of its place . . ."

- Isaiah 66:11, "that you may nurse and be satisfied from her consoling breast."

- 1 Corinthians 2:3–4, "And I was with you in weakness, and in fear, and in much trembling. 4 And my speech and my preaching were not in persuasive words of wisdom, but in demonstration of the Spirit and of power."

- 2 Corinthians 11:23, "Of the Jews five times received I forty stripes save one."

- 1 Thessalonians 3:13, ". . . at the coming of our Lord Jesus with all his saints."

- 1 Thessalonians 4:16, "For the Lord himself shall descend from heaven, with a shout, with the voice of the archangel, and with the trump of God . . . "

- 1 Thessalonians 5:1–6, wherein Paul explains the coming of the kingdom of God.

The Olivet discourse ends the major Pauline section of Mark's Original Gospel. The discourse draws from Dan 12 with the disciples asking the same question as asked at Dan 12:6. Dan 12:10 states that the wise will understand what is being said inspiring Mark to write, "Let the reader understand" at Mark 13:14. Mark makes reference to 2 Cor 11:23 about being flogged in synagogues, 1 Cor 2:3–4, about the Holy Spirit speaking through the disciples, and 1 Thess 5:1–6:

> 1 But concerning the times and the seasons, brothers, you have no need that anything be written to you. 2 For yourselves know perfectly that the day of the Lord will come as a thief in the night. 3 When they are saying, "peace and safety," then sudden destruction comes upon them, as pain upon a woman with child; and they shall in no way escape. 4 But you, brothers, are not in darkness, that that day should overtake you as a thief: 5 for you are all sons of light, and sons of the day, We are not of the night, nor of darkness; 6 so then let us not sleep, as do the rest, but let us watch and be sober.

Paul's explanation of the coming of the kingdom of God can be seen throughout the discourse: the time is near, no one knows the exact time, pain of childbirth, watch. Throughout the discourse there are quotes from Isaiah: the day of the Lord, the sun and moon will grow dark, earthquakes, the pain of child birth, nursing. Daniel is quoted about the abomination of desolation. Isaiah and Daniel were the sources of Paul's Eschatology.

"The Plot Against Jesus" (14:1–2)

"The Plot Against Jesus" has chief priests and scribes conspiring to kill Jesus. Psalms 41:7 is the source[28] saying, "All who hate me whisper together about me; they imagine the worst for me."

---

28. Price, "Midrash."

"Anointing with Oil in Bethany" (14:3–9)

In "Anointing with Oil in Bethany" a woman pours oil on Jesus's head as he reclines at dinner. In 1 Sam 9:22—10:1 Samuel meets Saul, invites him to dinner and pours oil on his head making him the first king of Israel. Jesus says the woman is preparing his body for burial, but the reader understands that Jesus is being anointed as the Messiah.

Here is the seventh time that Mark has reversed his OT source. But this time the stories that are consecutive in the OT are not consecutive in Mark. Mark used 1 Sam 10:11–12 as the source for Mark 6:1–6a "Jesus Is Rejected in His Own Country."

"Judas Joins the Plot" (14:10–11)

"Judas Joins the Plot" is the final third of another Markan intercalation and Mark continues the reference to Ps 41:9,[29] "Even my bosom friend in whom I trusted, who ate of my bread, has lifted the heel against me." This passage anticipates Judas eating with Jesus at "The Last Supper."

"Finding the Passover Room" (14:12–16)

Jesus sends two disciples to find a room in which they can eat the Passover meal. He tells them that they will meet a man carrying a pitcher of water and to follow him. The source for "Finding the Passover Room" is 1 Sam 9:10–22[30] wherein Saul and a servant are looking for his father's donkeys. They go to find the seer Samuel and see women carrying water. Samuel invites Saul to dinner. This has parallel elements with Jesus's two disciples finding a man carrying water who shows them where to eat the Passover meal. This pericope is the eighth occasion wherein Mark has reversed his OT source when using it in his Gospel.

"The Last Supper" (14:17–25)

"The Last Supper" is based on:

- 1 Corinthians 11:23–26, wherein Paul institutes the Eucharist.
- Exodus 24:8, ". . . "See the blood of the covenant that the Lord has made with you in accordance with all these words."
- Zechariah 9:11, "As for you also, because of the blood of my covenant with you, I will set your prisoners free from the waterless pit."

---

29. Ibid.
30. Ibid.

Mark uses Paul's Last Supper at 1 Cor 11:23–26, repeating many of the same words:

> 23 For I received of the Lord that which also I delivered to you, that the Lord Jesus in the night in which he was delivered up took bread; 24 and when he had given thanks, he broke it, and said, "This is my body, which is for you. Do this in remembrance of me." 25 Likewise after supper also the cup, saying, "This cup is the new covenant in my blood. Do this, as often as you drink it, in remembrance of me."

Paul's Jesus gives thanks over the bread while Mark's Jesus blesses the bread and gives thanks for the cup. Paul's Jesus tells those present to remember him knowing that he is going to his death. Mark's Jesus has not fully decided to go through with the crucifixion; therefore, Mark eliminates Paul's words of remembrance. Paul's Jesus says "new covenant in my blood" while Mark's Jesus says "my blood of the covenant being poured out for many." Mark's Jesus implies he may go through with the crucifixion. "Blood of the covenant" is from Exod 24:8 and Zech 9:11. This pericope has Mark's second reference to Exod 24 and Zech 9.

"Peter Will Deny Jesus" (14:26–31)

Jesus quotes Zech 13:7, ". . . Strike the shepherd, that the sheep may be scattered," as he tells his disciples they will abandon him.

"Praying At Gethsemane" (14:32–36)

The sources of this passage are:

- Genesis 18:14, "Shall anything be impossible with the Lord?"
- 2 Samuel 15:31, wherein David prays on the Mount of Olives that Absolom receive bad advice.
- Romans 8:15, "For you received not the spirit of bondage again unto fear; but you received the spirit of adoption, whereby we cry, 'Abba, Father.'"
- Galatians 4:6, "And because you are sons, God sent forth the Spirit of his son into our hearts, crying, 'Abba, Father.'"

As Mark's Jesus prays in Gethsemane he quotes Gen 18:14 that all things are possible with God. "Abba, Father" is a quote from Rom 8:15 and Gal 4:6, confirming Mark's Adoptionist Christology.

"Sleeping Disciples" (14:37–42)

In 2 Sam 18:24–27 the watchman posted by David alerts David twice of runners approaching. They are messengers with news of Absolom's death, ironically opposite of Jesus telling the disciples to keep watch for those who want to kill Jesus but they fall asleep three times.

"Jesus's Arrest" (14:43–49)

Jesus's arrest at Gethsemane has parallels with 2 Sam 16:9 as David flees from Absolom during Absolom's attempted deposing of David. Shimei begins to curse David and one of David's party threatens to cut off his head, parallel to someone cutting off the ear of the high priest's servant at Mark 14:47. At 2 Sam 16:20–22 David's counselor Ahithophel conspires with Absolom parallel to Judas delivering up Jesus at Mark 14:45.

14:50–52 "Naked Young Man"

This subpericope is sourced from:

- Amos 2:16, "And those who are stout of heart among the mighty shall flee away naked in that day, says the Lord."

- 2 Corinthians 5:1–3, wherein Paul writes that we pray for a home in heaven.

After Jesus is arrested a young man in a linen cloth runs away eluding the chief priest's men but loses the cloth and runs away naked. Amos 2:16 says that the courageous will flee away naked in that day. At 2 Cor 5:1–3 Paul says after the Parousia we shall not be found naked:

> 1 For we know that if the earthly house of our tabernacle is dissolved, we have
> a building from God, a house not made with hands, eternal, in the heavens.
> 2 Truly we groan for this, longing to be clothed in our habitation that is from
> heaven. 3 And being so clothed, we shall not be found naked.

According to Amos the brave will flee naked in that day, and according to Paul after the day of the Lord we shall not be found naked. Therefore, the naked young man who runs away is the same young man the women find in a luxurious robe after Jesus's resurrection.

14:53–72 "SANHEDRIN TRIAL, PETER'S DENIALS"

This long, intercalated pericope is an amalgamation of many sources:

- 1 Kings 22:24;[31] wherein Micah is slapped and asked to prophesy.

- Daniel 6:4,[32] wherein Daniel is tried, but no evidence could be found against him.

- Psalms 110:1, "The Lord says to my lord, 'Sit at my right hand until I make your enemies your footstool.'"

- Isaiah 50:6, "I gave my back to those who struck me, and my cheeks to those who pulled out the beard; I did not hide my face from insult and spitting."

- 2 Corinthians 5:1, ". . . we have a building from God, a house not made with hands, eternal, in the heavens."

- Galatians 2:11–14, wherein Paul exposes Peter as a hypocrite.

Jesus's trial before the Sanhedrin has many OT elements: a lack of evidence as in the trial of Daniel at Dan 6:4, being spit on as in Isa 50:6, being slapped and told to prophesy as in 1 Kgs 22:24. Jesus's third prediction of the Parousia has a new element of being at the right hand of God as in Ps 110:1.

In addition to the Pauline sources for the Parousia enumerated earlier in this chapter, there is a mention in the false evidence against Jesus that is a quotation from 1 Cor 5:1. A witness testifies that Jesus said he would build another temple in three days not made with hands (acheiropoiēton), the same word being used by both Paul and Mark. This word is also used in Colossians, and these are the only three times it is used in the NT.[33] There is an indirect Pauline reference as Peter denies Jesus three times showing his weak character as Paul described in Gal 2:11–14.

"THE TRIAL OF JESUS BEFORE PILATE" (15:1–15)

The second trial of Jesus is based upon:

- Isaiah 50:6, "I gave my back to those who struck me . . ."

- Isaiah 53:7, "He was oppressed, and he was afflicted, yet he did not open his mouth . . ."

- *Antiquities* 18:4:3, wherein Josephus reports that Vitellius released Jerusalem from paying taxes when he attended the Passover.

---

31. Price, "Midrash."
32. Ibid.
33. Strong, *Concordance,* 886.

Jesus's trial before Pilate also has OT references to being scourged as in Isa 50:6 and keeping silent as in Isa 53:7. Scholars report that there was no tradition for releasing prisoners at the Passover in Judaism.[34] However, Josephus reports that on one occasion the Roman president of Syria, Vitellius, released the residents of Jerusalem from paying tax on fruits and vegetables when he attended a Passover celebration. This occurred soon after Vitellius had sent Pilate back to Rome in 36 CE.

"SOLDIERS' ABUSE OF JESUS" 15:16–20

The source of "Soldiers' Abuse of Jesus" is 1 Macc 10:59–65, an ironic opposite to the treatment of Jesus by Pilate's soldiers. In the referenced passage Jonathan Maccabeus is invited to the palace by king Alexander, dressed in purple and given gifts. At this turn of events Jonathan's Jewish enemies flee. The previous reference to 1 Macc 10 was to 1 Macc 10:6–8 when the chief priests and elders asked Jesus by what authority he was doing things. Then the chief priests and elders discuss how to kill Jesus. The second reference of 1 Macc 10 comes at the culmination of the conspiracy as Jesus is convicted and sentenced to death. Mark made four references to First Maccabees, two about Simon Maccabeus and two about Jonathan Maccabeus. The two about Simon are parallel, Simon entered Jerusalem triumphantly and cleansed the temple as did Jesus, but the two references to Jonathan are opposites with Jonathan given authority and dressed in purple and given gifts, scattering his enemies. The parallel stories of Simon are included in reverse order in Mark, and the opposite stories of Jonathan are included in parallel order in Mark.

"THE CRUCIFIXION" (15:20B–39)

Many OT sources are found in "The Crucifixion" with a Pauline source at the climax.

- Psalms 22:1, "My God, my God why have you abandoned me?"
- Psalms 22:16, "For many dogs have compassed me: the assembly of the wicked doers has beset me round: they pierced my hands and my feet."[35]
- Psalms 22:17, "They counted all my bones; and they observed and looked upon me."[36]
- Psalms 22:18, "They parted my garments among themselves, and cast lots upon my raiment."[37]
- Isaiah 13:10, ". . . the sun will be dark at its rising . . ."

---

34. Cunningham, "Death of Jesus,"
35. LXX.
36. Ibid.
37. Ibid

- Isaiah 53:5, "But he was wounded for our transgressions, crushed for our iniquities. upon him was the punishment that made us whole, and by his bruises we are healed."

- Amos 2:12, "But you made the nazirites drink wine, and commanded the prophets, saying, 'You shall not prophesy.'"

- 2 Corinthians 3:16, "But when one shall have turned to the Lord, the veil is taken away."

Psalms 22 provides the outline of Jesus's crucifixion from "My God, my God why have you abandoned me," to being pierced by nails, to being scorned by observers, to soldiers casting lots for his clothes. Isaiah 13:10 says the sun will be dark. Isaiah 53:5 says, "he was wounded for our transgressions, . . . by his bruises we are healed." Amos 2 says that Judeans made the nazirites drink wine. The Romans offered Jesus, the Nazarene, wine and myrrh but he did not take it.

In 2 Cor 2:16 Paul says the veil of Moses is done away with by Christ, and as Jesus dies the temple veil is torn in two. In Greek the words for veil are different in the two passages because of the different sizes of the veils.

"The Burial of Jesus" (15:40–16:10)

The sources of "The Burial of Jesus" are:

- Isaiah 53:9, "They made his grave with the wicked and his tomb with the rich."

- Daniel 6:17, " A stone was brought and laid on the mouth of the den . . ."

- *Life of Flavius Josephus* 76, wherein Josephus reports that after seeing three friends being crucified he went to Titus and asked for them to be taken down. Two died and one survived.

Is it only a coincidence that Josephus reports three friends being crucified and he boldly goes in to Titus Caesar and asks that they be taken down, or did Mark know *Life of Flavius Josephus*? Jesus was placed in a rich man's tomb as prophesied by Isaiah, and a stone was placed against the door of the tomb parallel to the sealing of Daniel in the lions' den.

"The Women at Tomb" (16:1–8)

The sources for the last pericope in the Gospel are:

- Psalms 41:10,[38] "But you, O Lord, be gracious to me, and raise me up, that I may repay them."

---

38. Price, "Midrash."

- Genesis 18:15, "But Sarah denied, saying, I did not laugh, for she was afraid. And he said to her, but you did laugh."[39]

Psalm 41:10 asks God to raise up the psalmist after he has been conspired against and betrayed by his friend. The LXX version Gen 18:15 is quoted by Mark as the last words of the Gospel "for they were afraid" (ephobounto gar).

Conclusion

Mark used stories and quotations from the OT and Josephus to create the events in Jesus's life. Paul writes in his epistles that the story of Jesus's crucifixion as a salvific sacrifice was revealed to him through the OT. Mark made sure that the alert reader would understand that his story was based on the OT by referenceing to OT passages at least twice, and eight times in reverse order from that as found in the OT.

There are hundreds of stories in the OT, is it not possible that in anyone's life a clever author could find an OT parallel for every important event? The answer is that a parallel event from the OT could be found for some random events, but not for all of the important events. The proof that Mark used the OT to create events in Jesus's life lies in the small insignificant parallel details of the story, and his habit of reversing the order of the stories found close to each other.

Mark's stories and the source stories have small parallel details. When Saul is looking for Samuel in order to find his fathers lost donkeys, there are women carrying water and Samuel invites Saul to eat a meal. Jesus tells his disciples to find a man carrying a pitcher and ask him about a room to use for the Passover meal. In addition, it was the habit of Mark to take two consecutive stories from the OT and use them for events in Jesus's life but in reverse order from that found in the OT. Futher, events in Jesus's life in Act I are based on events in Elijah's life and in the early part of Act II they are based on events in Elisha's life. Once the Pauline section of Original Mark begins, neither Elijah nor Elisha are referenced by Mark. It is clear that the OT was Mark's primary source for the events in Jesus's life, not oral tradition handed down from disciples.

Traditional Christian history holds that Jesus preached in Palestine with his disciples and angered the authorities who had him crucified. The disciples told Paul the philosophy of Jesus and about his crucifixion. Paul then preached Christ crucified to the gentiles. The disciples passed down oral stories and teachings of Jesus that were collected by Mark who wove them into a narrative. It has been shown here that the events in Jesus's life were more than likely taken from OT stories and Psalms. With regard to the Pauline teachings of Jesus, the following list is the evidence that Mark used Paul as his source and not Jesus's teaching as passed down by his disciples:

---

39. LXX.

1. Paul's epistles were written before Mark's Original Gospel, so it is historically possible that Mark has a copy of the epistles.

2. Mark often uses the same significant words that Paul used when making a Pauline point (render; transfigured; clean; mystery, revealed, "Abba, Father").

3. Mark's Jesus quotes the same OT scripture Paul quotes (Ps 110, Ps 118, Is 29:13–14).

4. There are several passages in Paul that end up being events in the life of Mark's Jesus (baptism, Christians will be transfigured, Jews looking for signs, Christians will cry out Abba, Father).

5. In Gal 1:12 Paul denies that he learned anything about Jesus from any man. Unless Paul is lying, even though he met with the Jerusalem apostles, Peter, James and John, they told him nothing about Jesus.

6. Paul says he learned about Jesus through revelation. Paul quotes and refers to the OT over three hundred times in his epistles. His revelation must have come from interpreting the OT in new ways. Through the OT, God's word, God revealed to Paul his plan for the salvation of mankind. This becomes the reason why Mark used the OT as the source for events in the life of Jesus.

7. It is clear Mark loved chiastic structure. There is a Pauline section of Mark that refers to Paul's epistles chiastically. Mark 12:10–37 is a section of Pauline teachings spanning three full pericopae and two partial pericopae, where Mark quotes Ps 118 (quoted at Rom 8:31), Rom 13:1–7, 1 Cor 15:12–14, 1 Cor 15:35–51, Rom 13:8–10, Ps 110 (quoted at 1 Cor 15:25). It is too much of a coincidence to believe that based on stories collected from witnesses and disciples Mark happened to have a section constructed as follows:

> A Ps 118 (quoted in Rom)
> B Rom 13:1–7
> C 1 Cor 15:12–14
> C' 1 Cor 15:35–51
> B' Rom 13:8–10
> A' Ps 110 (quoted in 1 Cor)

In order to construct 12:10–37 Mark must have had copies of Romans and 1 Corinthians to use as sources for this passage. In this particular case Mark did not reverse the order of his source as he often does for OT stories, but used Romans in the same order and 1 Corinthians in the same order as Paul wrote them. In addition, the two Psalms quoted by Jesus in the passage were quoted by Paul in Romans and in 1 Corinthians.

Mark's Gospel is not history but literature based upon the OT and Paul's epistles designed to promote Paul's Christology.

17

Four Structures of the Original Gospel of Mark

As DOCUMENTED IN CHAPTER 1, NT scholars have been expounding on the structure of the Gospel of Mark for over one hundred years. There is no consensus. It has been shown herein that they have been at a tremendous disadvantage because they are trying to discern the structure of a literary work that has been distorted by a redactor. The scholars rightly concluded that Mark was a talented writer, and they assumed he must have had an overall structure in mind when he wrote his Gospel. They tried to discern it.

Mark did have a structure to his Original Gospel, in fact he had at least four separate, overlapping structures, but the redactor confused these structures. The four structures of the Original Gospel of Mark are:

1. The physical structure division into acts.

2. The plot structure

3. The geographic structure, and

4. The theological structure.

The Physical Structure – Three Acts

Mark divided his Gospel into three acts with a prologue and an epilogue as demonstrated in chapter 3. The author signaled these divisions with pericope-level chiastic structures that contain parallel centers. This is the physical division of the Original Gospel

Act I

    1:2–1:15 – Prologue

    1:16–4:41 – Remainder of Act I (not including 4:1–35)

Act II

    5:1–14:72 (including 4:1–35)

Act III

15:1–15:39 – Jesus' death

15:40–16:8 – Epilogue

The evidence for this is the parallel centered pericope chiasms at 1:14–20 delineating the prologue, the two parallel centered pericopae chiasms at 4:36–41 and 5:1–20 delineating the last pericope of the first act and the first pericope of the second act, the parallel centered pericope chiasm at 14:53–72 delineating the last pericope of the second act, and the parallel centered pericope chiasm at 15:20b–39 that also has a paralleled (C, C') stitch delineating the death of Jesus and the beginning of the epilogue.

In addition, the drama of the Gospel also points to this physical division. At the end of Act I Jesus has calmed the wind and sea and his disciples ask, "Who is this, then, that even the sea and wind obey him?" This is a perfect dramatic end to Act I. As it turns out in Mark's Original Gospel the disciples never figure out who Jesus really is, but the reader does. At the end of Act II Jesus has been convicted of blasphemy by the Council, and the cock crows for the second time just as Peter has denied knowing anything about Jesus for the third time. Peter realizes what he has done and breaks down crying, a dramatic end to Act II.

The end of Act III provides another dramatic and disturbing end as the women flee the tomb and say nothing about what they saw. As Fowler says, this ending is intended to engender an impulse in the reader to go out and tell the story of Jesus that the women failed to do. The physical structure heightens the drama of the Gospel.

The Plot Structure

Mark's Original Gospel has a plot structure much like that of a modern screenplay. Screenplays are typically one hundred twenty pages and run two hours on the screen. It takes about two hours to read the Original Gospel. A typical screenplay starts with what is called "the inciting incident." This is an event that happens to the protagonist that creates in him an objective or goal he wants to attain. This incident usually occurs in the first eight percent of the script, that is, by page ten. As the protagonist attempts to attain his goal, plot point one occurs setting up a major obstacle to his attainment of his goal. This occurs about twenty-five percent of the way into the script, about page thirty. There is a turning point in the middle of the script about page sixty, sometimes called "the pinch," where the protagonist makes a decision that leads him to the final confrontation. Then plot point two occurs at about page eighty-five to ninety, that is, about seventy-five percent of the way into the script. At plot point two an event occurs to the protagonist that compels him to confront his nemesis and proceeds to final resolution.[1]

In Mark's Original Gospel the inciting incident is Jesus's baptism that instills the spirit in him and propels him to proclaim the gospel of God. The first plot point occurs at the transfiguration where Jesus learns he is not only the Danielic Son of Man, but also the Suffering Servant of Isaiah, and cannot fulfill the Danielic prophecy until and unless he is killed and raised from the dead. This occurs at twenty-eight percent of the way into the Original Gospel, just past the twenty-five percent point advocated by modern screenwriters.

The turning point or pinch occurs in the Original Gospel when Jesus begins the trek to Jerusalem in the middle of Act II. This occurs very near the center, fifty-three percent of the way into the Gospel. Plot point two occurs at Jesus's arrest in Gethsemane, eighty-eight percent of the way into the Gospel. It is at this point the reader realizes that Jesus will not foment a revolution but has submitted himself to God's plan.

In *Poetics* Aristotle emphasizes plot as being the foremost quality of tragedy.[2] Aristotle advocated having a "reversal," his term for the screenwriter's plot point, coincide with the "recognition." Aristotle's recognition was the point at which the protagonist recognizes the truth of the situation. In Mark's Original Gospel Jesus fully recognizes and accepts who he is just before his arrest at Gethsemane. This occurs at the third temptation as he prays for guidance. Here he fully accepts that he is the fulfillment of the prophecy of the Suffering Servant of Isaiah, and he submits to God's plan. The recognition immediately results in his arrest—plot point two or the reversal, in Aristotle's terminology. Aristotle also said that good tragedy must have a scene of suffering, where a character dies or suffers injury on stage.[3] Mark's Gospel certainly has that.

The plot structure of the Original Gospel is as follows:

1:9–11 Baptism – Inciting Incident

9:2–13 Transfiguration – Plot Point One

10:32 Head for Jerusalem – Turning Point

14:43–49 Jesus's Arrest – Plot Point Two

15:22–39 Crucifixion – Scene of Suffering

The plot of Mark's Original Gospel has a chiastic structure with the Scene of Suffering balancing the Inciting Incident, the Plot Points balancing each other and it is centered on the Turning Point.

1. McKee, *Story*; Field, *Screenplay*.

2. Aristotle, *Poetics*, 6.

3. Ibid., 11.

Geographic Structure

Mark's Original Gospel has a clear geographic structure that even a casual reader can discern. The first half of the Gospel takes place in Galilee and the second half in Jerusalem. In Canonical Mark it appears that the first sixty percent is in Galilee and the last forty percent is in Jerusalem. Some scholars have advocated that Canonical Mark has a geographic structure.

What the casual reader will not grasp is that in the first half of the Original Gospel Jesus enters Capernaum three times, and in the second half he enters Jerusalem three times. In addition, in the first half of the Original Gospel Jesus enters three towns: Capernaum, Bethsaida and Caesarea Philippi. In the second half he also enters three towns: Jerusalem, Jericho and Bethany.

Then there are the specifically mentioned journeys. In the first half of the Original Gospel Jesus takes six boat trips. In the second half he makes six walking trips. By "specifically mentioned journeys" these are trips during which some incident takes place or an event occurs during or at the end of the journey. For example at 11:11 Mark says that Jesus and the twelve went out to Bethany. That is not counted as a walking trip because nothing happened. Mark says the next day that they came out of Bethany and saw the fig tree had withered. That is counted as a walking trip, because an event occurred during the trip.

The geographic structure is as follows:

1:21 Capernaum 1

2:1 Capernaum 2

8:22 Bethsaida

8:27 Caesarea Philippi

9:33 Capernaum 3

10:32 Turning point – End Galilee, begin Jerusalem section

10:46 Jericho

11:11 Jerusalem 1

11:15 Jerusalem 2

11:27 Jerusalem 3

14:3 Bethany

Jesus had to go to Jerusalem to either start the revolution of the Son of Man or be arrested by the central governmental authorities. Galilee is healing and spreading the word. Jerusalem is confrontation.

Theological Structure

Most important is the "Theological Structure" because it is based on the OT and Paul's epistles, setting out the events in Jesus's life and the theological import. Mark's Original Gospel has a theological structure that looks like a series of intercalations. Chapter 16 showed the sources of each pericope in Original Mark. Some pericopae were based mainly on the OT and other pericopae were based mainly on Paul's epistles. Analysis of those sources demonstrates that the first third of the Gospel from 1:2 to "The Parable Discourse" (4:1–34) is based generally upon the OT. The second third of the Gospel from "The Parable Discourse" to "The Olivet Discourse" (13:3–37) is based generally on Paul's epistles, and the last third of the Gospel from "The Olivet Discourse" to 16:8 is based again on the OT. Within this OT – Pauline – OT overall structure there are similar substructures. The first third has three parts: OT – Pauline – OT. There are four pericopae from 2:1–28 based on Pauline teachings about justification by faith, fasting and dietary restrictions, and Sabbath rules. The second third has three parts: Pauline – OT – Pauline, with the Pauline teachings being interrupted from 11:1–11:25 to use the OT to symbolically portray the end of Second Temple Judaism. Finally, the last third has three parts: OT – Pauline – OT beginning with the Olivet Discourse based on Dan 12 through the crucifixion based on Psalm 22 and the women keeping silent quoting Gen 18:15. Interrupting this OT section is the Last Supper derived from 1 Cor 11:23–26. Below is a segmented line showing the theological structure of Original Mark so that it can be visually appreciated. Old Testament based text is represented by segments labeled "*OT*," Pauline epistle based text is represented by segments labeled "*P*" or "*Paul*," the text of "The Parable Discourse" is labeled "*PD*" and the text of "The Olivet Discourse" is labeled "*OD*." The discourses are the boundaries of the major sections, and are a mixture of Pauline and OT sources. The length of the each segment is based on the number of words in each section.

| *OT* | *P* | *OT* | *PD* | *Paul* | *OT* | *Paul* | *OD* | *OT* | *P* | *OT* |

This graphic analysis demonstrates that there is an OT segment encompassing the first third of the Gospel ending with "The Parable Discourse" (PD). This predominantly OT third has a Pauline section about one third of the way in. Then there is a predominantly Pauline segment following "The Parable Discourse" and extending to "The Olivet Discourse" (OD) encompassing the middle of the Gospel. This Pauline section has a short OT section about two-thirds of the way in. The third major section matches the first major section, being basically an OT section with a Pauline middle. This theological structure is also chiastic.

A – OT

  B – Pauline

    C – OT

D – Discourse

E – Pauline

F – OT

E' – Pauline

D' – Discourse

C' – OT

B' – Pauline

A' – OT

Naturally, a Gospel written by Mark would have a basic chiastic structure. It is to be expected when each pericope has a chiastic structure and there are large chiastic structures through out the Gospel. The chiastic diagram above demonstrates that the turning point is the OT section in the middle of the Gospel as Jesus and his entourage head to Jerusalem beginning at 10:32. Those scholars who have written that Mark has a chiastic structure are correct. They have made incorrect matches because of the redaction.

This theological structure serves an additional purpose. The narrative sections moving the plot along are OT based and the teaching sections are Pauline based. In other words, as a basic construct, Mark got his stories about what happened to Jesus from the OT, and he got the teachings of Jesus from Paul's epistles.

Form criticism assumes that Mark got his stories about Jesus orally from Jesus's disciples or other witnesses. But that is just an assumption, based upon the further assumption that Jesus was an historical itinerant preacher who got in trouble with the authorities and was crucified. The oral basis of Gospel stories is an assumption on an assumption. The stories found in Mark's Original Gospel are literature designed to recruit new members to the Pauline branch of early Christianity.

Brilliant, creative NT scholars assume that Mark, Matthew, and Luke were cut and paste editors with little creative abilities. These scholars make the assumption that Mark was merely a collector of oral stories who put them into a semblance of order to tell the story of Jesus as his disciples knew it. One can excuse them because a clever redactor rearranged Mark's story and disrupted its flow, making it appear disorganized. The author of Mark was no editor of stories handed down to him. He used OT stories to create events in the life of his character, Jesus, the Nazarene. Then to teach Paul's message, he put Paul's words into Jesus's mouth.

When Mark used the OT in creating an event in the story of Jesus's life, he did not copy the OT story word for word. He creatively took the basis of each story and wove it into an event in the life of his character, Jesus, placing it in a definite historical context. Sometimes the stories are parallel and sometimes they have opposite effects. Since Matthew and Luke copied Mark basically word for word, doing some minor editing, NT scholars have made the unwarranted assumption that all gospel material was created beforehand and the Synoptic evangelists were mere editors piecing the stories together. With respect to Mark the handed down narrative from the early church fathers is that Mark collected oral stories and edited them into a Gospel.

Mark got the threads from the OT and then wove them into events in the life of his literary character. It is not surprising, then, that Mark transmuted Paul's teachings into Jesus's teachings. He created a situation where the teaching would be appropriate and had Jesus expound it. It is not a valid criticism to insist that Mark could not have been using Paul's epistles as a source, because he did not copy Pauline passages verbatim. He put the teaching situation into context in Jesus's life as he was creating it. Mark had his Jesus give the appropriate teaching based upon what Paul would have said if he had been in the situation Mark had created for Jesus. Word for word copying is not necessary to communicate Paul's message to the wider Christian world.

Conclusion

Mark's basic unit was the triplet. This can be seen in his intercalations, the three-act structure, the OT – Pauline – OT theological structure and his numerous triplets scattered through the text. Even his geographic Galilee – Jerusalem structure actually begins near Jerusalem with John Baptizing in the Jordan close enough to Jerusalem that the populace could go out to him. So one might say there is a Jerusalem – Galilee – Jerusalem structure. But within the Galilee half there are three entries into Capernaum and three named towns entered. Likewise for the Jerusalem half, Jerusalem is entered three times and three towns are entered. The plot structure also has a tripartite structure with inciting incident – plot point – turning point in the first half and turning point – plot point – scene of suffering in the second half. Mark's Original Gospel can be viewed as a fractal of threes.

18

Discovering the Original Gospel of Mark

FOR OVER ONE HUNDRED and seventy-five years NT scholars have suspected that Canonical Mark is not the original form of the Gospel According to Mark. By discovering large chiastic structures encompassing as much as half the Gospel and determining what goes where into those structures, we have seen that a redactor disrupted some of those structures by relocating pericopae and interpolating text into the Original Gospel.

Piecing the structures back together, we have reconstructed what may be close to the Original Gospel of Mark. The reconstructed Gospel is much more readable, smoother and tells a somewhat different story from Canonical Mark. The Original Gospel was Adoptionist in outlook and had a clear theological structure with a central Pauline message. The structure is consistent with Mark's triplets, intercalations and chiasms.

One can understand why a proto-Catholic redactor of the late first/early second century believing that Jesus had been a historical Son of God come to Earth would edit this master literary creation to de-emphasize its Adoptionist character. Additionally, the redactor attempted to rehabilitate bumbling, dense disciples Mark created for his Jesus by making what had been an Aristotelian false recognition, "Peter's Confession at Caesarea Philippi," into a recognition/turning point. Copious evidence has been given herein that the redactor was the author of the Gospel of Luke.

Not only were chiastic structures used to reposition and eliminate pericopae, textual confirmation of those actions has been produced by analyzing triplets and the contrasting writing styles of Mark and the redactor. Those tools were used also to detect smaller interpolations where the pericope-level chiastic structures did not have the crispness and flow of a Markan pericope.

In the process of analyzing triplets, structures were discovered in the Original Gospel that seemed to be unMarkan because they did not follow Mark's usual pattern of creating triplets. On closer analysis these structures appear to be puzzles laid out by the author for the reader to solve. Perhaps Mark did not intend them to be solved but thought they would have an unconscious affect on the reader. If there were only one of them, and not at least eight, one would pass it off as an interesting coincidence. But solutions have been found for the puzzles of the missing sixth Nazarene, the ninth

Moses and Elijah, and the fifteenth "Son of Man," "kingdom of God" and miracle, the third Isaiah and the extra "it is written." There may be more.

When this project began, the working hypothesis was that Mark created his entire Gospel as one chiastic structure from beginning to end. That proved to be erroneous, but the question arose why Mark would create these chiastic structures. And further why would he create these literary puzzles? Perhaps they satisfied his artistic sensibilities, and he did not care whether the reader or the hearers realized they existed. In other words, he did it because he could. He liked it, whether or not the readers appreciated it. On the other hand there may be a practical reason. He may have been setting literary traps for any would-be redactor, who would be exposed by discerning readers. If that is the reason, Mark hid his trap too well, and two thousand years would pass before the redactor was caught.

With regard to the Christology of the Original Gospel of Mark, besides being the adopted son of God, Mark's Jesus was an amalgamation of Isaiah's Suffering Servant and Daniel's Son of Man. In Mark's Christology, as in Paul's, Jesus first had to be crucified as an atonement sacrifice before he could be raised up to become the Son of Man with dominion over the kingdom of God. The disciples failed to understand that. They recognized him as only the Danielic Son of Man Messiah. Mark's plot line of the disciples never realizing that Jesus had to be crucified, points to the basis of the Christological battle between Paul and the Jerusalem apostles, James, Peter and John, referred to by Paul in Galatians and 2 Corinthians. The hint left by Paul is that in 2 Cor 11:4 he warned the congregation at Corinth about those who came preaching another Jesus. Who could another Jesus be? How would he be different from Paul's Jesus?

Paul answers that at 1 Cor 1:22 where he says he preaches Christ crucified, a stumbling block to Jews. The Jews he is talking about who cannot accept the crucified Christ are the Judaisers, those apostles sent by James, Peter and John, the Jerusalem apostles. After all, those are the Jews that Paul complains about in the other epistles, the ones he compares to "Satan" at 2 Cor 11:14. That means that James, Peter and John and all the Jerusalem apostles deny that Jesus Christ was crucified as Paul preached. They preached that the savior Jesus Christ was only the Danielic Son of Man, soon to be coming with the clouds to establish the Jewish kingdom of God on Earth. This is what the plot line in the Original Gospel of Mark conveys to the reader. No wonder the proto-Catholic redactor changed it.

The conclusion is inevitable, if James, Peter and John, those who supposedly were the disciples of Jesus, deny that Jesus was crucified, then the crucifixion never happened, the resurrection never happened, at least on Earth, and Mark's Jesus is only a character of literature, not a historical person who lived in the first century CE.

The author of the Original Gospel of Mark was a Pauline Christian, taking Paul's side in his dispute with the Jerusalem apostles. It is also clear that Mark was unaware of any oral stories about an earthly Jesus and resorted to the OT to reveal incidents in the life of Jesus leading to his crucifixion. Mark placed the teachings of Paul as written in his epistles in the mouth of Jesus. Mark strongly believed that Jesus as the Messiah would soon be coming to Earth with the clouds to gather the elect and establish the kingdom of God as Paul had preached. He wanted the readers and hearers of his Gospel to be faithful Pauline Christians so that they could enjoy ever lasting life with God in heaven.

I hope that others will consider the evidence and arguments presented here and subject them to scholarly scrutiny, correcting any errors, making additional discoveries and solving as yet undetected puzzles in The Gospel of Mark.

Appendix 1

The Original Gospel of Mark

1:1 The beginning of the gospel of Jesus Christ, Son of God

Prologue

A 1:2 As it is written in Isaiah the prophet,

    BA "Look, I send my messenger ahead of you,

    BB who will prepare your way."

    BA' 1:3 A voice proclaiming in the wilderness,

    BB' "Prepare the way for the Lord. Make his way straight."

A 1:4 Appeared John the Baptizer in the wilderness proclaiming the baptism of repentance for the forgiveness of sins.

    B 1:5 And all the country of Judea went out to him, and all of Jerusalem. And they were baptized by him in the Jordan River, confessing their sins.

        C 1:6 And John was dressed in camel's hair, and a leather belt around his hips.

        C' And he ate locusts and wild honey.

    B' 1:7 And he preached, saying, "After me there comes someone who is mightier than I. I am not fit to bend down and loosen the buckle of his sandals. 1:8 I baptized you in water; he will baptize you in the Holy Spirit."

A 1:9 And it happened in those days, that Jesus the Nazarene came from Galilee, and was baptized by John in the Jordan.

    B 1:10 And immediately coming up out of the water, he saw the heavens tearing open and the Spirit like a dove descending into him.

    B' 1:11 And a voice came out of the heavens, "You are my beloved son, in whom I am well pleased."

A 1:12 And immediately the Spirit drives him out into the wilderness.

    B 1:13 And he was in the wilderness forty days tempted by Satan.

    B' And he was with the wild animals. And the angels served him.

Act I

A 1:14 And after John was delivered up Jesus came into Galilee, proclaiming the gospel of God, 1:15 and saying, "The time is complete, and the kingdom of God is at hand. Repent, and believe in the gospel."

> BA 1:16 And passing by the sea of Galilee, he saw Simon and Andrew, the brother of Simon, throwing a net in the sea. For they were fishers.

> BB 1:17 And Jesus said to them, "Follow me, and I will make you fishers of men."

> BC 1:18 And immediately they left the nets and followed him.

> BA' 1:19 And going on a little farther, he saw James the son of Zebedee and John his brother and they were in the boat mending the nets.

> BB' 1:20 And immediately he called them.

> BC' And they left their father Zebedee in the boat with the hired servants and went after him.

A 1:21 And they go into Capernaum.

> B And immediately on the Sabbath he entered into the synagogue and taught.

>> C 1:22 And they were astonished at his teaching. For he taught them as having authority, and not as the scribes.

>>> D 1:23 And immediately in their synagogue there was a man with an unclean spirit.

>>>> E And he shouted, 1:24 saying, "What are we to you, Jesus, Nazarene? Have you come to destroy us? I know who you are—the Holy One of God."

>>>> E' 1:25 And Jesus admonished him saying, "Be silent and come out of him."

>>> D' 1:26 And having thrown the man into convulsions the unclean spirit shouted with a loud voice and came out of him.

>> C' 1:27 And they were all amazed such that they asked each other saying, "What is this? New teaching? He commands with authority, and the unclean spirits obey him."

> B' 1:28 And immediately the news about him went out everywhere into all the surrounding region of Galilee.

A 1:29 And immediately when they had come out of the synagogue they came into the house of Simon and Andrew with James and John.

> B 1:30 But Simon's mother-in-law was lying sick with a fever. And immediately they tell him about her.

>> C 1:31 And he came and took her by the hand and raised her up. And the fever left her, and she served them.

>>> D 1:32 And at evening when the sun went down, they brought all the sick to him and those that were possessed with demons.

D' 1:33 And the entire city was gathered together at the door.

C' 1:34 And he healed many that were sick with various diseases, and cast out many demons.

B' And he did not allow the demons to speak because they knew him.

A 1:35 And very early, a long time before daylight, he woke up and went out, and departed into a deserted place, and was praying there.

B 1:36 And Simon and those that were with him searched for him.

C 1:37 And they found him and say to him, "Everyone is looking for you."

C' 1:38 And he says to them, "Let us go some where else into the neighboring towns, so that I may preach there also.

B' For this is why I came."

A 1:39 And he went into their synagogues throughout all Galilee, preaching and casting out demons.

B 1:40 And there comes to him a leper begging him

C and kneeling down to him, and saying to him, "If you will, you can make me clean."

D 1:41 And being moved with compassion, he stretched forth his hand, and touched him, and says to him, "I will. Be clean."

E 1:42 And immediately the leprosy left him, and he was clean.

E' 1:43 And he strictly admonished him, and immediately sent him away.

D' 1:44 And he says to him, "See that you say nothing to any one, but go show yourself to the priest and offer the things which Moses commanded for your cleansing as a testimony to them."

C' 1:45 But he went out and began to proclaim it a great deal and to spread the word around. So much that he could no longer enter into a city openly, but was out in deserted places.

B' And they came to him from every quarter.

A 2:1 And after a few days he entered into Capernaum again. It was learned that he is at home.

B 2:2 And many were gathered together so that there was no longer room, no, not even at the door. And he was telling them the word.

C 2:3 And they come bringing him a paralytic being carried by four. 2:4 And not being able to come near to him because of the crowd, they removed the roof where he was.

D And after they had opened it up, they let down the pallet that the paralytic lay on.

EA 2:5 And seeing their faith Jesus says to the paralytic, "Child, your sins are forgiven."

EB 2:6 There were, however, some scribes sitting there and debating in their hearts.

EA' 2:7 "Why does this one speak like this? He blasphemes. Who can forgive sins but one, God?"

EB' 2:8 And immediately, recognizing in his spirit that they so debated within themselves, Jesus says to them, "Why do you debate these things in your hearts?

D' 2:9 Which is easier to say to the paralytic, 'Your sins are forgiven.' or to say, 'Arise, and pick up your pallet, and walk?'

C' 2:10 Just so you know that the Son of Man has authority on earth to forgive sins" (he says to the paralytic), 2:11 "I say to you, arise, pick up your pallet, and go to your home." And he arose.

B' 2:12 And immediately he picked up the pallet, and went out in front of all of them. Such that they were all amazed, and began to glorify God, saying, "We never saw such a thing."

A 2:13 And he went out again by the seaside, and the entire crowd came to him. And he taught them.

B 2:14 And passing by he saw Levi the son of Alphaeus sitting at the tax collector's booth, and he says to him, "Follow me."

B' And he arose and followed him.

A 2:15 And it happened that he was reclining at dinner in his house, and many tax collectors and sinners were reclining with Jesus and his disciples.

B For there were many, and they followed him.

C 2:16 And the scribes of the Pharisees, seeing that he was eating with the sinners and tax collectors, said to his disciples, "Why does he eat and drink with tax collectors and sinners?"

C' 2:17 And having heard this Jesus says to them, "Those that are healthy do not need a physician, but those that are sick.

B' I did not come to call the righteous, but sinners."

A 2:18 And John's disciples and the disciples of the Pharisees were fasting.

B And they come and say to him, "Why do John's disciples and the disciples of the Pharisees fast, but your disciples do not fast?"

B' 2:19 And Jesus said to them, "Can the sons of the bride chamber fast while the bridegroom is with them? As long as they have the bridegroom with them, they cannot fast. 2:20 But the days will come, when the bridegroom will be taken away from them. And then will they fast at that time. 2:21 No one sews a piece of unshrunken cloth on old clothing because the new patch would tear away from the old, and makes a worse tear. 2:22 And no one puts new wine into old wineskins because the wine will burst the wineskins. And the wine and the wineskins are destroyed. Put new wine into new wineskins."

A 2:23 And it happened that he was going through the grain fields on the Sabbath.

BA And his disciples began to pluck the ears as they went.

BB 2:24 And the Pharisees said to him, "Look, why do they do what is not lawful to do on the Sabbath?"

BA' 2:25 And he said to them, "Did you never read what David did when he was desperate and was hungry; he, and they that were with him? 2:26 How he entered into the house of God at the time Abiathar was high priest, and ate the bread of the presentation that it is not lawful to eat, except for the priests. And he also gave it to those that were with him?"

BB' 2:27 And he said to them, "The Sabbath was made for man, and not man for the Sabbath. 2:28 So that the Son of Man is even lord of the Sabbath."

A 3:1 And again he went into the synagogue; and there was a man there who had his hand withered.

B 3:2 And they were watching him, to see whether he would heal him on the Sabbath; that they might accuse him.

C 3:3 And he says to the man who had the withered hand, "Arise."

D 3:4 And he says to them, "Is it lawful to do good, or to do harm on the Sabbath? To save a life, or to kill?"

E But they were silent.

E' 3:5 And looking around at them with anger, being grieved at the hardness of their hearts,

D' He says to the man, "Stretch out your hand."

C' And he stretched it out; and his hand was restored.

B' 3:6 And having gone out, the Pharisees immediately consulted with the Herodians against him, how they might destroy him.

A 3:7 And Jesus withdrew with his disciples to the sea. And a great crowd from Galilee and from Judea, followed.

B 3:8 And from Jerusalem and from Idumea and beyond the Jordan, and about Tyre and Sidon a great crowd, hearing what great things he did came to him.

C 3:9 And he spoke to his disciples, that a small boat should wait on him because of the crowd, so that they could not press upon him. 3:10 For he had healed many. So much so that everyone who had diseases pressed upon him that they might touch him.

C' 3:11 And when ever the unclean spirits saw him, they fell down before him, and shouted, saying, "You are the Son of God."

B' 3:12 And he warned them many times that they should not make him known.

A 3:13 And he goes up into the mountain and summons those whom he wanted. And they went to him.

B 3:14 And he appointed twelve to be apostles, that they might be with him, and that he might send them out to preach, 3:15 and to have authority to cast out demons.

B' 3:16 And to Simon he added the name Peter. 3:17 And James the son of Zebedee, and John the brother of James; and for them he added the name Boanerges, which is sons of thunder. 3:18 And Andrew, and Philip, and Bartholomew, and

Matthew, and Thomas, and James the son of Alphaeus, and Thaddaeus, and Simon the Zealot, 3:19 and Judas Iscariot, who also delivered him up.

A 3:20 And he comes into a house. And the crowd comes together again, so that they could not even eat bread.

B 3:21 And when his family heard it, they went out to take custody of him. For they said, "He is out of his mind."

C 3:22 And the scribes who came down from Jerusalem said, "He is possessed by Beelzebul, and he casts out demons by the prince of the demons."

C' 3:23 And he called them to him, and said to them in parables, "How can Satan cast out Satan? 3:24 And if a kingdom be divided against itself, that kingdom cannot stand. 3:25 And if a house be divided against itself, that house will not be able to stand. 3:26 And if Satan has risen up against himself, and is divided, he cannot stand, but will come to an end. 3:27 But no one can enter into the house of the strong man, and plunder his goods, unless he first ties up the strong man. And then he will plunder his house. 3:28 Truthfully I say to you, all sins will be forgiven the sons of men, and their blasphemies when ever they may blaspheme. 3:29 But whoever blasphemes against the Holy Spirit will never have forgiveness, but is guilty of an eternal sin."

B' 3:30 Because they said he has an unclean spirit.

A 3:31 And his mother and brothers arrive.

B And standing outside they sent to him, calling him.

C 3:32 And a crowd was sitting around him; and they say to him, "Look, your mother, brothers and sisters are outside looking for you."

C' 3:33 And answering them he says, "Who is my mother and my brothers?"

B' 3:34 And looking at them that sat round around him, he says, "Look, my mother and my brothers! 3:35 For whoever does the will of God, he is my brother, and sister, and mother."

A 4:36 And leaving the crowd, they take him with them in a boat.

B And other boats were with him.

CA 4:37 And there arises a large windstorm, and the waves washed into the boat, so that the boat was already filling.

CB 4:38 And he was in the stern sleeping on the cushion. And they awaken him, and say to him, "Teacher, do you not care that we are going to die?"

CA' 4:39 And awakening and admonishing the wind, he said to the sea, "Silence, be still." And the wind ceased, and there was a great calm.

CB' 4:40 And he said to them, "Why are you afraid? Do you not have faith yet?"

B' 4:41 And they were very afraid, and said one to another, "Who is this then, that even the wind and the sea obey him?"

Act II

A 5:1 And they came to the other side of the sea, into the region of the Gerasenes.

B 5:2 And immediately coming out of the boat, out of the tombs a man with an unclean spirit met him there 5:3 who was living in the tombs. And no one could bind him any longer, not even with a chain.

C 5:4 Because he had often been tied up with shackles and chains, and the chains had been broken by him, and the shackles broken in pieces. And no one had strength to subdue him. 5:5 And all night and day in the tombs and in the mountains, he was shouting out, and cutting himself with stones.

D 5:6 And seeing Jesus from a distance, he ran and fell on his knees in front of him.

E 5:7 And shouting with a loud voice, he says, "What have I to do with you, Jesus, son of the Most High God? I implore you by God, do not torment me."

F 5:8 For he said to him, "Come out, unclean spirit, out of the man."

G 5:9 And he asked him, "What is your name?"

HA And he says to him, "My name is Legion; for we are many."

HB 5:10 And he begged him many times that he would not send them out of the country.

HA' 5:11 Now there was on the mountainside a large herd of swine feeding.

HB' 5:12 And they begged him, saying, "Send us into the swine, that we may enter into them."

G' 5:13 And he yielded to them.

F' And the unclean spirits leaving him entered into the swine, and the herd rushed down the precipice into the sea, about two thousand; and they were drowned in the sea.

E' 5:14 And those feeding them fled, and told it in the city and in the country.

D' And they came to see what had happened. 5:15 And they come to Jesus and see him who was possessed with demons, he that had the legion, sitting, dressed and of sound mind. And they were afraid. 5:16 And those that saw it told them how it happened to him that was possessed with demons, and about the swine.

C' 5:17 And they began to beg him to depart from their region. 5:18 And as he was entering into the boat, he who had been possessed with demons asked him that he might be with him. 5:19 And he did not permit him, but says to him, "Go to your house to your family, and tell them how much the Lord has done for you, and that he had mercy on you."

B' 5:20 And he went his way. And he began to proclaim in the Decapolis how much Jesus had done for him, and all were amazed.

A 5:21 And Jesus having crossed over again in the boat to the other side, a great crowd was gathered around him; and he was beside the sea.

B 5:22 And one of the leaders of the synagogue, named Jairus comes, and seeing him, falls at his feet. 5:23 And he begs him a great deal saying, "My little daughter is at the point of death. You must come and lay your hands on her, that she may be cured and live."

C 5:24 And he went with him; and a great crowd followed him, and they pressed on him.

D 5:25 And a woman had an issue of blood twelve years. 5:26 And she had endured many things from many physicians, and had spent all she had, and was no better. But rather she was worse. 5:27 Having heard things about Jesus, she came in the crowd behind and touched his robe.

E 5:28 For she said, "If I just touch his robe, I will be cured."

E' 5:29 And immediately the flow of blood was dried up. And she realized in her body that her affliction was healed

D' 5:30 And immediately Jesus realizing that the power had gone out of him, turned around to the crowd, and said, "Who touched my robe?"

C' 5:31 And his disciples said to him, "You see the crowd pressing on you, and you ask, 'Who touched me?'" 5:32 And he looked around to see her who had done this.

B' 5:33 But the woman fearing and trembling, seeing what had been done to her, came and fell down in front of him, and told him the truth. 5:34 And he said to her, "Daughter, your faith has cured you. Go in peace, and be free of your affliction."

A 5:35 As he spoke, they come from the house of the leader of the synagogue saying, "Your daughter is dead. Why trouble the teacher any further?"

B 5:36 But Jesus, hearing what they said, says to the leader of the synagogue, "Do not be afraid. Only believe."

B' 5:37 And he did not allow any one to follow him except Peter, and James, and John the brother of James.

A 5:38 And they come to the house of the leader of the synagogue. And he sees a commotion, and loud weeping and wailing.

B 5:39 And when he was entered he says to them, "Why do you make such a commotion, and weep? The child is not dead, but is sleeping."

C 5:40 And they laughed at him.

D But he, putting them all out, takes the father of the child and her mother and those that were with him, and goes in to where the child was.

D' 5:41 And taking the child by the hand, he says to her, "Talitha cumi." Which is translated, "Little girl, I say to you, arise."

C' 5:42 And immediately the girl arose, and walked. For she was twelve years old. And they were instantly overcome with a great amazement.

B' 5:43 And he admonished them strongly that no one should know this. And he said that she should be given something to eat.

A 6:1 And he went out from there. And he comes into his own hometown. And his disciples follow him.

B 6:2 And on the Sabbath, he began to teach in the synagogue.

C And many hearing him were astonished, saying, "Where have these things come from, and what wisdom has been given to him, and are such marvelous works done by his hands? 6:3 Is this not the carpenter, the son of Mary, and brother of James, and Joseph, and Judas, and Simon, and are not his sisters here with us?"

D And they took umbrage at him.

D' 6:4 And Jesus said to them, "A prophet is not without honor, except in his own hometown, and among his own family, and in his own house."

C' 6:5 And he could not do any marvelous work there, except that he laid his hands upon a few of the sick, and healed them.

B' 6:6 And he wondered at their lack of faith.

A And he went round about the villages teaching.

B 6:7 And he summons the twelve, and began to send them out two by two; and gave them power over the unclean spirits. 6:8 And he instructed them that they should take nothing for their journey, except only a staff; no bread, no bag, no money in their purse. 6:9 But put on sandals and do not put on two tunics.

B' 6:10 And he said to them, "When ever you enter into a house, stay there until you leave that place. 6:11 And if a place will not receive you, nor hear you, as you leave, shake off the dust from under your feet as testimony to them."

A 6:12 And going out they preached that all should repent.

B 6:13 And they cast out many demons, and anointed many that were sick with oil, and healed them.

C 6:16 But Herod, when he heard about it, said, "John, whom I beheaded, is risen."

D 6:17 For Herod himself sent out men who laid hold of John, and locked him in prison on account of Herodias, the wife of his brother Philip because he had married her.

D' 6:27 And immediately the king sent an executioner and commanded him to bring his head.

C' And he went and beheaded him in the prison. 6:29 And hearing about it, his disciples came and took his body.

B' And they laid it in a tomb.

A 6:30 And the apostles gather together with Jesus. And they told him about everything, what they had done, and what they had taught.

B 6:31 And he says to them, "Come down into the desert and rest a while."

B' For many were coming and going, and they had no opportunity to even eat.

A 9:2 And after six days Jesus takes with him Peter, and James, and John, and brings them up into a high mountain by themselves.

B And he was transfigured in front of them. 9:3 And his tunic became radiant, exceeding white, such as no launderer on earth can whiten it.

C 9:4 And there appeared to them Elijah with Moses. And they were talking with Jesus.

D 9:5 And Peter answers and says to Jesus, "Rabbi, it is good for us to be here. And let us construct three tents: one for you, and one for Moses, and one for Elijah."

D' 9:6 For he knew not what to answer. For they became afraid.

C' 9:7 And there came a cloud enveloping them. And there came a voice out of the cloud, "This is my beloved son. Listen to him."

B' 9:8 And suddenly looking around, they no longer saw anyone, but Jesus alone with themselves.

A 9:9 And as they were coming down from the mountain, he instructed them that they should tell no one what things they had experienced, until the Son of Man should rise from the dead.

B 9:10 And they pondered the words, discussing among themselves, "What is rising from the dead?"

C 9:11 And they asked him saying, "Why do the scribes say that Elijah must come first?"

C' 9:12 And he said to them, "Elijah indeed having come first restores all things. And why is it written of the Son of Man, that he should suffer many things and be despised?

B' 9:13 But I say to you that Elijah has come, and they did to him what they wanted to, just as it is written of him."

A 9:14 And when they came to the disciples, they saw a great crowd around them, and scribes arguing with them.

B 9:15 And immediately all the crowd upon seeing him were greatly amazed, and running to him, greeted him.

C 9:16 And he asked them, "What were you arguing with them about?"

D 9:17 And one of the crowd answered him, "Teacher, I brought my son to you. He is possessed by a mute spirit. 9:18 And when it seizes him, it throws him down. And he foams, and grinds his teeth, and he is pining away. And I spoke to your disciples that they might cast it out. But they were not able to."

E 9:19 And answering them he says, "Oh faithless generation, how long must I be with you? How long must I endure you? Bring him to me."

F 9:20 And they brought him to him. And when he saw him, immediately the spirit convulsed him, and he fell on the ground, and rolled around foaming.

G 9:21 And he asked his father, "How long has he been like this?"

G' And he said, "From childhood. 9:22 And often it has cast him both into the fire and into the water in order to destroy him. But if you can do anything, have compassion on us, and help us."

F' 9:23 And Jesus said to him, "If you can? All things are possible to him that believes."

E' 9:24 Immediately the father of the child cried out and said, "I believe; help my faithlessness."

D' 9:25 And when Jesus saw that a crowd gathered together, he admonished the unclean spirit, saying to him, "You mute and deaf spirit, I order you, come out of him, and do not enter him again."

C' 9:26 And crying out, and greatly convulsing him, he came out. And the boy became lifeless, so that many said, "He is dead."

B' 9:27 But Jesus taking him by the hand awakened him; and he arose.

A 9:28 And entering into a house,

B his disciples asked him privately, "Why were we not able to cast it out?"

B' 9:29 And he said to them, "This kind can come out only by prayer."

A 4:1 And again he began to teach by the seaside. And there is a very large crowd gathered around him, so that he entered into a boat, and sat in the sea. And all the crowd were on the land close to the sea.

B 4:2 And he taught them many things in parables, and said to them in his teaching,

C 4:3 "Listen! Look, the sower went out to sow 4:4 And it happened as he sowed some fell by the way side, and the birds came and devoured it. 4:5 And other fell on the rocky ground where it did not have much earth; and immediately it sprang up. Because it had no depth of soil 4:6 when the sun rose, it was scorched. And because it had no root, it withered away. 4:7 And other fell among the thorns, and the thorns grew up, and choked it. And it yielded no fruit. 4:8 And others fell into the good soil, and yielded fruit, growing and increasing; and one bore thirty, and one sixty, and one a hundred. 4:9 And he said, "Who has ears to hear, let him hear."

D 4:10 And when he was alone, those that were around him with the twelve asked him about the parables. 4:11 And he said to them, "The mystery of the kingdom of God has been given to you. But to those that are outside, all things are done in parables 4:12 so that seeing they might see, and not perceive; and hearing they might hear, and not understand; they might never turn again, and it be forgiven them." 4:13 And he says to them, "Do you not understand this parable? And how will you understand all the parables?

E 4:14 The sower sows the word. 4:15 And these are those along the road where the word is sown. And when they have heard it, immediately

Satan comes and takes away the word that has been sown in them. 4:16 And these likewise are those that are sown upon the rocky places, who, when they have heard the word, immediately receive it with joy. 4:17 And they have no root within themselves, but are only temporary. Then when tribulation or persecution comes because of the word, immediately they stumble. 4:18 And others are those that are sown among the thorns. These are those that have heard the word 4:19 and the cares of the world, and the deceit of riches, and the desires of other things entering in choke the word and it becomes unfruitful. 4:20 And those that were sown upon the good soil, such as hear the word, and accept it, and bear fruit, one thirty, and one sixty, and one a hundred."

F 4:21 And he said to them, "The lamp is not brought to be put under the bushel, or under the bed, but to be put on the lamp stand. 4:22 For there is nothing hidden unless it is made manifest. Neither was anything made secret, without it coming to light.

G 4:23 If any man has ears to hear, let him hear."

G' 4:24 And he said to them, "Be careful what you hear.

F' With what measure you measure it will be measured to you, and more will be given to you. 4:25 For he that has, to him will be given. And he that has not, from him will be taken away even that which he has."

E' 4:26 And he said, "So is the kingdom of God, as if a man should throw seed upon the earth, 4:27 and should sleep and rise night and day. And the seed should sprout up and grow, he does not know how. 4:28 The earth bears fruit by herself; first the blade, then the head, then the full grain in the head. 4:29 But when the grain is ripe, immediately he sends the sickle, because the harvest is come."

D' 4:30 And he said, "To what can we liken the kingdom of God? Or in what parable can we present it?

C' 4:31 It is like a seed of mustard when it is sown upon the earth, it is the smallest of all the seeds that are upon the earth. 4:32 Yet when it is sown grows up and becomes greater than all the garden plants and puts out great branches. So that the birds of the heavens can nest in its shade."

B' 4:33 And he spoke the word to them with many such parables, as they were able to hear it. 4:34 And he did not speak to them without a parable, but privately to his own disciples he explained every thing.

A 4:35 And on that day when evening arrived he says to them, "Let us go over to the other side." 6:32 And they went away in the boat to their private desert place.

B 6:33 And many saw them going, and recognized them.

B' And they all ran there on foot from all the cities, and got there before them.

A 6:34 And he got out and saw a large crowd. And he had pity on them because they were as sheep without a shepherd. And he began to teach them many things.

B 6:35 And when the hour became late his disciples came to him and said, "This place is desolate, and the hour is late. 6:36 Dismiss them, so that they may go into the surrounding country and villages round about, and buy themselves something to eat."

    C 6:37 But he answered and said to them, "You give them something to eat."

        D And they say to him, "Should we go and pay two hundred denarii for bread, to give them to eat?"

            E 8:5 And he asked them, "How many loaves do you have?"

            FA And they said, "Seven."

            FB 8:6 And he instructs the multitude to sit down on the ground. And taking the seven loaves, and giving thanks, he broke, and gave them to his disciples, so that they might serve them; and they served them to the crowd.

            FA' 8:7 And they had a few small fish.

            FB' And having blessed them, he told them to serve these also.

            E' 8:8 And they ate and were satisfied.

        D' And they took up seven baskets of broken pieces that remained.

    C' 8:9 And there were about four thousand.

  B' And he dismissed them.

A 8:10 And immediately he got into the boat with his disciples, and came into the region of Dalmanutha.

  B 8:11 And the Pharisees went out and began to discuss with him, looking for a sign from heaven from him, testing him.

  B' 8:12 And sighing deeply in his spirit, he says, "Why does this generation seek a sign? Truthfully I say to you, no sign will be given to this generation."

A 8:13 And sending them away, and again embarking into the boat he departed to the other side.

  B 8:15 And he admonished them, saying, "Watch out. Beware of the leaven of the Pharisees and the leaven of Herod."

    C 8:16 And they discussed among themselves saying, "We have no bread."

        D 8:17 And realizing it he says to them, "Why do you discuss about having no bread? Do you not yet perceive nor understand? Are your hearts hardened?

        D' 8:18 Having eyes, do you not see? And having ears, do you not hear? And do you not remember? 8:20 When I broke the loaves among the four thousand, how many basketfuls of broken pieces were left over?"

    C' And they say to him, "Seven."

  B' 8:21 And he said to them, "Do you still not understand?"

A 8:22 And they come to Bethsaida. And they bring to him a blind man, and beg him to touch him.

B 8:23 And he took hold of the blind man's hand, and brought him out of the village.

    CA And spitting into his eyes, and laying his hands on him, he asked him, "Do you see anything?"

    CB 8:24 And looking up, he said, "I see men; for I see them as walking trees."

    CA' 8:25 Then again he laid his hands upon his eyes,

    CB' And he opened them, and was restored, and saw everything clearly.

B' 8:26 And he sent him home, saying, "Do not even enter the village or tell anyone in the village."

A 8:27 And Jesus and his disciples went into the villages of Caesarea Philippi. And on the way he questioned his disciples, saying to them, "Who do men say that I am?"

    B 8:28 And they told him, saying, "John the Baptizer, and others Elijah, but others, one of the prophets."

      C 8:29 And he asked them, "But who do you say I am?"

        D Peter answers and says to him, "You are the Christ."

          E 8:30 And he admonished them that they should tell no one about him.

            F 8:31 And he began to teach them, that it is necessary that the Son of Man suffer many things, and be rejected by the elders, and the chief priests, and the scribes, and be killed, and after three days rise.

            F' 8:32 And he spoke these words plainly.

          E' And taking him, Peter began to admonish him.

        D' 8:33 And turning around and seeing his disciples, he admonished Peter, and says, "Get behind me, Satan. Because you are minding not the things of God, but the things of men."

      C' 8:34 And summoning the crowd with his disciples, he said to them, "If any man wishes to come after me, he must deny himself, and take up his cross, and follow me. 8:35 For whoever would preserve his life will lose it. And whoever will lose his life for my sake and that of the gospel will preserve it. 8:36 For what does it benefit a man to gain the whole world and forfeit his soul? 8:37 For what should a man give in exchange for his soul? 8:38 For whoever might have been ashamed of me and of my words in this adulterous and sinful generation, the Son of Man also will be ashamed of him, when he comes in the glory of his Father with the holy angels."

    B' 9:1 And he said to them, "Truthfully I say to you, there are some standing here who will in no way taste of death, until they see the kingdom of God coming with power."

A 9:30 Leaving there, they passed through Galilee. And he did not want that anyone should know it.

    B 9:31 For teaching his disciples he said to them, "The Son of Man is delivered into the hands of men, and they will kill him. And when he is killed, after three days he will rise."

B' 9:32 But they did not understand the saying, and were afraid to ask him.

A 9:33 And they came to Capernaum. And coming into the house he asked them, "What were you discussing on the road?"

B 9:34 But they were silent. For they had arguing with each other on the road about who was the greatest. 9:35 And sitting down he summoned the twelve and he says to them, "If any man wants to be first, he will be last of all, and servant of all."

C 9:36 And taking a little child, he set him in the middle of them. And taking him in his arms, he said to them, 9:37 "Whoever will receive one such little child in my name receives me. And whoever receives me, does not receives me, but the one that sent me."

D 9:38 John said to him, "Teacher, we saw someone who does not follow us casting out demons in your name, and we forbade him."

D' 9:39 But Jesus said, "Do not forbid him. For no man who does a mighty work in my name will be able easily to speak evil of me. 9:40 For he that is not against us is for us.

C' 9:41 For whoever will give you a cup of water to drink, because you are in Christ's name, truthfully I say to you, he will in no way lose his reward.

B' 9:42 And whoever causes one of these little ones believing in me to stumble, it would be better for him if a heavy millstone were put around his neck, and he were thrown into the sea. 9:43 And if your hand cause you to stumble, cut it off. It is better for you to enter into life maimed, than having your two hands to go into Gehenna, into the unquenchable fire. 9:44 9:45 And if your foot cause you to stumble, cut it off. It is better for you to enter into life lame than having your two feet to be thrown into Gehenna. 9:46. 9:47 And if your eye cause you to stumble, throw it away. It is better for you to enter into the kingdom of God with one eye, than having two eyes to be thrown into Gehenna. 9:48 Where the worm does not die and the fire is not quenched. 9:49 For every one will be salted with fire. 9:50 Salt is good: but if the salt becomes unsalty, what will you season it with? Have salt in yourselves, and be at peace with one another."

A 10:1 And rising from there he comes into the region of Judea and beyond the Jordan. And again crowds come together around him.

B And as he was accustomed to, he taught them again.

C 10:2 And coming to him the Pharisees questioned him, "Is it lawful for a man to divorce his wife?" Testing him.

D 10:3 And answering he and said to them, "What did Moses command you?"

D' 10:4 And they said, "Moses permitted a man to write a bill of divorce, and to send her away."

C' 10:5 But Jesus said to them, "Because of your hardness of heart he wrote you this commandment.

B' 10:6 But from the beginning of the creation, male and female He made them. 10:7 Therefore, a man will leave his father and mother, and will join with his wife.

10:8 And the two will be one flesh, so that they are no longer two, but one flesh. 10:9 What, therefore, God has joined together, man may not separate."

A 10:10 And in the house the disciples asked him again about this.

B 10:11 And he says to them, "Whoever may divorce his wife and marry another, commits adultery against her.

B' 10:12 And if a woman herself may divorce her husband and marry another, she commits adultery."

A 10:13 And they were bringing to him little children so that he would touch them.

B And the disciples admonished them.

C 10:14 But Jesus seeing it became indignant, and said to them, "Allow the little children to come to me. Do not forbid them. For the kingdom of God belongs to such as these.

C' 10:15 Truthfully, I say to you, Whoever will not receive the kingdom of God as a little child, there is no way he will enter into it."

B' 10:16 And he took them in his arms, and blessed them, laying his hands upon them.

A 10:17 And going on the journey one ran up to him and kneeled to him, and asked him, "Good Teacher, what should I do that I may inherit eternal life?"

B 10:18 But Jesus said to him, "Why call me good? None is good except one, God. 10:19 You know the commandments. Do not murder. Do not commit adultery. Do not steal. Do not testify falsely. Do not defraud. Honor your father and mother."

C 10:20 But he said to him, "Teacher, I have kept all these things from my youth."

D 10:21 But Jesus looking upon him loved him, and said to him, "One thing you lack. Go sell everything you have, and give it to the poor. And you will have treasure in heaven. And come, follow me."

E 10:22 But his face fell with these words, and he went away sadly, for he had many possessions.

FA 10:23 And Jesus looked around him, and says to his disciples, "How difficult it is for those that have riches to enter into the kingdom of God!"

FB 10:24 But the disciples were wondering at his words. But Jesus answering again says to them, "Children, how difficult is it for those that trust in riches to enter into the kingdom of God!

FA' 10:25 It is easier for a camel to pass through the eye of a needle than for a rich man to enter into the kingdom of God."

FB' 10:26 But they were exceedingly astonished, saying to each other, "Then who can be saved?"

E' 10:27 Looking upon them Jesus says, "With men it is impossible, but not with God. For all things are possible with God."

D' 10:28 Peter began to say to him, "Lo, we have left all, and have followed you."

C' 10:29 Jesus said, "Truthfully I say to you, There is no one that has left house, or brothers, or sisters, or mother, or father, or children, or lands, for my sake, and for the sake of the gospel, 10:30 but he will receive a hundred fold now in this time, houses, and brothers, and sisters, and mothers, and children, and lands, with persecutions, and in the world to come eternal life.

B' 10:31 But many first will be last; and the last first."

A 10:32 But they were on the road going up to Jerusalem, and Jesus was going ahead of them. And they were amazed. And they that followed were afraid.

B And again he took aside the twelve, and began to tell them the things that were to happen to him,

B' 10:33 "Look, we are going up to Jerusalem; and the Son of Man will be delivered to the chief priests and the scribes. And they will condemn him to death, and will deliver him to the gentiles. 10:34 And they will ridicule him, and will spit upon him, and will flog him, and will kill him. And after three days he will rise."

A 10:35 And James and John, the sons of Zebedee, approach him saying to him, "Teacher, we want that you will do for us what ever we may ask."

B 10:36 But he said to them, "What do you want me do for you?"

CA 10:37 And they said to him, "Grant us that we may sit, one on your right hand, and one on your left hand, in your glory."

CB 10:38 But Jesus said to them, "You do not know what you are asking. Can you drink the cup that I drink? Or be baptized with the baptism that I am baptized with?"

CA' 10:39 But they said to him, "We can."

CB' But Jesus said to them, "The cup that I drink, you will drink. And with the baptism that I am baptized with you will be baptized. 10:40 But to sit on my right hand or on my left hand is not mine to give; but for whom it has been prepared."

B' 10:41 And hearing this the ten became indignant toward James and John.

A 10:42 And summoning them to him

B Jesus says to them, "You know that they who seem to rule over the gentiles lord it over them, and those powerful men exercise authority over them. 10:43 But it is not so among you. But whoever wishes to become great among you, will be your servant; 10:44 and whoever would be first among you will be a slave of all.

B' 10:45 For the Son of Man also did not come to be served, but to serve, and to give his life as a ransom for many."

A 10:46 And they come to Jericho. 7:1 And there are gathered together around him the Pharisees, and some of the scribes, coming from Jerusalem. 7:2 And they see that some of his disciples are eating their bread with dirty hands, that is, unwashed.

B 7:3 For the Pharisees and all Jews, do not eat unless they wash their hands diligently, observing the tradition of the elders. 7:4 And when they come from the market place they do not eat unless they wash themselves. And there are many other things that they observe: washings cups, and pots, and brass vessels and eating tables. 7:5 And the Pharisees and the scribes ask him, "Why do your disciples not act according to the tradition of the elders, but eat their bread with dirty hands?"

CA 7:6 But he said to them, "Rightly prophesied Isaiah about you hypocrites, as it is written,

CB This people honors me with their lips, but their heart is far away from me. 7:7 But in vain do they worship me. Teaching as their doctrines the precepts of men.

CC 7:8 You ignore the commandment of God, and observe the tradition of men."

CA' 7:9 And he said to them, "Rightly do you ignore the commandment of God, so that you may keep your tradition.

CB' 7:10 For Moses said, 'Honor your father and your mother.' and, 'He that speaks evil of father or mother, will be put to death.'

CC' 7:11 But you say, 'If a man says to his father or his mother, "What ever you might have gotten from me is Corban, that is, a gift to God."' 7:12 You no longer require him to do anything for his father or his mother, 7:13 making void the word of God by your tradition, which you have handed down. And many similar things you do."

B' 7:14 And summoning the crowd again, he said to them, "Hear me all of you, and understand. 7:15 There is nothing from outside the man that going into him can defile him. But the things proceeding out of him are the things that defile the man." 7:16.

A 7:17 And when he went into the house away from the crowd, his disciples asked him about the parable.

B 7:18 And he says to them, "Are you so without understanding also? Do you not realize, that whatever goes into the man from outside cannot defile him 7:19 because it does not go into his heart, but into his belly, and into the drain?" Making all food clean.

B' 7:20 And he said, "Things that proceed out of the man are what defiles the man. 7:21 For from within, out of the heart of men, evil thoughts proceed: fornications, thefts, murders, adulteries, 7:22 covetous desires, wickedness, deceit, lasciviousness, envy, slander, pride, foolishness. 7:23 All these evil things proceed from within, go out and defile the man."

A 10:46b And as he and his disciples were going out from Jericho, along with a large crowd, the son of Timaeus, Bartimaeus, a blind beggar, was sitting beside the road.

B 10:47 And hearing that it is Jesus the Nazarene, he began to shout out and to say, "Jesus, son of David, have mercy on me."

C 10:48 And many admonished him, that he should be silent.

D But he shouted out all the more, "Son of David, have mercy on me."

E 10:49 And Jesus stopped, and said, "Call him."

F And they call the blind man, saying to him, "Cheer up. Arise. He calls you."

F' 10:50 And he, throwing away his tunic, leaped up, and came to Jesus.

E' 10:51 And answering him Jesus said, "What do you want me to do for you?"

D' But the blind man said to him, "Rabbi, that I might see."

C' 10:52 And Jesus said to him, "Go on your way; your faith has cured you."

B' And immediately he could see, and followed him on the road.

A 11:1 And when they approached Jerusalem, to Bethphage and Bethany, towards the Mount of Olives, he sends two of the disciples 11:2 and says to them, "Go into the village that is in front of you. And immediately entering into it, you will find a colt tied, that no man ever yet sat upon. Untie it, and bring him. 11:3 And if any one say to you, 'Why do you this?' say, 'The Lord has need of him, and immediately he will send him back.'"

B 11:4 And they departed.

C And they found a colt having been tied at the door outside on the street.

D And they untie him.

D' 11:5 And some of those standing there said to them, "What are you doing, untying the colt?"

C' 11:6 But they said to them what Jesus had told them.

B' And they let them go.

A 11:7 And they bring the colt to Jesus, and throw on him their tunics. And he sat upon him.

B 11:8 And many spread their tunics on the road, and others branches, which they had cut from the fields.

B' 11:9 And those in front and those that followed cried, "Hosanna. Blessed is he who comes in the name of the Lord. 11:10 Blessed is the coming kingdom of our father David. Hosanna in the highest."

A 11:11 And he entered into Jerusalem, into the temple. And when having looked around at every thing, since it was late, he went out to Bethany with the twelve. 11:12 And on the next day when they were come out from Bethany, he was hungry.

B 11:13 And seeing a fig tree in the distance having leaves, he went to see if he will find anything on it.

C And when he came to it, he found nothing but leaves.

C' For it was not the season of figs.

B' 11:14 And responding he said to it, "No man may eat fruit from you from now on." And his disciples heard him.

A 11:15 And they come to Jerusalem.

B And entering into the temple he began to throw out those selling and those buying in the temple.

 C And he overturned the tables of the moneychangers, and the seats of those selling doves.

  D 11:16 And he would not allow any man to carry a pitcher through the temple.

  D' 11:17 And he taught, and was saying to them, "Is it not written, 'My house will be called a house of prayer for all the nations?' But you have made it a den of thieves."

 C' 11:18 And the chief priests and the scribes heard it, and searched for a way they might kill him.

B' For they feared him; for everyone in the crowd was astonished at his teaching.

A 11:19 And when evening arrived he left the city.

B 11:20 And passing by the next morning, they saw the fig tree had been withered away from the roots.

 C 11:21 And remembering Peter says to him, "Rabbi, look, the fig tree that you cursed is withered away."

 C' 11:22 And answering Jesus says to them, "Have faith in God. 11:23 Truthfully, I say to you, whoever says to this mountain, 'Be taken up and thrown into the sea.' and does not doubt in his heart, but believes that what he says will happen, it will be.

B' 11:24 Therefore, I say to you, whatever you pray for, believe that you will receive it, and you will have it. 11:25 And whenever you stand praying, forgive, if you have anything against any one. So that your Father who is in heaven may forgive you your trespasses." 11:26

A 11:27 And they come again to Jerusalem.

B And as he was walking in the temple, the chief priests and the scribes and the elders come to him. 11:28 And they said to him, "By what authority are you doing these things? Or who gave you this authority to do these things?"

 C 11:29 And Jesus said to them, "I will ask you one question. Answer me, and I will tell you by what authority I do these things. 11:30 The baptism of John, was it from heaven, or from men? Answer me."

  D 11:31 And they discussed among themselves, saying, "If we say, 'From heaven;' He will say, 'Why then did you not believe him?' 11:32 But should we say, 'From men . . .'" They feared the people for everyone truly held John to be a prophet.

  E 11:33 And answering Jesus they say, "We do not know."

  E' And Jesus says to them, "Neither will I tell you by what authority I do these things."

  D' 12:1 And he began to speak to them in parables. "A man planted a vineyard, and put a fence around it, and dug a pit for the winepress, and built a tower, and rented it to farmers, and went abroad. 12:2 And at the proper time he sent to the farmers a servant, that he might receive from the farmers the fruits of the vineyard. 12:3 And taking him they and beat him, and sent him away empty handed. 12:4 And again he sent to them another servant. And him they beat him on the head, and dishonored him. 12:5 And he sent another and him they killed: and many others, beating some, but killing some. 12:6 Further he had a beloved son. Finally, he sent him to them, saying, 'They will have respect for my son.' 12:7 But those farmers said to each other, 'This is the heir. Come, let us kill him, and the inheritance will be ours.' 12:8 And taking him they killed him, and threw him out of the vineyard. 12:9 What then will the lord of the vineyard do? He will come and destroy the farmers, and will give the vineyard to others.

C' 12:10 Have you not read even this scripture, 'The stone that the builders rejected, this was made the corner stone. 12:11 This was from the Lord. And it is wonderful in our eyes?'"

B' 12:12 And they wanted to take him, and they feared the crowd. For they realized that he spoke the parable against them.

A And leaving him they went away.

B 12:13 And they send to him some of the Pharisees and of the Herodians, that they might ensnare him in his words.

C 12:14 And arriving they say to him, "Teacher, we know that you are truthful, and are not concerned about any one, for you do not discern the surface of a person, but truly teach the way of God. Is it lawful to pay taxes to Caesar, or not? 12:15 Should we pay, or should we not pay?"

DA But he, knowing their hypocrisy, said to them, "Why do you test me? Bring me a denarius, that I may see it."

DB 12:16 And they brought it.

DA' And he says to them, "Whose is this image and inscription?"

DB' And they said to him, "Caesar's."

C' 12:17 And Jesus said to them, "Render to Caesar the things that are Caesar's, and to God the things that are God's."

B' And they marveled at him.

A 12:18 And Sadducees arrive, who say that there is no resurrection.

B And they asked him, saying, 12:19 "Teacher, Moses wrote to us, 'If a man's brother die, and leave a wife behind him, and leave no child, that his brother should take his wife, and raise up an heir for his brother.' 12:20 There were seven brothers. And the first took a wife, and dying left no heir. 12:21 And the second took her, and died, leaving no heir behind him. And the third likewise. 12:22 And the seven left no heir. Last of all the woman also died. 12:23 In the resurrection whose wife will she be? For the seven had her as a wife."

B' 12:24 Jesus said to them, "Is not this the reason why you err, that you do not know the scriptures, nor the power of God? 12:25 For when they rise from the dead, they neither marry, nor are given in marriage, but are as angels in heaven. 12:26 But concerning the dead that they are awakened: have not you read in the book of Moses, about the bush, how God spoke to him, saying, 'I am the God of Abraham, and the God of Isaac, and the God of Jacob?' 12:27 He is not the God of the dead, but of the living. You do greatly err."

A 12:28 And approaching one of the scribes heard them discussing together. And realizing that he had answered them well, he asked him, "What commandment is the first of all?"

B 12:29 Jesus answered, "The first is, Hear, O Israel. The Lord our God, the Lord is one. 12:30 And you will love the Lord your God with all your heart, and with all your soul, and with all your mind, and with all your strength. 12:31 The second is this: you will love your neighbor as yourself. There is no other commandment greater than these."

   C 12:32 And the scribe said to him, "Correct, Teacher, you have spoken the truth that He is one, and there is no other but Him. 12:33 And to love Him with all the heart, and with all the soul, and with all the mind, and to love one's neighbor as oneself, is greater than all burnt offerings and sacrifices."

   C' 12:34 And seeing that he replied wisely, Jesus said to him, "You are not far from the kingdom of God."

B' And after that no one dared question him.

A 12:35 And teaching in the temple Jesus answered and said, "Why do the scribes say that the Christ is the son of David? 12:36 David himself said in the Holy Spirit, 'The Lord said to my Lord, "Sit on my right hand until I make your enemies a footstool for your feet."' 12:37 David himself calls him Lord. So how is he his son?"

B And the large crowd heard him with pleasure.

B' 12:38 And in his teaching he said, "Beware of the scribes, desiring to walk in long robes, and receiving greeting in the marketplaces, 12:39 and honorable seats in the synagogues, and chief places at feasts. 12:40 They are devouring widows' houses, and for a pretence make long prayers. These will receive abundant judgment."

A 12:41 And sitting down over in front of the treasury, he saw how the crowd threw money into the treasury.

B And many of the rich threw in a lot.

   C 12:42 And coming a poor widow threw in two lepta, which amount to a kodrantes.

   C' 12:43 And summoning his disciples, he said to them, "Truthfully I say to you, this poor widow threw in more than anyone who is throwing into the treasury.

B' 12:44 For they all threw in their extra. But out of her poverty she threw in all that she had, all her livelihood."

A 13:1 And he is leaving the temple.

B One of his disciples says to him, "Teacher, look. What wonderful stones and what wonderful buildings!"

B' 13:2 And Jesus said to him, "See these great buildings? There will not be left here one stone upon another that will not be torn down."

A 13:3 And he is sitting on the mount of Olives in front of the temple.

B Peter and James and John and Andrew asked him privately, 13:4 "Tell us, when will these things happen? And what is the sign that these things are all going take place?"

C 13:5 And Jesus began to say to them, "Be careful that no one leads you astray. 13:6 Many will come in my name, saying, 'I am he;' and many will be lead astray. 13:7 But when you hear of wars and rumors of wars, do not be alarmed. These things must happen, but it is not yet the end. 13:8 For nation will rise against nation, and kingdom against kingdom. There will be earthquakes in various places. There will be famines. These things are the beginning of birth pains.

D 13:9 But watch out for yourselves. They will deliver you up to councils. And in synagogues you will be flogged. And you will stand before governors and kings for my sake, as a witness to them. 13:10 And the gospel must first be proclaimed to all the nations. 13:11 And when they lead you away and deliver you up, do not be worried beforehand what you will say. But whatever comes to you at that time, say it. For it is not you speaking, but the Holy Spirit. 13:12 And brother will deliver up brother to death, and the father his child. And children will rise up against parents, and put them to death. 13:13 And you will be hated by all men for my name's sake. But those enduring to the end will be saved. 13:14 But when you see the abomination of desolation standing where it should not—let the reader understand—then those who are in Judea must flee to the mountains. 13:15 And he who is on the housetop must not go down, nor enter to take anything out his house. 13:16 And he who is in the field must not return to fetch his tunic. 13:17 But woe to those who are pregnant and to those who are nursing in those days! 13:18 And pray that it does not happen in the winter. 13:19 For those days will be an affliction such as there has never been since the beginning of the creation that God created until the present. And never will be. 13:20 And if the Lord had not shortened the days, no flesh would have been saved. But because of the elect, whom he chose, he shortened the days.

D' 13:21 And then if any man says to you, 'Look, here is the Christ,' or 'Look there.' Do not believe it. 13:22 For there will arise false Christs and false prophets, and they will give signs and wonders to lead the elect astray, if possible.

C' 13:23 But take care. I have told you all things beforehand. 13:24 But in those days after the affliction, the sun will be darkened, and the moon will not give her light. 13:25 And the stars will be falling from heaven, and the powers that are in the heavens will be disturbed. 13:26 And then they will see the Son of Man coming in clouds with great power and glory. 13:27 And then he will send the angels, and will assemble his elect from the four winds, from the ends of the earth to the ends of heaven. 13:28 But from the fig tree learn the parable. When the branch becomes tender, and sprouts its leaves, you realize that the summer is close. 13:29 You too, when you see these things happening, know that it is near, at the doors.

B' 13:30 Truthfully, I say to you, this generation will not pass away, until all these things happen. 13:31 Heaven and earth will pass away. But my words will not pass away. 13:32 But when that day or that hour comes no one knows, not even the angels in heaven, nor the son, but the Father. 13:33 Take care, stay awake. For you do not know when the time is. 13:34 Like a man going abroad having left his house, and given authority to his servants, to each one his work. And he commanded the porter to keep watch. 13:35 Be vigilant, then, for you do not know when the lord of the house comes, whether in the evening, or at midnight, or at cockcrowing, or in the morning. 13:36 Unless coming unexpectedly, he should find you sleeping. 13:37 And what I say to you I say to all. Be vigilant."

A 14:1 After two days was the Passover and the feast of the unleavened bread.

B And the chief priests and the scribes looked for a way they might take him with treachery and put him to death.

B' 14:2 For they said, "Not during the feast because there would be a disturbance of the people."

A 14:3 And being in Bethany in the house of Simon the leper reclining at dinner.

B There came a woman having an alabaster flask of ointment of very costly pure nard.

C Having broken the alabaster flask, she poured it over his head.

D 14:4 But there were some that were indignant saying to each other, "Why has there been a waste of the anointing oil? 14:5 For this oil might have been sold for more than three hundred denarii, and given to the poor."

D' And they made noises against her.

C' 14:6 But Jesus said, "Leave her alone. Why do you bother her? She has done a good deed for me. 14:7 For you always have the poor with you, and whenever you desire, you can do them good. But you will not always have me. 14:8 She has done what she could; she has anointed my body in anticipation for my burial.

B' 14:9 But truthfully I say to you, wherever the gospel will be proclaimed throughout the whole world, what this woman has done will be told in memory of her."

A 14:10 And Judas Iscariot, one of the twelve, went to the chief priests that he might deliver him to them.

B 14:11 But when they heard it, they were glad, and promised to give him money.

B' And he looked for how he might conveniently deliver him.

A 14:12 And on the first day of unleavened bread, when they sacrificed the Passover lamb.

B His disciples say to him, "Where do you want us to go and prepare for you to eat the Passover?"

C 14:13 And he sends out two of his disciples, and says to them, "Go into the city, and you will meet a man carrying a pitcher of water. Follow him. 14:14 And where ever he enters say to the master of the house, 'The Teacher says, "Where is my guest room, where I might eat the Passover with my disciples?"'

C' 14:15 And he will show you a large upstairs room furnished and ready. Prepare for us there."

B' 14:16 And the disciples went out and came into the city, and found as he had told them. And they prepared the Passover.

A 14:17 And evening having arrived, he comes with the twelve.

B 14:18 And as they reclined eating, Jesus said, "Truthfully, I say to you, One of you who is eating with me will deliver me up."

C 14:19 They became to be sorrowful, and to say to him one by one, "Not I, is it?"

D 14:20 But he said to them, "It is one of the twelve who dips with me in the bowl. 14:21 For the Son of Man goes as it has been written of him. But woe to the man by whom the Son of Man is delivered! It would be better for that man if he had not been born."

D' 14:22 And as they were eating, taking bread, and blessing it, he broke, and gave it to them, and said, "Take it. This is my body." 14:23 And taking a cup, and giving thanks, he gave to them. And they all drank it.

C' 14:24 And he said to them, "This is my blood of the covenant, being poured out for many.

B' 14:25 Truthfully I say to you, I will not drink of the fruit of the vine, until that day when I drink it anew in the kingdom of God."

A 14:26 And having sung a hymn, they went out to the Mount of Olives.

B 14:27 And Jesus says to them, "All you will stumble for it is written, I will strike the shepherd, and the sheep will be scattered.

C 14:28 But after I am risen I will go before you into Galilee."

D 14:29 But Peter said to him, "Even if everyone will stumble, I will not."

D' 14:30 And Jesus says to him, "Truthfully I say to you, that today, this night, before the cock crows twice, you will deny me three times."

C' 14:31 But he spoke vehemently, "If it is necessary that I die with you, I will not deny you."

B' And likewise they all spoke.

A 14:32 And they come to a place that was named Gethsemane.

B And he says to his disciples, "Sit here while I pray."

C 14:33 And he takes with him Peter and James and John. And he became greatly awe struck, and deeply troubled. 14:34 And he says to them, "My soul is extremely sorrowful even to death. You stay here, and watch."

D 14:35 And going on a little farther he fell on the ground, and prayed that, if possible, the hour might pass by him.

E 14:36 And he said, "Abba, Father, all things are possible for you. Remove this cup from me. But not what I desire, but your will."

F 14:37 And he comes, and finds them sleeping, and says to Peter, "Simon, are you asleep? Could you not watch one hour?

F' 14:38 Watch and pray that you do not enter into temptation. The spirit indeed is willing, but the flesh is weak."

E' 14:39 And again going away, he prayed, saying the same words.

D' 14:40 And again coming he found them sleeping for their eyes were very heavy. And they did not know what to answer him.

C' 14:41 And he comes the third time, and says to them, "Are you still sleeping and taking your rest? Enough. The hour is at hand. Look, the Son of Man is delivered into the hands of sinners.

B' 14:42 Wake up, let us be going. Look, he that delivers me is coming."

A 14:43 And immediately, while speaking of him, Judas, one of the twelve comes and with him a bunch from the chief priests and the scribes and the elders with swords and clubs.

B 14:44 Now the one delivering him up had given them a signal saying, "Whoever I kiss, he is the one. Take him, and lead him away safely."

C 14:45 And immediately on arriving, he came to him and says, "Rabbi."

D And he kissed him.

E 14:46 And they laid hands on him, and took him.

F 14:47 But one of them standing by drawing his sword struck the servant of the high priest.

F' And he cut off his ear.

E' 14:48 And answering Jesus said to them, "Did you come out as against a robber, with swords and clubs to arrest me? 14:49 I was with you in the temple teaching every day, and you did not take me. But let the scriptures be fulfilled."

D' 14:50 And leaving him, they all fled.

C' 14:51 And a certain young man was following him, having a linen cloth thrown around his naked body.

B' And they lay hold of him. 14:52 But leaving the linen cloth he fled naked.

A 14:53 And they led Jesus away to the high priest. And there come together all the chief priests and the elders and the scribes.

B 14:54 And Peter had followed him at a distance up to inside the court of the high priest. And he was sitting with the servants, and warming himself at the fire.

C 14:55 Now the chief priests and the entire council looked for evidence against Jesus to put him to death. And they did not find any.

D 14:56 For many testified falsely against him. And their testimony was inconsistent.

E 14:57 And some rising gave false testimony against him, saying, 14:58 "We heard him saying, 'I will destroy this temple that is made with hands, and in three days I will build another made without hands.'"

F 14:59 And none of the testimony was the same.

G 14:60 And standing up in the middle of them, the high priest questioned Jesus, saying, "Do you answer nothing? What is it that these testify against you?"

H 14:61 But he was silent and answered nothing.

I Again the high priest questioned him, and says to him, "Are you the Christ, the son of the Blessed?"

J 14:62 And Jesus said, "I am. And you will see the Son of Man sitting at the right hand of Power, and coming with the clouds of heaven."

KA 14:63 And the high priest tore his tunic, and says, "What further need do we have for witnesses? 14:64 You have heard the blasphemy. What is your decision?"

KB And they all condemned him to be deserving death.

KA' 14:65 And some began to spit on him, and to cover his face, and to punch him, and to say to him, "Prophesy."

KB' And the servants slapped him.

J' 14:66 And Peter was down under in the courtyard. There comes one of the servant girls of the high priest. 14:67 And having seen Peter warm himself,

I' She looked at him and says, "You also were with the Nazarene, Jesus."

H' 14:68 But he denied, saying, "I neither know, nor understand what you are saying." And he went out into the porch.

G' 14:69 And the servant girl seeing him again, began to say to them that standing there, "This is one of them."

F' 14:70 But he again denied it.

E' And after a little while again those standing there said to Peter, "Truly you are one of them. For you are a Galilean."

D' 14:71 But he began to curse and swear, "I do not know this man you are talking about."

C' 14:72 And immediately the cock crowed a second time.

B' And Peter remembered the words that Jesus said to him, "Before the cock crows twice, you will deny me three times." And breaking down, he wept.

Act III

A 15:1 And immediately in the early morning the chief priests with the elders and scribes, and the Sanhedrin, held a consultation.

  B And binding Jesus they led him away. And they delivered him up to Pilate.

    C 15:2 And Pilate interrogated him. "Are you the King of the Jews?"

      D And he answering says to him, "So you say."

        E 15:3 And the chief priests were accusing him of many things.

          F 15:4 And Pilate again questioned him, saying, "Do you have nothing to say? Look how many things they accuse you of."

            G 15:5 But Jesus answered nothing; so that Pilate was amazed.

              H 15:6 But at the feast he used to release to them one prisoner whom they requested.

                I 15:7 Now there was one called Barabbas, captured with the rebels who had committed murder in the insurrection.

                  J 15:8 And the crowd went up and began to petition him to follow his customary practice.

                  J' 15:9 And Pilate answered them, saying, "What do you want me to do with the King of the Jews?"

                I' 15:10 For he realized that the chief priests had delivered him up because of envy.

              H' 15:11 But the chief priests stirred up the crowd, that he should release Barabbas to them instead.

            G' 15:12 And Pilate again answered and said to them, "What then should I do to him whom you call the King of the Jews?"

          F' 15:13 And they shouted back, "Crucify him."

        E' 15:14 And Pilate said to them, "What evil has he done?"

      D' But they cried out vehemently, "Crucify him."

    C' 15:15 But Pilate, wanting to appease the crowd, released Barabbas to them.

  B' And having flogged Jesus, he delivered him to be crucified.

A 15:16 But the soldiers took him inside the court, that is, the Praetorian; and they summoned the entire cohort.

  B 15:17 And they dressed him in a purple tunic, and braiding a crown of thorns, they put it on him.

    C 15:18 and they began to salute him, "Hail, King of the Jews!"

    C' 15:19 And they struck his head with a rod, and spat upon him. And on bended knees they worshipped him.

  B' 15:20 And when they had ridiculed him, they took off the purple, and put on him his own tunic.

A And they lead him out to crucify him.

B 15:21 And they compel a passer by coming from the country, Simon of Cyrene, the father of Alexander and Rufus, to carry his cross. 15:22 And they take him to Golgotha which is being translated, "The place of a skull."

CA 15:23 And they gave him wine mingled with myrrh. But he did not take it.

CB 15:24 And as they were crucifying him.

CC They divided his garments among them, throwing dice for them, what each should take.

D 15:25 And it was the third hour, and they crucified him.

E 15:26 And the inscription of the charge against him was written above, "The King of the Jews."

F 15:27 And with him they crucify two robbers; one on his right hand, and one on his left. 15:28.

GA 15:29 And those that passed by called him names, shaking their heads, and saying, "Ha! you that destroys the temple, and builds it in three days.

GB 15:30 Save yourself, and come down from the cross."

GA' 15:31 Likewise also the chief priests ridiculing him among themselves with the scribes said, "He saved others; he cannot save himself.

GB' 15:32 Let the Christ, the King of Israel, now come down from the cross, that we may see and believe."

F' And those being crucified with him insulted him.

E' 15:33 And at the sixth hour darkness came over the entire land until the ninth hour.

D' 15:34 And at the ninth hour Jesus shouted with a loud voice, "Eloi, Eloi, lama sabachthani?" Which is, being translated, "My God, my God, why have you abandoned me?"

CA' 15:35 And some of those that standing there, hearing it, said, "Look, he calls Elijah." 15:36 And one ran and filled a sponge full of vinegar, put it on a rod, and gave it to him to drink, saying, "Let him have it. See if Elijah comes to take him down."

CB' 15:37 And Jesus uttered a loud sound, and the spirit departed from him.

CC' 15:38 And the curtain of the temple was torn in two from the top to the bottom.

B 15:39 And the centurion standing across from him, seeing that the spirit departed from him said, "Truly this man was a Son of God."

Epilogue

A 15:40 And there were also women looking on from a distance: among whom Mary Magdalene, and Mary the mother of James the less and of Joseph, and Salome. 15:41 Who, when he was in Galilee, followed him and served him. And many other women came up with him to Jerusalem.

B 15:42 And evening had arrived, since it was the Preparation, that is, the day before the Sabbath.

C 15:43 Came Joseph from Arimathaea, a Sanhedrin member of honorable estate, who also himself was expecting the kingdom of God. And he boldly went in to Pilate, and petitioned for the body of Jesus.

D 15:44 And Pilate wondered if he were already dead. And calling the centurion to him, he questioned him whether he was already dead. 15:45 And learning of it from the centurion, he granted the corpse to Joseph.

D' 15:46 And buying a linen cloth, and taking him down, he wrapped him in the linen cloth, and laid him in a tomb which had been hewn out of a rock. And he rolled a stone against the door of the tomb.

C' 15:47 And Mary Magdalene and Mary the mother of Joseph saw where he was laid.

B' 16:1 And with the Sabbath passing Mary Magdalene, and Mary the mother of James, and Salome bought spices, that they might come and anoint him.

A 16:2 And very early on the first day of the week, they come to the tomb after the sun had risen.

B 16:3 And they were saying to each other, "Who will roll the stone away from the door of the tomb for us?"

C 16:4 And looking up, they see that the stone has been rolled back for it was extremely large.

D 16:5 And entering into the tomb, they saw a young man sitting on the right, dressed in a white robe.

E And they were astonished.

E' 16:6 And he says to them, "Do not be astonished.

D' You are looking for Jesus, the Nazarene, who was crucified. He is risen. He is not here.

C' Look at the place where they laid him! 16:7 But go, tell his disciples and Peter, he goes ahead of you into Galilee. You will see him there just as he told you."

B' 16:8 And going out they fled from the tomb. For trembling and astonishment had came over them. And they told no one anything for they were afraid.

Appendix 2

Triplets in the Original Gospel of Mark

THIS APPENDIX SETS OUT the triplets and sextets discovered to date in Mark's Original Gospel. The first column identifies the word, phrase or concept that is repeated, the second column shows the chapter and verse where the word or phrase is found, and the third column identifies how the middle element differs from the first and third elements. Mark's structure of making the middle element different from the first and third elements in his triplets is parallel to his intercalated pericopae wherein the first story is interupted to tell a second story and then the first is completed.

Triplet	Locations	Middle Element
1. Major Temptations	1:13 8:33 14:36–38	There are three major temptations and three minor temptations (or testings) in Original Mark. In the first element of the major temptation triplet Jesus was "being tempted"(peirazomenos) by Satan. In the third element the noun form "temptation" is used (peirasmon). In the middle element neither the verb nor the noun is used. The temptation is implied. The persceptive reader knows that Peter has tempted Jesus from Jesus's reaction to Peter's rebuke.
2. Prophet	1:2 6:4 11:32	In the middle element of this triplet Jesus calls himself a prophet. In the first and third elements the narrator tells the reader that Isaiah was a prophet and that the people thought John the Baptizer was a prophet.
3. "In those days"	1:9 13:17 13:24	The middle element has the event before "in those days." The first and third elements state the event after "in those days."
4. Satan		This is a chiastic sextet. All the chiastic matching words or phrases are placed before the word "Satan."
4. Satan	1:13	A Tempted by Satan
4. Satan	3:23	B . . . in parables, "How can Satan
4. Satan	3:23	C cast out Satan?"
4. Satan	3:26	C' "cannot stand . . . If Satan . . ."
4. Satan	4:13–15	B' "all the parables? . . . Satan comes
4. Satan	8:33	A' "Get behind me, Satan

Triplet	Locations	Middle Element
5. Peter, James, John get special treatment.	5:37 9:2 14:33	The middle element in this triplet says, "Jesus takes with him." In the first and third elements Jesus is identified by pronouns.
6. Miracle witnesses exclamation	1:27 2:12 4:41	While there is a crowd reaction in almost all the miracles, there are only three in which the words of the witnesses are quoted. In the first and third elements of this triplet the witnesses use the term "obey" (hupakouō). In the middle element they do not.
7. Recognizing (epiginōkō)	2:8 5:30 6:33	In the middle element of this triplet the person recognizing (Jesus) precedes the verb. In the first and third elements (Jesus, many) the recognizer follows the verb.
8. "I (Son of Man) came"	1:38 2:17 10:45	This is an interesting triplet in that the first two elements (1 and 2) Jesus calls himself "I." In the last two elements (2 and 3) Jesus uses a "not . . . but" construction. So the middle element is unique in that it uses both "I" and the "not . . . but" construction. In addition, in the middle element the "not" precedes the subject "I." In the third element Jesus calls himself "Son of Man."
9. Gospel	1:14 1:15 8:35 10:29 13:10 14:9	This is a sextet or double triplet with the first two having "proclaim" and "says believe" preceding "gospel" the next two having "sake" preceding "gospel," and the last two having "proclaim " preceding "gospel." There is a popular theory among exegetes that "proclaim the gospel" at 13:10 is a later redaction. This sextet proves that theory wrong.
10. "Son of God"	3:11 5:7 15:39	In the middle element the unclean spirit calls Jesus the "Son of the most high God." In the first and third elements Jesus is called the "Son of God."
11. Pharisees and Herodians	3:6 8:15 12:13	The middle element of this triplet uses the word "Herod" while the first and third elements use "Herodians."
12. Reclining	2:15a 2:15b 14:3	The first and third elements contain "at dinner" while the middle element does not.
13. Sinners and Tax Collectors	2:15 2:16a 2:16b	This is a typical pericope triplet in which a key element is repeated three times. The middle element of this triplet is "sinners and tax collectors" while the first and third elements are "tax collectors and sinners."
14. Enter Capernaum	1:21 2:1 9:33	The middle element in this triplet has the third person singular "he" entered Capernaum. The first and third elements use the third person plural "they" go or came into Capernaum.
15. First half towns: Capernaum, Bethsaida, Caesarea Philippi	1:21 2:1 8:22 8:27 9:33	In Capernaum Jesus goes into a house or a synagogue, but in Bethsaida and Caesrea Philippi he is not in a particular building. He is outside.
16. Enter synagogue	1:22 3:1 6:2	In the middle element Jesus did not teach in the synagogue. In the first and third elements Jesus taught in the synagogue.

Triplet	Locations	Middle Element
17. Three disciples with epithets	3:16 3:17a 3:17b	Peter, James, and John are the three favorite disciples. They are the only ones to whom Jesus gave an additional name. After Peter and John the text says, "he added the name." This phrase does not appear after James, the second named disciple.
18. Seaside	2:13 5:21 4:1	The middle element of this triplet does not have the words "again" (palin) and "teach" (didaskō). The first and third elements say that Jesus is *again* by the sea and he *taught* the crowd.
19. First boat triplet	3:9 4:36 4:1	All three elements of this triplet contain the words "crowd" and "boat." Only in the middle element of this first *boat* triplet does a second "boat" follow "boat" In the first and third elements "crowd" follows "boat." This confirms that 4:1 followed 4:36 in the original Gospel. The first boat triplet ends as the Pauline section begins and the second boat triplet is in the Pauline section.
20. Second boat triplet	6:32 8:10 8:13	In the first and third elements of this second *boat* triplet Jesus goes "away" (apēlthen). In the middle element "come" (erchomai) is used instead of "away."
21. First power triplet	5:30 9:1 12:24	In this first *power* triplet the middle element has "with power" (en dynamei). The first and third elements have "the power" (tēn dynamin).
22. Second power triplet	13:25 13:26 14:62	In the second *power* triplet the middle term does not have the word "heaven" (ouranos) following it. The first and third elements precede the word "heaven."
23. Aramaic phrase	5:41 15:22 15:34	The middle element of this triplet of Aramaic phrases is in the words of the narrator. The Aramaic phrases in the first and third elements are spoken by Jesus.
24. Daughter	5:23 5:34 5:35	This triplet is contained in the "Healing the Woman with Blood Flow"/"Jairus's Daughter Is Dead"/"Healing Jairus's Daughter" intercalation. Jesus speaks the word "daughter" in the middle element while others say "daughter" in the first and third elements.
25. "Risen" outside the Passion predictions	6:16 9:9 16:6	Jesus predicts his death three times and says that he will rise from the dead. Outside of those predictions Mark has "risen" in connection with rising from the dead three additional times. In this triplet the first and third elements have "ēgerthē" meaning "is risen," and in the middle element Mark uses "anastē" for "is risen."
26. Go to deserted, solitary place (erēmon topon)	1:35 1:45 6:31	The middle element of this triplet is plural while the first and third elements are singular.
27. First run triplet	5:6 6:33 15:36	The middle element of this triplet is "run together" (suntrechō), The first and third elements use "run" (trechō).
28. Second run triplet	9:15 9:25 10:17	The first and third elements use "run to" (prostrechō) while the middle element uses "run together again" (episuntrechō). This second *run* triplet is imbedded within the first *run* triplet, an unusual structure for Mark.

Triplet	Locations	Middle Element
29. Noun of address – Satan, Abba, Simon	8:33 14:36 14:37	The first and third elements are both directed at Peter and both start with an S (sigma). The middle element is directed to God.
30. All things are possible	9:23 10:27 14:36	The middle element has "with God." The first and third elements use pronouns (him, you).
31. Hand, foot, eye causes stumble	9:43 9:45 9:47	The middle element does not mention unquenchable fire (pyr to asbeston) while the first and third do.
32. First "kingdom of God" triplet	4:11 4:26 4:30	This is a pericope level triplet confined to "The Parable Discourse." The middle element does not have the word "parable" following "kingdom of God," while the first and third elements do.
33. Second "kingdom of God" triplet	9:47 10:14 10:15	The first element of the triplet has the word "enter" before "kingdom of God." The third element has the word "enter" after "kingdom of God." The middle element does not use the word "enter."
34. Third "kingdom of God" triplet	10:23 10:24 10:25	The middle element in this triplet is spoken about those who "trust in riches" (pepoithotas epi chrēmasin) while the first and third elements pertain to those who have riches.
35. Forgiveness of sins (aphesin hamartiōn)	1:4 2:5 3:28	Three pericopae contain the phrase "forgiveness of sins." The first and third pericopae have quoted words from 2 Kgs 1:2–16 associated with it, the middle pericope, "Healing the Paralytic," (2:1–12) tells a story that is the reverse of 2 Kgs 1:2–16. "Healing the Paralytic" contains the phrase "forgiveness of sins" four times, making two triplets occurring in these three pericopae. See triplet numbers 62 and 63 below.
36. First, last, last, first	9:35 10:31 10:43–44	The middle element of this triplet does not use the word "servant" (diakonos) or "slave" (doulos). Also the middle element reverses first, last so that it is a chiasm (the first shall be last and the last, first). The first and third elements only have first shall be last (or slave).
37. Entries into Jerusalem and the temple	11:11 11:15 11:27	In this triplet Jesus enters Jerusalem and the temple three times. In the middle element he clears the temple, while in the first and third elements Jesus is looking around and walking in the temple.
38. Second half towns: Jericho, Jerusalem, Bethany	10:46 (7:1–2) 11:11 11:15 11:27 14:3	In the first and third elements Jesus is eating in a building (7:1–2 follow 10:46a.) In the middle element, Jesus's entries into Jerusalem, he is looking, walking or casting out sellers. All of the entries into Jerusalem fall between coming to Jericho and being in Bethany.
39. Go up a mountain (up to Jerusalem, Mt. Zion)	3:13 9:2 10:32	In the first and third elements the verb is "go up" (anabainō) first person singular in the first element and third person plural in the third element. In the middle element the verb is "bring up" or "lead up" (anapherō) with Jesus taking the three disciples with him.

Triplet	Locations	Middle Element
40. "Son of David"	10:47 10:48 12:35	The first element is "Jesus, son of David" the third element is "Christ is the son of David" while the middle element only has "son of David," without saying that it is Jesus or Christ.
41. "Defiles the man"	7:15 7:20 7:23	This is another pericope triplet with Jesus making his point three times. The middle element of this triplet uses "cleansing" (katharizōn) before "defiles the man." The first element uses "to defile" (koinōsai) before "defiles the man," and the third element uses "evils" (ponēra) before "defiles the man." So that the middle element "cleansing" is opposite of "to defile" or "evils."
42. Passion predictions	8:31 9:31 10:32	The middle element of this triplet says only that the Son of Man will be killed. In the first element Jesus says the Son of Man will suffer many things and in the third element Jesus details the things the Son of Man will suffer.
43. Parousia predictions	9:1 13:26 14:62	The middle element of this triplet uses "great power" (dynameōs pollēs) while the first and third elements use only "power" (dynameōs).
44. Denarii	6:37 12:15 14:5	The middle element of this triplet uses the singular "denarius," while the first and third elements use the plural "denarii."
45. Jesus goes to pray	1:35 14:35 14:39	In the middle element of this triplet Jesus's exact words are given while in the first and third elements the reader is told only that Jesus prayed.
46. Sleeping disciples	14:37 14:40 14:41	In the middle element of this triplet there is no quote of Jesus, while in the first and third elements Mark tells the reader what Jesus said to the disciples.
47. Peter's denials	14:68 14:70 14:71	In the middle element of this triplet the reader is not told exactly what Peter said, while in the first and third elements Mark tells the reader what Peter said to his accuser.
48. Women named	15:40 15:47 16:1	In the middle element of this triplet only two women are named while in the first and third elements three women are named.
50. Three women at Jesus's tomb	16:1	Three women went to Jesus's tomb. The middle named woman is identified by the name of her son.
51. "They were afraid"	10:32 11:18 16:8	This triplet is built around "they were afraid" (ephobounto, the third person plural imperfect indicative middle or passive). All three elements occur in the second half of the Original Gospel, at the turning point, clearing the temple and women fleeing Jesus's tomb. All three instances are combined with a word of amazement (ethambounto, exeplēsseto, or ekstasis). In the middle element the word of amazement follows "they were afraid" while in the first and third elements the word of amazement precedes "they were afraid."

Triplet	Locations	Middle Element
52. "As it is written" (kathōs gegraptai)	1:2 9:13 7:6	The middle element of this triplet has "Elijah" preceding "as it is written." The first element has "Isaiah" following "as it is written," and the third element has "Isaiah" preceding the phrase. Isaiah – Elijah – Isaiah. This triplet is about OT prophets. In Original Mark 7:6 comes after 9:13. 7:1–23 was originally located between 10:46a and 10:46b. In fact 9:13 is approximately mid way between 1:2 and 7:6 in Original Mark. This OT prophet triplet is additional evidence that that 7:1–23 has been moved from its location in Original Mark.
53. "Have you read"	2:25 12:10 12:26	The middle element of this triplet does not name an OT person. The first element specifies David and the third element specifies Moses.
54. Fear the people	11:32 12:12 14:2	This is another triplet where the middle element is a combination of the first and third elements. The triplet escalates the threat to Jesus after he enters Jerusalem. In the first element Mark only states that the authorities feared the people. In the middle element Mark says they wanted to lay hold of Jesus, but they feared the people. In the last element Mark says the authorities wanted to take Jesus by stealth and kill him, but there might be a disturbance or riot of the people if they did it during the feast. Only in the middle element are there both the word "fear" and a desire to arrest Jesus.
55. First Christ triplet	8:29 9:41 12:35	There are two triplets using the words "Christ" and "say" (legō). In both triplets the middle element has "say" coming after "Christ," and in the middle element of both triplets Jesus is the person saying "Christ." In the first and third elements someone else says "Christ" and "say" comes before Christ. Peter says, ". . . the Christ," "Christ's name, truly I (Jesus) say," "Scribes say that the Christ"
56. Second Christ triplet	13:21 14:61 15:32	In the second *Christ* triplet we find the same pattern as in the first one. "If any man says to you . . . the Christ," "Are you the Christ? . . . and Jesus said," Chief priests . . . said, "Let the Christ "
57. Beginning	10:6 13:8 13:19	The middle element of this triplet is the "beginning of birth pains." The first and third elements are "the beginning of creation."

Triplet	Locations	Middle Element
58. Kill Jesus	3:6 11:18 14:1	This is an interesting triplet in that the first element has the Pharisees and the Herodians wanting to destroy (apolesōsin) Jesus. The middle element has the chief priests and scribes wanting to destroy (apolesōsin) Jesus. The third element has the chief priests and scribes wanting to kill (apokteinōsin) Jesus. The middle element is the one where the chief priests and scribes want to destroy Jesus, combining the first and third elements. That is, only one part of the first element is found in the other two, and only one part of the third element is found in the other two, but both parts of the middle element are found in the other two.
59. Minor temptations (peirazontes)	8:11 10:2 12:15	The middle element of this triplet does not use the verb "to give." In the first element Jesus says no sign from heaven will be given (dothēsetai). In the third element the Pharisees ask three times if it is lawful to give to Caesar (dounai). In addion, in the middle element Jesus "answers" (apokrinomai) them, while in the first and third elements Jesus "says" (legō) to them. All three of these minor temptations give Jesus an opportunity to expound a Pauline lesson.
60. Repent (metanoeite)	1:4 1:15 6:12	While the last two elements are verbs and the first one is a noun, the first and third elements are preceded by "preach" (kērussō) and the middle element is preceded by "saying" (legōn).
61. Into Galilee (eis tēn Galilean)	1:15 14:28 16:7	In the first and third elements the name of a person (John, Peter) comes before the phrase and in the middle element the name (Peter) comes after the phrase.
62. First 'forgiveness of sins" (aph-esin hamartiōn) triplet	1:4 2:5 2:7	In the first *forgiveness of sins* triplet the first and third elements have "sins" immediately following "forgiveness," while in the middle element the Greek wording has the possessive "of you" between "forgiveness" and "sins."
63. Second "forgiveness of sins" triplet	2:9 2:10 3:28	The second *forgiveness of sins* triplet has the opposite construction from the first one. The middle element of this triples has "sins" immediately following "forgiveness," and the first and third elements having the personal possessive, telling whose sins are being forgiven, between "forgiveness" and "sins."
64. Loaves	8:5 8:6 8:20	The first and third elements have the word "seven" after "loaves," while the middle element has "seven" before "loaves."
65. Hard of heart	3:5 8:17 10:5	Mark uses three different expressions to mean "hard of heart." The first and third elements are declarative statements to Pharisees and the middle element is a question to the disciples.

Triplet	Locations	Middle Element
66. First way, road, journey (hodos) triplet	1:2 1:3 12:14	There is a fifteen element structure using the Greek word "hodos" (way, road or journey). There seem to be five triplets with a unique structure in that two of the elements are found very near each other and the other one is some literary distance away. In this first *road* triplet there is "the way of you" (sou) at 1:2 with "you" assumed to mean "the Christ" in this context, "The way of the Lord" (Kyrios) at 1:3 and "the way of God" (Theou) at 12:14. The middle element "Lord" could mean either Christ or God in Christian parlance.
67. Second way, road, journey (hodos) triplet	2:23 10:52 11:8	This second *road* triplet has "began to make their way" (ērxanto hodon poiein), "followed him on the way" (ēkolouthei autō en tē hodō) and "spread in the road" (estrōsan eis tēn hodon). The middle term has "hodō" the dative case, while the first and third elements have "hodon," the accusative case. Again the first element is long literary distance away from the second and third elements, which are very near each other.
68. Third way, road, journey (hodos) triplet	6:8 10:17 10:32	This third *road* triplet has "they take nothing in the journey" (mēden airōsin eis hodon), "He setting out in the journey" (ekporeuomenou autou eis hodon), and "they were on the journey" (Ēsan de en tē hodō). The middle element is third person singular and the first and third elements are third person plural. The first element is a literary distance away from the second and third elements.
69. Fourth way, road, journey (hodos) triplet	4:4 4:15 10:46b	This fourth *road* triplet all have "beside the road" (para tēn hodon). The first and third elements have an active verb (fell and sitting) while the middle element has a being verb (were). The first two elements are close to each other and the last element is a literary distance away.
70. Fifth way, road, journey (hodos) triplet	8:27 9:33 9:34	The fifth and final *road* triplet all have "on the way" (en tē hodō), with the first and third elements being part of a statement and the middle element being part of a question. All three of these elements are relatively close together.
71. Secret conversations with Jesus.	1:12 9:4 8:32	This triplet consists of three conversation others have with Jesus wherein the reader is not told what is said: Satan temps Jesus, Jesus talks with Elijah and Moses and Peter chides Jesus at Caesarea Philippi. In the middle element there are two conversants with Jesus, while in the first and third elements there is only one. The middle element of this triplet is in "The Transfiguration" pericope and the third element is in the "Peter's Confession at Caesarea Philippi" pericope. This triplet shows positively that "The Transfiguration" comes before "Peter's Confession at Caesarea Philippi" in the Original Gospel.
72. Voice (phōnē)	1:3 1:11 9:7	In elements one and three the voice gives a command. In the middle element the voice makes a statement.

Triplet	Locations	Middle Element
73. Gehenna	9:43 9:45 9:47	Gehenna is used as a synonym for "hell." It is the Greek transliteration of a valley, Gehinnom, outside Jerusalem where child sacrifice took place in ancient Judea. Modern textual critics have eliminated 9:44 and 9:46 from Mark's Gospel as being not authenticated. I assume they are correct in that judgment. Therefore, the middle element of this triplet does not have "unquenchable fire" (pyr to asbeston) or "the fire not queched" (pyr ou sbennytai) following it as do the first and third elements.
74. "Arise and pick up your pallet"	2:9 2:10 2:12	This is a pericope level triplet using "arise and pick up your pallet." In the first and third elements the wording is "arise (or arose) and pick up (or having picked up)" while in the middle element there is no "and" (kai).
75. First demon or demon possessed triplet	1:34a 1:34b 1:39	Mark uses demon (diamonion) twelve times in the Original Gospel. There are four triplets. This first triplet has in the first and third elements "cast out" following "demon." The middle element does not use "cast out" associated with "demons."
76. Second demon or demon possessed triplet	3:15 3:22a 3:22b	This second *demon* triplet is much like the first except in the first and third elements "demon" follows "cast out." This is a reversal of the first triplet, and a Markan trait. Like the first triplet "cast out" is not found associated with "demons" the middle element.
77. Third demon or demon possessed triplet	1:32 5:15 5:18	This third *demon* triplet is one of "demon possessed" (diamonizomai). This third *demon* triplet is marked by the word "city" (polis). The first and third elements have "city" following "demon." In the third element the word used is "Decapolis," and area of ten Greek towns east of the Sea of Galilee. The middle element of this triplet has "city" placed before "demon."
78. Fourth demon or demon possessed triplet	5:16 6:13 9:38	The fourth *demon* triplet uses both "demon" and "demon possessed." It also combines the previous three triplets in having the middle element with the word "city" coming before it and "cast out" after it, In the first and third elements characters "saw" using the aorist (past) tense of "see" (horaō). All twelve elements of the structure are in the Galilee half, first half, of the Gospel.
79. First three triplet: "after three days rise"	8:31 9:31 10:34	In the first *three* triplet the first and third elements have the words "chief priests and scribes" before "after three days rise" and the middle element has "men" before "after three days rise."
80. Second three triplet: three buildings or constructions.	9:5 14:72 15:29	In the second *three* triplet the first and third elements have "construct" or "build" coming before "three" and in the middle element "build" comes after "three."
81. Third three triplet: combined with another number	14:5 14:30 14:58	The third *three* triplet combines "three" with another number. There are two times mentioned that Peter will deny knowing Jesus three times before the cock crows twice and the expensive nard could be sold for three hundred denarii, combining three and a hundred (triakosioi). In the first and third elements there is a short dramatic sentence coming after the word "three:" "And they made noises against her," and "and breaking down he wept." In the middle element Peter vehemently protests Jesus's prophecy.

Appendix 3

Pericopae of the Original Gospel of Mark

	1:1	Incipit

Prologue – Act I

1.	1:1–3	Messenger to Prepare the Way
2.	1:4–8	John the Baptizer at the Jordan
3.	1:9–11	Baptism of Jesus
4.	1:12–13	Temptation
5.	1:14–20	Calling the First Four Disciples
6.	1:21–28	Unclean Spirit in the Synagogue
7.	1:29–34	Healing Simon's Mother-in-Law
8.	1:35–38	Finding Jesus
9.	1:39–45	Healing the Leper
10.	2:1–12	Healing the Paralytic
11.	2:13–14	Calling Levi
12.	2:15–17	Eating with Sinners
13.	2:18–22	Lesson on Fasting
14.	2:23–28	Plucking Grain on the Sabbath
15.	3:1–6	Healing the Man with a Withered Hand
16.	3:7–12	Crowd at the Sea; Demons Know the Son of God
17.	3:13–19	Appointing the Twelve
18.	3:20–30	Controversy on Beelzebul
19.	3:31–35	Who Are My Brothers
20.	4:36–41	Calming the Sea

Act II

21.	5:1–20	Healing the Gerasene Demoniac
22.	5:21–34	Healing the Woman with Blood Flow
23.	5:35–37	Jairus's Daughter Is Dead
24.	5:38–43	Healing Jairus's Daughter
25.	6:1–6a	Jesus Is Rejected in His Own Country
26.	6:6b–11	Sending Out the Twelve
27	6:12–29	Killing John the Baptizer
28.	6:30–31	Return of the Twelve
29.	9:2–8	The Transfiguration
30.	9:9–13	Leaving the Mountain
31.	9:14–27	Healing the Epileptic
32.	9:28–29	Answering the Disciples
33.	4:1–34	The Parable Discourse
34.	4:35, 6:32–33	Running Ahead of Jesus
35.	6:34–37, 8:5–9	Feeding the Multitude
36.	8:10–12	Seeking a Sign
37.	8:13–21	Leaven of the Pharisees
38.	8:22–26	Healing the Blind Man of Bethsaida
39.	8:27–9:1	Peter's Confession at Caesarea Philippi
40.	9:30–32	Second Passion Prediction
41.	9:33–50	Teaching the Disciples, Millstone Award
42.	10:1–9 `	Controversy on Divorce
43.	10:10–12	Remarriage Is Adultery
44.	10:13–16	Entering the Kingdom of God
45.	10:17–31	The Rich Man
46.	10:32–34	Heading to Jerusalem, Third Passion Prediction
47.	10:35–41	Request of James and John
48.	10:42–45	Being a Servant
49.	10:46a, 7:01–7:15	Controversy on Tradition
50.	7:17–23	Eating Does Not Defile

51.	10:46b–52	Healing Blind Bartimaeus
52.	11:1–6	Getting a Colt For Jesus
53.	11:7–10	Entering Jerusalem
54.	11:11–14	Cursing the Fig Tree
55.	11:15–19	Clearing the Temple
56.	11:20–25	The Withered Fig Tree
57.	11:27–12:12a	Questioning Jesus's Authority
58.	12:12b–17	Rendering unto Caesar
59.	12:18–27	Controversy on Resurrection
60.	12:28–34	The Greatest Commandment
61.	12:35–40	Beware of the Scribes
62.	12:41–44	The Widow's Mite
63.	13:1–2	Wonderful Buildings
64.	13:3–37	The Olivet Discourse
65.	14:1–2	The Plot Against Jesus
66.	14:3–9	Anointing with Oil in Bethany
67.	14:10–11	Judas Joins the Plot
68.	14:12–16	Finding the Passover Room
69.	14:17–25	The Last Supper
70.	14:26–31	Peter Will Deny Jesus
71.	14:32–42	Praying at Gethsemane, Sleeping Disciples
72.	14:43–52	The Arrest of Jesus

Act III – Epilogue

73.	14:53–72	The Sanhedrin Trial, Peter's Denials
74.	15:1–15	The Trial of Jesus Before Pilate
75.	15:16–20a	The Soldiers' Abuse of Jesus
76.	15:20b–39	The Crucifixion
77.	15:40–16:1	The Burial of Jesus
78.	16:1–8	The Women at the Tomb

Appendix 4

Pericopae of Canonical Mark

	1:1	Incipit
1.	1:1–3	Messenger to Prepare the Way
2.	1:4–8	John the Baptizer at the Jordan
3.	1:9–11	Baptism of Jesus
4.	1:12–13	Temptation
5.	1:14–20	Calling the First Four Disciples
6.	1:21–28	Unclean Spirit in the Synagogue
7.	1:29–34	Healing Simon's Mother-in-Law
8.	1:35–38	Finding Jesus
9.	1:39–45	Healing the Leper
10.	2:1–12	Healing the Paralytic
11.	2:13–14	Calling Levi
12.	2:15–17	Eating with Sinners
13.	2:18–22	Lesson on Fasting
14.	2:23–28	Plucking Grain on the Sabbath
15.	3:1–6	Healing the Man with a Withered Hand
16.	3:7–12	Crowd at the Sea; Demons Know the Son of God
17.	3:13–19	Appointing the Twelve
18.	3:20–30	Controversy on Beelzebul
19.	3:31–35	Who Are My Brothers
20	4:1–35	The Parable Discourse
21.	4:36–41	Calming the Sea
22.	5:1–20	Healing the Gerasene Demoniac
23.	5:21–34	Healing the Woman with Blood Flow

24.	5:35–37	Jairus's Daughter Is Dead
25.	5:38–43	Healing Jairus's Daughter
26.	6:1–6a	Jesus Is Rejected in His Own Country
27.	6:6b–11	Sending Out the Twelve
28	6:12–29	Killing John the Baptizer
29.	6:30–31	Return of the Twelve
30.	6:32–33	Running Ahead of Jesus
31.	6:34–44	First Feeding the Multitude
32.	6:45–52	Walking on Water
33.	6:53–56	Healing in the Marketplace
34.	7:1– 7:15	Controversy on Tradition
35.	7:17–23	Eating Does Not Defile
36.	7:24–30	Healing the Syro-Phoenician Woman's Daughter
37.	7:31–36	Healing the Deaf Mute
38.	8:1–9	Second Feeding the Multitude
39.	8:10–12	Seeking a Sign
40.	8:13–21	Leaven of the Pharisees
41.	8:22–26	Healing the Blind Man of Bethsaida
42.	8:27—9:1	Peter's Confession at Caesarea Philippi
43.	9:2–8	The Transfiguration
44.	9:9–13	Leaving the Mountain
45.	9:14–27	Healing the Epileptic
46.	9:28–29	Answering the Disciples
47.	9:30–32	Second Passion Prediction
48.	9:33–50	Teaching the Disciples, Millstone Award
49.	10:1–9 `	Controversy on Divorce
50.	10:10–12	Remarriage Is Adultery
51.	10:13–16	Entering the Kingdom of God
52.	10:17–31	The Rich Man
53.	10:32–34	Heading to Jerusalem, Third Passion Prediction
54.	10:35–41	Request of James and John
55.	10:42–45	Being a Servant

56.	10:46–52	Healing Blind Bartimaeus
57.	11:1–6	Getting a Colt for Jesus
58.	11:7–10	Entering Jerusalem
59.	11:11–14	Cursing the Fig Tree
60.	11:15–19	Clearing the Temple
61.	11:20–25	The Withered Fig Tree
62.	11:27–12:12a	Questioning Jesus's Authority
63.	12:12b–17	Rendering unto Caesar
64.	12:18–27	Controversy on Resurrection
65.	12:28–34	The Greatest Commandment
66.	12:35–40	Beware of the Scribes
67.	12:41–44	The Widow's Mite
68.	13:1–2	Wonderful Buildings
69.	13:3–37	The Olivet Discourse
70.	14:1–2	The Plot Against Jesus
71.	14:3–9	Anointing with Oil in Bethany
72.	14:10–11	Judas Joins the Plot
73.	14:12–16	Finding the Passover Room
74.	14:17–25	The Last Supper
75.	14:26–31	Peter Will Deny Jesus
76.	14:32–42	Praying at Gethsemane, Sleeping Disciples
77.	14:43–52	The Arrest of Jesus
78.	14:53–72	The Sanhedrin Trial, Peter's Denials
79.	15:1–15	The Trial of Jesus Before Pilate
80.	15:16–20a	The Soldiers' Abuse of Jesus
81.	15:20b–39	The Crucifixion
82.	15:40–16:1	The Burial of Jesus
83.	16:1–8	The Women at the Tomb

Appendix 5

Luke Edits of Mark

THE FOLLOWING TABLE CONTAINS the Luke edits of Mark's Original Gospel as they appear in The Gospel of Luke. These edits add detail to Mark's description, show character motivation or clear up Markan ambiguity. The table is arranged in the order the passages are found in Canonical Mark.

Mark	Luke
1:10	3:22
1:14	4:15
1:21	4:31
1:26	4:35
1:30–31	4:38–39
1:34	4:40
1:36–37	4:42
2:2–4	5:17–19
2:14–15	5:27–29
2:17	5:32
2:18	5:33
2:22	5:37–39
2:23	6:1
3:1	6:6
3:5–6	6:8–11
3:10	6:19
3:27	11:21–22
4:4–5	8:5–6
4:14	8:11
4:17	8:13
4:20	8:15
4:21	8:16
4:25	8:18

Mark	Luke
4:35–38	8:22–24
5:1–3	8:26–27
5:4	8:29
5:9	8:30
5:15	8:35
5:17	8:37
5:25–34	8:43–48
5:36	8:50
6:1–2	4:16–17
6:7	9:1–2
8:15	12:1
9:2	9:29
9:7	9:34
9:17	9:38
9:20, 9:27	9:42
10:22	18:23
10:47	18:36–38
10:49–52	18:40–43
11:3	19:31
11:6	19:34
11:18	19:48
11:32	20:6
12:1	20:9
12:17	12:25–26

Appendix 5: Luke Edits of Mark

Mark	Luke		Mark	Luke
12:25	20:35–36		15:3	23:2
12:36	20:42		15:4	23:5
13:8	21:10–11		15:10	23:22
13:15–16	21:21–22		15:15	23:25
13:29	21:31		15:21	23:26
14:10–11	22:4–6		15:39	23:47
14:22	22:15–16		15:46	23:53
14:43	22:47		15:47	23:56
14:47	22:50		16:7	22:46–48
14:54	22:55			

Comparing all of the above edits in Luke's Gospel with those passages in Canonical Mark that have been suggested as having been interpolated into Mark, will lead the reader to agree that the suggested interpolations that I have identified herein display a style more akin to Luke than to Mark.

Bibliography

Achtemeier, Paul J. *Mark*. Proclamation Commentaries. Philadelphia: Fortress, 1984.

Aristotle. *Poetics* translated by S. H. Butcher ca. 350 BCE. No pages. Online http://classics. mit.edu//Aristotle/poetics.html

Bowman, John. *The Gospel of Mark: The New Christian Jewish Passover Haggadah*. Studia Post-Biblica 8. Leiden: E.J. Brill, 1965.

Brett, L.F.X. "Suggestions for an Analysis of Mark's Arrangement," in C.S. Mann. *Mark: A New Translation with Introduction and Commentary*, 174-90. New York: Doubleday, 1986.

Brenton, Lancelot C. L. *The Septuagint with Apocrapha: Greek and English*. London: Samuel Bagster & Sons Ltd., 1851. No pages. Online: http://ecmarsh.com/lxx/

Burkett, Delbert. *The Son of Man Debate*. Cambridge: Cambridge University Press, 1999.

Carrington, P. *The Primitive Christian Calendar: A Study in the Making of the Markan Gospel*. Cambridge: Cambridge University Press, 1952.

Crais, Robert. *The Promise*. New York: G. Putnam & Sons, 2015.

Cummins, S.A. *Paul and the Crucified Christ in Antioch*. Cambridge: Cambridge University Press, 2001.

Cunningham, Philip. *The Death of Jesus: Four Gospel Accounts*. STM Online: Crossroads Mini-Courses. No Pages. Online http://www.bc.edu/schools/stm/crossroads/resources/ deathofjesus.html

Derrett, J.D.M. *The Making of Mark: The Scriptural Bases of the Earliest Gospel*. Shipston-on-Stour: Drinkwater, 1985.

Dewey, Joanna. *Markan Public Debate*. Society of Biblical Literature Dissertation Series Chico, CA: Scholars, 1980.

Doherty, Earl. *Jesus Neither God nor Man*. Ottawa, Canada: Age of Reason, 2009.

Dykstra, Tom. *Mark, Canonizer of Paul*. St. Paul, MN: OCABS, 2012.

Eisenman, Robert. *James, The Brother of Jesus*. New York: Penguin Group, 1997.

Ehrman, Bart D. *Forged*. New York: HarperCollins, 2011.

———. *The Orthodox Corruption of Scripture*. New York: Oxford University Press, 2011.

Eusebius of Caesarea. *Ecclesiastic History*. ca 325. No pages. Online http://www.ccel.org/ccel/ schaff/npnf201.toc.html

Farrer, Austin E. *A Study in Mark*. Westminster: Dacre, 1951.

Feldman, L.H. "Josephus," in *The Anchor Bible Dictionary*, edited by Freedman, David Noel, Vol 3: 981-88. New York: Doubleday, 1992.

Field, Syd. *Screenplay*. New York: Dell, 1982.

Fowler, Robert M. *Let the Reader Understand*. Minneapolis, MN: Fortress Press, 1991.

France, R.T. *The Gospel of Mark*. NIGTC. Grand Rapids, MI: Eerdmans, 2002.

Gnilka, J., *Das Evangelium nach Markus*. EKKNT, 2.1. Neukirchen–Vluyn, Germany: Neukirchner Verlag, 5th edn, 1998.

Goldberg, Gary J. *The Flavius Josephus Home Page.* "Life of Josephus." No pages. Online http://www.josephus.org/life.htm

Goodacre, Mark. *The Case Against Q.* Harrisburg, PA: Trinity, 2002.

_____ "The Rock on Rocky Ground: Matthew, Mark and Peter as Skandalon" in Philip McCosker (ed.), *What Is It That the Scripture Says?: Essays in Biblical Interpretation, Translation, And Reception in Honour of Henry Wansbrough Osb.* 61-73, Library of New Testament Studies. London & New York: Continuum, 2006

Goulder, Michael D. *Midrash and Lection in Matthew.* Eugene, OR: Wipf and Stock, 2004.

Guelich, R.A., *Mark 1–8.26.* WBC, 34a. Dallas: Word, 1989.

Hedrick, C.W. "What is a Gospel? Geography, Time and Narrative Structure," *PRSt* 10 (1983) 255-68.

Heil, J.P. *The Gospel of Mark as a Model for Action: A Reader-Response Commentary.* New York: Paulist, 1992.

Helms, Randel. M., *Who Wrote The Gospels?* Ann Arbor, MI: Millennium, 1997.

Hobbs, E.C., 'The Gospel of Mark and the Exodus' PhD diss., University of Chicago, 1958.

Holtzmann, H.J. *The Synoptic Gospels: Their Origin & Historical Character* (1863). No pages. Online http://virtualreligion.net/primer/holtz.html

Humphrey, H. *He is Risen? A New Reading of Mark's Gospel.* New York: Paulist, 1992.

Iverson, K., "A Further Word on Final γάρ (Mark 16:8)," *Catholic Biblical Quarterly*, 68/1 (2006) 79–94.

Josephus. *Antiquities of the Jews.* 93 CE. No pages. Online http://earlyjewishwritings.com/text/josephus/ant1.html

Kata Biblon. *Greek Septuagint and Wiki English Translation.* No Pages. Online http://en.katabiblon.com/us/index.php?text=LXX.

Koester, Helmut. *Ancient Christian Gospels.* Harrisburg, PA: Trinity, 1990.

Krantz, J.H. "Mark's Chiastic Gospel Structure." No pages. Online http://www.preachingpeace.org/news/25-articles-ebooks/articles-by-friends-of-preaching-peace/74-mark-s-chiastic-gospel-structure.html

Ladd, G. E. *The Theology of the New Testament.* Grand Rapids, MI: Eerdmans, 1993.

Lane, W. *The Gospel According to Mark.* NICNT. Grand Rapids, MI: Eerdmans 1974.

Larsen, Kevin W. "The Structure of Mark's Gospel: Current Proposals." *Currents in Biblical Research 3.1* (2004) 143-164.

Manicardi, E. *Il cammino di Gesù nel Vangelo di Marco: Schema narrativo e temacristologico.* AnBib, 96. Rome: Pontifical Biblical Institute, 1981.

McCoy, Brad. "Chiasmus: An Important Structural Device Commonly Found in Biblical Literature." No pages. Online http://www.onthewing.org/user/BS_Chiasmus%20-%20McCoy.pdf.

McKee, Robert. *Story.* New York: Harper-Collins, 1997.

Meagher, John C. *Clumsy Constructions in Mark's Gospel.* New York: Mellen, 1979.

Moloney, Francis J., *Gospel of Mark, A Commentary*, 2002

Myers, C. *Binding the Strong Man: A Political Reading of Mark's Story of Jesus.* Maryknoll, NY: Orbis, 1988.

Nineham, D.E. *The Gospel of St. Mark.* Penguin New Testament Commentary. New York: Penguin, 1963.

Peace, R.V. *Conversion in the New Testament: Paul and the Twelve.* Grand Rapids, MI: Eerdmans 1999.

Perrin, N. "Towards an Interpretation of the Gospel of Mark," in *Christology and a Modern Pilgrimage,* edited by H.B. Betz, 7-13. Missoula, MT: SBL and Scholars, 1974.

Price, Robert M. "1 Corinthians 15:3-11 As A Later Interpolation," *Journal of Higher Criticism* 2/2 (1995), 69-99.

———. "New Testament Narrative as Old Testament Midrash." In *Encyclopedia Of Midrash: Biblical Interpretation In Formative Judaism,* edited by Jacob Neusner, et al. Leiden: Brill, 2005.

Rhoads, D., et al. *Mark as Story: An Introduction to the Narrative of a Gospel.* Minneapolis MN: Fortress, 1999.

Robbins, V.K., *Jesus the Teacher: A Socio-Rhetorical Interpretation of Mark.* Philadelphia: Fortress, 1984.

Schmidt, K.L. *Der Rahmen der Geschichte Jesu: Literarkritische Untersuchungen zur ältesten Jesusüberlieferung.* Berlin: Trowitzsch & Sohn, 1919.

Scott, M.P. "Chiastic Structure: A Key to the Interpretation of Mark's Gospel." *BTB* 15 (1985) 17-26.

Schweitzer, Albert. *Mystery of the Kingdom of God.* New York: Dodd, Mead and Co., 1914.

Shepherd, T. *Markan Sandwich Stories: Narration, Definition, and Function.* Andrews University Seminary Doctoral Dissertation Series, 18. Berrien Springs, MI: Andrews University Press (1993)

Smith, David Oliver. *Matthew, Mark, Luke and Paul.* Eugene, OR: Wipf and Stock, 2011.

Standaert, B. *L'évangile selon Marc: Composition et genre littéraire/* Bruge: Sint-Andriesabdij, 1978.

Strong, James. *The Exhaustive Concordance of the Bible.* No pages. Online http://biblehub. com/interlinear/mark/1.htm

Stuhlmacher, P. *Das paulinsche Evangeliumz; I. Vorgeschichte.* FRLANT 95. Göttingen: Vandenhoeck & Ruprecht, 1968.

Swartley, W.M. "The Structural Function of the Way (*Hodos*) in Mark's Gospel," in *The New Way of Jesus,* edited by W. Klassen, 73-86. Topeka, KS: Faith and Life, 1980.

Taylor, V. *The Gospel According to St. Mark.* London: Macmillan, 1952.

Teleford, W. *The Barren Temple and the Withered Tree: A Redactional-Critical Analysis of the Cursing of the Fig-tree Pericope in Mark's Gospel and its Relation to the Cleansing of the Temple Tradition.* JSNT Supp, 1. Sheffield: JSOT, 1980.

Tertullian, *The Five Books Against Marcion,* 208 CE. translated by Dr. Holmes, in *Ante-Nicene Fathers Volume 3,* edited by Allan Menzies. Grand Rapids, MI: Eerdmans (1868).

Tolbert, Mary Ann. *Sowing the Gospel: Mark's World in Literary-Historical Perspective.* Minneapolis MN: Fortress, 1989.

Turton, Michael A. *Historical Commentary on the Gospel of Mark.* No pages. Online http:// www.michaelturton.com/Mark/GMark_index.html

Vivano, B.T. *Kingdom of God in History.* Eugene, OR: Wipf and Stock, 1988.

Watts, Rikki. *Isaiah's New Exodus in Mark.* Biblical Studies Library. Grand Rapids: Baker Book House, 2000.

Weeden, T.J. *Mark, Traditions in Conflict.* Philadelphia: Fortress, 1971

Weisse, Christian.H. *The Gospel History Examined Critically and Philosophically.* Leiden: Breitkopf and Hartel, 1838.

Witherington, B. *The Gospel of Mark: A Socio-Rhetorical Commentary.* Grand Rapids: Eerdmans, 2001.

Subject/Name Index

Scripture Index